POLITICAL ECONOMY OF AGRARIAN REFORM IN CENTRAL
AND EASTERN EUROPE

Political Economy of Agrarian Reform in Central and Eastern Europe

Edited by
JOHAN F. M. SWINNEN

Ashgate

Aldershot • Brookfield USA • Singapore • Sydney

Published by
Ashgate Publishing Ltd
Gower House
Croft Road
Aldershot
Hants GU11 3HR
England

Ashgate Publishing Company
Old Post Road
Brookfield
Vermont 05036
USA

British Library Cataloguing in Publication Data

Swinnen, Jo
 Political economy of agrarian reform in Central and Eastern
 Europe.

 1.Land reform - Europe, Eastern 2.Agriculture and state -
 Europe, Eastern 3.Land reform - Europe, Central
 4.Agriculture and state - Europe, Central
 I.Title
 333.3'1'47

Library of Congress Catalog Card Number: 97-71710

ISBN 1 85972 560 0

Printed and bound by Athenaeum Press, Ltd.,
Gateshead, Tyne & Wear.

Contents

Tables

Contributors

Štefan Bojnec is assistant professor of agricultural economics at the University of Ljubljana and former advisor to the Government at the Ministry of Agriculture, Food, and Forestry, Ljubljana, Slovenia. Previously he was post-doctoral researcher at Leuven Institute for Central and East European Studies, visiting research associate at the UC Berkeley (USA) and at the University of Manchester (UK). He holds a Ph.D. in economics from the University of Zagreb and finished economics at the University of Ljubljana.

Azeta Cungu holds a B.Sc. in financial economics from the University of Tirana and a M.Sc. in agricultural economics from Wye College, University of London. She is currently Ph.D. student at the Department of Agricultural Economics, K.U.Leuven.

Konrad Hagedorn is professor at the Institute of Agricultural Policy, Marketing and Agricultural Development, College of Agriculture and Horticulture, Humboldt University of Berlin, Germany. He holds a Ph.D from the University of Göttingen and has written extensively on agricultural reform in Central and Eastern Europe.

Marvin Jackson holds a Ph.D. in economics from Berkeley and is a professor in economics at the Katholieke Universiteit Leuven (previously at the University of Arizona) and director of the Leuven Institute for Central and East European Studies (LICOS). He has written extensively on economic development and reform in Central and Eastern Europe.

Isabelle Lindemans is a researcher at LICOS, specialized in the political economy of agricultural policies. She holds a Master in engineering in agriculture from the K.U.Leuven.

Erik Mathijs holds a Master in engineering in agriculture from the K.U.Leuven, and is currently a Ph.D. student at the Department of Agricultural Economics, K.U.Leuven. His Ph.D. research is on the economics and politics of agricultural privatization and farm restructuring in Central and Eastern Europe.

Ewa Rabinowicz is associate professor at the Department of Economics, The Swedish Agricultural University. She has written extensively on agricultural sector modeling, agricultural policy, political economy, and CEEC agricultural transition. She is currently a member of the Economic Council of Sweden and President of the European Association of Agricultural Economists.

Johan F. M. Swinnen has a Ph.D. in agricultural economics from Cornell University and is assistant professor of agricultural economics and food policy, Katholieke Universiteit Leuven (K.U.Leuven) in Belgium. Previously, he was senior research economist at the Leuven Institute for Central and East European Studies (LICOS).

Don Van Atta has a Ph.D. in political science from the University of California at Berkeley and has written widely on the politics of Soviet and post-Soviet agriculture. Formerly the desk officer for the NIS countries in the Directorate of Food, Agriculture and Fisheries of OECD, he now directs the Center for Privatization Research.

Preface and Acknowledgements

This volume studies agricultural privatization, decollectivization, and land reform programs in twelve Central and Eastern European countries (CEECs). Contributors to this volume compare the reform processes and use a political economy framework to explain and interpret similarities and differences found in the various countries.

This project also reflects the basic framework of endogenous institutional change and endogenous policy analysis. In particular, our approach joins traditional Marxist analysis of production factor ownership with neoclassical public choice theory and institutional economics. Neoclassical institutional economists focus their attention on allocative efficiency improvements in discussing institutional change, whereas Marxists often emphasize how institutions change or do not change depending on surplus appropriations to a dominant class. In particular, progress towards a more efficient institution may be blocked if it reduces the control of surplus by this class. This focus on how institutional change influences control of surplus by a particular class suggests that efficiency-improving institutional change cannot really be separated from redistributive institutional change. Our study accepts this inherent link between redistribution and efficiency as a starting hypothesis for understanding choices of agrarian reform processes in the CEECs.

From the start, this research project had two objectives. The first objective was to collect raw material on the processes of reform and on the political and economic situations influencing the discussions, choices, and implementation of reforms. This objective is reflected in the extended discussions of reform legislation, political changes, and reform backgrounds. The collection of this 'raw material' was intended (a) to contribute to a greater insight into the actual reform processes and (b) to provide a base for future research on related issues.

The second, and more ambitious, objective was to develop a comparative perspective on reform processes in CEECs and, if possible, to explain the reform choices for various countries. Initially we set out to explain differences and remarkable variations between countries, but we soon had to rephrase our hypotheses in terms of the remarkable similarities between CEECs' reform processes that began to emerge.

This volume is organized into three parts. The first part introduces readers to the main theoretical and conceptual issues involved in land reform, privatization, and decollectivization and surveys past agrarian reforms in Central and Eastern Europe. Part two presents country studies giving in-depth analyses of the reform processes and the political, economic, and historical factors affecting them. The focus is on agricultural privatization, land reform, and decollectivization. The individual country studies provide (a) a description of the general political and macroeconomic changes; (b) a description of the policy and regulatory changes and a discussion of the (potential) impacts of these changes; and (c) an attempt to explain/relate the (lack of) policy changes to changes in political balances within a country. The book's final part compares the various countries' processes and presents political economy hypotheses to explain differences and similarities.

This research project began in the summer of 1992. In a hotel room in Sofia, Bulgaria, Andy Schmitz asked me to write a chapter on the political economy of Bulgarian reform for a book he was preparing with Allan Buckwell, Sophia Davidova, and Kirby Moulton on agricultural reforms in Bulgaria. After finishing this study, I convinced colleagues at the Leuven Institute of Central and East European Studies (LICOS) and the Department of Agricultural Economics at the Katholieke Universiteit Leuven to extend this study to other CEECs, to analyze whether my hypotheses on the political economy of agrarian reform in Bulgaria were more generally apllicable. All of these efforts resulted in the chapters here by Marvin Jackson on Romania, by Isabelle Lindemans on the Czech and Slovak Republics and on Poland, by Stefan Bojnec on Slovenia, and by Erik Mathijs on Hungary. Our preliminary results and hypotheses were presented at a workshop in June 1994 in Leuven. This meeting induced enthusiasm in other researchers. Konrad Hagedorn and Ewa Rabinowicz added studies on East Germany and the Baltic countries (Latvia and Lithuania), respectively. Azeta Cungu contributed an analysis of Albanian agricultural reforms. Finally, Don Van Atta updated his earlier work on the politics of Russian agrarian reform into a chapter for this book.

We gratefully acknowledge financial support for this project from the Belgian National Science Foundation (NFWO), from the EU Commission (ACE and COST programmes), from Almanij Antwerpen, from the Leuven Institute for Central and East European Studies, and from the Department of Agricultural Economics at the Katholieke Universiteit Leuven. I thank Andy Schmitz, Allan Buckwell, and Sophia Davidova for getting me started and for their many critical comments and their encouragement. I thank Marvin Jackson for making scarce LICOS funds available to get the project running and Katrien Verhelst for administrative assistance. Josee Verlaenen and Odette Moria patiently went through numerous revisions of most chapters. Danny Verhaegen assisted with the initial formatting and editing, and Ria Uyttebroeck helped with the final formatting of the manuscript. Catherine Taylor carefully edited all chapters from Albanian English, Belgian English, German English, Swedish English, Slovenian English, etc., into American English. I also want to thank Leo Simon, Gordon Rausser, Bob Lyons, Betty Sadoulet, Alain de Janvry, Scott Pearson, Marcel Fafchamps, Tim Josling, Karen Brooks, Csaba Csaki, Zvi Lerman, Richard Burcroff, Harry de Gorter, Tomáš Ratinger, Alexander Sarris, and participants at seminars in IFPRI, Berkeley, Stanford, Cornell, the World Bank, Sinaia and Edinburgh for critical comments and encouragements on this project. I thank James Garrett and Alison Burrell for critical reviews of the prelimary conclusions. Finally, Erik Mathijs developed, in the course of this and related projects, into one of Europe's prime experts on CEEC privatization, land reform, and farm restructuring. He reviewed the entire manuscript and contributed substantially to the conclusions of this project.

> Jo Swinnen
> December 1996
> Leuven

Abbreviations

CEEC	Central and Eastern European country
OECD	Organization for Econmic Co-operation and Development

Chapter 1

NIE	New institutional economics
RICB	Restitution in comparable boundaries
RIHB	restitution in historical boundaries

Chapter 2

CEE	Central and Eastern European
CEEC	Central and Eastern European countries

Chapter 3

APC	Agricultural Producer Cooperative
CP	Communist Party
DLDC	Land distribution council at the district level
DP	Democratic Party
GAO	Gross agricultural output
HJO	Historical Justice Option
IFDC	International Fertiliser Development Centre
INSTAT	Albanian Institute of Statistics
LDC	Land distribution council
MAF	Ministry of Agriculture and Food
MRO	Minimal Reform Option
NLDC	Land distribution council at the national level
RP	Republican Party
SDP	Social Democratic Party
SEO	Social Equity Option

SF	State farm
SP	Socialist Party
VLDC	Land distribution council at the village level

Chapter 4

CARD	Center for Agricultural and Rural Development
CSCE	Conference on Security and Cooperation in Europe
FSU	the former Soviet Union
LCP	Latvia's Communist Party
LDLP	Lithuanian or Latvian Democratic Labor Party
LFU	Latvia's Farmer's Union
LNNK	The National Independence Movement of Latvia
MARS	Municipal Agrarian Reform Services
PFL	Peoples' Front of Latvia

Chapter 5

BANU	Bulgarian Agricultural National Union
BBB	Bulgarian Business Bloc
BCP	Bulgarian Communist Party
BSDP	Bulgarian Social Democratic Party
BSP	Bulgarian Socialist Party
BBN	Bulgarian Business News
LALOLU	Law for Agricultural Landownership and Land Use
LC	Liquidation council
MLC	Municipal land council or commission
MRF	Movement for Rights and Freedom
NCC	UDF's National Coordinating Council
PU	Popular Union
UDF	Union of Democratic Forces

Chapter 6

CDA	Civic Democratic Alliance
CDP	Civic Democratic Party
CDU	Civic Democratic Union
CF	Civic Forum
ChDM	Christian Democratic Movement
ChDMS	Christian Democratic Movement for Slovakia
ChDP	Christian Democratic Party
ChDU	Christian Democratic Union
CM	Civic Movement
CP	Communist Party

CPBS	Slovak Communists and the Communist Party for Bohemia and Moravia
DPL	Democratic Party of Labor
MDS	Movement for a Democratic Slovakia
NFWO	National Foundation for Scientific Research
PAV	Public Against Violence
PDL	Party of Democratic Left
PP	People's Party
SChDM	Slovak Christian Democratic Movement
SNP	Slovak National Party

Chapter 7

ADR	Alternative dispute resolution
BVVG	Bodenverwaltungs- und verwertungsgesellschaft (Land Administration and Utilization Company)
DM	German Mark
EALG	Entschädigungs- und Ausgleichsleistungsgesetz (Indemnification and Compensation Act)
GDR	German Democratic Republic
LPG	Landwirtschaftliche Produktionsgenossenschaft (cooperative farm)
THA	Treuhandanstalt (Privatization Agency)
VEG	Volkseigenes Gut (State farm)

Chapter 8

AFD	Alliance of Free Democrats
AYD	Alliance of Young Democrats
CDP	Christian Democratic Party
CDPP	Christian Democratic People's Party
HDF	Hungarian Democratic Forum
HSP	Hungarian Socialist Party
HSWP	Hungarian Socialist Workers' Party
ISCP	Independent Smallholders' and Civic Party
ISP	Independent Smallholders' Party
MOSZ	National Federation of Agricultural Producers
SDP	Social Democratic Party
GDP	Gross domestic product
HUF	Hungarian Forint
USD	United States Dollar

Chapter 9

| AAPST | Agency of the Agricultural Property of the State Treasury |

PA	Peasant Alliance
PPP	Polish Peasant Party
UPP	United Peasant Party

Chapter 10

DAF	Democratic Antitotalitarian Forum
DAP	Democratic Agrarian Party
DCR	Democratic Convention of Romania
DNSF	Democratic NSF
GSD	Group for Social Dialogue
HDFR	Hungarian Democratic Federation
HDUR	Hungarian Democratic Union of Romania
NCED	National Convention for the Establishment of Democracy
NLP	National Liberal Party
NSF	Council for National Salvation
PCA	Party of Civic Alliance
PCNU	Provisional Council of National Unity
POFs	private ownership funds
PRNU	Party of Romanian National Unity
PSDR	Party of Social Democracy of Romania
SOF	State ownership fund

Chapter 11

| RSFSR | Russian Soviet Federated Socialist Republic |

Chapter 12

DEMOS	Democratic United Opposition of Slovenia
FALF	Fund of Agricultural Land and Forests
LDS	Liberal Democratic Party
LSC	Yugoslav Law on Social Capital
OG SLO	Official Gazette of the Republic of Slovenia
OG YU	Official Gazette of the former Yugoslavia
	People
	Renewal
SKD	Slovenian Christian Democrats
SKZ	Slovenian Farmers Alliance
SLS	Slovenian People's Party
SNS	Slovenian National Party
SY SLO	Statistical Yearbook of Slovenia
SZS-SZDL	Socialist Alliance of Slovenia-Socialist Alliance of Working
ZKS-SDP	League of Communists of Slovenia-Party of Democratic

| ZL | Unity List |
| ZSMS-LS | League of Socialist Youth of Slovenia-Liberal Party |

Chapter 13

BANU	Bulgarian Agricultural National Union
BSP	Bulgarian Socialist Party
BVVG	Land Utilization and Administration Company
CP	Communist Party
FSU	former Soviet Union
HSP	Hungarian Socialist Party
LDLP	Lithuanian Democractic Labor Party
MARS	Municipal Agrarian Reform Services
MRF	Movement for Rights and Freedoms
NSF	National Salvation Front
SP	Socialist Party
UDF	Union of Democratic forces

1 Political economy of privatization and decollectivization of Central and East European agriculture: Definitions, issues and methodology

Ewa Rabinowicz and Johan F. M. Swinnen

Introduction

Privatization of property rights and transformation of the production organization have been two key decisions in the agrarian reform process for all Central and Eastern European countries (CEECs). Policymakers have had various strategic options to choose from. Their policy choices have important and long-lasting economic and political implications and have therefore been the subject of intense political debate. One could argue that there has been relatively little discussion about the need for private ownership to improve allocative efficiency in the economy. The main issues in these debates have been (a) who would be the 'new' private owners of agricultural assets, and (b) what farm structures should replace the state and cooperative farms.[1] These have been sensitive issues, fueled by the perceived danger that assets might fall in the wrong hands or the future performance of agriculture be impaired.

The purpose of this chapter is to define some fundamental concepts related to this debate to identify and discuss the key issues, and, finally, to sketch the theoretical framework underlying the country studies in the chapters that follow.

Definitions

Barzel (1989) defines *property rights* of individuals over assets as 'the rights, or the powers, to consume, to obtain income from, and to alienate these assets'. Legal rights, as a rule, enhance economic rights, but the former are neither necessary nor sufficient for the existence of the latter.[2] Furthermore, the rights people have over assets are not constant. Such rights are a function of the owners' direct efforts at protection, of other people's capture attempts, and of

1

government protection. Obligations or responsibilities, which in some cases are imposed by government regulations or by traditions, also contribute to the relative nature of property rights.

This specification of property rights has implications for the analysis in this book. In most CEECs, in contrast to the former Soviet Union, land in collective farms was still formally owned by individuals who had joined collectives during collectivization or by their heirs. However, these formal owners had virtually no authority over the use of the land. This fact provides a good illustration of legal ownership rights not being a sufficient condition for the existence of effective property rights.

Privatization in the CEECs has had to do more with the transfer of property rights than with (legal) ownership rights. In most cases, privatization concerns the allocation of both legal ownership rights and effective property rights to individuals or private institutions. Privatization can occur by various methods – for example, free distribution of assets, sales of assets, usufruct divestment, or restitution. Most of these methods allow for specific groups to be targeted and encompass various technical options. For example, sales of assets can be by general auctions or by in-house sales to workers or management. Different methods of privatization can also be combined by allowing various means of payment at sales, such as general vouchers (part of a mass privatization package), special vouchers valid only for a particular enterprise (distribution to workers), and cash. A combination of different means of payment was applied for example in the privatization of collective farm assets in Lithuania.[3]

Property rights are fully restored only if all three rights (user, income, and alienation rights) are given to the owners. Not all privatization schemes fullfil these criteria. For example, farms created on a usufruct basis in the Baltic countries had no right to sell the land. Another example of incomplete property rights is the land restitution implementation in several CEECs which specifies that an 'equivalent' piece of land be given to individuals wanting to retrieve their land from the (reformed) collective farm. Important transaction costs are involved in the assignment of an 'equivalent' or 'comparable' plot of land. The plot has to be assigned by the management of the reformed farm. The claimant can go to court if he disagrees with the assignment. *Ex ante* property rights that are restituted are clearly incomplete in this process because of the high transaction costs. Whether the process generates full property rights *ex post* depends on whether the claimant is actually able to successfully retrieve the property and use it according to the three criteria mentioned above.

From this perspective, one should be careful in interpreting the data on 'private' assets in CEEC agriculture since the transition. In some cases, neither legal (ownership) rights nor property rights are private; in other cases, land titles have not yet been distributed, but new owners are already determining what is being done with the assets and have acquired some property rights. In other cases, ownership rights have been transferred to individuals, but private property rights are incomplete because owners have only limited power over the use and transfer of the assets.

Restitution is a form of privatization that returns property rights to those defined as 'legitimate' owners. Restitution of assets is limited by the fact that many original assets no longer exist. The main exception is land and real estate. However, land has sometimes changed dramatically in qualitative terms. Plots that had little infrastructure might now have drainage and irrigation facilities or even buildings on them. The collectivization process, moreover, often resulted in a consolidation of fields, in a new infrastructure, and in the destruction of old buildings and roads and the construction of new ones. Plots of land which prior to collectivization were adjacent to a road might now be in the middle of a vast grain field. The social infrastructure has changed as well. Plots previously located close to villages might now be far away. Such change in quality and use of land creates administrative difficulties in restituting land to previous owners. It also induces compensation claims. Nonlandowning members and management of collective farms often claim that they should be compensated if the quality of the land has been improved and the land is restituted to its previous owners.

Transformation refers to the conversion and restructuring of collective and state enterprises into enterprises compatible with a market economy. This is, in part, a legal conversion and, in part, an organizational restructuring of the entities into viable business units. The available options are specified in laws and typically include conversion of collective and state farms into joint stock companies, limited liabilities companies or producer cooperatives. Transformation includes management reform to increase efficiency (for instance, by creating profit-oriented subdivisions). Farm restructuring can involve enlargement of subsidiary plots, separation of individual farms from collective farms, or a complete dismantling of large farms (Csaki and Lerman, 1994). A useful definition of *decollectivization* is Pryor's (1992):

> the breakup of large-scale farms, *organized either as cooperatives or state enterprises*, into individually operated farms and their creation as autonomous production units independent of the government. A change of ownership of these farms, for example, a conversion into a cooperation in which the workers or others hold stock but the essential farming operations remain roughly the same, is quite a different matter and can occur with much greater ease.

Transformation and, in particular, decollectivization – the creation of individually operated farms – can be encouraged or discouraged by the government. The process is directly affected by laws, that provide explicit

3

rules for designing the transformation. Facilitating farmers to withdraw from agricultural production cooperatives can be done through various incentives, for example by providing individual private farmers with preferential credit arrangements (e.g., low interest credit and loan guarantees), by canceling their share of the collective farm debt, or by providing training and extension facilities to support the development of individual farming. Some countries have included a series of regulations that tend to discourage farmers from leaving the cooperatives. We refer to the set of government policies and regulations which attempt to influence process as the *transformation policy* or *decollectivization policy*.

Transaction costs and economic efficiency

Privatization and economic efficiency

The classic argument for privatization and restoration of property rights is that the allocative efficiency of the productive assets will increase under private ownership. Private ownership allows market transactions to take place and provides the basis for value maximization of assets. Without privatization, market trades are inhibited by the absence of property rights, and decision-makers who are not true residual claimants of profits lack incentives to monitor production and use resources efficiently.[4] An additional argument is that the effective conduct of stabilization policy requires privatization (Hillman 1992; Hinds, 1991). Relationships between ownership, incentives, and efficiency are complex (Vickers and Yarrow, 1991). The change of ownership in CEECs does not guarantee efficiency. Lack of knowledge and experience by management as well as insufficient control by new owners can minimize improvements in performance.

In discussions about privatization, the concept of *economic efficiency* can also relate to the timing of reforms (see, e.g., the discussions on gradual versus big-bang approches).[5] *Efficiency* is also used when discussing the distortions caused by the *process* of privatization (e.g., restitution versus vouchers or sales) and in discussions on the *outcome* of the privatization process, that is, the optimality of the resulting farm organization and structure.[6] It is often argued that the redistribution of land according to historical boundaries is inconsistent with the goal of efficiency, where efficiency does not refer to the general goal of private ownership but to the resulting optimal farm structure.

4

Privatization and transformation as defined in the preceding section are two different concepts. The former relates to change in the ownership and property rights structure, the latter to the organization of assets for productive use. A fundamental issue is how the two are related. The answer depends on the precedence of transaction costs.[7] More specifically, the potential for the existing management to keep their production entity similar to its pre-privatization state after property rights to agricultural assets have been assigned to individuals depends strongly on (a) how the privatization process affects transaction costs for the various partners (legal owners, potential users) in a potential exchange of the assets, (b) transaction costs involved in monitoring the reform implementation, and (c) incentives for individuals to start an individual farm and leave the cooperative farms (Mathijs and Swinnen, 1996a).

Without transaction costs, it does not matter, from an efficiency point of view, who owns the assets because assets will invariably be used where their marginal return is highest.[8] In such a world, the privatization process, as long as it turns all ownership rights over to private individuals, might not affect the farm structure and the transformation process beyond the change from a socialist to a capitalist mode of production.

With positive transaction costs in land and asset markets, the transformation process will be affected by the privatization process. The main reason is that by allocating to individuals the private property rights to production factors used by the farms, the farms must then set up (formal and informal) contracts with those individuals for the use of the assets. Property rights are uncertain during a transition period, increasing the difficulties and uncertainties for farms in the use and allocation of their production factors. These difficulties and uncertainties increase when information is less available and transaction costs are higher. The privatization process will have an important impact here. Disruption (in terms of increasing information costs and other transaction costs) is higher for restitution of production factors to former owners, and more so if the land is restituted according to historical boundaries and if the initial distribution is very fragmented. Voucher privatization and sales have a less disruptive effect.

Problems arise on both sides of the market. New (or potential) owners have difficulties selling or renting their restituted land. Monitoring the restitution process and searching for the best potential use of the land can be costly for an individual who is not closely involved in the collective farm. These costs tend to stimulate disruption in the production system and its structures. Thus, with positive transaction costs, privatization and transformation policies are not independent.[9]

Transaction costs and imperfect (asymmetric) information in *reform implementation* may have a negative effect on decollectivization. The implementation of transformation policies takes place at the decentralized level by special institutions, such as collective farm transformation councils. Those institutions are often influenced by local preferences and biased towards the interests of management and employees who are closely involved in the decisions and activities of the institutions. In the areas of information and monitoring, management and workers of the collective and state farms have an advantage over the dispersed (often urban) asset owners. The higher the transaction costs, the more the current management will be able to reorganize the farm according to its own preferences.

The role of land and input markets

Restitution according to historical boundaries typically leads to an ownership structure that mirrors the (very) fragmented pre-World War II land distributions (see Mathijs, 1997). This fragmentation is exacerbated by the creation of private plots based on private gardens under the Communist regime. Moreover, nonland assets have often been privatized differently, predominantly distributed to the former members of the collective farms. What implications have fragmentation and lack of coordination in the privatization of different types of assets on the outcome of the process of transformation? In this discussion, one should be careful to distinguish between (initial) asset *ownership* and asset *use*. In a world of perfect markets, (i.e., a world without transaction costs, information costs, and other distortions), asset ownership and use can be perfectly separated. For example, in some Western countries farmers do not own most of their land,[10] but rent it. In addition, initial landownership does not necessary imply continued ownership, because land can be sold and bought. According to these arrangements, the land markets or the market for rental services of land, machinery, or feed purchase can solve the problems of land fragmentation and confused asset ownership. What is necessary for the CEECs is to establish clear property rights and well-functioning markets.

A first comment on this argument is that it is taking a long time for land titles to be distributed in Central and Eastern Europe. Verifying land claims and resolving conflicts between claimants is particularly time-consuming. In the meantime, chaotic conditions and large uncertainties have prevailed.

But even if land titles are assigned and distributed, efficient land allocation does not always result. This can be seen in some better-developed market economies where land markets have generally not functioned well in the past. In these countries, land market imperfections result from credit market imperfections, the underdevelopment of capital markets, the presence of

6

considerable risks (production and price risks, as well as the risk of losing nonland assets), and the absence of insurance markets (Platteau, 1992). Land is viewed as a portfolio investment with few alternatives, as an inflation hedge, a secure form of wealth in an uncertain environment, or as a form of luxury consumption that provides social prestige and political influence to the holder (Ellis, 1988). Poorer members of society are concerned even more than the rich with holding a relatively secure form of wealth and retaining their traditional source of livelihood. In general, they are very reluctant to part with their land unless they are forced to do so under distress sale conditions, because ownership of a small plot of land makes it possible to retreat to subsistence farming to escape unemployment in the cities or other economic hardship. Another problem is that as farmers need the land as collateral for working capital, they cannot use the same land as collateral for a loan to purchase the land. As a result, land needs to be financed out of savings (Binswanger and Rozenzweig, 1986). In summary, as a consequence of market imperfections, land sales are mainly limited to distress sales. Such sales tend to foster accumulation in the hands of people with already high landownership (Rosenzweig et al., 1988).

Another general observation is that land consolidation to improve farm structures has often required government intervention in countries with rather egalitarian land distributions. For the reasons mentioned above, the land market has not resulted in improved structures. For example, fragmentation of land, which came about for various reasons (e.g., because of inheritance rules), has often not been remedied by the land market.

Thus, it can be concluded that fragmented initial landownership will most likely have long-lasting effects on future landownership and on the emerging structure of production in CEECs.

Efficiency implications

Many economists have argued that restitution of land to former owners conflicts with efficiency. Among the reasons for this view are dispersion and fragmentation of landownership, the inherent potential destruction of existing infrastructure, and a distribution of nonland assets that does not support the distribution of land. If all assets are privatized by sale, the problem of complementarity is easily solved because the potential buyer will try to assure himself a proper package. If more than one method of privatization is used to distribute assets that are complementary in production, efficiency may be impaired. For example, if some assets are restituted to 'rightful owners' while others are distributed to present users, the result can easily be that land is privatized without machinery and vice versa, that livestock is privatized without resources for raising feed, etc. Problems also emerge when a large share of productive assets are held by retired ex-members of collective farms. It is highly improbable that such circumstances will result in the succesful grouping of farmland and resources. In such cases, the privatization process starts from a disequilibrium position, which will eventually have to be corrected. Transaction costs are decisive here, but even at a low level of transaction cost, efficiency losses seem unavoidable, particularly in the short run, before markets for land and services develop.

Another issue relates to maintaining of the existing capital stock and protecting it against destruction during the transition. The uncertainty of future ownership reduces the incentives for current managers to maintain the capital stock. In addition, in some CEECs, the property of collective and state farms in transition is put under temporary management for some time. All this encourages poor maintenance or even outright theft. While some might argue that the latter is a form of spontaneous privatization, it can also lead to destruction of assets.

However, the efficiency implications of land reform and privatization choices are still a matter of debate. For example, Mathijs and Swinnen (1996b) argue that land restitution induces a consolidation of the large-scale structures in the short-run. As a consequence, disruptions in technology and land fragmentation are reduced which may have a positive effect on long run efficiency.

Choice, implementation, and outcome of reform policies

Reform policy choice

We characterize privatization through vouchers and sales as a nonradical policy option because it allows more flexibility in terms of asset ownership allocations and has a less restrictive impact on restructuring. Restitution in comparable boundaries (RICB) allocates ownership rights to specific land plots to the former owners or their heirs, but it limits property rights in the sense that new owners are not allowed to use or rent their plot of land without the cooperative's confirmation. The alternative is for owners to be assigned full property rights over a comparable land plot after negotiation with the cooperative. The most radical (and most disruptive) privatization policy is restitution in historical boundaries (RIHB), through which property rights to land plots are returned to their previous owners.

Consistent with our earlier definitions, we define radical transformation or decollectivization policies as those that attempt to break up the existing production organizations and force a radical restructuring of the agricultural production system. Smooth transformation policies are more concerned with changing the formal organization (for example by changing the collective into a joint-stock company or a 'private' cooperative) but want to avoid major disruption to the existing production structures.[11]

Assume that the government has made the decision to privatize assets in agriculture and to transform the farms.[12] The choice of RIHB and a radical transformation policy is intended to yield a radical decollectivization of the farm structure. When the government picks a nonradical transformation policy in combination with RIHB, it allows for the establishment of family farms in combination with new types of large-scale 'private' cooperative production units. While this approach might coincide with a substantial reduction in the average size and activities of the cooperative farms, it differs strongly from radical decollectivization, which usually entails the breakup of collectives into individually operated ('Western-style') family farms.

Reform implementation

The most radical policies on paper may result in little effective change unless they are well implemented. While the government has control over the choice (the design) of the policy, it may have less control over its implementation. The first problem is information. Typically implementing the policy requires either decentralized actions or actions by the central administration. However, when a relatively new government is in charge – as is typically the case when reform-minded governments have taken over – they are often confronted with central and local administrations that are hostile towards the reforms. In particular, in a situation where legislation is unclear, or even inconsistent, the ability of the local or central administration to act according to its own interests or preferences increases. Given the asymmetry of information, that is, the fact that local administrations are usually much better informed, it is often very difficult for a government to implement its reforms. Lack of information also makes it hard for a government to intervene if it suspects that the reforms are being sabotaged, because delays might also be due to the complexity of the process and actual difficulties in implementation.

Hayami (1991) argues that (1) using simple, transparent, and uniform rules and (2) limiting the scope of discretionary government involvement in implementation are two key variables in a succesful land reform. Both seem important in CEECs. Little progress has been achieved in some reform programs because the rules were unclear, insufficient incentives for change were provided by a little committed government, and reform was blocked by collective farm management.

Other factors are *timing* and *government credibility*. The problem of credibility is fundamental for all public decision making, and to some extent the problem is unsolvable. All decisions made in democratic fashion can be

9

reversed in the same way. Solutions to this problem involve various institutional arrangements (such as delegating some policy functions to independent bodies, demanding qualified majorities for important changes of legislation, etc.) to make reversals difficult or impossible in the short run. The problem is greater in the CEECs because of their high level of political instability. The privatization and transformation processes require much time, even when all parties support the reforms. Therefore, there exists a real chance that before reforms are finished, or even well under way, the government will be replaced by another which may be less supportive of the reforms. While the new government may not choose to change the privatization process decision (which is a major decision), it may very well introduce a number of regulations and policies – minor decisions, that have an important impact on the speed and extent of the reform implementation. As a consequence, local administrations and executing institutions may feel less inclined to obey government orders and regulations that they privately oppose, knowing that enforcement procedures may only come into effect if the government is replaced (Swinnen, 1995).

Reform outcome

Decollectivization implies a tremendous change of production technology and a major restructuring of human capital. A modern farmer in a Western country combines many skills, while members of collectives farms often possess very narrow skills. Newly established farmers need a wide variety of skills and knowledge, some of which cannot be learned quickly from books but only develop with the accumulation of experiences over time. Therefore, important incentives are necessary to encourage individuals to set up their own farms. Agricultural privatization is, in general, more complicated than similar processes in other sectors of the economy. For instance, *small privatization* often simply means that production of some service is now run by private owners, hopefully using fewer resources and achieving better quality. Even in the privatization of heavy industry (*large privatization*) the goal is a more efficient operation using the existing stock of capital in ways that often involve less labor and better management, rather than dividing, say, a large steel mill into two smaller ones.

The economic environment will affect the opportunities and risks for emerging private farmers and, thus, the incentives for individuals to set up their own farms or to stay with a reformed cooperative or state farm. Two major economic forces affect this process: the first is short-term and inhibits decollectivization, the second is long-term and stimulates decollectivization.

The short-term economic environment is characterized by falling terms of trade for agriculture, depressed farm incomes, high inflation, lack of inputs (especially credit), inappropriate technology and human capital, production declines, and widespread uncertainty (Jackson and Swinnen, 1995; OECD, 1994a). The combination of these factors probably explains the widespread lack of enthusiasm of collective farm members and employees to start up their own private farms. These short-term factors have a negative impact on decollectivization. One short-term factor which tends to stimulate private activity in agriculture occurs when agriculture temporarily absorbs surplus labor in countries with high unemployment, as was the case in Poland and Romania.

In the longer run, however, one can expect a development towards a farm structure with fewer cooperatives in production and with smaller farms. The reasons for this are the same as those that determine optimal farm size and organization in market economies. Farming in most Western market economies is dominated by family farms which on average are much smaller than the former cooperative and state farms in CEECs. It is important in this discussion to distinguish between *size* (large versus small scale) and *organization* (family farm, corporate farm, cooperative farm).

Many economists argue that agricultural production cooperatives are economically unviable (Hagedorn, 1992; Csaki and Kislev, 1993; Schmitt, 1993). A somewhat different perspective is suggested by the OECD (1994b, p. 80): 'Successful farming cooperatives may not evolve under market conditions but this does not prove that 'cooperatives' created without market considerations and by coercion cannot survive as free cooperatives under market conditions'. The standard argument against cooperative organization is that it is incapable of controlling moral hazard and adverse selection problems (Platteau, 1992). The existence of asymmetric information suggests that while sufficient linking of labor input and reward may be possible in theory, it is too difficult and costly in reality. This is particularly true in the case of agricultural operations. Labor quality matters greatly in many agricultural operations and is very costly to monitor effectively (Pollak, 1985). Typically, before transition, many collectives had a symbiotic arrangement with employees who took over part of the animal husbandry activities and fruit and vegetable production, activities where labor quality and monitoring cost matter greatly, in their private farms (gardens) (Juhasz, 1989).

In terms of *size*, the transaction cost argument mainly applies to the difference between family labor and hired labor, with transaction costs increasing rapidly when the farm hires labor from outside the family. Available evidence indicates that long-run cost curves in agriculture are L-shaped, allowing family farms to capture most of the scale effects with their labor capacity. This labor capacity has increased dramatically with technological innovations. The combination of these factors explains the 'optimality of family farms' (Schmitt, 1993).

11

The optimality of small-scale family farms in Western Europe is, however, to some extent dependent on the institutional environment and on a series of regulations that explicitly favor family farming (Swinnen et al., 1994). In an environment where both institutional arrangements (extension services, machine services, etc.) and favorable government policies towards farming would be missing, family farming may turn out to be less competitive than might be expected based on evidence from western countries. With capital relatively scarce in the CEECs, this suggests that in the short- and medium-term, large-scale farming, with employed workers may remain a general feature of CEEC agriculture.

Most experts do foresee a gradual evolution of the new cooperatives into more family-type farms. The time dimension for this is quite important. The process will likely be a gradual one which could gather momentum after a few years as new and better educated farming entrepreneurs learn from each other. Cooperative structures, however, may survive in the medium run if they learn to adapt to the market, together with corporate or family farms (OECD, 1994b). Csaki and Lerman (1995) claim that in the foreseeable future a multiplicity of production and ownership forms in agriculture is likely to prevail. Those might include subsistence farms or enlarged household plots, family farms, large private farms, new cooperatives, and corporate farms. Moreover, the composition would most probably vary from country to country.

Distributional aspects: equity, historical justice and social class structure

The choice of the agricultural privatization process is sometimes presented as a choice requiring an important trade-off between economic efficiency objectives and income distribution (Brooks et al., 1991). Income distribution includes social ('equity') objectives and legal ('historical justice') demands. This trade-off varies substantially between countries, among other reasons, because of differences in precollectivization land distribution and in postcollectivization ownership structure.

The concern for 'historical justice', that is, compensation to former owners whose land and assets were confiscated by the Communists or who were made to participate in the collectivization, and the 'equitable' or 'fair' distribution of assets are objectives not independent of one another, and may conflict. For example, the pre-collectivization land distribution in Bulgaria was rather egalitarian. This was much less the case in Bohemia (Czech Republic). Also, land distribution has been changed in all CEECs by various land reforms since the end of the nineteenth century. The issue of fairness or of undoing social injustice may be clouded by disputes about finding the proper reference point, that is, defending what kind of justice is to be restored. Land reforms were conducted in several CEECs before and just after the Second World War, prior to collectivisation (Mathijs, 1997) by democratic governments. The debates over which date to take as the basis for compensation or restitution of land reflect concern about the resulting distribution of wealth.

Another important aspect of this debate relates to the legitimacy of different policies. Fairness, social justice, and democratic legitimacy are some of the *raison d'êtres* of the new democratic regimes. Redistribution policies which clearly violate those principles endanger the survival of the new system, and policies that can be presented as undoing historical injustices can be expected to have a good chance of general approval.

An important effect of privatization and reallocation of property rights and decollectivization is the induced change in the distribution of income, wealth, and political influence in CEECs. This effect depends strongly on the privatization and the decollectivization *process* (Hillman, 1992). The design of transformation policies also has clear distributional implications. It will, for example, influence the ability of current management to remain in charge of the transformed cooperative farm. It will also affect the chances for current employees to remain employed or to become private individual farmers. Transformation policies therefore influence the distribution of future income streams and economic rents.

Several factors are relevant for determining if a person is going to win or lose from the reforms. Among individual variables one can list the following (Roland, 1992): individual skills, social position under Communism, the amount of job rents, and consumption rents. In addition to these, individuals differ with respect to the size of their claims on past property. Winners of restitutions are past owners or their heirs. In particular, people with large claims on land who possess skills in farming unutilised that would be valved in a privatized system are clear winners. Losers on the other hand, can be found among the management of the former collective farms and unskilled workers who have enjoyed job rents in the shelter of collective farming. Consumption rents were sizable as well, and particulary important to the large number of retired people living on collective farms, because state and collective farms were not only economic but also social centers.

The relative size of the winners and losers depends on several factors, such as the structure of agriculture and the larger economy at the time of the Communist takeover as well as the speed of structural transformation of the society during the Communist period. For example, large numbers of losers from land restitution, such as landless people employed on the former collective farms, can be found in CEECs with large numbers currently employed in agriculture, which had skewed land distribution in the pre-Communist period.

Finally, agrarian reform in CEECs also influences the social class structure in the rural areas and the rural political organization, which is partly based on the social and economic structure. The privatization and decollectivization process affects large landowners, landless agricultural workers, family farms, large corporate or cooperative farms, and small peasants in the emerging social structure. This emerging class structure affects the political preferences of the rural electorate: for example, the interests of large landowners and tenants coincide on output prices, but conflict over regulating land markets and land tenure. Typically differing organizations emerge to defend their interests. In some countries rural interests have been defended/captured by one party (for example, the Christian Democrats in Belgium). In other countries different parties and socio-political organizations have emerged (regarding France, see Tracy, 1989).

An important social factor is the potential development of a middle class in rural areas, based on private landownership and family farms if decollectivization is successful. The development of such a class of small property owners would not only potentially form the base for a long-term right-wing constituency, but would be an important base for securing political and economic reforms (Prosterman and Riedinger, 1989). On the other hand, small farmers with little comparative advantage are likely to end up as a low-income group and may support left-wing policies on taxation and social benefits. Such examples of agrarian-labor coalitions abound in the Nordic countries.

A political economy analysis of privatization and decollectivization

The importance of distributional effects

The distributional effects of agrarian reforms are a key issue in government decision making. The redistribution of assets or wealth involved in privatization is potentially much larger than current distribution of surpluses. What is redistributed are future income streams during the lifetime of the asset. Furthermore, once given away, assets can hardly be reclaimed by a democratic government which respects property rights. Redistribution of assets also involves redistribution of economic power and political influence and therefore has long-term implications for the future political structure of the country. A reform's potential distributional effects will determine to what extent various groups in society will support or oppose reform policies proposed by the government. Equity, fairness, and efficiency considerations may have played a role in both the rhetoric and the strategies of politicians and parties. However, those considerations have not solely been objectives, but have also served as instruments and ideological arguments used for political purposes. This is well captured by the assertion of Minchev et al. (1991) that '[b]ehind the ideological rethorics and moralizing, the [fight] between the interests of the current and potential economic and political elites is actually the main factor that [determines] the process of privatization'.

The emphasis on the distributional aspects of agrarian reform to explain the CEEC government choices is consistent with the basic assumption of political economy analyses of land reform. Analyses by de Janvry (1981a,b) of Latin American land reforms and by Hayami (1991) of Asian land reform attempts to discuss land reform primarily as a distributional – and therefore political – issue. Similarly, Allen (1982) concludes that the major consequence of the enclosure of open fields in eighteenth-century England was not to raise agricultural output but to redistribute existing income. Or as another writer puts it: 'Enclosure (when all the sophistications are allowed for) was a plain enough case of class robbery' (Thompson, 1963, quoted in Eggertson, 1990).

The inherent link between efficiency and distributional issues brings together Marxist and neoclassical thinking on institutions and institutional change:[13]

> neoclassical institutional economists focus their attention on allocative efficiency-improving institutions, whereas Marxist often emphasize how institutions change or do not change depending on considerations of surplus appropriation of a dominant class. ... The emphasis on the effect of an institutional change on control of surplus by a particular class also suggests that the question of efficiency-improving institutional change cannot really be separated from that of redistributive institutional change (Bardhan, 1989, p. 10-11).

Bardhan further stresses that it is important to understand the rationale of the formation of these institutions, how one was selected over another, and how in the historical-evolutionary process the underlying rationale changes and the institutional forms adapt and mutate in response to the changed circumstances. Our project attempts to contribute to this question by studying explicitly the origins and the choice mechanism that lie behind a particular process of institutional change, for example, property rights restoration and decollectivization in CEEC agriculture.

A public choice perspective

The main hypothesis of the public choice approach (i.e., the application of neoclassical economic analysis to political decisionmaking) is that individuals or organizations pursue their proper interests in the political arena. In this framework, strategies and actions of the agents (voters, politicians, interest groups, parties) are endogenously determined (Mueller, 1989). The actions follow from the agents' rational attempt to achieve their objective, given the constraints imposed by the political, economic and institutional environment. The implication for our analysis is that the choice of the reform process can be explained by analyzing the constraints, the proper objectives, and the strategies of the different agents involved in the political decisionmaking process. The actions of the agents must be consistent with their objectives, given the constraints imposed by the institutional environment. Important to realize is that the political process and changing institutional constraints can lead to an outcome of the process which may have little in common with the agents' objective.[14] Even if their objective is to implement the economically most efficient policies, they may not be able to do so because of political constraints. Overwhelming evidence supports this assumption in market economies and democratic regimes, and the case studies in this volume indicate that this assumption is valid as well in the CEECs.

In general, research on the political economy of transition is still at an early stage. We are far from having an integrated theory of political economy of reform (Roland, 1993). Our methodological approach relates to several strains of literature: the political economy of public debt and macroeconomic stabilization, political economy of trade policies, and theories of agrarian reforms, as well as political-science-based analyses of party competition.

As argued above, a key aspect of agrarian reform is redistribution. Therefore, the analysis can draw on existing public choice theories on redistributive policies such as protection or taxation. The study of the political economy of price and trade policies has learned that a trade-off between income (or wealth) distributional effects and economic efficiency is likely to affect decisionmaking about economic policies. Research on the political economy of trade and price policies, which was based on the public choice literature and has found widespread application in the agricultural economics literature, started from the observation of widespread occurrences of 'suboptimal' trade and price policies.[15] Much of the initial analyses were based on Becker's (1983) and Olson's (1965) models linking the size of the redistributive transfers to the effectiveness of various interest groups in controlling free-riding in collective action. Recent contributions focus on the influence of economic structure on the distributional impacts of price and trade policies as a key factor in explaining suboptimal policymaking. Changes in the distribution of costs and benefits of agricultural policies induce changes in political incentives and reactions, which lead to an adjustment of equilibrium policies (Swinnen, 1994a; Anderson, 1995). This is an important insight for our CEEC agrarian reform analysis where we observe a similar interaction between efficiency and distributional effects.

However, the application of trade political economy models is not straightforward. The models are typically of a static nature, analyzing long-term equilibrium outcomes. The equilibrium emerges either through the balancing of pressures that are put on the government by different interest groups or by the existence of sufficient political competition to force the government to reflect the marginal preferences of the electorate. However, the problem of CEEC privatization has a more discrete nature than models based on continuous choice problems. Furthermore, agricultural privatization in Central and Eastern Europe is a one-time event. The decision to privatize, the 'major decision', cannot be reversed. But the design and implementation of the process can be adjusted. Privatization laws have been revised or amended several times, in some cases more than ten times (OECD, 1994a). Moreover, by altering the decollectivization policies, governments may considerably encourage or discourage the privatization process, thereby making the process more than a one-time event and creating a process resembling to a continuous choice problem.

Another problem is that the dynamic objectives and constraints play a crucial role in the political game, which cannot be captured due to the static nature of most trade political economy models. Finally, the transition period between Communist rule and a parliamentary democracy has not been characterized by the political constraints that typically ensure a long-run equilibrium solution.

Some important insights come from the emerging literature on the political economy of economic transition. The choice between radical and smooth privatization as defined above is related to the choice between 'big-bang' and 'gradual' reforms of the economy (see Dewatripont and Roland, 1995, for a survey). Lyons et al. (1996) summarize the literature as follows: the arguments in favor of big-bang reforms are essentially political arguments, while the arguments in favor of gradual change are economic. However, Dewatripont and Roland (1995) argue that gradualism may be politically optimal as clever sequencing of the reform process may create constituencies for further reforms. If policy is designed in that way, it may be chosen even by reformers. Related analyses on the political acceptability of Pareto-improving reforms are Wyplosz (1993) and Roland and Verdier (1994). The latter model the probability of a political backlash against privatization in Eastern Europe as being endogenously determined by the level of privatization. The key factor is a critical mass effect due to economies of scale in privatization. Once full privatization is achieved, its efficiency gains will outweight the costs, making the process irreversible. Multiple equilibria may, however, arise. Other papers on the political economy dynamics of the privatization and transformation policies that focus on optimal design of reform programs include Haggard and Webb (1993) and Przeworski (1991).[16]

The importance of land restitution in the agrarian reform process reduces the immediate relevance of the general reform studies (focused often on sales and voucher privatization). An interesting formal model which is relevant to our approach is Lyons et al.'s (1994) analysis of Bulgarian agrarian reform (and generalized in Lyons et al., 1996). They model reform decisionmaking in which a prior decision affects the institutional constraints at a later level of decisionmaking. They formally derive a trade-off between disruption and continuity where the nomenklatura plays a crucial role as providers of indispensable human capital in agriculture and as a potential rent-extracting group. They identify conditions under which the quality of the transition is enhanced by coupling the nomenklatura's acquisition of political power to the magnitude of rents that they extract.

The impact of ideology

Many political economy models ignore ideology and partisanship in voting. Personal preferences of the policymakers are irrelevant in the world of perfect political competition of Becker (1958). Neither does a support-maximizing politician care about who is gaining or losing from a policy. What matters is that the support from the winners is greater than opposition from the losers. Median voter models assume that parties are spatially mobile, that is, without ideology. In contrast, partisan political business cycle theory is based on the assumption that it makes a difference whether a right-wing or a left-wing party is in power (Hibbs, 1977). Similarly, in some political science literature, parties are distinguished by different ideologies and represent different segments of the population:

> The most influential accounts of political conflicts in Western democracies have focused on the effects of pre-existing social cleavages on the development of the party system. According to these accounts voting is primarily an expression of social position and well-established values and interests associated with it: parties develop in order to express these interests (Evans and Whitefield, 1993, p. 523).

Evans and Whitefield further argue that issues of redistribution of income and wealth, unemployment and inflation, public ownership and welfare state, etc., have been found to be consistently and strongly related to partisanship in voting.

A key question in this literature is whether or not the structure of party competition emerging in the new CEEC democracies will resemble that commonly found in the West. Some argue that this will be the case (e.g., Kitschelt, 1992). Arguments against this view are that the formation of social

18

classes has been inhibited by egalitarian economic policies and disaggregation of economic and social resources such as property and wealth, as well as education and status in the past. People in several CEECs have been found to have difficulties placing themselves in a left-right dimension.

As pointed out above, ideology is ignored in many political economy models. A change of a policy is seen as the result of a change of supply or demand forces on the political market (or of relative pressure exerted by competing groups) and *not* as a result of *a change of the government per se.* Other theories (e.g., partisan business-cycle theories) predict that different governments would (or may) apply different policies. Under the conditions of dramatic changes of governments and policies, it appears that such linkage cannot be ignored. The ongoing battle between the former Communists and anti-Communist reformers can be expected to be important here, and agricultural privatization should be seen as a vital part of such a battle.

The role of political organization

The ability of winners and losers of privatization and transformation policies to organize differs. Both groups may not be equally successful in influencing the policies. Most collective farm members are still living within the former collective farms and are thus relatively concentrated. Preexisting labor unions of agricultural workers may also be useful in lobbying against the privatization of collective farms assets. Members of the former nomenklatura may rely on past organizational contacts. Many former owners (or heirs) live in urban areas, which makes it more difficult for them to form an organization and increases the cost of collective action.

An important factor is the gap in the organizational structure of the various parties. The formation of alternative political elites and the existence of alternative social structures were impaired by past oppression, while the ex-Communist party typically has relied on its well established formal or informal organizations. Some of these organizations were severely shaken by the unexpected and dramatic political events in 1989 and 1990. However, most have recovered to some extent and are now using their organizational strength for securing votes in the elections. In several countries the rural areas have turned out to be large support bases for former Communist parties, among other reasons because a large share of elderly people who worry about the reform impacts on their pensions live in rural areas. There is no doubt that political organization based on the structure of collective farms has played an important role in securing this rural political support.

Another closely related issue, which has been widely discussed, is the question of whether former Communist Party officials and related managers (the so-called *nomenklatura*) should be allowed to play a major role in post-

Communist society. There is also the issue of the extent to which the (ex-) Communist elite can hold on to power. A hold-to-power-strategy can be both economic and political. The political strategy is focused on remaining in power, if necessary under a different name and an 'adapted' program, as many former Communist and now Socialist parties have attempted to do. The economic strategy is to remain in charge of the economy by obtaining control over the privatized property rights of economic assets. The privatization strategy will seriously affect the potential for the former Communists to achieve this objective.

It is clear that the future structure of political competition in the CEECs will depend on a successful process of transformation to a market economy. Successful transition could result in similar types of socioeconomic cleavages as those observed in the West and in a similar party structure. However, if a failed transition simply makes almost everybody worse off, the likelihood of populist and extremist parties rising to prominence would increase. The idea of democracy still seems to be weakly rooted in the populations' values and expectations and is very dependent on the government's ability to produce acceptable living conditions. Under economic depression, new, vulnerable democracies risk breakdowns. Since the CEECs have been very different at the outset of the transition and are likely to develop at different speeds, it is highly probable that the process of party competition will differ substantially from country to country.

A radical land reform and decollectivization program, if well implemented, would have a reasonable chance of dismantling the social and economic structure that formed the backbone of the Communists' organizational strength in the rural areas and of thereby securing democratic and economic reforms. A radical privatization and decollectivization addresses three key strategies for radical reformers: (1) it damages the organizational structure from which the ex-Communists have been deriving their remarkable electoral strength; (2) it creates a long-term political support base for reforms; and (3) it removes the nomenklatura from the key positions that might allow them to block the implementation of reforms (Swinnen, 1994c).

Additional complication in the analysis of the privatization process, particularly in the Baltic countries, relates to the instability of institutions, especially constitutional institutions. What makes the analysis of the political competition in the transition economies difficult is that institutions have been changing as well. The constitutional institutions usually provide stability to the system. Such institutions can often be assumed to be exogenous, especially in the short run, due to high degree of inertia, which follows from extreme high set-up cost.

Ethnic nationalism has emerged as one of the most difficult issues in the transition process, particularly within the former Soviet Union. There are two interpretations of Communism's role in the present ethnic conflicts in the CEECs and former Soviet Union. The first suggests that ethnic nationalism was suppressed or 'frozen' by Communist regimes and has simply become visible again with freedom of expression. The second argument is that Communism not only contributed to the maintenance of ethnic claims but might be held responsible for the promotion, persistence, and virulence of new movements. Lingle (1992) has argued for the second explanation, referring to such features of Communist societies as encouragement of collectivist mentality, the presence of systematic political compulsion, systemic shortages, and economic insecurity, and the purposeful repression or neglect of the role of the entrepreneur. Without necessarily subscribing to all above mentioned points, one could add a very simple and obvious reason for increased ethnic tensions, namely the changed ethnic composition of many regions. This argument applies mainly to the former Soviet Union due to Soviet policies of forced resettlement for many groups and promotion of Russian migration to non-Russian regions.

The analysis of privatization becomes more complicated when ethnic tensions are present. Privatization now entails redistribution between socioeconomic cleavages and also between ethnic groups. The key question is whether or not the asset-competing groups share the same ethnicity. In countries where ethnic tensions are very severe, ethnic issues may dominate over socioeconomic conflicts. This is, in particular, a case when the statehood of a new country is only weakly established. A related issue is how the distributional conflicts within one sector, in our case, agriculture, relate to the distributional conflicts at large, in particular when such a conflict is based on ethnicity. The Baltic countries constitute interesting cases where such differences can be found.

Conclusion: a pragmatic approach

In conclusion, the authors of this collection use a rather general and pragmatic public choice framework to interpret and explain agrarian reform choices in CEECs. We assume that the actors rationally pursue their objectives. No doubt lack of experience and imperfect information have played a role in the debate and the decisionmaking in CEECs. The rational choice and revealed policy preference approach must therefore be applied with care, because of the enormous complexity involved and the CEECs' lack of previous experience with large-scale economic and social transition. Developments in these

21

economies has been surprising in many respects to foreign experts (Nuti and Portes, 1993) and might be even more confusing to domestic decisionmakers without previous experience with a market economy. Unlike trade policies, which have been present for a long period of time and whose effects are in general fairly well understood, privatization and decollectivization are more like a one-time event, in which one can expect that the *consequences* of policy decisions might be less understood. On the other hand, agricultural privatization has been debated much more widely and more intensely in those countries than trade policies usually are. Therefore, people in CEECs are likely to be better informed on the *decision* itself.

It is reasonable to assume that many political decisions are made with limited or imperfect information as well as with bounded rationality. Under such conditions, the subjective models of actors modified by very imperfect feedback and by ideology will shape the path (North, 1990). A proper analysis of the political process should thus concentrate on reconstructing the actual environment in which decisions are made, including the decision makers' subjective perceptions, beliefs, and ideological biases. One should allow for mistakes, unforeseen effects, or genuine surprises for all involved.

However, it seems too easy to explain suboptimal policymaking by putting it in the imperfect information basket or assigning it to irrationality. Furthermore, when information is costly and/or limited, it may well be that unintentional results or by-products emerge. However, in this case we would expect either to find governments trying to adjust the process and the implementation to correct for those unintended by-products (in case they want to stimulate the original policy) or to observe, after a change in government, a less supportive government stimulating those policies that create negative by-products. Both actions have been rather consistently observed in the various CEECs and are consistent with our 'rational choice, learning-by-doing' perspective.

Our study relates the political developments since the end of the 1980s and the objectives and strategies of the various political actors (ex-Communists, reformers, and an increasing number of new parties) and interest groups to the agrarian reforms. We apply a revealed policy preference approach. Instead of focusing on the rhetoric, we analyze the positions taken in decisionmaking – which laws and regulations were approved under which governments and how they have (or have not) been implemented.

We focus on several key factors that might affect decisionmaking regarding agricultural privatization and transformation policies and their implementation. We have found that political reform and changes in governments should be variables to consider when analyzing policy choice and government decisionmaking. Reform of political institutions and the consequent election results affect both the decisionmaking process and the distribution of influence among the major political actors and parties. Examples include the number of seats in Parliament (ex-)Communists maintain or whether radical reformers can form a government with or without more moderate coalition partners.

A key factor is the distributional effects of the agricultural privatization and decollectivization program. These distributional effects raise reactions from various groups of the population (the constituency). Therefore, distributional effects influence the demand side of the political market in which privatization and decollectivization are the 'political commodities' (policies) exchanged between the government that supplies the policies and various groups in the economy that demand the policies. These distributional effects are influenced themselves by the precollectivization land distribution. Factors such as the equality of precollectivization land distribution, the share of land owned by organizations such as the Catholic Church, the share of land owned by foreigners, etc., all influence effective demand for land reform and land restitution.

Distributional effects are also influenced by the importance of agriculture in export earnings, in providing employment, and in securing the domestic food supply. In addition, it is likely that the economic performance of agriculture under the Communist system will influence popular opinion about whether dramatic reforms are needed to restructure the system and make it more efficient.

Notes

1. Alain de Janvry (1981a) argues that land reform aims at changing the agrarian structure, defined as (a) a system of social relations (i.e., *modes of production* and their corresponding *social class structure*) and (b) a system of land tenure. Considered from this framework, there was general agreement in Central and Eastern Europe on the need to change from a socialist to a capitalist mode of production in agriculture. The main discussion centered on how this could best be achieved, and key issues were how the process would change the class structure and land tenure patterns.

2. The concept of property rights is closely related to that of transaction costs. If transaction costs are associated with the transfer, capture, and protection of rights, and if each of these costs is positive and rises with the actions, rights to assets cannot be perfectly delineated. Assets have many attributes that are typically not well known to at least one of the partners in a potential exchange. Access to information is usually uneven, present owners or users are better informed. The transfer of assets entails costs, resulting from both parties' attempts to determine the valued attributes of

assets. Exchanges that otherwise would be attractive may be abandoned because of such exchange costs (Barzel, 1989).

3   The simultaneous use of several approaches often generates conflict and inconsistencies, especially when the privatization strategy is altered while the process is going on. For example, privatization in Latvia started during the Soviet period with the creation of private farms on a usufruct basis. Not all the farmers were former owners, some received somebody else's land. When the Latvian government decided to restitute agricultural land to former owners, conflicting claims on land were frequent, as were conflicts between land claims and privatization of farm enterprises. Such conflicts leave more to the discretion of local administrations. Furthermore, conflicting claims, court procedures, and inherent uncertainty impede the progress in privatization and stimulate the decline of production (Rabinowicz, 1997).

4   For a brief discussion of market socialism, i.e., the functioning of the market without privatization, see Hillman (1992).

5   See Dewatripont and Roland (1995) for a survey of the discussion.

6   Schumpeter (1942), Hayek (1945), and more recently, North (1990) and Williamson (1992) further argue that in a *static* framework the question of economic optimality is less important. Instead, the main issue in economics should be change and adaptation. The objective of economics should therefore not be 'allocative efficiency', but rather 'adaptive efficiency' or 'dynamic efficiency', and there is no a priori reason why both should coincide (Williamson, 1992). Moreover, a trade-off may exist between static efficiency and adaptability when considering questions of institutional choice.

7   Within the neoclassical economics literature different schools emphasize information, monitoring, and enforcement costs (Williamson, 1985; Bardhan, 1989; North, 1990; Eggertson, 1990). The original discussion of transaction costs is usually traced back to Coase (1960), despite the fact that Coase himself never used the expression.

8   The original point (while not presented as a theorem) was made in Coase (1960). For a discussion of the (mostly unintended and, according to Coase, mostly irrelevant and incorrect) implications of the discussion, see Coase (1989).

9   Privatization and transformation are also interdependent because both have distributional impacts. The distributional impacts of privatization are straightforward, as the distribution of property rights will affect future income streams. The transformation policy will affect restructuring of farms and will therefore influence how former management and employees can retain their position in the restructured enterprises. Therefore, both privatization and transformation policies are important in determining the

24

distributional effects and the transformed organizations that result from reforms.

10 The importance of land tenureship varies tremendously, even between countries with relatively similar characteristics. For example, in Belgium 72 percent of agricultural land is rented compared with less than 10 percent in Ireland. Government interventions in the form of tenure contract regulations play an important role in explaining these differences in land tenureship.

11 It is possible for a government (or a party platform) to combine radical price liberalization with smooth decollectivization policies. For example, the Czech government under Vaclav Klaus could be characterized as implementing radical price and trade liberalization policies while supporting smooth transformation of the agricultural production entities. On the opposite side, several peasant parties have supported more radical privatization and decollectivization policies that create a family-farm-based agricultural structure, while demanding price support and subsidies for farmers.

12 The problem as represented here is independent of whether the privatization choice is made prior to or after the transformation choice. In reality, the privatization choice often preceeds the transformation choice at the government level, but implementation could start with transformation. However, while the privatization program choice can be amended, it is much more a 'one time decision' than is transformation policy, which can be adjusted regularly. An example is credit and debt policy. Most agricultural collectives are loaded with debts. When members are leaving the collective to start their own private farm they must take with them a share of the debt, which is divided over the assets, as is the case in the Czech and Slovak Republic. This provides an important negative incentive for members wanting to leave the cooperative. Agricultural credit is a problematic issue in all CEECs during transition. Credit supply is limited and nominal interest rates are very high, increasing uncertainty and production risk. Policies that provide more or less subsidized credit for cooperative versus family farms can influence individual decisions to stay within the cooperative farms or to attempt to start their own farms. Such policies can be regularly adjusted by new governments.

13 The latter refers to the emerging field of new institutional economics. Standard neoclassical theory in general ignores institutions such as markets and property rights: it assumes they exist and are perfect. New institutional economics (NIE) encompasses a series of subfields (see Eggertson, 1990). However, the NIE paradigm which studies institutions, including property rights, as endogenous outcomes of individuals and groups trying to maximize their utility, has some important shortcomings.

Institutions are too often considered efficient because they are hypothesized to emerge because they minimize transaction costs. NIE often unthinkingly implies the application of market analogy of competitive equilibrium to the social choice of institutions or the biological analogy of natural selection in the survival of the fittest institution (Bardhan, 1989). Yet, even with rational behavior, there is no assurance that an institutional arrangement will come into being simply because it is more efficient than existing alternatives. See Platteau (1992) for an excellent discussion. Lipton (1993) has a somewhat different, though related, perspective. North (1990) has attempted to address some of these shortcomings.

14 For example, in a world of 'perfect political competition' the personal preferences of the policymakers are irrelevant, because the only way they can survive in office is by reflecting the electorate's preferences (Becker, 1958). The argument has a strong analogy to the classic case for profit maximizing as a derived objective for firms in a competitive market (Alchian and Demsetz, 1972).

15 The public choice literature is largely based on the seminal work of Downs (1957), Olson (1965) and Buchanan and Tullock (1962). For a survey of its application on price and trade policies, see Hillman (1989) and Baldwin (1989); for its application to agricultural policies, see Swinnen and van der Zee (1993).

16 In general, these studies concentrate on the 'macro' aspects of privatization and are closely related to the literature on political cycles in macroeconomic policies. The political economy of macroeconomic policy is surveyed in Persson and Tabellini (1991). This approach contributes important insights on the role of strategic government behavior and the role of government credibility in dynamic and short-run political cycles. However, the application to privatization is not straightforward because privatization is a one-time policy, while macroeconomic policy is an ongoing problem. Furthermore, the political institutional environment is exogenous and fixed in most of these models. Some of this literature does analyze the impact of institutions, such as degree of central bank independence on budget deficits and macroeconomic outcomes.

References

Alchian, A. and Demsetz, H. (1972), 'Production, Information Costs, and Economic Organization', *American Economic Review,* Vol. 62, pp. 777-795.
Allen, R. (1982), 'The Efficiency and Distributional Consequences of Eighteenth Century Enclosures', *Economic Journal*, Vol. 92, pp. 937-953.

Anderson, K. (1995), 'Lobbying Incentives and the Pattern of Protection in Rich and Poor Countries', *Economic Development and Cultural Change*, Vol. 43, No. 2, pp. 401 - 423.

Baldwin, R. (1989), 'The Political Economy of Trade Policy', *Journal of Economic Perspectives*, Vol. 3, No. 4, pp. 119-135.

Bardhan, P. (ed.) (1989), *The Economic Theory of Agrarian Institutions,* Clarendon Press: Oxford.

Barzel, Y. (1989), *Economic Analysis of Property Rights*, Cambridge University Press: Cambridge.

Becker, G. (1958), 'Competition and Democracy', *Journal of Law and Economics*, Vol. 1, pp. 105-109.

Becker, G. (1983), 'A Theory of Competition Among Pressure Groups for Political Influence', *Quarterly Journal of Economics*, Vol. 68, No. 3, pp. 371-400.

Binswanger H. and Rosenzweig, M. (1986), 'Behavioral and Material Determinants of Production Relations in Agriculture', *Journal of Development Studies*, Vol. 22, No. 3, pp. 5-21.

Brooks, K., Guasch, J. L., Braverman, A. and Csaki, C. (1991), 'Agriculture and the Transition to the Market', *Journal of Economic Perspectives*, Vol. 5, No. 4, pp. 149-161.

Buchanan, J. and Tullock, G. (1962), *The Calculus of Consent*, University of Michigan Press: Ann Arbor.

Coase, R. H. (1960), 'The Problem of Social Cost', *Journal of Law and Economics*, Vol. 3, No. 1, pp. 1-44.

Coase, R. H. (1989), *The Firm, The Market and The Law*, University of Chicago Press: Chicago.

Csaki C. and Kislev, Y. (eds.) (1993), *Agricultural Cooperatives in Transition*, Westview Press: Boulder.

Csaki, C. and Lerman, Z. (1994), 'Land Reform and Farm Sector Restructuring in the Former Socialist Countries in Europe', *European Review of Agricultural Economics*, Vol. 21, No. 3-4, pp. 553-576.

Csaki, C. and Lerman, Z. (1995). 'Agricultural Transformation in Central and Eastern Europe and the Former USSR: Issues of land Reform and Restructuring', unpublished manuscript, The World Bank: Washington D.C.

de Janvry, A. (1981a), 'The Role of Land Reform in Economic Development: Policies and Politics', *American Journal of Agricultural Economics*, Vol. 63, May, pp. 384-392.

de Janvry, A. (1981b), *The Agrarian Question and Reformism in Latin America*, The Johns Hopkins University Press: Baltimore and London.

Dewatripont, M. and Roland, G. (1992), 'Economic Reform and Dynamic Political Constraints', *Review of Economic Studies*, Vol. 59, pp. 703-730.

Dewatripont, M. and Roland, G. (1995), 'The Design of Reform Packages under Uncertainty', *American Economic Review*, Vol. 85, No. 5, pp. 1207-1223.

Downs, A. (1957), *An Economic Theory of Democracy*, Harper and Row Publishers: New York.

Eggertson, T. (1990), *Economic Behavior and Institutions*, Cambridge University Press: Cambridge.

Ellis, F. (1988), *Peasant Economics. Farm Households and Agrarian Development*, Cambridge University Press: Cambridge.

Evans, G. and Whitefield, S. (1993), 'Identifying the Bases of Party Competition in Eastern Europe', *British Journal of Political Sciences*, Vol. 23, pp. 521-548.

Hagedorn, K. (1992), 'Transformation of Socialist Agricultural Systems', *Journal of International and Comparative Economics*, Vol. 1, pp. 103-124.

Haggard, S. and Webb, S. (1993), 'What Do We Know About the Political Economy of Economic Policy Reform?', *The World Bank Research Observer*, Vol. 8, No. 2, pp. 143-68.

Hayami, Y. (1991), 'Land Reform', in Meier, G. (ed.), *Politics and Policy Making in Developing Countries. Perspectives on the New Political Economy*, ICS Press: San Francisco, pp.155-171.

Hayek, F. (1945), 'The Use of Knowledge in Society', *American Economic Review*, Vol. 35, pp. 519-530.

Hibbs, D. A. (1977), 'Political Parties and Macroeconomic Policy', *American Political Science Review*, Vol. 71, pp. 1467-87.

Hillman, A. L. (1989), *The Political Economy of Protection*, Harwood Academic Publishers: New York.

Hillman, A. L. (1992), 'Progress with Privatization', *Journal of Comparative Economics*, Vol. 16, pp. 733-749.

Hinds, M. (1991), 'Incentives and Ownership in Socialist Countries in Transition', in Hillman, A. L. (ed.), *Markets and Politicians: Politicized Economic Choice*, Kluwer: Boston and Dordrecht.

Jackson, M. and Swinnen, J. (1995), *A Statistical Analysis and Survey of the Current Situation of Agriculture in Central and Eastern European Countries*, Report to EU Commission DG-I, LICOS, K.U.Leuven.

Juhasz, J. (1989), 'Hungarian Agriculture: Present Situation and Future Prospects', *European Review of Agricultural Economics* (Conference Proceedings), Vol. 18, No. 3, pp. 399-416.

Kitschelt, H. (1992), 'The Formation of Party System in East and Central Europe', *Politics and Society*, Vol. 20, pp. 7-50.

Lingle, L. (1992), 'Ethnic Nationalism and Post-Communist Transition Problems', in Somogyi, L. (ed.), *The Political Economy of the Transition Process in Eastern Europe*, Edward Elgar Publishing.

Lipton M. (1993), 'Land Reform as Commenced Business: The Evidence Against Stopping' (in de Janvry, A., Sadoulet E. and Thorbecke, E. (eds.), State, Market, and Civil Organizations: New Theories, New Practices, and Their Implications for Rural Development), *World Development*, Vol. 21, No. 4, pp. 641-658.

Lyons, R., Rausser, G. and Simon, L. (1994), 'Disruption and Continuity in Bulgaria's Agrarian Reform', in Schmitz, A., Moulton, K., Buckwell, A., and Davidova, S. (eds.), *Privatization of Agriculture in New Market Economies: Lessons from Bulgaria*, Kluwer Academic Publishers: Boston, London, and Dordrecht.

Lyons, R., Rausser, G. and Simon, L. (1996), 'Political Economy of Transition', unpublished manuscript, Department of Agricultural and Resource Economics, University of California: Berkeley.

Mathijs, E. (1997), 'An historical overview of Central and Eastern European land reform', chapter 2 in this volume.

Mathijs, E. and Swinnen, J. (1996a), 'The Economics of Agricultural Decollectivization in Central and Eastern Europe', Working Paper Series of the joint Research Project: *Agricultural Implications of CEEC Accession to the EU*, Working Paper No. 3/1, Department of Agricultural Economics, K.U.Leuven.

Mathijs, E. and Swinnen, J. (1996b), 'The Efficiency of Privatization and Decollectivization Policies in Central and Eastern European Agriculture', unpublished manuscript, Department of Agricultural Economics, K.U.Leuven.

Minchev, O., Young, D. and Prigorova, M. (1991), 'Editorial Comment', *Bulgarian Quarterly*, Vol. 2, pp. 5-10.

Mueller, D. (1989), *Public Choice II*, Cambridge University Press: Cambridge.

North, D. (1990), *Institutions, Institutional change and Economic Performance*, Cambridge University Press: Cambridge.

Nuti, D. M. and Portes, R. (1993), 'Central Europe: The Way Forward', in Portes, R. (ed.), *Economic Transformation in Central Europe: A Progress Report*, Butler & Tanner Ltd: London and Luxembourg.

OECD (1994a), *Agricultural Policies, Markets and Trade in the Central and Eastern European Countries, The New Independent States, Mongolia and China: Monitoring and Outlook 1994*, OECD: Paris.

OECD (1994b), *Review of Agricultural Policies: Hungary*, OECD: Paris.

Olson, M. (1965), *The Logic of Collective Action*, Harvard University Press: Cambridge.

Persson T. and Tabellini, G. (1991), *Macroeconomic Policy, Credibility and Politics* (Fundamentals of Pure and Applied Economics), Harwood Academic Publishers: Chur.

Platteau, J.-P. (1992), *Land Reform and Structural Adjustment in Sub-Saharan Africa: Controversies and Guidelines* (FAO Economic and Social Development Paper 107), FAO: Rome.

Pollak, R., (1985), 'A Transaction Cost Approach to Families and Households', *Journal of Economic Literature*, Vol. 23, June, pp. 581-608.

Prosterman, R. L. and Riedinger, J. M. (1989), *Land Reform and Democratic Development*, The Johns Hopkins University Press: Baltimore and London.

Przeworski, A. (1991), *Democracy and the Market: Political and Economic Reform in Eastern Europe and Latin America*, Cambridge University Press: New York.

Pryor, F. L. (1992), *The Red and the Green. The Rise and Fall of Collectivized Regimes*, Princeton University Press: Princeton.

Rabinowicz, E. (1997), 'Political economy of agricultural privatization in the Baltics', chapter 4 in this volume.

Roland, G. (1992), 'Issues in the Political Economy of Transition in The Economic Consequences of the East', Report of a conference organized by the Centre for Economic Policy Research.

Roland, G. (1993), 'The Political Economy of Restructuring and Privatization in Eastern Europe', *European Economic Review*, Vol. 37, pp. 533-540.

Roland, G. and Verdier, T. (1994), 'Privatization in Eastern Europe. Irreversibility and Critical Mass Effects', *Journal of Public Economics*, Vol. 54, pp. 161-183.

Rosenzweig, M., Binswanger, H. and McIntire, J. (1988), 'From Land Abundance to Land Scarcity -- the Effects of Population Growth on Production Relations in Agrarian Economies', in Lee, R., Arthur, W., Kelley, A., Rodgers, G. and Srinivasan, T. N. (eds.), *Population, Food and Rural Development*, Clarendon Press: Oxford.

Schmitt, G. (1993), 'Why Collectivization of Agriculture in Socialist Countries Has Failed: A Transaction Cost Approach', in Csaki C. and Kislev, Y. (eds.), *Agricultural Cooperatives in Transition*, Westview Press: Boulder.

Schumpeter, J. (1942), *Capitalism, Socialism and Democracy*, Harper & Bros: New York.

Swinnen, J. (1994a), 'A Positive Theory of Agricultural Protection', *American Journal of Agricultural Economics*, Vol. 76, No. 1, pp. 1-14.

Swinnen, J. (ed.) (1994b), *Policy and Institutional Reform in Central European Agriculture*, Avebury: Aldershot.

Swinnen, J. (1994c), 'Political Economy of Reform in Bulgarian Agriculture', in Schmitz, A., Moulton, K., Buckwell, A., and Davidova, S. (eds.), *Privatization of Agriculture in New Market Economies: Lessons from Bulgaria*, Kluwer Academic Publishers: Boston, London, and Dordrecht.

Swinnen, J., Christiaensen, L. and Felton-Taylor, L. (1994), 'Agricultural Production Structures and Their Determinants', in *Agricultural Cooperatives and Emerging Farm Structures in Hungary*, OECD: Paris.

Swinnen, J. (1995), 'Does Compensating for Disruptions Stimulate Reforms? The Case of Agrarian Reform in Central Europe', *Discussion Papers on the Economic Transformation: Policy, Institutions and Structure*, Working Paper 43/1995, Leuven Institute for Central and East European Studies: Leuven.

Swinnen, J. and van der Zee, F. (1993), 'The New Political Economy of Agricultural Policies: A Survey', *European Review of Agricultural Economics*, Vol. 20, No. 3, pp. 261-290.

Tracy, M. (1989), *Governments and Agriculture in Western Europe 1880 - 1988*, Granada Publishers: London.

Thompson, E. P. (1963), *The Making of the English Working Class*, Random House: New York.

Vickers, J. and Yarrow, G. (1991), 'Economic Perspectives on Privatization', *Journal of Economic Perspectives*, Vol. 5, No. 2, pp. 111-132.

Williamson, O. (1992), 'Economic Institutions: Spontaneous and Intentional Governance', *Journal of Law, Economics and Organization*, Vol. 7, pp. 159-187.

Wyplosz, C. (1993), 'After the Honeymoon. On the Economics and the Politics of Economic Transformation', *European Economic Review*, Vol. 37, pp. 379-386.

2 An historical overview of Central and Eastern European land reform

Erik Mathijs[1]

Introduction

Central and Eastern Europe witnessed four major waves of land reform in this century. After both the First and the Second World War, land reform was legislated partly to compensate the victims and punish the losers of the war, but also to change the ownership distribution of land (which affected the political preference structure in society). Land reform in the 1920s was intended both to break ties with the feudal past and to anticipate the threat of Communism. Land reform after the Second World War can be regarded as the first phase of the collectivization of Central and Eastern European (CEE) agriculture, as it was passed by governments dominated by Communists in the presence of the Red Army. The collectivization of CEE agriculture constituted a third land reform movement, and it radically changed the face of agriculture. Finally, democratic changes at the end of the 1980s are leading to the decollectivization of CEE agriculture. This chapter provides a brief overview of the background, the motives and the effects of the first three land reform movements that preceded the current land reforms.

Twentieth century land reforms in Central and Eastern Europe

The interbellum land reforms (1919-1939)

The several land reform measures taken or attempted in the 1920's had in common the background of World War I, the breakthrough towards democracy that followed or appeared to follow upon it, and the shadow of the revolution in Russia (Dovring, 1965, p.258).

A strong demand for land reform existed after the First World War as interwar CEE agriculture was characterized by overpopulation and poverty. Okey (1982) described the CEE countryside between the two world wars as 'a hopelessly under-capitalized, overpopulated bottom rung of the European economy'. Overpopulation was considered the fundamental problem of Central Europe's peasantry by Seton-Watson (1986) (see table 2.1). He reports that in 1918 the proportion of peasants in the total population was 80 percent in Bulgaria, 78 percent in Romania, 63 percent in Poland, 55 percent in Hungary, and 34 percent in Czechoslovakia. Furthermore, in all Central and Eastern European countries (CEECs) except Bulgaria, landownership was highly unequal. In what could be considered a feudal system, landless peasants worked on large estates owned by the aristocracy. Around 1930, the percentage of the land in farms (see table 2.2) smaller than 5 hectares was 2.3 in Latvia, 3.7 in Lithuania, 16.3 in Poland, 20.1 in Hungary, 28 in Romania and Yugoslavia, and 30 percent in Bulgaria (Moore, 1945; Berend, 1985). Inherent social conflicts were exacerbated during World War I. The demand for land redistribution to improve the situation of the peasants became so strong that land reform was inevitable to keep the support of the peasants.

Table 2.1
Proportion of peasants in the total population

Country	Percentage of peasants
Bulgaria	80
Czechoslovakia	34
Hungary	55
Poland	63
Romania	78

Source: Seton-Watson, 1986.

Most CEECs were rural societies, and during the First World War peasants organized themselves and were armed. In most of these countries, this resulted in significant political power for the peasants after the war. Peasant parties such as the Agrarian Party in Czechoslovakia and the National Peasant Party in Romania increased their power, and some even won elections and formed governments (for example, the National Smallholders' Party in Hungary and Stamboliski's Agrarian Union in Bulgaria). These governments were eager to implement land reform.

34

Table 2.2
Percentage of land in farms smaller than 5 hectares

Country	Percentage of land
Bulgaria	30.0
Hungary	20.1
Latvia	2.3
Lithuania	3.7
Poland	16.3
Romania	28.0
Yugoslavia	28.0

Source: Moore, 1945; Berend, 1985.

Three other factors played a role in land reform: the democratization of politics, the consequences of World War I, and the threat of Communism. Democratic elections were held in all CEECs and resulted in a brief period of democratic governments.   The power of the aristocracy declined, the bourgeoisie took over.   Hence, the interwar land reforms had an antifeudal slant.   But the interwar land reforms also had an anti-Communist slant. 'Bourgeois' governments feared that the Communist Revolution in Russia would spread to Central Europe. Giving some land to the poor and the landless was therefore a strategy to take away the breeding ground for Communist revolt. The antifeudal element of the land reforms was induced by the First World War, which ended in defeat for Germany and the Austro-Hungarian Empire.[2] The conditions imposed on Hungary were settled in the Trianon Peace Treaty, signed in 1920. Three new 'successor' states were created out of the Austro-Hungarian Empire: Hungary, Czechoslovakia, and Yugoslavia. Big parts of the former dual monarchy were also divided among the other Allied countries. Table 2.3 gives an overview of the extreme division of Hungary that constituted the severe peace conditions imposed by the Allies. Hungary not only lost twothirds of its area, but also onethirth of its native Magyar population.   In these areas land reform (essentially expropriating a foreign aristocracy) was easiest to pursue.

Table 2.3
Area and population losses of Hungary after World War I
based on statistics extrapolated from the 1910 census

	Area (in '000 sq.km.)	Population (in '000)	Magyars (in '000)
Hungary before World War I (without Croatia-Slavonia)	283	18,265	9,945
Benefitors:			
Austria	4	292	26
Czechoslovakia	62	3,518	1,067
Poland	0.6	24	0.2
Romania	103	5,257	1,662
Yugoslavia	21	1,509	452
Italy	0.021	50	6
Total losses	190	10,649	3,214
Postwar Hungary	93	7,615	6,731

Source: Rothschild, 1974.

Interwar land reforms had different impacts in the different CEECs. Several factors influenced the impact of land reforms on peasants' welfare:

1 Inheritance rules hindered the development of a viable agricultural sector. In most regions, it was the custom to divide land between all sons when the owner died. Hence, strong fragmentation occurred. Only in western Poland, the Czech lands, and parts of Hungary, was the Napoleontic code used, which stipulated that the eldest son inherited all the land.

2 The Great Depression of the 1930s shifted terms of trade against the agricultural sector.

3 CEE governments failed to create the institutions to support the new landowners (Cochrane, 1993). They failed to invest in a series of measures to improve agricultural productivity, such as technical education, supply of credit, regrouping of the existing strip holdings into more rational units, cultivation of different crops, development of local and international transport, public works, and the organization of

efficient cooperatives. They also failed to improve the shift of surplus labor to other sectors. Without these measures, land reforms proved insufficient to solve the 'peasant problem' (Seton-Watson, 1986).

4 In all CEECs, except Czechoslovakia, democracy ended in dictatorship: Admiral Horthy in Hungary; Pilsudski and, after him the 'Government of the Colonels' in Poland; King Carol II in Romania; King Zog in Albania, and King Alexander in Yugoslavia. As these dictators based a great deal of their power on the aristocracy, the implementation of the land reform legislation passed by earlier democratic governments was first slowed down and eventually stopped.

Three types of rural societies emerged as a result of the interwar land reform just before the Second World War in Central and Eastern Europe: (1) countries dominated by small, unviable farms emerged as a result of radical land reforms in the interwar period (Romania, Czechoslovakia) or before the First World War (Albania, Bulgaria); (2) countries where viable farms were created through land reform (Latvia and Lithuania); (3) and countries where big estates survived (Hungary and Poland).

Hence, in most CEECs, the rural economic and social problems were not solved. As democratic regimes were replaced by dictatorships, except in Czechoslovakia, promises of land reform were not fulfilled, and as Swain and Swain (1993, p. 2) contend:

Such a combination of circumstances was bound to provide a good breeding ground for communism among East European intellectuals. The region was backward, prey to the whims of foreign capitalists when it came to investment decisions, and ruled by self-interested cliques: what Lenin's followers seemed to be achieving in peasant Russia in the inter-war years, spectacular economic growth on the basis of peasant co-operative farms, was bound to be attractive. A generation of young people grew up in inter-war Eastern Europe convinced that Lenin's message had meaning for them.

The land reforms immediately after the Second World War (1945-1948)

The Second World War ended on 8 May 1945 with the defeat of Nazi Germany and its allies Italy, Hungary, Bulgaria, and Romania. All CEECs were liberated by the Soviet Red Army and started postwar reconstruction under provisional governments dominated by the Communists. Before formal Communist rule, land reforms were passed, as were a set of other economic reforms, by these provisional governments. Communist and socialist parties were supported by smallholders in implementing a land reform and in expropriating land owned by 'the enemy'. However, it soon became clear that the Communists also considered rich peasants, or kulaks, their enemy.

Lenin believed that collectivization would occur voluntarily over time as the poor peasants came to see the advantages of large-scale mechanized production. He therefore advocated a gradual transition from peasant farming to collective farming. In his view, no force should not be needed to make peasants join the collectives. Nevertheless, the village became a battleground for the rural bourgeoisie and the rich farmers (kulaks) on the one hand, and the rural proletariat, the poor peasants, and the landless on the other hand. Thus, the peasantry had to be split in order for collectivization to win the support of the poor. Lenin also emphasized the importance of the worker-peasant alliance: urban workers were to be sent to the countryside to educate the peasants and bring them revolution. In a first phase of collectivization, those identified as kulaks had to face land confiscation and even deportation, and their land was given to the poor. Indebted to the state, the poor peasants who were the recipients of this land then had a strong incentive to join the collectives (Sokolovsky, 1990).

Ideas regarding peasant class structure and the relationship between the peasantry and the socialist state that were applied in Russia's collectivization in the 1920s were used as a guide for collectivization policy in Central Europe. In all of the Central European countries, collectivization was preceded by one or more land reforms. The land that was confiscated and partly redistributed first was that of large estates belonging to Germans or collaborators. But also the land of the rich, not only of kulaks but also of the Catholic Church, was taken without compensation. Table 2.4 indicates in more detail the sources of land which were available after the Second World War. As can be seen from table 2.4, only in Hungary and Romania was the expropriation of property belonging to native landowners the principal source of land. In Poland and Czechoslovakia, most land came from former German ownership, constituting in Poland almost onethird of the total country's area, and a quarter in Czechoslovakia (Brus, 1986).

Communists took power in Central Europe in three different ways. In Bulgaria and Yugoslavia the Communists had won a revolution through war and were disdainful of the need to legitimize their regimes through the procedures of 'bourgeois' democracy. They believed that democracy expressed through a popular front was a fairer way of gauging popular support. In Romania and Poland, Stalin decided to use force to establish Communist rule and to settle the border disputes with these countries. In Hungary and Czechoslovakia, Stalin was initially pleased with the role the Communists played in the respective coalition governments. But after President Truman declared his doctrine and launched the Marshall Plan, Stalin feared Hungary and Czechoslovakia would disappear from his sphere of influence. Only after the establishment of the Cominform did the Communists take total control in Hungary and Czechoslovakia.

Table 2.4
Sources of land available for the agrarian reforms after the Second World War

Origin of area under land reform (in %)

	Total area (in million ha)	Estates above the legal limit	German ownership	Collaborators and war criminals	Other
Hungary	3.2	29	71	-	-
Poland	13.1	24	76	-	-
Czechoslovakia	4.2	90	-	10	-
Romania	1.5	73	24	-	-
Yugoslavia	1.6	22	41	6	31

Source: Brus, 1986.

Nevertheless, land reforms were implemented in all CEECs, initiated by Communists who had been inspired by the Soviet example of the 1920s, and supported by the smallholders. Land reform legislation was passed by coalition governments in Bulgaria, Hungary, and Czechoslovakia and by a Communist government in Yugoslavia, Albania, Poland, Romania, Latvia, and Lithuania. As a result, 64 percent of the total land was redistributed in Hungary, 50 percent in Poland, 17 percent in Czechoslovakia, 8 percent in Romania, 6 percent in Yugoslavia and 2 percent in Bulgaria (Brus, 1986).

Collectivization (1948-1989)

In 1948 Stalin founded the Cominform to strengthen the imposition of his ideas on Central Europe. Land reform after World War II was soon followed by the collectivization of agriculture. The aim of collectivization was to simultaneously achieve political supervision and economic regulation of the whole economy. Because of the economies of scale and the increased efficiency due to an accumulation of capital, economic performance and development was improved (Schmitt, 1993) or, as Cochrane (1993) contends, agriculture experienced a period of 'arrested development'. After Stalin's death in 1953, Communist rule under Khrushchev resulted in a slowdown of collectivization. Political unrest culminated in the short Hungarian revolution in 1956. Khrushchev was replaced by Brezhnev in 1964, and the economic and political regime was tightened.

In the 1920s, Preobrazhensky had introduced the concept of 'primitive socialist accumulation' into the debate about economic policy in the Soviet Union. He argued that the establishment of socialism in a country surrounded by enemies depended on expansion of the state-owned industrial sector. Sokolovsky (1990) calls this 'collectivization as control of economic resources'. It aimed at the transformation of private property into state property through a phase of collective property.

Collectivized agriculture was to be organized into four types of production units: (1) the state farm, owned by the state, where farmers worked as wage laborers and which was seen as the highest form of collective; (2) the collective farm, a transitional form between the state farm and individual peasant plots; (3) machine-tractor stations, concentrations of agricultural machinery hired by the rural enterprises for specific tasks; and (4) private farms, linked to government planning through tax, credit, and pricing policies (Sokolovsky, 1990).

Five phases can be identified in the general pattern of collectivization in the different CEECs. A first step constituted the postwar land reform described earlier. In a second step, the initial collectivization drive, was begun in the period 1948-49. Third, a period of retreat and the introduction of the Soviet New Course under Malenkov followed Stalin's death in 1953. Fourth, there was a brief resumption of collectivization in 1955 under Khrushchev. The final push toward collectivization followed in the late fifties. General collectivization was achieved by 1962 in Bulgaria, Czechoslovakia, Romania, and Hungary. In Bulgaria collectivization was achieved most forcefully and most quickly. In Poland and Yugoslavia the second drive was never implemented, mainly due to political developments.

The Soviet model of collectivization was never applied in its most radical form in Central and Eastern Europe, as it was in China up to 1978 and in Cuba. Most CEECs, including the Soviet Union itself, chose for 'a more or less reformed orthodox type of collectivization', as Wädekin (1990) calls it. He considers the Hungarian model a third type of Communist agriculture. Key factors in the collectivization of agriculture are the level of economic development and the natural endowment. Wädekin defines four groups according to the share of agricultural in total active population in 1986:

less than 10 percent	Czechoslovakia and East Germany
10-30 percent	Hungary, Soviet Union, Cuba, and Bulgaria
30-45 percent	North Korea, Mongolia, and Romania
more than 45 percent	China, Albania, and Vietnam

Agriculture can be collectivized most easily when it is already a small sector and when resources and industrial inputs are already available, as was the case in Czechoslovakia. The same argument can be used for decollectivization. Pryor (1992) argues that decollectivization depends on economic, social, and political factors. It is most difficult in countries with a high level of agricultural technology, where collectivized agriculture dominated for many decades, and where state farms predominate.

A brief overview of land reforms in Central and Eastern Europe

Albania

Among the succession states of the Turkish Empire, Albania was liberated last. It proclaimed its independence in 1912, but only gained full independence in 1920, after various occupations. Being a predominantly Moslem area, Albania retained more of the social structure inherited from the Turks than was the case in other parts of the Balkans (Dovring, 1965). In 1924, the six-month government of the democrat Fan Noli fell after failing to implement various promised reforms, including land reform. Fan Noli was succeeded by clan chieftain Ahmed Zogu, who in 1928 assumed the title of King Zog I (Rotschild, 1974). Around 1930, another land reform was planned, but never implemented. The main reason was resistance by owners of the large estates (Dovring, 1965). In 1945, 60.4 percent of the land was cultivated in medium and small holdings, 23.2 percent by 'well-to-do-peasant' households, 12.7 percent by the state, including royal lands, and 3.7 percent on latifundia (Berend, 1985).

In October 1944, Enver Hoxha formed his Provisional Democratic Government, later named the Democratic Front, which was recognized by the Allies in November 1945. Tirana was liberated in November 1944. Elections were held on 2 December 1945. An overwhelming majority voted in favor of the Democratic Front. In the beginning of its Communist period, Albania followed the Yugoslav line in determining its policies (Swain and Swain, 1993). Land reform was carried out by two acts. The first (30 August 1945) provided for (1) the expropriation (without compensation) of all land owned by persons employing only hired labor; (2) the expropriation of land in excess of 7 hectares owned by those letting to tenant farmers; and (3) the expropriation of all land in excess of 40 hectares. The beneficiaries were entitled in principle to 5 hectares each and were obliged to pay compensation equivalent to 10 quintals of wheat over a period of ten years. The second act (27 May 1946) declared that all those not personally working on the land lost their right to ownership. Holdings were limited to approximately 5 hectares per head of a

41

farming family and approximately 2.5 hectares for each married couple belonging to an extended family and living under the same roof. All together, about 300,000 hectares were distributed among some 21,500 landless and 49,000 smallholders' families. Moreover, the act stipulated that land not be alienated (Berend, 1985).

By a decree of 27 March 1947, 18 state farms were established, mainly based on the former Italian agrarian colonies. Collectivization began in 1948 with the nationalization of draft animals, followed by nationalization of forests, grazing pasture, and water resources. Collectivization became a mass movement in 1955 and was completed in 1967 (Bland, 1992). Strictly following Stalin's principles, Albania started to convert its collectives to state farms in 1971. The number of cooperatives increased from 90 in 1950 to 1,484 in 1960, but declined to 417 in 1987 as a result of the amalgamation of cooperatives into larger units. The average area of these cooperatives increased from 232 hectares in 1950 to 1,205 hectares in 1987 (Bland, 1992). In 1983, of Albania's total cultivated land, 78.4 percent of land was in collectives, 21.1 percent in state farms, and 0.5 percent in private farms (Pryor, 1992).

Bulgaria

Interbellum Bulgarian agriculture was characterized by small peasant holdings, a structure it had inherited from the Turkish rule in the nineteenth century. Turkish landlords held land that had formally belonged to the Turkish crown. Hence, when Bulgaria became independent in 1848, most of the land was granted to the cultivating peasants (Dovring, 1965). As a result, Bulgaria had the most egalitarian landownership distribution of all Central European countries, and demand for land reform from the rural population was weak. Pressure for land reform came in the person of Alexander Stamboliski and his Agrarian Union (Lampe and Jackson, 1982). It was also in the interest of the liberal bourgeoisie to support a land reform that might destroy the power base of their Communist opponents.

The Bulgarian government passed land reform legislation in 1921. A maximum of 30 hectares per household was set in general, 50 hectares in mountainous regions. This land reform resulted in the transfer of about 333,000 hectares or 6 percent, of agricultural land, mostly from state holdings (Lampe and Jackson, 1982). Compensation was settled under the law of 1 August 1924 at 50 percent of 1923 land prices, and was progressive, based on the amount of land expropriated. A spontaneous land redistribution also occurred as the rural population rapidly increased. Between 1926 and 1934, the number of farms under 5 hectares rose by 31 percent, strengthening the role of farms with small plots (Berend, 1985).

During the Second World War, resistance against the Bulgarian pro-Hitler government came mainly from Communist partisans. The Communist resistance could not seize power until the arrival of the Red Army in September 1944. The Fatherland Front government, established on 9 September 1944, was a coalition that included four Communists. A number of radical reforms, including land reform, were implemented quickly (Swain and Swain, 1993).

As the structure of landownership was already quite equitable, the scope of a land reform could only be limited. A law of 12 March 1946 fixed an upper limit of 20 hectares for those cultivating their own land, of 30 hectares in Southern Dobrogea (ceded by Romania in 1940), and of 10 hectares for those letting more than 40 percent of their property. Added to the 45,000 hectares thus confiscated, were 120,000 hectares taken from church holdings. Together these constituted 2 percent of cultivated land. Of these 165,000 hectares, 130,000 hectares were allotted to some 120,000 families. The remainder was taken over by the state. Some small amount of compensation was paid (Brus, 1986).

Paradoxically, although Bulgarian agriculture was characterized by the most egalitarian farm structure, Bulgarian collectivization was the most violent of all in Central Europe. Bulgaria was also the first to achieve full collectivization (Sokolovsky, 1990). In the early 1970s, state and cooperative farms were combined to form agro-industrial complexes. As these most resembled state farms, they were classified as such. In the 1980s, they were broken down again into their constituent units (Pryor, 1992).

Czechoslovakia

Czechoslovakia was the most industrialized of all CEECs. As in the rest of the former Austro-Hungarian empire, Czechoslovakia's agriculture was characterized by large estates. Problems of rural poverty and landlessness were more important in Slovakia than in Bohemia and Moravia, where agriculture was more advanced and industry absorbed the abundant rural workers. Rural unrest and traditional sympathy for Russia was considered a threat to Czechoslovakia's ruling regime. Hence, the liberal government had strong incentives to pass a land reform. Destruction of the aristocrats' power base was easy, because the nobility was German and Hungarian and had lost the war. The first aim of land reform was therefore to distribute the estates of the German and Hungarian landlords among the Czech and Slovak peasants (Dovring, 1965).

The land reform legislation was settled in three acts: the Confiscation Act of April 1919, the Distribution Act of January 1920, and the Compensation Act of April 1920. Compensation was based on rather high prices. The government, intending to expropriate all estates of over 150 hectares of agricultural land and 250 hectares of nonagricultural land, thus transferring about 34 percent of total agricultural land, set a period of thirty years for the implementation. By 1931 only 300,000 hectares had been transferred. By 1937, however, more than four million hectares (of which 1.3 million hectares were arable land) had been confiscated and redistributed, thus transferring about 16 percent of all agricultural land (Berend, 1985). Czechoslovakia took an intermediate position in Central Europe in the extent of its land reform.

As in most CEECs, the Communists dominated the resistance movement in Czechoslovakia during the Second World War. Moreover, the Communist Party of Czechoslovakia was the most influential of all prewar Communist parties. The situation was very different for the Czech region, which was incorporated into Germany, and for Slovakia, which was independent. In Slovakia, Communist partisans started an insurrection against the pro-German government in August 1944. This Slovak National Uprising was ended by government forces. After liberation from the Nazis by the Red Army and the reunification of Czechoslovakia in 1945, the Communist Party could have seized power, backed by a large part of the population. However, Stalin instructed Party leaders to settle for a role in a coalition government. The Communist Party took part in a coalition government with the Socialist Party, the National Socialist Party, the People's Party, and the Democratic Party. The Communists strengthened their power by winning the 1946 elections with 38 percent of the vote. Together with their socialist allies, they made up the majority in the 1946 coalition government (Swain and Swain, 1993).

This coalition government voted a land reform in three stages. A first law of June 1945 concerned only 'enemy-owned land' belonging to Germans and Hungarians or to traitors and collaborators. Nearly 1.8 million hectares were thus confiscated: 1.4 million hectares in Czech 'borderlands', 100,000 hectares in the Bohemian interior, and 275,000 hectares in Slovakia. Some three quarters of this land was distributed among Czech and Slovak settlers. In July 1947, a second law completed the prewar land reform (upper limit of 250 hectares of total area and 150 hectares of agricultural land). Hence, a further 700,000 to 800,000 hectares were expropriated. Finally, a third law brought the upper limit down to 50 hectares in March 1948. This resulted in an extra 700,000 hectares of expropriated land. Compensation was granted only in the two latter cases. Of the 4.2 million hectares confiscated, only 1.7 million hectares, a quarter of the cultivable area, were distributed among some 350,000 families, most of which were landless. As a result, each family received more than 4 hectares on average, significantly more than families received in Romania, Bulgaria, and Yugoslavia (Brus, 1986).

Like Bulgaria, Czechoslovakia was one of the forerunners of collectivization. Unlike Bulgaria, less force was used in Czechoslovakia, because collectivization there met with less resistance in the countryside. Collective farms dominated the Czechoslovakian agricultural sector during the seventies and eighties: Pryor (1992) reports that in 1985 63.5 percent of the land was owned by collectives, 30.4 percent by state farms, and 6.1 percent was in private hands. Czechoslovakian agriculture witnessed no real reform efforts during the Communist period.

Hungary

After World War I, Hungarian agriculture was dominated by large estates, and most rural people were landless. During the short Communist revolution of Bela Kun in 1919, all land was nationalized. However, after the intervention of foreign troops, the Communists were defeated. The 1920 democratic elections were won by the National Smallholders' Party. After the monarchy was restored with Admiral Miklós Horthy as regent, and the Trianon Peace Treaty was signed in 1920, a government led by Prime Minister Count Pál Teleki passed land reform legislation.

Under the Hungarian land reform of 1920, only 6 percent of all arable land, or 300,000 hectares, was redistributed to some 400,000 peasant families, 250,000 of which had been landless. Peasants had to pay 30-40 percent more than the market price for these lands. Many of the holdings thus created were not viable, because peasants received, on average, plots of less than a hectare. As a result some 67,000 peasant farms were auctioned between 1926 and 1938 (Berend, 1985), and semifeudal structure survived in Hungary.

At the end of the Second World War, almost half of Hungary's people earned their living in agriculture. Most did not own their land or possessed holdings under 2.8 hectares. In contrast, the 1,000 wealthiest families owned a quarter of all arable land, and the Catholic Church held over half a million hectares.

The Red Army marched into Hungary at the end of September 1944. A provisional government of Communists, Socialists, and Smallholders was formed which implemented several reforms. The National Peasants' Party, which was manipulated by the Communists, published its land reform plans on 14 January 1945. These plans were adopted by the Communist Party to tackle the rural poor's growing impatience. Under a decree issued on 15 March 1945, large estates of more than 575 hectares, land owned by 'traitors of the fatherland' and 'Horthy Fascists' and land owned by the Catholic Church were expropriated. An upper limit for holdings was set at 50 hectares for the gentry and 115 hectares for peasants. Of the 3.2 million hectares confiscated, 1.9 million hectares were given to 642,000 people (110,000 former farmhands, 261,000 agricultural laborers, and 214,000 dwarfholders, along with smallholders and village tradesmen). The Communists succeeded in overturning the social structure in the countryside, 95 percent of the rural population owned small plots with an average farm size under 3 hectares (Brus, 1986).

It took a relatively long time to collectivize Hungarian agriculture. As in Poland, collectivization was abandoned in 1953, following the New Course from Moscow. It was only after the 1956 Revolution that the Hungarian countryside was fully collectivized. Rather than being dominated by collective farms, Hungarian agriculture was characterized by a symbiosis between small- and large-scale farms. According to Pryor (1992), in 1987, 71.4 percent of land was in collective hands, 14.9 percent in state farms, and 13.7 percent in private hands. Cochrane (1988) reports that private agriculture accounted for 15 percent of arable land and 31 percent of gross farm output in 1975 and for 13 percent of arable land and 34 percent of gross farm output in 1985.

In 1968, Hungary introduced what were considered the most radical reform efforts in Central and Eastern Europe. The main characteristics of these reforms, called the New Economic Mechanism, were the replacement of compulsory deliveries by a set of financial instruments, greater enterprise autonomy, and, most of all, the symbiotic relationship between the socialized sector and private farmers. Reform efforts were renewed in 1980, which made Hungary a gradual reformer even before the fall of Communism. These reforms have resulted in the relative success of Hungary as a net exporter of food products.

Latvia and Lithuania[3]

In the nineteenth century and in the beginning of the twentieth century, the Baltics were part of the Russian Empire. The provinces corresponding to what is now Estonia and Latvia were dominated by large estates more of which had been preserved intact than in any other part of the Russian Empire and which were owned by German gentry. These German nobles had enjoyed special consideration from the Czar ever since they had helped Russia to conquer the Baltics in the eighteenth century. Lithuania, like adjacent Belorussia, was also influenced by German colonization, although to a lesser extent than the northern Baltic regions. Some agrarian reforms were already on their way in Latvia in the eighteenth century, when Baltic German nobles gave peasants rights on their own estates, hoping to create a more secure power base by emancipating the native Baltic peasants. In Lithuania, this emancipation was delayed until 1861, as it was in the rest of the Russian Empire. Major land reform measures were introduced in the Russian Empire in 1906, the so-called Stolypin Land Reform. Lithuanian peasants were able to profit more from these reforms than were their Latvian neighbors, but in general the reforms had less impact in the Baltic countries than in the rest of the Russian Empire.

After the First World War, the Baltic states became independent. The two major forces in the parliaments of both Latvia and Lithuania were the Peasant Party, representing smallholders, and the Socialist Party, representing the working class and the landless. A wide range of smaller parties reflected the ethnic diversity of the Baltic republics. Russians formed the largest minority in Latvia (12 percent of the population), while Jews were the largest minority in Lithuania (7.6 percent). Although population pressure was moderate and the man-land ratio relatively favorable, radical land reforms were implemented both in Latvia and in Lithuania. In both countries, the government's intention was to create a new landowning peasantry to counter the Communist threat. Former landowners (Baltic Germans in Latvia and Poles and Russians in Lithuania) were expropriated and lost most of their wealth. New farms were made large enough to employ both a farm family and a family of hired workers. Agricultural progress was remarkable after the reforms in Latvia and was followed by a vigorous start towards industrialization.

After a short period of independence, the Baltic states once again became part of Russia after Soviet occupation in 1940. The 'Sovietization' of the Baltics met with determined resistance until the early 1950s, especially in the countryside. Between 1945 and 1985, the ethnic balance of Latvia and Lithuania shifted through the large-scale immigration of industrial workers from other parts of the Soviet Union, especially from the Russian Federal Republic. Agricultural land had been confiscated and distributed among landless peasants after the initial Soviet takeover in 1940, creating the pattern of very small farms which had preceded collectivization in other parts of the Soviet Union. Farms larger than 30 hectares disappeared completely, and the number of farms was increased considerably. Only the smallest units, those under 1 hectare in size, diminished both in number and area, while those between 1 and 5 hectares remained stable in number and increased in area.

Poland

Before the First World War, Polish agriculture was also characterized by large estates. Roughly onethird of the rural population was landless, and only 17 percent of peasant families owned farms that could provide their livelihood. The 1919 elections for the first Sejm (Polish Parliament) were won by the National Democrats, the party of the Catholic middle class. Ambitious schemes of reform were discussed in Parliament during the first years after the war, but while the parties quarreled little was done to put reforms into practice. The land reform law that finally passed was very conservative and provided only for a gradual transfer of land to peasants. In 1926, Pilsudski, the leader of the Polish Socialist Party, staged a coup that kept him in power until his death in 1935. Although he had led the Socialists, Pilsudski allied himself with industrialists and large landowners. Consequently, land reform slowed under his leadership. His successors, the Government of the Colonels, further suppressed peasant movements, such as the united Popular Party established in 1930 (Thompson, 1993).

Poland's first land reform law was passed on 10 July 1919 and took effect on 15 July 1920. Maximum holding size was set at between 60 and 180 hectares in industrial areas or around big cities and at 300 hectares in the eastern provinces. Compensation was paid on an individual basis according to the estimated values of the estates. However, implementation was slow, and a new land reform law was voted in on 28 December 1925 to allot 200,000 hectares annually between 1926 and 1935. But once again the reform was slowed down, especially during the depression. Compensation regulations were rather moderate with the price of redistributed land limited to half its free market price. Of the 2 million hectares identified for redistribution, only 1.4 million hectares were allotted by 1935. In total, 2.7 million hectares were redistributed between 1919 and 1938, only 10 percent of Poland's agricultural land. (The share was one third if one takes into account the 5.4 million hectares which were handed over to peasants who already had small farms). As a result, 734,100 new farms were established, but many large estates survived the reform. Moreover, the land reform was not able to solve the problem of a steadily increasing rural population, and many peasants remained landless (Berend, 1985).

The Red Army crossed the border into Poland in July 1944, and Communists took power without the support of a broad popular front. The Polish Committee for National Liberation became Poland's provisional government. Radical reforms were supported by the Socialist and the Peasant parties (Swain and Swain, 1993). As the result of a decree on 6 September 1944, 9.3 million hectares, or almost half of Poland's agricultural area, was confiscated. Six million hectares were distributed to 1,070,000 families. One fifth (1.1 million hectares) came from estates expropriated in the 'old' territories and 4.9 million hectares from German holdings in the 'regained' territories. The remaining land constituted the basis for state farms, which were formed mainly in the regained territories. Holding sizes were set at 100 hectares of total area or 50 hectares of agricultural area. No compensation was granted; former owners had the right to a small independent farm outside the expropriated estate or to a small pension. The recipients of land paid a price similar to that required in other countries (Brus, 1986).

Because of strong resistance from the peasants, Polish agriculture was never fully collectivized. Private agriculture remained predominant after the decollectivization of the 1950s. No efforts were made to recollectivize agriculture as happened in Hungary. In Poland, private agriculture accounted for 80 percent of arable land and 80 percent of gross farm output in 1975 (Cochrane, 1988).

Romania

The Romanian countryside was characterized by huge overpopulation. One of Marx's few references to agrarian conditions was about the Romanian peasantry because theirs was an extreme example of class oppression (Dovring, 1965). Landowning nobles managed to exercise far-reaching authority over the local peasantry as they maintained their position under the loose and remote Turkish Empire. Demand for land reform was thus very strong after the First World War. Moreover, the new government was eager to provide land reform legislation. First, it wanted to expel non-Romanian landlords in Transylvania and Bessarabia, new provinces of postwar Romania where the landowning class was Hungarian or Russian. But the native aristocracy of the old kingdom of Romania also lost much of its political power with the approval of universal suffrage (Seton-Watson, 1986). Second, the government wanted to tackle the Communist threat. The poor conditions of Romanian peasants constituted a major breeding ground for Communist agitation. Land reform was first implemented in the annexed province of Bessarabia, where the Communist threat was most imminent. In the 1927 elections the National Peasant Party, formed in 1926, received 75 percent of the vote. The party remained important until 1937, when King Carol II imposed a dictatorship. He pretended an interest in peasant welfare, but made no real agricultural reforms (Thompson, 1993).

After the government's declaration on 1 December 1918, the enactment of reform in Romania soon followed (16 December 1918). The law was strengthened and expanded in July 1921. Limits to the size of holdings were set at between 100 and 500 hectares depending on the region. All land occupied by non-Romanian citizens and by landowners living abroad was expropriated. Compensation was as follows: 20 percent of the value of the land was to be paid immediately, 35 percent was to be paid by the state, and the remaining 45 percent was to be paid in installments over twenty years. Of the 6.3 million hectares of land expropriated, 3.8 million hectares were redistributed among 1.4 million peasant families and 1.2 million hectares were used to create state reserves. The rest was used for further settlement. As a result, Romanian land reform was quite radical. Two thirds of the large estates were broken up. Only 0.4 percent of the estates owned more than 100 hectares, however, those occupied 28 percent of the land (Berend, 1985).

Territorial dispute about Moldavia (annexed from the Soviet Union in 1940) dominated domestic politics after the Second World War. Traditional parties wanted to return to pre-1939 borders. The Communists did not. A coup by

King Michael overturned pro-Nazi dictator Antonescu on 23 August 1944. A demonstration by Communists and Socialists on 24 February 1945 was suppressed by shooting and resulted in an intervention by the Red Army. The National Democratic Front, a coalition of Communists and Socialists formed a government on 6 March 1945 and quickly passed land reform legislation (Swain and Swain, 1993). The law of 22 March 1945 limited the size of holdings to 50 hectares. All land belonging to German settlers, Fascists, and war criminals was confiscated. A Romanian landowner could get compensation for an expropriated surplus over 50 hectares. Beneficiaries had to pay the value of an average year's harvest over ten to twenty years. Eight percent of the total cultivable area, or 1.1 million hectares, was distributed to over 900,000 families. Royal lands, other land remaining in large estates, and 'model' capitalist farms were untouched by the 1945 law and only confiscated in 1948-49 (Brus, 1986).

Of all countries with a collectivized agricultural sector, Romania was characterized by the largest share of private agriculture. According to Pryor (1992), 15.6 percent of the land was in private ownership in 1987. According to Cochrane (1988), 14 percent of the land was privately owned both in 1975 and 1985. Still, Romanian agriculture was dominated by collective farms (54.7 percent of the land). Minor reform efforts were of no importance.

Slovenia

After World War I, a new state was formed: Yugoslavia. Its agriculture was a mix of different farming systems inherited from the Austro-Hungarian Empire and the Turkish domination. Serbian peasant agriculture coexisted with the Moslem latifundia system of Bosnia, Kosovo, and Macedonia, the Austro-Hungarian estates in Slovenia and Vojvodina, and the properties of the Croatian nobility. The most important political parties, the Serbian Radical Party and the Croatian Peasant Party, had much support from the countryside, and land reform was high on the agenda (Thompson, 1993).

A land reform act was passed on 25 February 1919, and a Ministry of Land Reform was set up to execute the law in February 1920. Almost every estate larger than 50 to 300 hectares was expropriated. No precise regulations were issued about compensation until 31 July 1925. From then on, compensation was optional, based on a voluntary agreement between landlord and peasant. Only on 24 June 1933 a decree was issued to regulate the price of land according to the net income per hectare and at a rate of one half to one third of existing land market prices. Peasants were able to pay in installments from 1933 onwards for up to thirty years. As a result, a radical land reform gave about 2.5 million hectares to 650,000 peasant families between 1920 and 1938. In Slovenia more than 200,000 hectares were expropriated (Berend, 1985).

Communist partisans, led by Tito, played an important role in the liberation of Yugoslavia from the Nazi regime. Tito garnered enough support from the population to establish a provisional government. At the Yalta Conference in February 1945, Tito agreed to merge his Popular Front government with the Government-in-Exile. On 7 March 1945 the Allies recognized the National Liberation Committee, later renamed the People's Front, as Yugoslavia's government. Only one third of the seats went to non-Communist groups. Even before the November 1945 elections, in which the People's Front received 90 percent of the votes, a land reform was initiated (Swain and Swain, 1993).

Under the land reform decree of 23 August 1945, 1.6 million hectares, or 6 percent, of the national territory were expropriated, mainly from Germans or collaborators. Fewer than 400,000 hectares belonged to Yugoslav landlords. Limits to holding size were set at 45 hectares of total area or 25-35 hectares of cultivated land. About half of the land available for redistribution went to 180,000 smallholders and 70,000 landless peasants (Brus, 1986).

Former Yugoslavia followed its own course, one different from the Soviet model, and did not collectivize its agriculture. Only some 'social' farms were established. In the whole of Yugoslavia, private agriculture accounted for 83 percent of arable land and 76 percent of gross farm output in 1975, and for 80 percent of arable land and 69 percent of gross farm output in 1985 (Cochrane, 1988).

Conclusion

CEEC land reforms are a good example of institutional change following a major crisis. War is the extreme case of a crisis leading to institutional change. Demand for land reform was high after both World Wars. Politicians were eager to provide legislation to redistribute land. Or, as Seton-Watson (1986) remarks, 'there was a general feeling ... that as the peasantry had borne the brunt of war, and had proved itself in the greatest crisis yet known in human history to be in fact the backbone of the nation, it deserved to be given its share of the wealth of the nation'. Land reforms after World War I marked the transition from feudalism to democracy, while those after the Second World War were a sign of the transition from Fascism to Communism. The later reforms were more radical and successful than the former in achieving their goals of breaking the power base of the rich, because they were backed by the Red Army.

Slow or incomplete implementation and lack of a proper institutional environment characterized interwar land reforms. Hence, in most CEECs land reform was an unfinished business at the beginning of the Second World War. Postwar coalition governments, manipulated by the Communists, finalized the reforms. The land reforms were a precursor to the collectivization of agriculture under the Communist regime. Except in Yugoslavia and Poland, where collectivization failed, mainly collective farms replaced CEE peasant agriculture. Some forty years later, policymakers were faced with the legacy of their predecessors when they had to decide on the fourth, and final, land reform of the twentieth century.

Notes

1   I gratefully acknowledge Jo Swinnen for comments on earlier versions of the chapter.
2   The Austro-Hungarian Empire was established in 1867 as a dual monarchy. Both countries had separate constitutions, but the same head of state: the emperor of Austria was also the king of Hungary. After the war the dual monarchy was ended. A separate peace treaty was signed with Hungary in 1920.
3   Based on Dovring (1965) and Hiden and Salmon (1991).

References

Berend, I. T. (1985), 'Agriculture', in Kaser, M. C. and Radice, E. A. (eds), *The Economic History of Eastern Europe 1919-1975. Volume I: Economic Structure and Performance Between the Two Wars*, Clarendon Press: Oxford.

Bland, W. (1992), 'Albania After the Second World War', in Winnifrith, T. (ed.), *Perspectives on Albania*, MacMillan: London.

Brus, W. (1986), 'Post-War Reconstruction and Socioeconomic Transformation', in Kaser, M. C. and Radice, E. A. (eds), *The Economic History of Eastern Europe 1919-1975. Volume II: Interwar Policy, the War and Reconstruction*, Clarendon Press: Oxford.

Cochrane, N. J. (1988), 'The Private Sector in East European Agriculture', *Problems of Communism*, March-April, pp. 47-53.

Cochrane, N. J. (1993), 'Central European Agrarian Reforms in a Historical Perspective', *American Journal of Agricultural Economics*, Vol. 75, pp. 851-856.

Dovring, F. (1965), *Land and Labor in Europe in the Twentieth Century: A Comparative Survey of Recent Agrarian History*, Nijhoff: The Hague.

Hiden, J. and Salmon, P. (1991), *The Baltic Nations and Europe: Estonia, Latvia and Lithuania in the Twentieth Century*, Longman: London.

Lampe, J. R. and Jackson, M. R. (1982), *Balkan Economic History, 1550-1950, From Imperial Borderlands to Developing Nations*, Indiana University Press: Bloomington.

Moore, W. E. (1945), *Economic Demography of Eastern and Southern Europe*, League of Nations: Geneva.

Okey, R. (1982), *Eastern Europe 1740-1980: Feudalism to Communism*, Hutchinson: London.

Pryor, F. L. (1992), *The Red and the Green. The Rise and Fall of Collectivized Agriculture in Marxist Regimes*, Princeton University Press: Princeton.

Rotschild, J. (1974), *East Central Europe Between the Two World Wars, A History of East Central Europe volume IX*, University of Washington Press: Seattle.

Schmitt, G. H. (1993), 'Agrarian Reform in Eastern Europe After World War II', *American Journal of Agricultural Economics*, Vol. 75, pp. 845-850.

Seton-Watson, H. (1986), *Eastern Europe Between the Wars 1918-1941*, Westview Press: Boulder.

Sokolovsky, J. (1990), *Peasants and Power. State Autonomy and the Collectivization of Agriculture in Eastern Europe*, Westview Press: Boulder.

Swain, G. and Swain, N. (1993), *Eastern Europe Since 1945*, Macmillan: London.

Thompson, S. (1993), 'Agrarian Reform in Eastern Europe Following World War I: Motives and Outcomes', *American Journal of Agricultural Economics*, Vol. 75, pp. 840-744.

Wädekin, K.-E. (1990), 'Determinants and Trends of Reform in Communist Agriculture: A Concluding Essay', in Wädekin, K.-E. (ed.), *Communist Agriculture. Farming in the Soviet Union and Eastern Europe*, Routledge: London and New York.

3 Agricultural privatization and decollectivization in Albania: A political economy perspective

Azeta Cungu and Johan F. M. Swinnen

Introduction

Agrarian reform was a very important part of the overall economic reforms in Albania, because agriculture is a significant part of this country's economy. The reform resulted in a complete decollectivization of farms and a radical shift to private ownership of land. These changes have been impressive both in their conception and in their extraordinarily rapid implementation. In light of such radical change, it is logical to ask whether such reform was desirable and whether it provided a solution to the problems it was supposed to address. Although a comprehensive answer to this question is not the main concern of this chapter, we recognize that many experts would agree that Albania's agricultural reform did not completely succeed in achieving its economic goals. It did provide a quick solution for halting decline and disintegration in the agricultural sector and creating a more dynamic rural economy. However, the reform did not manage to establish the basis for long-term, sustainable growth. In fact, the highly fragmented structure of holdings that emerged from land distribution hardly allows for further gains in efficiency or for substantial increases in productivity. Why, then, was the reform designed and implemented the way it was?

This chapter uses a political economy framework to explain the adoption of the policies that made up Albania's agrarian reform. We focus on the motivations of policymakers and the political and institutional constraints affecting the reform choice. We argue that Albania's agricultural privatization choice resulted from a political bargaining process between former owners, farm workers, and the rural nomenklatura. Further, we show that the reform choice and the resulting decollectivization were influenced by changes in the political institutions, Albania's dramatic economic situation at the beginning of the 1990s, the structure of its economy, and the historical and legal status of agricultural assets under privatization.

This chapter is organized as follows. The first sections discuss the general political and economic reforms, the importance of agriculture in the Albanian economy, and the history of land tenure rights in Albania. The next sections review the policy debate and discuss alternative options for agricultural privatization, problems in reform implementation, and policy responses. We then present our political economy framework for examining a number of determinants of the reform design. In the last section we explain the impact of these (and other) factors on the choice of the privatization process and the resulting decollectivization.

Political and economic reforms since 1989

Albania is a small country situated on the southwestern side of the Balkan Peninsula and sharing its borders with Montenegro, Serbia, Macedonia, and Greece. The western part of the country, facing Italy, lies on the Adriatic and Ionian coasts of the Mediterranean Sea. Before 1991, the country was isolated from the rest of the world, and the economy was centrally planned. Albania had the lowest per capita income in Europe (Grace, 1995). In 1990/91, the combination of a critical economic situation, increased political tensions, social unrest, and the collapse of Communist regimes throughout CEECs induced students and university teachers to demonstrate in Tirana. This marked the creation of the first opposition party, the Democratic Party (DP). The first democratic elections (March 1991) brought the democrats for the first time into Parliament with a third of the seats. An important factor in this election was that the anti-Communist coalition lacked the necessary structures and linkages in the rural areas and in small provincial cities, mainly because the elections were held only three months after the creation of the first opposition party (DP). As a result, the ex-Communists, who then organized in the Socialist Party (SP), obtained the majority due to the support they enjoyed in rural areas where most of the Albanian population still lives.

A lack of stability and public order followed the elections. In March and August 1991, thousands of Albanians migrated to Italy and many others left for Greece. A four-week general strike in which the majority of urban workers participated caused the Socialist government to resign. A coalition government took over in June 1991. Later, economic stagnation and the lack of political stability led to the opposition's withdrawal from the government and to new elections.[1] A caretaker government of technocrats led the country to new elections in March 1992. This time, the three opposition parties obtained 69.9 percent of the votes. Moreover, the DP missed a two-thirds

56

majority in Parliament by only one seat, as it won 62.4 percent of the votes. The Republican Party (RP) received 3.1 percent, and the Social Democratic Party (SDP), 4.3 percent, while the Socialist Party (SP) won 25.6 percent (see table 3.1). Sali Berisha was elected president and, since then, Meksi's Democratic Party (DP) government has been leading the country.

Table 3.1
Major political developments since 1990

1990	Dec	Creation of the first opposition party (Democratic Party)
1991	March	First democratic elections
		(ex-CP) Socialist Party obtains majority and forms SP-Government
	June	SP-Government resigns after strikes and upheaval
		Coalition Government (including SP, DP, SDP) takes over
	Fall	Opposition parties leave the government
		New elections are announced; caretaker government takes over
1992	March	Second democratic elections
		Democratic Party (DP) 62.4%
		Republican Party (RP) 3.1%
		Social Democratic Party (SDP) 4.3%
		Socialist Party (SP) 25.6%
		Other Parties 4.5%
		DP falls just short of 2/3 majority in Parliament
		DP Government (Prime Minister Meksi) rules

The Democratic Party government was reasonably stable in its early years. There was little threat from ex-Communists. It managed to restore public order and launched a program of radical economic reforms by adopting a shock-therapy approach. This was initially associated with massive unemployment, high inflation rates, drastic cuts in public spending, collapse of industries, and rapid withdrawal of the state from the economy. Political competition increased as various interest groups became better organized in parties or associations. Once the 'fight against the Communists' relaxed, the diversity of the underlying interest groups became an important source of opposition.

Agriculture in the economy

One of the most debated issues of the economic reform proposals was the privatization of asset property rights in agriculture.[2] In fact, agriculture was the first sector to be privatized. As early as begin 1991, farmers began dismantling the agricultural producer cooperatives (APCs) and distributing land, livestock, and other assets among themselves. While this signaled the beginning of transition in agriculture, the debate on agricultural privatization and land reform remained at the top of the political agenda because of the large vested interests and the overwhelming importance of agriculture in Albania.

Agriculture is well distributed within the country, but is most intensive in the western coastal lowland. Farmland covers 25 percent of the total land area, 35 percent is forests, and another 40 percent is made up of pastures and unproductive land (Xhamara, 1995b). Before the reforms, agriculture was the main source of foreign exchange earnings and employed half of the country's labor force, with 65 percent of the population living in the rural areas. In 1986 it produced 50 percent of GDP, but this share fell sharply to 33 percent just before the reforms, when agricultural output collapsed at the end of the 1980s and the beginning of the 1990s, resulting in food shortages.

Since the reforms, agriculture and food have gained in importance in the economy. The share of agriculture in GDP had increased to 56 percent, and employment in agriculture has increased as well (table 3.2). Growth in agriculture has exceeded that of GDP in each year since the reforms (Christensen, 1994). After an aggregate decline in gross agricultural output (GAO) of 25 percent in the two years before the reforms (1990 and 1991), GAO increased by 18 percent, 14 percent and 8 percent in the next three years (OECD, 1995). The low level of income is reflected in the dramatic figures on food spending per average household: the already high share of 56 percent in 1989 increased to more than 70 percent in 1994 (table 3.2).

Table 3.2
Importance of the agro-food sector in the economy

	1986	1989	1994
Share of agriculture in GDP (%)	49.7	33.0	56.0
Share of agriculture in total employment (%)	-	40.9	42.5
Share of household income spent on food (%)	-	56.5	72.0

Source: INSTAT, 1996, and IFDC, 1994.

58

Prior to the reforms, almost all production took place on state farms (SFs) and agricultural producer cooperatives (APCs). In 1989, 29 percent of total agricultural production was generated from 160 SFs which owned 24 percent (170,000 hectares) of the total arable land. The state farm size varied from 500 hectares to 2,000 hectares with an average size of 1,070 hectares. APCs numbering 492 contributed 50 percent of the total agricultural production and cultivated over 70 percent of the arable land. The private sector, which operated only 4 percent of the total arable land in 1990 (table 3.3 and Christensen, 1993), produced 21 percent of the total agricultural output (compared with only 9 percent in 1985).

Table 3.3
Agricultural land use, 1989-1992

	1989	1990	1991	1992
		(In thousands of hectares)		
Area of agric. land	706.2	704.0	702.7	701.3
		(Share of total land use %)		
Area of agric. land	100	100	100	100
- State farms	24	24	24	18
- Cooperatives	73	72	35	7
- Private Plots	3	4	41	75

Source: IMF, 1994.

As table 3.3 shows, the share of privately used land increased sharply in 1991, reflecting widespread 'spontaneous privatization'. Before we address the reasons for this and the government regulations on land reform and decollectivization since 1991, it is important to look at the historical evolution of landownership. The (changes in) precollectivization land distribution(s) have strongly affected the current debate.

History of landownership in Albania

Landownership prior to 1945

At the turn of the nineteenth century, the landownership system in Albania was dominated by 'çiflig'-based feudal relations, which were characteristic of the Ottoman Empire. Under çiflig land tenure, peasants were obliged to contribute labor and produce for a private landlord, for the state, or for a religious institution. This traditional form of tenancy continued until the end of 1945, when it was abolished by the Communist reforms.

Table 3.4 shows the landownership pattern in Albania just before independence from the Turks (1912). In his 'Die Landwirtschaft Albanien', E. C. Von Sedlmayer (quoted in Xhamara, 1995a) notes a big inequality in land distribution among the Albanian rural population right after independence (1913). The vast majority of agricultural land was controlled by five families, each owning about 60,000 hectares of farmland and forestland.

Table 3.4
Landownership pattern in 1912

Ownership	Total area	
	Ha	%
Large estates owned by the state or the sultan	56,287	14.7
Private estates	140,000	36.7
Religious institutions' ownership	13,700	3.6
Peasant ownership	171,789	45.0
TOTAL	381,776	100

Source: Xhamara, 1995a.

There were two attempts at land reform prior to 1945. The first, in 1924, was never carried out because the government collapsed shortly after announcing the reform. The second attempt, by King Zog in 1930, also failed to reach its objective of establishing a more equitable distribution of wealth in the countryside. The government limited itself to buying some land from the big landlords. Altogether, some 8,100 hectares of land were distributed, of which 3,400 hectares were state owned. Large estates were not substantially affected (Xhamara, 1995a).

Between 1925 and 1945, an embryonic land market developed together with a division of big estates into slightly smaller ones through inheritance (Civici, 1994). Brandt (1994) writes that in 1944 many large landowners started to sell their properties. These lands were bought and paid for in gold, by small- and medium-size proprietors interested in increasing their own farming network.

However, table 3.5 shows that the landownership pattern prior to Communist land reform in 1945 was still very skewed, with 3 percent of the population owning 27 percent of the land. Moreover, the inequality was strongest on the most fertile and productive land in the country. There, agriculture was predominantly organized in large estates owned by a few landlords, the pre-Communist state, and religious institutions. Land was highly concentrated among seven large families, six of whom owned lowland and good quality estates while the seventh family owned land in the hills and forests in the region of Mirdita (Civici, 1994). The vast majority of small- and medium-size landholders operated on marginal land or in less fertile holdings in the low and hilly areas.

Table 3.5
Landownership pattern in 1945

Ownership	Number	%	ha	%	Average per family (ha)
Big landlords	7	0.0	14,554	3.7	2,079
Rich farmers	4,713	3.0	91,133	23.2	19
State property	-	-	50,000	12.7	-
Small- and medium-size landowners	128,961	83.1	237,668	60.4	1.8
Landless	21,544	13.9	0	0	0

Source: Xhamara, 1995a.

At present, some 44 percent of Albania's agricultural land is lowland, 18.5 percent is mountainous, and 37.5 percent is hills. The area of lowland and hillside agricultural land has doubled over the last fifty years due to state investments in drainage, land reclamation, and terracing. Therefore, the marginal mountainous land made up a much higher percentage of the total agricultural land in 1945 than it does today.

Between 1944 and 1976, Albanian agrarian structure changed from semifeudal to socialist. In fact, immediately after World War II, the Communists introduced quick and radical reforms in agriculture. Agricultural policy after 1945 was characterized by the distribution of land to peasants, collectivization of assets, and a focus on production relations and attempts to achieve self-sufficiency in food.

Collectivization was preceded by a two-stage land reform which denied ownership rights to large landholders. In 1945 and 1946, the Communist government confiscated land from large landowners and distributed it to landless families or to those who only possessed tiny plots. Owners of large- and medium-sized holdings were allowed to retain 5 hectares of arable land. A law enacted in August 1945 and its amendment in May 1946 constituted the legal basis for these actions. By 1947, all peasants had their own land and generally were on equal grounds. Shortly after this, mass collectivization was introduced, requiring farmers to pool their recently acquired land and assets into cooperatives. For many, this severely discredited the 1946 reform: '... many villagers now view the 1946 reform as a disguised first step towards collectivisation, used to offer a more palatable way of establishing the right of the state to separate the peasants from their traditional land holdings' (Lemel et al., 1993).

The collectivization of agriculture as well as other reforms in that sector brought about the creation of the state farms (SFs), agricultural producer cooperatives (APCs), and 'the individual plot'. The latter was a small area of land allowed for the private use of APC members. Pryor (1992) argues that the choice between APCs and SFs depended considerably upon the organization of agriculture prior to collectivization. In countries that ended up with primarily a system of collective farms, postwar (1945) landownership was usually highly concentrated in large landholdings rented out to tenants. Albania, certainly, inherited such a pattern from the past. On the other hand, big land estates owned by the pre-Communist state or the Church, were confiscated and transformed into SFs. The process of agricultural reform was accompanied by the extension of the SFs and APCs alongside the gradual contraction of personal plots.

Collectivization began on the coastal plain with the creation of the first APC in 1946. In the mid-1950s collectivization was extended into the hilly and mountainous areas. SFs were established simultaneously. The final stage of collectivization began in 1965. Its goal was to fully collectivize, to completely abolish private farming, and to increase the amount of arable land. This final stage resulted in the nationalization of all land, as sanctioned by Albania's 1976 Constitution. While the average size of the APCs was 175 hectares in

1959, it was 1,320 hectares by 1983. By 1983, most of the agricultural land (78.4 percent) was being cultivated by the APCs, 21.1 percent by SFs, and a trivial 0.5 percent was left in private use (Pryor, 1992).

Throughout the process, agriculture was managed to achieve 'self-sufficiency with little regard to comparative advantage, efficiency, or sustainability' (Ministry of Agriculture and Food, 1995b). This led to severe constraints on economic and agricultural development, resulting in serious food shortages and a steady deterioration in the living standards of the population, especially for peasants who were the most discriminated against. In the 1980s, the Communist government searched for instruments to mitigate the decline in the economy and particularly in agriculture. It launched a series of new measures and regulations conceding some degree of decentralization and autonomy for individual economic structures and shifted more resources into the more efficient areas of agricultural production.

Agricultural reforms under the Communists: too little, too late

After the break with China in 1978, there was no more aid to help oil the rusty mechanism of the political and economic machine that had jammed in the way of development. The economy was suffering the consequences of an accumulated misallocation of domestic resources and the resulting inefficiencies. Profound symptoms of the system's decay appeared after 1985, including widespread shortages of almost all basic food ingredients. The foreign debt exploded as Albanian politicians tried to solve the problem by further borrowing abroad. The economic disaster, and an overall political and institutional crisis were the source of growing opposition and discontent among the population. In 1988, this culminated in thousands of Albanians climbing the walls of foreign embassies in Tirana, looking for a better future outside the country.

The government responded with a series of plenums of the Communist Party (CP). Directives were issued granting some degree of liberalization in society. The existence of political parties other than the CP was still condemned. As far as the economy was concerned, the most striking measure was the implementation of the 'New Economic Mechanism', which granted more autonomy to individual enterprises by advocating self-administration and management of resources. In attempts to improve the allocation of resources and induce stronger labor incentives, subsidies to state enterprises were reduced and most of these enterprises were, subsequently, closed down. Their large inefficiencies had only constituted a massive drain on the state budget. These inefficiencies were reflected in one policy that paid employees 80 percent of their normal salaries in cash even though they were staying at home. This was estimated to be less costly although workers and management were not contributing any labor.

By the late 1980s, agricultural policies were once again changed in a continuing effort to make production more efficient. In July 1988, provisions were made for each rural family (member of the APCs) to receive '0.1-0.3 hectares of land, one cow, or ten heads of sheep and/or goats' (Civici, 1994). The state also reestablished private marketing for most agricultural products. Yet the efforts to reform in the late 1980s were superficial and did not stop the economy's decline. These measures were unproductive hybrids of a socialist economy with a vague market orientation, including only limited decentralization and restricted private ownership in agriculture. These actions, moreover, were not given a legal basis. Consequently, uncertainty, especially regarding the rights to distributed assets, led to confusion, hesitation, and fear of a potential new reversal in policies. Individual farmers were reluctant to engage seriously in farming. The measures also failed to have any major impact on increasing efficiency or productivity in the collective and state sectors. By their very nature, late 1980s' reforms could not improve farmers' contribution to the APCs, as they did not solve the incentive problem of free-riding: farmers were more interested in extracting revenues from their private plots and livestock. The disintegration of the agricultural sector continued during 1990-91. Its almost complete collapse and the threat of food shortages seriously jeopardized the stability of the country. By 1991, Albania was totally depending on food aid. Agricultural stagnation and spontaneous destruction of plantations, orchards, stables, and irrigation systems were characteristics of the moment (IMF, 1994).

The new Socialist government, which took office in March 1991 after winning the first democratic elections, recognized the need for much deeper reforms. Unfortunately, its views did not go beyond a limited internal reorganization of exisiting agricultural structures and a relaxation of absolute state controls over the agricultural sector. The new government replaced a few managers, preserved the collectives, and was opting for the transformation of the SFs into 'private' companies, which would (miraculously) make them very efficient. Experiments with agriculture thus continued and an extremely intense political debate over the proposed reforms took place. However, under increasing pressure from dramatic changes in other CEECs, coupled with severe economic conditions and food shortages, the spontaneous privatizations taking place in the rural areas, and strong opposition from the urban population, the Socialist government had to step down. A coalition government with more radical reformers was formed, and under this government the basic laws for asset privatization and the decollectivization and dismantling of the APCs were passed.

Post-Communist land reforms

Economic efficiency, social equity, historical justice, and politics

The impact of the land reform on the Albanian economy was expected to be twofold. First, the privatization of property rights in agriculture was to prevent further disintegration of this sector and also to clear the ground for its sustainable development. Second, it would provide the basis for a major redistribution of wealth in the rural areas and the integration of the greatest part of the population into the transition to a market economy. As such, land reform in Albania addressed social equity, economic efficiency, and historical justice concerns. But politics also played an important role. More specifically, as far as economic considerations were concerned, land reform would ensure a better allocation of resources in the rural economy and reduce disincentives and inefficiencies associated with the former ownership system and production organization. These would, in turn, lead to increases in productivity and profitability in farming as well as boost production, which would be the basis for sustainable growth and development. The social goals were dominated by concerns over employment, food security, and equity of asset ownership. Historical justice was most important for those expropriated by the previous regime. Finally, the political objectives were very important. Depending on the process adopted, the reform could constitute a means to restore lost credibility for the Communists in power while preserving the basis of their support in the countryside. In contrast, the anti-Communist coalition would use land reform to destroy this support base.

The combination of all these considerations placed the 'agrarian question' on top of the political agenda and made it the point of attention for any ruling government. Obviously, it would be very unrealistic to think that all of these objectives could be achieved within the frame of a land reform package. Moreover, some of the above goals were at odds with each other. For example, in the Albanian context, equity of asset distribution conflicts with historical justice and, as demonstrated extensively in the political economy literature, economic and political rationalities can differ considerably.

The land reform debate

By 1991, all parties accepted the need for private ownership and for farm restructuring in agriculture. The main areas of controversy related to the speed of the process and to how radical the reform should be. The debate on agrarian reform reflected conflicts between the political demands of various interest groups. Each of these groups came up with solutions of their own, which, converged into two main streams:

1 Those who advocated the preservation of the previous structures (i.e., the Socialists), and

2 Those who opted for more fundamental changes through decollectivization.

The second group was divided into the 'democrats', who supported efficiency through privatization and decollectivization, and social equity through an egalitarian distribution of agricultural land and other assets among farmers, and the 'republicans' who emphasized historical justice. The republican (RP) preference was to physically restitute land up to a certain limit to legitimate owners (i.e., those who were expropriated after 1945) or their heirs and to financially compensate for the remainder. In contrast, the democrats argued that '...restituting land to owners of before 1945, means a return back to feudalism... because, in order to satisfy the interests of a small group of ex-landowners (only 3 percent of agricultural landholders at that time) at least another 47,000 peasant families would remain landless and thus forced to work as laborers...' (DP representative quoted in Civici, 1994). The democrats (DP) proposed an egalitarian distribution of land among current farmers and promised financial compensation to former owners for part of their properties confiscated by the Communist state.[3]

Until mid-1991, the SP desperately tried to hold on to power, and little progress was made on agrarian reform. With political instability and economic chaos, farmers simply divided land and livestock among themselves in some areas. In June 1991, the SP lost absolute control over the government, and under pressures from the field and extremely heated parliamentary debates, the first law on land reform was passed in July 1991. After the election of a DP government in March 1992, policies aimed at complete decollectivization in agriculture by distributing land property rights to farm workers and the liberalization of all agricultural input and product prices were initiated. Privatization in agriculture contrasted with the process of privatizing urban properties through restitution.[4]

From mid-1991 to 1992, a remarkable legislative output provided the legal basis for the reform. These early laws together with later decrees are crucial for understanding the reform approach and policy reactions to implementation problems. They also give insights into the objectives of the reform and the views and intentions of its designers.

The basic legal framework for agricultural privatization and land reform

A framework for land privatization in Albania was established by the Land Law (Law No. 7501 of 19/07/1991), and by the Law On the Sanctioning and Protection of Private Property, Free Initiative and Independent Private

Activities, and Privatization' (Law No. 7512 of 10/08/1991) which declares agriculture open to private activity. The Land Law specifies the following:

1 Agricultural land can be granted 'as property of or for the use of' Albanian legal or natural persons, free of charge (Art.3).

2 'Families which have been members of an agricultural cooperative have the right to secede and operate on their own, becoming owners of the agricultural land provided to them' (Art.5).

3 For the purposes of assigning land in ownership or usufruct to physical or juridical persons, prior landownership, its precollectivization size, and boundaries are not recognized (Art.8).

4 Agricultural land may only be used for agricultural purposes (Art.11).

5 Failure to use land for agricultural purposes for more than one year may lead to withdrawal of the right of use (Art.15).

6 Agricultural land can be inherited according to inheritance rules to be provided (Art.25).

7 Land cannot be bought or sold (Art.2) while 'foreign juridical or physical persons can rent land to build on' (Art.4).

More detailed directions on farmland and orchard distribution were provided in the government decision on the criteria for the distribution of the agricultural land (Decision No. 255 of 08/08/1991). This decision specifies that ex-cooperative land is to be distributed to each family on a per capita basis proportional to the total area of land available in the cooperative. In cooperatives composed of several villages, the land is first to be broken up among the villages on the basis of their per capita size. Rural residents permanently working in the nonagriculture sector are only eligible for use rights to land equivalent to half the size allocated to cooperative members. Agricultural land within village residential boundaries is also assigned with user rights only. These use rights give the beneficiary the right to cultivate land and benefit from it for an undefined period of time. The user is not obliged to contribute any produce to the state, which retains ownership of such land. The user has no other rights to land such as inheriting it, renting, or selling it to a third party. Use is restricted to agricultural purposes only.

Decision No. 255 also defines the criteria for distributing irrigated and nonirrigated land according to specific conversion factors. Orchards and vineyards are to be distributed according to the same criteria that regulate the distribution of arable land.

A series of other decisions and directives which supplemented the Land Law included:

1 Decision No. 229 of 23 July 1991 on livestock distribution,

2 Decision No. 230 of 23 July 1991 on the creation of land commissions,

3 Decision No. 256 of 2 August 1991 on regulations for the registration, changes and transfers in state lands and cadastral changes,

4 Decision No. 377 of 11 October 1991 on the dismantling of the machinery and tractor stations and the creation of firms for agricultural machinery,

5 Decision No. 378 and 379 of 11 October 1991 on regulating and reorganizing animal husbandry and veterinary services.

The government decision on the distribution of the agricultural cooperatives' assets (No. 266 of 08/08/1991) outlined the procedures for the distribution of assets and for the liquidation of the APCs. It specifies that 'the distribution of the money equivalents and products is not made until all debts are paid' (par. 6a) and that 'if the cooperative is not capable of paying back its debts, these debts should be charged to its members in proportion to the land they have received' (par. 6c).

Other pieces of legislation provided for the distribution of land belonging to SFs, the financial compensation of ex-owners of agricultural land, the setting up of a new cadastral system and registration of real estate, and creation of a market for agricultural land. Specific features of these laws and issues related to their implementation are discussed below.

Compensation for former owners

By the beginning of 1993, opposition from pre-1945 landowners to the land distribution increased strongly. Their lobbying power grew as they organized in the Property with Justice movement and were more efficiently represented in political parties. A petition signed by 20,000 citizens was presented to Parliament in an attempt to change the Land Law. Parliament rejected any fundamental changes in the Land Law and opted instead for financial indemnity, by either direct compensation or by vouchers for participation in future sales of state enterprises.

Three laws regulating compensation of former landowners were passed. The first law (No. 7698 of 1 April 1993) provided for the restitution of nonagricultural land to former owners. The second law, the Financial Compensation of Former Owners of Agricultural Land Law (No. 7699 of 21/04/1993) recognized former property rights to agricultural land for financial compensation purposes only. It specified the following:

1 All ex-owners are to be compensated for expropriation of land based on the pre-1945 cadastre (Art.1).

2 Former owners and their heirs who have already received land on the basis of the Land Law are only eligible for compensation for the difference between land in their possession pre-1945 and the area already assigned to them in the framework of the current reform (Art.6).

3 Former owners are entitled to 'full' compensation for a maximum of 15 hectares of land (Art.8/1).

4 For parcels between 15 and 1,100 hectares, compensation is to be paid on a decreasing-scale basis (Art.8/2a,b).

5 For any claimed area of over 1,100 hectares, no additional compensation will be paid (Art.8/2c).

6 Financial compensation should in no case exceed the equivalent amount paid for 43.5 hectares of land (Art.8).

7 Compensation is to be paid by vouchers fully guaranteed by the state, freely transferable and tradable for cash or at face value in future sales of state-owned enterprises. A State Council for Compensation and district offices to deal with the practical side of distributing the compensation will be created (Art.13).

A third law, On the Price of the Agricultural Land for Compensation Purposes (No. 7836), specified how the price of the land was to be determined for compensation and also the procedures, rules, and deadlines for former owners to submit compensation claims.

Implementing these laws proved very difficult. Property with Justice, the association of former owners, rejected the idea of compensation and insisted on full and physical restitution of properties. There were also debates over the form of payment and how to estimate the value of 1945 properties whose records were only partially available and could not be physically assessed

(Stanfield and Kukeli, 1995). Moreover, the administration and bureaucracy involved in the collection and evaluation of claims and in resolving disputes, registering property, assessing the value of compensation to be paid, issuing vouchers, etc. was complex and costly. The continued opposition of former owners, in combination with the large technical difficulties in implementing the Law On the Financial Compensation of Former Owners of Agricultural Land increased pressure on the government. In attempting to introduce new dynamics and authority in carrying out the reform, the minister of agriculture was changed three times in less than eighteen months beginning in 1993. Disputes over the restoration of ownership rights caused a second split of the Democratic Party.[5] The faction that split off created the Right Democratic Party, which is very radical in its request for restitution of properties to pre-1945 owners. Also, the Republican Party and the Nationalists do represent, by and large, the interests of former owners. This growing political power of former owners has increased the uncertainty over property rights in agriculture. The legislation of the Land Market Law in July 1995 (see further) was intended to secure full property rights and security of ownership to new owners who received land under the distribution program. However, former owners objected to the law. Following extremely vigorous political debates, the case was sent to the Constitutional Court, which rejected the request, allowing the Land Market Law to remain unchanged. As a compromise to the former landowners, the government decided to distribute the old seaside and tourist site properties to them. Although the law does not itself specify what segment of former landowners is eligible for such compensation, it is obvious that former agricultural landholders are targeted to effectively benefit from this law because urban former owners have already been restituted their properties or else have been physically compensated.

Reform implementation

Agricultural cooperatives. Land distribution councils (LDCs) were established to manage, supervise, and coordinate the distribution program at the village (VLDC), district (DLDC), and national (NLDC) levels. Nationally, there were 531,000 hectares of arable land available from the former cooperatives for distribution to approximately 375,000 families (Stanfield et al., 1992). The amount of land to be allocated to each family was therefore extremely limited.[6]

The privatization of ex-APC land proceeded very rapidly with almost 87 percent of the land used by APCs distributed by October 1992 (Stanfield et al., 1992). By the end of August 1993, 91.5 percent of ex-APC land was assigned. The remaining 8 percent was unproductive land that the NLDC judged not suitable for use by farming families (IFDC, 1994). Ownership certificates were given to those who received land as part of the decollectivization process. The process of formal titling, however, proceeded more slowly than the physical distribution of land because of demands for restitution by ex-owners and other disputes.

In principle, 'land distribution' meant conceding ownership or use rights to land and other agricultural assets to farm workers, APC members, and other rural residents.   In terms of effective rights, however, ownership was practically limited to usufruct rights. The only difference was that those who were granted ownership certificates could inherit the assets. The evolution of those rights towards effective full property is discussed later.

State farms. The legal basis for the privatization of SFs was developed only after the breakup of the APCs, with Government Decision No. 452 of 17/10/1992 on Restructuring the agricultural enterprises (state farms).   A number of factors explain the government's reluctance to dismantle the state farms:

1   The land/population ratio in SFs was so low that per capita division would result in miniplots, which would, in turn, lead to the creation of subsistence-oriented agriculture on some of the best land in the country (Stanfield et al., 1992).

2   Given the complete breakup of the APCs with privatization, the government hoped to preserve SFs as production structures in order to guarantee at least a minimum of continuity in agricultural production.

3   It was hoped that SFs would attract foreign investment in the sector.

Nonetheless, technicians concluded that almost half of the SFs were not viable as large units. It was therefore decided to distribute 50,000 hectares of SF land to former employees and pool the remainder into joint ventures as part of foreign investment programs. In November 1992, the Central Agency for the Privatization of the State Farms was set up by the Ministry of Agriculture and Food (MAF) to manage, coordinate, and supervise the process in all districts. In those SFs created by merging several cooperatives together, land was to be distributed on the basis of Land Law No. 7501 and Decision No. 255. In SFs where the state financed important land improvement projects or which were based on expropriated large estates, former workers would get usufruct rights, but the state would retain ownership of the land. In some cases, beneficiaries were given a formal 'use right' certificate giving them the right to use the land for an indefinite period without charge. Elsewhere they were granted possession of the land without such a certificate (Stanfield and Jazo, 1995).

According to official estimates from the MAF, by August 1993, 78.8 percent of SF land had been leased to former specialists and workers or pooled into joint ventures (MAF, 1994). The same sources indicate that about 92 percent of the total land available for distribution had been assigned by the end of that year, including 93 percent of former APC land and 91 percent of former SF land.

Problems with reform implementation

Spontaneous privatization. As previously mentioned, during March-April 1991, (after the Socialists won the first elections), many APCs were spontaneously broken up and assets distributed among villagers. When the Socialist government resigned the coalition government that took over introduced the Land Law and related decrees. The coalition government tried to control the reform process and establish some consensus between the government and the peasant population. In some villages, however, properties were still being illegally taken over by people. In the process, irrigation facilities and other rural infrastructure was damaged.

Rural nomenklatura attempts to obtain economic power. The egalitarian distribution of land and assets to farmers was jeopardized by attempts of the nomenklatura to capture most of the benefits of agricultural privatization. Decree No. 266 specified that APC directors and managers were to organize the process of distributing assets as well as the liquidation of the APCs. This authority was widely abused. Many cases were reported where managers retained the best part of the assets for themselves or their friends and where they manipulated the assets' values. This threatened the reform's main features of fairness and equity. In addition, managers delayed reforms by slowing down administration in liquidating the APCs, as they were very reluctant to lose their jobs and privileges.

Lack of administrative capacity. A serious bottleneck was created by the bureaucratic inability to cope with the large volume of administrative work necessary for the implementation of the land reform. There were delays in processing and preparing the required documentation for the distribution of the property, for land registration, and especially land titling. In 1994, only 57.6 percent of the total assigned area titles was titled, whereas 77.7 percent of total land area was privately used (table 3.6). In the ex-ACPs, the process of land titling proceeded much faster than in the ex-SFs, with about 68.3 percent of the APCs' land titled compared with only 19 percent in ex-SFs. Field surveys showed that there were important differences between the 'de facto ownership' of land and what the Land Commissions' ownership certificates assigned to new owners. This was, partly, due to administrative problems and partly due to informal land transactions which were taking place in the absence of a formal land market.

Return to old boundaries. The land distribution program was opposed by the rural population in some parts of the country. In many northern villages, land was not distributed in conformity with the law and government directives. Instead it was restituted to former owners in old boundaries. Stanfield et al. (1992) argue that this was because collectivization occurred relatively recently in these areas and because the moral code of traditions, which recognizes private property as somebody's moral belonging, was still very strong. In some villages people who were excluded from the land distribution process because their families had no claim to land from before collectivization often accepted their fate without complaint, since they believed they had no legitimate claim.

Table 3.6
Progress in the privatization of the agricultural land

Type of land	Ex-SFs hectares	Ex-APCs hectares	Total hectares	% of total area
Total agricultural land	154,083	547,922	702,005	100
Undistributed, state-owned land				
- Land of low quality	13,507	100,199	113,706	16.2
- State retained	10,097	6,131	16,228	2.3
- Joint ventures	1,808	0	1,808	0.3
Total state owned land	25,412	106,330	131,742	18.8
Available for distribution	128,671	441,592	570,263	81.2
Distributed in fact	119,649	425,958	545,607	77.7
In process of distribution	9,022	15,634	24,656	3.5
Titling process:				
- Number of titles issued	19,379	248,788	268,167	
- Area covered by titles	23,445	290,948	314,393	
- Distributed land area not yet titled	96,204	135,010	231,214	
- Area titled as % of area distributed	19.6	68.3	57.6	

Source: Stanfield and Kukeli, 1995, and MAF, 1995a.

73

Land refusal. MAF data reveal that more than 100,000 hectares of land have been refused by the would-be owners, because the land was marginal or far from home and because of personal disputes in the process of redistribution and lack of enthusiasm for farming (Korra, 1994). The bulk of the refused land is, however, rejected because of poor quality and lack of access to reliable irrigation water. Potential solutions, such as agro-forestry, are investigated to make this land attractive for privatization.

Failure of joint ventures in agriculture. The area of land occupied by joint ventures was 24,400 hectares in the spring of 1993. However, it has been drastically reduced due to failure of these partnerships. This led to the 'use right' distribution of joint venture land and Albanian assets to farm workers and agricultural specialists who are now individually cultivating such land.

Rural migration. Due to, among other things, unfavorable land conditions and a very low ratio of land per capita, a massive migration of people from mountainous areas to more fertile regions has occurred since 1991, increasing population pressure in some areas. Although 8,200 hectares of land were used by the state to accommodate this anticipated population movement towards more fertile areas and coastal plains, in some cases illegal land capturing induced conflicts over land use between local villagers and the newcomers.

Legislative responses

Legislative response to the above problems was dynamic. Government policies have focused on eliminating administrative constraints, on speeding up the implementation, reducing uncertainty and, recently, on providing full property rights and security of tenure and transactions. The first amendment to the Land Law (Law No. 7715 of 02/06/1993) stipulates that 'owners of agricultural land are free to lease out their plots to any local or foreign natural and legal persons' (Art.3a). It defines the procedures and deadlines for accepting or refusing the title to land distributed under the Land Law, beyond which land reverses to the state. It also provides stronger administrative and legal measures in case of illegal land capturing and devastations. A second amendment to the Land Law (Law No. 7855 of 29/07/1994) recognizes the need to speed up the process of distribution, especially land titling. It provides detailed also administrative procedures for the completion of relevant documents and administrative measures against those civil servants who obstruct implementation.

In addition, the government approved legislation to put in place the prerequisites of a land market by passing the Law for the Creation of the Real Estate Registration System (Law No. 7843 of 13/07/1994) and for the Taxation of Agricultural Land (Law No. 7805 of March 1994). Also, the passage of a bill permitting the transfer of rights to farmland from 'use rights' to 'ownership rights' was intended to accelerate the process in SFs. However, this law does not extend such rights to land belonging to failed joint ventures until their disputes are settled.

Reform outcomes

Privatization in agriculture brought about considerable changes in the incentives structure and in motivations. It reduced free-riding behavior of individuals and waste of scarce resources in the farming economy. Agricultural output responded well to privatization and price liberalization. During the first two years after the initiation of the reform program (1992 and 1993), total agricultural output grew by 28 percent compared with 1991 (MAF, 1994). Strong growth continued in 1994 and 1995 (OECD, 1995). There is good reason to believe that this development was due to improvements in incentives induced by privatization. However, further growth and productivity increases are seriously restrained by a highly fragmented pattern of farm holdings, restricted access to credit, the remaining uncertainty over property rights, and by high external transaction costs due to underdeveloped market institutions and upstream and downstream sectors.

Fragmentation. Land privatization has created about 490,000 new private holdings. These are fragmented into at least 1.9 million separate parcels of land, with an average of about 3.3 separately located parcels for each family (IFDC, 1994). The average farm size is 1.05 hectares, ranging between 1.29 hectares in valley and foothill regions to 0.8 hectares in the mountains (Grace, 1995). This tiny household structure of farming makes it difficult to use mechanization, which is not suited to such a small scale of operations. As a result, a primitive form of cultivating, with most operations carried out manually, prevails.

Uncertainty over property rights. Uncertainty over land property rights has come from pressure from pre-1945 landowners and their growing political power. Delays in the process of assigning land litles and restrictions on ownership rights adds to these uncertainties. This, coupled with limited access to credit, has resulted in a significant lack of investment and maintenance, the use of low-quality seeds and restricted application of chemical fertilizers, especially in the mountainous area.

Absence of a land market. The absence of an effective, formal market for land has significantly constrained the development of agriculture as a whole. It has limited individuals' choices to stay in or to leave agriculture and has encouraged the development of a subsistence form of farming producing little marketed surplus. Restrictions on land transactions have blocked the process of land consolidation, with negative consequences on productivity and viability of farming. It has also added to the already critical problem of uncertain property rights by limiting property right to usufruct rights.

The Law on the Buying and Selling of Agricultural Land, Meadows and Pastures (No. 7983 of 27/07/1995), which provided for the creation of a land market, is not operational yet, but it is expected to contribute to the removal of the above constraints. This law prohibits transfers of ownership to land until such land is registered. Registration is well underway, but is not likely to be completed for the entire country until 1998 (Stanfield, 1995). It is unlikely, however, that a land market will immediately result in reduction of fragmentation. For example, much will depend on the evolution of the process of compensating ex-owners of agricultural land.

An explanation of the choice of the land reform process

At this stage of the reform, it is still difficult to draw conclusions about the size and form of farm organizations that will prevail by the end of the transition period. It is also beyond the scope of this chapter to analyze whether the reform outcome is economically optimal. However, whatever the theoretical 'optimal' size and form of farm organization, many economists agree that the egalitarian approach adopted in Albania may not have been the best choice from an economic standpoint. While privatization and liberalization have induced important output increases, subsistence agriculture is emerging as a result of fragmentation of land and production structures coupled with high uncertainty, undeveloped markets, and institutions of property rights, difficult access to inputs (especially credit), restricted information and extension services, limited savings, lack of managerial skills, and farmers inexperienced in running their own farms. This allows for very restricted use of mechanization and inhibits innovation and introduction of new technology, severely limiting the scope for expanding production and raising productivity.

As long as growth in other sectors is not sufficient to absorb labor released from agriculture, the large number of unviable farms is likely to prevail. To the extend that off-farm opportunities will be limited and, therefore, the opportunity costs of farm labor low, farmers will be reluctant to give up their land, which would constitute their major, if not their only, source of livelihood.

The questions we need to answer are:

1 Why has Albania preferred distribution of land to the rural population, instead of restitution of land as in most other CEECs?

2 Why has Albania, unlike most other CEECs, chosen such a radical decollectivization process, one that has resulted in the complete breakup of its APCs?

Which factors have determined the choice of this reform process? Some might attribute this choice to lack of knowledge, inadequate understanding of economics, and poor management. In fact, it is hardly plausible that these are the only, or even most important, explanations. In this section we analyze what motivated Albanian policymakers and what constraints they faced while choosing from alternative approaches. We search for reasons behind the choice of the Albanian reform in the interaction between social, political, and economic factors and institutions affecting the process. We argue that the answer lies in the politics of the choice and in institutional arrangements which constrain the scope of government in selecting economically optimal options. More specifically, besides political and institutional changes since 1989, several exogenous factors have been important determinants of land reform and decollectivization choices in Central and Eastern Europe (Swinnen, 1997). These include the precollectivization asset ownership distribution, asset ownership status on the eve of the current reforms, the ethnicity of potential owners, and the impact of decollectivization on the (rural) political equilibrium. We will analyze the impacts of these and other factors for the Albanian case after introducing the general framework of analysis.

A political economy perspective

The 'new' or 'neo-classical' political economics studies the interactions between economic and political markets by focusing on the role of political preferences, the influence of pressure groups, and interactions between voters, politicians, and bureaucrats. Applying the language and assumptions of neoclassical economics to institutions and political behavior gives insights into the way policies are determined. The theory is based on the assumption of informed agents who rationally pursue their interests and attempt to maximize their objectives, subject to constraints. It assumes that man is a rational utility maximizer also in political activities, and applies itself to understanding his endeavor to relate means to ends as efficiently as possible (Staniland, 1985; Swinnen and van der Zee, 1993).

Policies are considered to be traded in a political market whereby agents meet to exchange political goods and seek to maximize returns to their political involvement. Equilibrium is reached when marginal political returns to all agents are equal. On the demand side, voters are treated as 'consumers' demanding favorable policies to maximize their own utility function. On the supply side, governments and political parties are alternative 'suppliers' competing to produce public policies. Policies are bought and paid for by voters with the political support they provide to politicians. In choosing among alternative policies, decision makers end up doing a political cost-benefit analysis. If political costs are larger than benefits, the proposed policy is not pursued, and policies that are likely to receive more political support from various groups are chosen and implemented. In this process policies are determined endogenously.

The reform options

One can describe the government's reform policy choice as a choice from the following options:

1 Minimal Reform Option (MRO), which implies the privatization of asset ownership, with more autonomy to enterprises and minimal restructuring but without decollectivization;

2 Social Equity Option (SEO), which consists of full decollectivization with equal distribution of assets among farm workers;

3 Historical Justice Option (HJO), with full decollectivization and restitution of asset property rights to former owners.

Wealth distribution and the demand for land reform

The three most important groups on the political demand side in Albanian land reform were:

1 Farm workers and rural families who owned little or no land before 1945, ('farmers' or 'farm workers'),

2 Pre-1945 owners of land ('former owners' or 'pre-1945 owners'), and

3 Communist leaders who were in charge of the APCs and SFs ('rural nomenklatura').

In reality, additional interest groups and internal exist within these three groups. For example, state farm workers had a better status than APC workers and are sometimes affected differently by the reforms. Also, pre-1945 landowners included both landlords with large estates and smaller farmers. Further, 1946-1948 landowners were also former owners, but quite different from the pre-1945 landowners. As explained before, the 1946-1948 land distribution followed the expropriation of land from the large landowners who dominated Albanian agriculture prior to 1945, and from people who owned more than 5 hectares. Land was given to small and landless peasants.

In the following analysis, we concentrate primarily on the three most vocal and important interest groups in the land reform debate: the farm workers, the former owners, and the rural nomenklatura. When the groups' internal heterogeneity or a more nuanced separation of interests is important for the explanation, we will be more specific in our discussion. The discussion will also explain why other groups were less important players in the debate.

Land reform affects future income streams of both gainers and losers from the process. Given Albanian farm workers' low incomes, and thus high marginal utility of income, the effects of land reform on this group is substantial. The vested interest of former owners is high ℁ they stand to gain or loose much because pre-1945 landownership was very concentrated. The rural nomenklatura who were in charge of both APCs and SFs prior to the reforms stand to lose their jobs and privileges through decollectivization.

From the positions taken by representatives of the farm workers and the former owners in the agrarian reform debate, we can conclude that both these groups preferred full decollectivization to the minimal reform option. Only the rural nomenklatura supported the MRO, because decollectivization would imply a loss in their economic, social, and political status. The main debate within the decollectivization camp was how to privatize assets, mainly the land. Distributing assets equally among farm workers (the social equity, or SEO, option) was preferred by those who actually farmed the land and by other rural people (who, along with farm workers, made up 65 percent of the population). This SEO option discriminated against pre-1945 large landowners and their heirs, who made up approximately 3 percent of the population and who were to receive financial compensation.[7]

Large landowners and their heirs preferred full and physical restitution of expropriated assets (the historical justice option, or HJO). This option would transfer large estates of some of the best land of the country to a few families. In addition to the large landlords, small farmers owned some land, mostly in less favored areas. The income differences between the SEO and HJO would be much smaller for these former small landowners, especially when the transaction costs of submitting valid claims to former property are considered. Therefore, small farmers were less committed to pressuring for HJO. In general, however, most rural families would end up without landownership under the HJO policy.

Each group wanted the government to choose a reform policy with the most favorable income and wealth redistribution for themselves. They tried to influence the government's decisionmaking through political actions, such as demonstrations, by voting in favor of or against the party in government, making financial or labor contributions to electoral campains, etc. A standard assumption is that the intensity of these political (re)actions are proportional to the welfare impacts of the policies (Swinnen, 1994).

The three groups on the demand side of the Albanian political market for land reform have had different comparative advantages in trying to influence the political decisionmaking. Farm workers make up the majority of the population and, in an electoral system, the number of their votes represents a major power factor. Former landowners have a big stake on a per capita basis, and the benefits of restitution are very concentrated. This increases their investment in political activities to influence the decision and reduce their political organization costs (Olson, 1965). The rural nomenklatura can rely on a well-established organizational and political network to influence the decisions. This organizational advantage is likely to be strongest in the beginning of the reforms, but tends to erode gradually. The declining performance of the Socialist Party in the two elections was probably influenced by this factor.

The political supply side and reform choices

On the political supply side, politicians in government or in Parliament have to make the decisions. While politicians have their own preferred policy, which depends on their objectives and motivations, they may not be able to choose the reforms according to their proper preferences. This depends on the political institutions and on the distribution of the decision making power within these institutions. In other words, a government needs a minimum of political support to push policies through, and the amount of support it needs to remain in charge is determined by the political institutions. For example, the pre-1990 political system allowed the Communist Party to govern with much less support from the population than is possible under the current electoral system. Therefore, since the beginning of the reforms, the government increasingly has to take the political reactions of various groups on the demand side of the political market into account, as these will determine the political support for the governmnent. Changes in institutions and in political preferences will therefore change the reform policy picked by the government.

The Socialist government's minimal reform policies (MRO) reflected the main objective of the Socialists, which was to retain control in rural areas by relying on the traditional structures of political, economic, and social organization – the APCs and SFs. This strategy proved effective in the first elections, in which the SP managed to obtain the majority of parliamentary seats thanks to the support they received from rural areas. Organizational advantages and lack of information from sources other than the highly politicized governmental ones were probably the main reason for the above result. The opposition had little access to the rural areas and small provincial cities due to limited resources, lack of the necessary structures and linkages in those areas, and (ex-)Communist control of the media. Also, intellectual contacts and the level of education in rural areas were lower than in urban areas.

If reforms were unavoidable, from the SP's point of view, retaining control would be most effective if the reforms were organized while the Socialists were still in power. This would ensure that the rural nomenklatura was in the best position either to obstruct the reforms or to manipulate them in order to turn political power into economic power.

In contrast, a fundamental objective of the DP reformers in both governments was privatizing agricultural assets by distributing them (especially land) to farm workers. This process would ensure the support of a large part of the rural constituency (65 percent of the population), that showed reluctance to abandon the Communists and was skeptical of the new political process and reform parties. For the DP reformers, distributing land on an equal per capita basis to farm workers and supporting decollectivization and liquidation of APCs would also destroy the basis for Communist support in the countryside and provide for a long-term political support base for right-wing forces.

In this environment, the spontaneous privatizations of APCs in spring 1991, which contributed to the fall of the Socialist government, played an important role. They evidently reflected the strong disbelief of farmers in the future of the APC structures that extremely impoverished them. It is an interesting question whether this process was initiated as an ultimate reaction to the extreme decline of the agricultural sector in 1989 and 1990 and the resulting food shortages, or whether it was a deliberate action to influence the political debate on the choice of a reform process, which was taking place at that time.

The questions of why Albania differed from most other CEECs in its land privatization (choosing distribution instead of restitution) and the intensity of cooperative farm decollectivization need to be addressed further. To answer these questions, we analyze how a series of exogenous factors characteristic of Albania have affected post-Communist land reform decisions.

The impact of the postcollectivization landownership status

A key difference between Albania and other CEECs is that agricultural land in Albania was formally state owned on the eve of the reforms, while in most other CEECs the land remained formally in private hands throughout the collectivization period, even if all effective decisionmaking authority was taken away from the private owners. It turns out that this legal factor played a very important role in all CEECs. Without exception, property rights to land that was formally still privately owned in 1989 have been returned to the former (or formal) owners (Swinnen, 1997). With land in state ownership, the Albanian government had more options than the other CEEC governments.

The impact of the precollectivization landownership distribution

The restitution option requires a decision regarding the reference date for restitution, because there is more than one 'former owner' for most of the agricultural land. As in other CEECs, the reference date played an important role in Albania's restitution debate. Post World War II land reforms, often implemented under a Communist-led government, induced a more egalitarian landownership in several CEECs prior to collectivization. In most of these CEECs, restitution of land was based on the ownership situation just before collectivization, but after the Communist-inspired land reforms (Swinnen, 1997). Assuming the same reference date, had land restitution been chosen by the Albanian government, it would have been based on the 1948 ownership situation. However, it is remarkable that in the Albanian debate 1948 owners have been much less vocal than in many other CEECs and less opposed to distribution than Albania's pre-1945 owners. Why is this?

The first reason is that restitution based on 1948 ownership would have had results similar to the redistribution option. Most 1948 owners were to receive land under the distribution program. This was because the structure of the APCs in terms of member families did not change much over the years due to restrictions in labor mobility. After 1948 farming families voluntarily or by force pooled their land into the APCs and remained there ever since. Moreover, in some cases, the area of land assigned to families under the land distribution program was larger than what they would have received under a restitution program. This was due partly to increases in arable land area and improvements in land quality resulting from state investments, and partly because restituted land would have to be divided among other heirs.[8]

A second reason restitution was not chosen might be that the 1946-1948 land reform was considered a Communist action and a first step towards collectivization. As such, those who received land in the framework of Communist reforms may somehow have felt that they had no legitimate claim to the land. These considerations might also have played a role in the anti-Communist sentiments in the early 1990s.

A third reason is that for the small landowners the marginal costs of lobbying and of submitting valid claims per hectare of land to be restituted (or to be compensated for) were high compared with the expected additional benefits.

These three reasons also explain the much more vigorous opposition of the pre-1945 owners to land distribution. They had much more to gain from restitution in comparison with what they receive under the actual reform program, even with the costs of lobbying and submitting restitution claims. In addition, pre-1945 owners feel they are the legitimate owners of land that was violently taken away from them by the Communists.

The traditional political organization cost argument would predict that former owners would be much more influential on the decisionmaking level than would farm workers. Former owners have all the characteristics that reduce transaction costs in political organization: they are a much smaller group with highly concentrated benefits, compared with the enormous group of farm workers who have much more diluted benefits (Olson, 1965). Then why did the reformers in government choose land distribution over restitution? Why were pre-1945 owners less influential than the peasants in determining the reform choice?

The most important explanation, we believe, has to do with reform impacts and the low income level of farm workers. While the income effect of the land reform choice might have been smaller for farm workers than for pre-1945 owners, being given a piece of land had a very substantial effect on farm workers' utility. Even a relatively small plot of land had a big welfare impact on farm workers in their situation of very low opportunity costs for their labor. Moreover, in an uncertain environment, land is viewed as a secure form of wealth and income security (Ellis, 1988). Poorer members of society are often more concerned than wealthier people with holding a secure form of wealth and retaining their traditional source of livelihood (Binswanger and Rosenzweig, 1986).

Because of its large impact on marginal welfare and on income security, the land reform choice strongly influenced peasants' political reactions. A vast number of people (50 percent of the labor force and 65 percent of the population living in the rural areas) benefited to some extent from land distribution, and many of this group, would have reacted vehemently against restitution to pre-1945 owners. Only 3 percent of the population would benefit from restitution to pre-1945 owners. Thus, the important marginal utility effect of distribution reforms for the many peasants offset the 'land dilution effect'. In combination with the vast numbers difference, this more than offsets the concentration and organizational cost advantages.[9]

A related factor is the likely opposition most people would have shown to the restoration of a feudal structure in the best agricultural areas that would occur by restituting a very large share of this land to the heirs of a handful of families. Another consideration might have been that land distribution is technically much easier to organize and to implement than restitution to former owners especially in the absence of land maps indicating the previous borders. These factors combine to explain Albania's choice of land distribution over the restitution option.[10]

Why was there an important difference in privatization of SFs and APCs?

Differences in the structure of farm organization, land use, and pattern of asset ownership explain why privatization methods differed for APCs, SFs, and individual plots. Small individual plots remained private. Privatization of SFs was different and more gradual than in APCs. The APCs' status and organization under central planning was different from that of the SFs. At least in theory, the means of production in APCs were collectively owned, except for land that was state property after 1976. Land used by APCs was previously privately owned by peasants and then pooled into the collectives which were created all over the country, including in the mountainous areas. What the APCs produced was divided up among members, while a special quota went to the state and surpluses were sold in cities.

Unlike the APCs, SFs were operated like any other state enterprises. Everything was state owned and workers (mostly urban residents) were government employees. Their benefits were much higher than those of APC members. Some SF activities produced exportables. The state invested intensively in such farms by providing special facilities, including greenhouses, high-quality inputs, irrigation water, and agricultural machines. Mechanization stations, which provided services to the APCs on a contract or rental basis, were owned by SFs. Moreover, SFs were created on big estates confiscated from the Church or from the pre-Communist state, often on the best land of the country. Some SFs were also created by merging APCs together.

While APCs were privatized (and decollectivized) quickly, the privatization of SFs started later and proceeded more slowly. The reasons for this include the following:

1 There was relatively less pressure from state farm workers to privatize the farms and distribute the land because of their relatively better situation and benefits;

2 In most cases there were no former owners demanding land restitution;

3 Privatization of state farms was technically more complicated because more land improvements and investments, including nonland asset constructions, had occurred over the previous forty years; and

4 Given the complete breakup of the APCs and the fragmentation of land the government hoped to preserve SFs as large production structures to attract foreign investment.

Why was the breakup of collective farms much more radical than in other CEECs?

Albania's difference from most other CEECs is remarkable. While spontaneous privatization occurred to some extent in virtually all CEECs, the extent to which this spontaneous process contributed to a complete breakup of the collective farms in Albania is unique. The only country which comes close to Albania in this respect is Romania. In most CEECs, most farm workers have not left the cooperative-under-transformation during the first years of transition (Swinnen, 1997). What is the reason for the difference in Albania?

The main reason seems to be the less advantaged situation of Albania's cooperative members. Albania had the lowest per capita income in Europe, and the APC members' incomes were even lower than average incomes. In addition, the virtual collapse of the agricultural sector between 1988 and 1991 further worsened their situation, inducing a radical reaction from APC farm workers in an environment of reduced social control and political instability. The fact that a complete breakup of the APCs resulted from this spontaneous privatization and the consequent officially organized land distribution programs indicates that farm workers preferred small individual farms over continued farming within a reformed APC framework. This shift to individual farms occurred despite all the problems associated with credit supply, lack of machinery, etc., which in many other CEECs discouraged individuals from leaving the cooperative framework. This emphasizes APC members' lack of confidence in, and expected poor benefits from, remaining in the cooperative framework.

This argument is consistent with the remarkable observation of strong growth in gross agricultural output (GAO) since 1992: GAO increased 30-40 percent between 1992 and 1994 (OECD, 1995). In most other CEECs, the GAO did not pick up until 1994, despite their earlier start on reforms. This argument is also consistent with the less extreme reactions of SF workers and the less radical decollectivization of these farms.

Finally, the ethnicity of the potential beneficiaries is also important. In agriculture foreigners are denied any property rights on land. The law does not recognize their ancient rights, and it is not clear whether they could be eligible for any degree of compensation in the future. The bill on the creation of a land market stipulates that agricultural land is not to be sold to foreigners. But foreigners can rent land for agricultural purposes, even on a long-term basis. There is some uncertainty regarding the situation of the Greek minority in Albania. As Albanian citizens they were distributed land. However, many of them have obtained permanent working permissions in Greece. This has created a vacuum of labor in the southern part of the country, where land and fruit plantations are not looked after.

Conclusion

Agricultural privatization in Albania included the distribution of agricultural land on an equal per capita basis to the rural population. Furthermore, agrarian reform resulted in a complete decollectivization of collective farms. Both facts contrast with the rest of Central and Eastern Europe, where restitution of land was the most commonly chosen privatization process and where decollectivization was modest in the first years of transition.

We have explained these differences from a political economy perspective. We argue that the privatization choice results from political bargaining between former owners, farm workers, and the rural nomenklatura. The choice is influenced by changes in the political institutions, the economic structure, and the historical and legal status of the assets under privatization. More specifically, the fact that land used by cooperative farms was state owned, the large rural population share, and the very unequal pre-1945 land distribution have all affected the choice of the privatization process. Further, with low opportunity costs of agricultural labor and large uncertainties, the distribution of even small plots of land had large impacts on the marginal welfare and income security of farm workers. The size and intensity of this political constituency was more influential than the lobbying efforts of the very concentrated vested interests in favor of land restitution to pre-1945 owners.

In addition, the extremely low incomes of collective farm workers induced a radical decollectivization of cooperative farms in the environment of a dramatic collapse of agricultural production, food shortages, reduced social control, political instability, and uncertain land reform legislation that characterized the early 1990s.

Notes

1. From 1990 to mid-1992, output shrank by 50 percent. The industrial sector collapsed. State enterprises, awaiting privatization, closed down.
2. For a comprehensive discussion of the economic and political case for privatization, see Estrin (1994).
3. The Social Democratic Party, which was created in 1991 by liberal elements from the Communist Party, took a centrist position in the reform debate.
4. Normally, urban properties were restituted, where possible, to legitimate owners or their heirs. In cases where this was not possible, another form of compensation was introduced. Urban properties for which no claims were received were sold to the public. Enterprises built during the period of central planning were also sold either by direct sales or auction, although former workers were given preferential access in the process.
5. The first split occured in November 1992 when the Democratic Alliance, consisting of ex-DP members, was established.
6. In those areas where peasant families could not get the necessary minimum of agricultural land, 'the state takes measures so that other sources of livelihood are guaranteed to them by the Council of Ministers' (Article 5 of the Land Law).
7. The population has increased, and the number of those who would have a claim on properties which before 1945 belonged to large landowners has increased also. However, proportionally, the number has not changed much.
8. In fact, since then, the area of arable land doubled and population more than tripled (1.9 percent annual growth). Moreover, population growth rates for rural areas were much higher than the national average rate.
9. See de Gorter and Swinnen (1995) for a similar discussion applied to price and trade policies.
10. The pre-1945 owners did succeed in receiving financial compensation for part of their lost property, as was also the case in Hungary.

References

Albanian Institute of Statistics (INSTAT) (1996), *Albanian Statistics 1995*, Tirana, Albania.

Binswanger H. and Rosenzweig, M. (1986), 'Behavioral and Material Determinants of Production Relations in Agriculture', *Journal of Development Studies*, Vol. 22, No. 3, pp. 5-21.

Brandt, H. (1994), 'Albania's Development Problems Between Land Reform and Large-Scale Privatization', Report prepared for the German Development Institute GDI: Berlin.

Caputo, E. and Christy, L. (1994), 'Joint Ventures and Foreign Investment in Albanian Agriculture and Agri-Businesses', Report Commissioned by the FAO: Tirana-Rome.

Christensen, G. (1993), 'Review of the Subsidy and Support System for Wheat and Bread in Albania', FSG-University of Oxford, Report Commissioned by the FAO.

Christensen, G. (1994), 'Policy Issues for the Agricultural Sector in Albania', FSG- University of Oxford, Report Commissioned by the FAO.

Civici, A. (1994), *La Question Forcière Dans La Restructuration De L'Economie Agricole En Albanie*, Université de l'Agriculture: Tirana, Albania.

de Gorter, H. and Swinnen, J. (1994), 'The Economic Polity of Farm Policy', *Journal of Agricultural Economics*, Vol. 45, No. 3, pp. 312-326.

de Gorter H. and Swinnen, J. (1995), 'The Economic Polity of Farm Policy: Reply', *Journal of Agricultural Economics*, Vol. 46, No. 3, pp. 403-414.

Ellis, F. (1988), *Peasant Economics: Farm Household and Agrarian Development*, Cambridge University Press: Cambridge.

Estrin, S. (1994), 'The Economic Transition and Privatization: The Issues', in Estrin, S. (ed.), *Privatization in Central and Eastern Europe*, Longman: London and New York.

Grace, C. (1995), *The Hill and Mountain Farmers of Albania*, SARA/USAID, Ministry of Agriculture and Food: Tirana, Albania.

International Monetary Fund (IMF) (1994), 'Economic Review - Albania', No. 5, July 1994, International Monetary Fund: Washington DC.

International Fertiliser Development Centre (IFDC) (1994), *Agricultural Production in Albania, Socio-Economic Survey, 1993-1994*, Tirana, Albania.

Korra, L. (1994), *Agricultural Policy and Trade in Albania*, Ministry of Agriculture and Food: Tirana, Albania.

Lemel, H., Gandle, D. and Stanfield, D. (1993), 'Albania's Land Distribution Programme: Problems of Tirana, Kavaja and Lushnje Districts, and Options for Overcoming Them', unpublished manuscript, Land Tenure Center, University of Wisconsin-Madison.

Ministry of Agriculture and Food (MAF) (1994), 'Food and Agriculture Statistics of Albania' in *1993 Annual Yearbook*, Tirana, Albania.

Ministry of Agriculture and Food (MAF) (1995a), *Mid-term Progress Report for the Implementation of the Agricultural Sector Adjustment Credit*, Agriculture Programme Office: Tirana, Albania.

Ministry of Agriculture and Food (MAF) (1995b), *Albanian Agriculture: Towards a Europe Agreement*, Agriculture Programme Office: Tirana, Albania.

OECD (1995), *Agricultural Policies, Markets and Trade in Transition Economies: Monitoring and Outlook 1995*, OECD: Paris.

Olson, M. (1965), *The Logic of Collective Action*, Harvard University Press: Cambridge.

Pryor, F. (1992), *The Red and the Green. The Rise and Fall of Collectivized Agriculture in Marxist Regimes*, Princeton University Press: Princeton.

Stanfield, D. (1995), *Comments on Law 7983, of 27/07/1995: Buying and Selling of Agricultural Land, Meadows and Pastures*, PMU/IPRS: Tirana, Albania.

Stanfield, D. and Jazo, A. (1995), 'Privatization of Immovable Property and the Creation of Land Market Institutions in Albania', paper presented at the 1995 ACSM/ASPRS Convention in Charlotte, North Carolina, 27 February-2 March 1995.

Stanfield, D. and Kukeli, A. (1995), 'Consolidation of the Albanian Agricultural Land Reform Through a Programme for Creating an Immovable Property Registration System', paper prepared for the GIS/LIS 1995 Central Europe Conference, Budapest, Hungary, 12-16 June 1995.

Stanfield, D., Lastarria-Cornhiel, S., Bruce, J. and Friedman, E. (1992), *Consolidating Property Rights in Albania's New Private Farm Sector*, Land Tenure Center, University of Wisconsin-Madison.

Staniland, M. (1985), *What is Political Economy? A Study of the Social Theory and Underdevelopment*, Vail-Ballou Press: New York.

Swinnen, J. (1994), 'Political Economy of Reform in Bulgarian Agriculture', in Schmitz, A., Moulton, K. Buckwell, A. and Davidova, S. (eds.), *Privatization of Agriculture in New Market Economies: Lessons from Bulgaria*, Kluwer Academic Publishers: Boston, London and Dordrecht.

Swinnen, J. (1997), 'The Choice of Privatization and Decollectivization Processes in Central and Eastern Europe', chapter 13 in this volume.

Swinnen, J. and Van der Zee, F. (1993), 'The Political Economy of Agricultural Policies: A Survey', *European Review of Agricultural Economics*, Vol.20, pp. 261-290.

Xhamara, I. (1995a), *Land Reform in Albanian and Its Macroeconomic and Social Impacts*, Ministry of Agriculture and Food: Tirana, Albania.

Xhamara, I. (1995b), *Economical and Environmental Impact of Land Registration in Albania*, Ministry of Agriculture and Food: Tirana, Albania.

4 Political economy of agricultural privatization in the Baltic countries

Ewa Rabinowicz[1]

Introduction

This chapter provides a comparative study of agricultural privatization in Latvia and Lithuania. It focuses on the policy environment and the mechanics of the process of privatization and on competition between involved interest groups. The issues addressed are the choice of the privatization method and the speed and sequencing of the privatization process.

The Baltic countries have been Soviet Republics and not independent states. They have heterogeneous populations and ethnic conflicts play a major role in political competition and in the process of regaining independence. Therefore, this chapter focuses on ethnic tensions, which vary in source and in degree in Lithuania and Latvia, as an important factor in understanding the mechanics of privatization in each country. The differences in their privatization strategies can be explained by differences in both ethnic composition and in agrarian structures. Both affect the balance of power between the winners and losers of various privatization schemes.

In Lithuania, ethnic conflicts are less pronounced because ethnic Lithuanians form the vast majority and because of the country's more clearly established statehood. Here, privatization has been primarily driven by distributional conflicts between former landowners and the collective farms and the related political struggle between Communists (or their descendants) and the anti-Communist opposition (later transformed into a conservative party). The Communists have supported collective farms (and smallholders) while anti-Communists are associated with the landowners. In Latvia, ethnic competition for political influence and national wealth has been the overriding struggle. Privatization in agriculture has been part of a larger distributional conflict there. Ethnic diversity and breakaway status in Latvia have affected class structure and distributional cleavages.

Methodological approach

For this study of Lithuania and Latvia, I use a partial model, treating developments outside agriculture as exogenous factors and disregarding possible feedbacks. The analysis does not render an accurate test of a specific theory. By necessity, the approach is more of a 'story telling'. A theoretical framework is used to organize the story in a consistent fashion. My methodological approach relates to several strains of literature, briefly reviewed here.

Privatization is an issue of *political economy*, for privatization is really about redistribution of assets or wealth. Since the essence of privatization is redistribution its analysis can draw on existing public choice theories regarding redistributive policies such as protection or taxation. A number of alternative paradigms addressing the basis of endogenous policy behavior are available in the literature.

One class of models concentrates on voting behavior (median voter model, simple majority redistribution coalition). This approach describes how political equilibrium is reached, but, it can be argued, under very unrealistic conditions (Strömberg, 1994). Another class of models can be described as political influence models, where policies reflect a balance between winners and losers. Two alternative approaches to modeling how such balance is reached are usually distinguished. The first concentrates on political support-maximizing behaviors of politicians and has a relatively mechanical view of pressures on them. This approach is based on Downs (1957) and has been further developed by Stigler (1971) and Peltzman (1976). Hillman (1989) has used this model for trade policy analysis. The second approach (pressure group model), proposed by Becker (1983), treats government as a black box whose inputs are the pressures exerted by competing groups.

The median voter approach and pressure group models generate different conclusions with respect to important issues such as economic efficiency and the size of the group that benefits from policies. Political influence models downplay the importance of size. Small, effective groups are considered important because their comparative advantage in controlling free-riding outweighs the relatively small number of votes these groups may deliver in an election. In the median voter model, on the other hand, small special interests have little political influence relative to more general mass interests. A primary implication of the median voter hypothesis is that political competition is unlikely to generate efficient public policies. This would only happen in unusual circumstances when the median voter would prefer an efficient outcome (Abrams and Lewis, 1987). In contrast, Becker's pressure group approach implies that policies that raise economic efficiency are more likely to be adopted than policies that lower efficiency.

Several studies of the political economy of privatization in Eastern Europe are based on the median voter approach (Bolton and Roland, 1994). However, this approach is not well suited to an analysis of privatization in one sector of the economy affecting only a subsection of the population. Moreover, the issue is a discrete choice from few options, each producing identifiable winners and losers. Thus, it is more appropriate to analyze privatization in terms of conflicting interests, making a careful identification of interest groups as important input to the analysis (see next section).

Since decisions about privatization are being made under indirect democracy, it should be recognized that losing and winning groups will attempt to affect the privatization process in their favor and may be able to do so to different degrees. The ability of groups to organize themselves and to articulate a position must thus be considered. The latter is facilitated by the possibility of using consensus-generating arguments, for example by focusing on justice or fairness. Since fairness, social justice, and democratic legitimacy are *raison d'être* of the new democratic regimes, in contrast to the oppression in the past, such arguments can be highly effective.

Some groups may be able to capture the support of preexisting organizations originally designed for other purposes, such as labor unions of agricultural workers. The efficacy of small groups (Olson, 1965) may not hold in societies without preexisting private wealth. A high potential gain is generally believed to facilitate formation of an organized group, but a small group of potential winners, consisting of individuals without financial resources can hardly be influential since borrowing against possible future stakes may not be possible.

Many political economy models ignore *ideology and partisanship in voting*. Personal preferences of policymakers are irrelevant in the world of perfect political competition of Becker (1958). Nor does an incumbent support-maximizing politician of Stigler/Peltzman care about who is gaining or losing with a policy. Not all economists subscribe to this world without ideology, however. Partisan political business cycle theory developed by Hibbs (1977, 1982) is based on the assumption that whether a right-wing or a left-wing party is in power makes a difference (see also Alesina and Roubini, 1992). Hibbs finds that in the UK party allegiance has a clear class-oriented base. Hibbs' analysis of political cycles refers to macroeconomic issues and has been based on an econometric analysis of unemployment and inflation. A somewhat similar approach has been used by Lindahl (1995) and Rabinowicz (1996) in an analysis of agricultural policy in the Nordic countries. Their analysis emphasizes the role of agrarian parties, recognizing parties as representatives of distinct economic interests, and links agricultural policy reforms to the composition of the government.

The same approach will be followed in this study. I will link changes of policies to changes of the government in search of a systematic pattern. Under conditions of dramatic changes of governments and policies such a linkage cannot be ignored. Redistribution of assets involves redistribution of economic power and political influence, with long-term implications for the future political structure of the country. The ongoing battle between the former Communists and anti-Communist reformers comes to the forefront because some methods of privatization may destroy the power base of Communist or ex-Communist parties while benefiting other parties. Agricultural privatization, in particular, is a vital part of such a battle.

This does not discount the influence of special interest groups regarding policy, but emphasizes that the success of lobbying activities may be dependent on the political persuasion of the government. Moreover, systematic relations between organized pressure groups and political parties may emerge. *Interactions between pressure groups and political parties* (in particular between agrarian parties and farm organizations) have been important in the Nordic countries, and such a relationship is worth examining in the Baltic countries as well, since there exists a long tradition of agrarian parties there. Another relationship to explore in this context is that of the old nomenklatura with Communist or ex-Communist parties.

Recognizing partisanship in voting and the existence of special interest parties opens the way for an analysis of coalition formation in which farm interests interact with other forces and privatization in agriculture can be seen from a general equilibrium perspective (see Ström and Leipart (1993) for a discussion of coalition theory). Our approach is more modest and looks at implications of a change in government for the process of privatization, without trying to explain why the government has changed in the first place.

A political science paradigm represents a perspective on the issue of political competition that is fundamentally different from the mainstream political economy approach. Parties are distinguished by different ideologies and represent different segments of the population.

> The most influential accounts of political conflicts in Western democracies have focused on the effects of pre-existing social cleavages on the development of the party system. According to these accounts voting is primarily an expression of social position and well established values and interests associated with it: parties develop in order to express these interests (Evans and Whitefield, 1993, p. 523).

The partisan model I will apply is quite close to the political science perspective on political activity.

The key question in applying this approach to Eastern Europe is whether the structure of party competition emerging in the new democracies will resemble that commonly found in the West. Some authors (Kitschelt, 1992) argue that this will be the case. Several arguments can be advanced against this view, however. Formation of social classes has been inhibited by egalitarian economic policies and the disaggregation of economic and social resources such as property and wealth as well as education and status in the CEECs' Communist-dominated past. People in several CEECs have been found to have difficulties placing themselves in a left-right dimension. Hard-line regimes have prevented the emergence of alternative elites. Furthermore, right-left competition can also be inhibited by the influence of Western organizations such as IMF and the World Bank, since the foreign credits (or financial assistance in general) on which these countries are highly dependent have as a prerequisite the move to a market economy resulting in a commitment (at least at the level of rhetoric) to a similar ideology by all major parties.

Another very important issue is the country's *ethnic composition*. Ethnic conflicts are likely to cut through socioeconomic groups and alter party formation. This is particularly the case when the statehood of a new country is only weakly established. Ethnic nationalism has emerged as one of the most difficult issues in the transition process, in particular within the former Soviet Union (FSU) (Lingle, 1992). Soviet policies of forced resettlement of many ethnic groups and promotion of Russian migration to non-Russian regions have strongly contributed to this development. In the context of transition in the FSU, the problem of national independence appears to be the focus of competition between ethnic-based pressure groups. For this reason, one could claim that some of the ethnic conflicts within the FSU, particularly those involving the national independence of previous republics or autonomous regions, exhibit strong similarities to anticolonial movements in Africa and Asia.

Ethnic conflicts can, otherwise, be analyzed in terms of pressure or interest group competition. The objectives of pressure groups based on ethnic selectivity are in several aspects similar to those of any other interest groups, namely, redistribution of both monetary and nonmonetary rewards to their members. Ethnicity goes of course much deeper than a simple redistribution of assets, privileges, or other benefits. Ethnic groups sometimes exhibit a preference for revenge, particularly in the case of groups that have experienced discrimination. For this reason it is possible to interpret some ethnic activity as the expression of an electorate not very experienced in mainstream political participation. For this reason such groups can also be vulnerable to populist appeals by politicians relying on nationalistic retorics (Lingle, 1992).

The major economic reason a regional majority might want to create an independent nation is that redistribution in favor of the majority, even if it is based on correcting historical injustice at expense of the Russian minority, is difficult if not impossible as long as the Russian minority has powerful allies in other regions of the same nation. Of course discriminatory redistributive policy, such as extending certain groups from participating the asset distribution schemes, cannot be unlimited even if the ethnic majority manages to create an independent nation, or the new nation will not achieve the international respectability and good relations it needs to have with its neighbors. Redistributive policies are also influenced by the relative size of the competing groups. Discriminatory policies may not be worthwhile for a large majority. The stakes are too small to outweigh such costs as loss of international reputation with possible implications for support, credits, etc.

What complicates this analysis of privatization is that two types of conflicts of interest are involved. The first is related to socioeconomic cleavages. The second involves redistribution between ethnic groups. Ethnicity usually proves stronger than class when groups compete for assets. Related to these is the very important issue of how privatization in agriculture is affected by, and can also influence, such a major process as the regaining of independence in the Baltic countries. In the interaction of these two processes – national independence and economic privatization – the power struggles between different interest groups, including ethnic groups, clearly emerge.

A complication in the analysis of the process of the privatization in the Baltic countries relates to the instability of institutions, in particular *constitutional institutions*. Such institutions define the rules of the political game: who is allowed to participate, who finances electoral campaigns, any entry barriers to political markets, etc. What makes the analysis of political competition in transition economies difficult is that their institutions have been changing as well. Constitutional institutions are intended to provide stability in the system. Even during a transition, such institutions can often be assumed to be exogenous, particularly in the short run, due to the high degree of inertia, that follows from extremely high set-up costs. At the formative stages of political development, which the economies of transition are going through now, political competition is not only about redistribution of assets within a fixed set of institutions but also about the structure of those institutions. The struggle for the structure of institutions is a long-term competition for influence, but it also has direct implications for present redistribution. The most fundamental issue in this context is eligibility for participation in the political activity, i.e., the issue of citizenship. Here the issue of ethnic competition can be directly translated into competition regarding to the structure that political institutions will take. Making it more difficult for ethnic minorities to acquire citizenship or even excluding them completely has direct implications for the redistribution assets, and noncitizens have as a rule been excluded from privatization schemes.

The incidence of privatization

Privatization's impact relates to *efficiency, equity* or income distribution, and revenues or *financial position* of the state, all of which influence the motives and goals of a privatization process. The process can be guided by the desire to achieve greater efficiency, constrained by availability of financial means, or driven by competition between winners and losers of a particular scheme. In our analysis, we put the main emphasis on the distributional and political impacts of agricultural privatization.

Several factors are relevant for determining if a person is going to win or lose from the transition to a market economy. Among individual variables one can list the following (Roland, 1992): individual skills, social position under Communism, and the amount of job rents and consumption rents. In addition, individuals differ with respect to the size of claims on past property (including zero claims). Winners of restitutions are past owners or their heirs. Such claimants can choose to engage in farming, or the land can be claimed for future sale as a hedge against inflation, a kind of insurance against unemployment (making it possible to retreat to subsistence farming), or for recreational use, etc. Size of the claim is of course decisive. People having large claims on land and possessing skills in farming unutilized under the preprivatization system are clear winners. Losers can be found among the nomenklatura of the former kolchozes (collective farms) and unskilled workers who enjoyed an easy income (job rent) in the shelter of collective farming. Consumption rents could be quite sizable as well and have been particulary important to large numbers of retired people living on collective farms. State and collective farms were not only economic but social centers. They used to sponsor educational and cultural activities. Interfarm associations of health centers and rest homes for farmers were well known and popular (Poviliunas, 1993). These benefits would disappear if all land were claimed and the collective farms ceased to exist. Restructuring of collective farms may to some extent produce similar losses of benefits as it may involve redundancies, radical changes in methods of production, etc. Such changes can hardly be expected to benefit unskilled workers or workers possessing limited skills.

The relative number of winners and losers depends on several factors, such as the structure of agriculture and the economy as a whole at the time of the Communist takeover as well as the speed of the structural transformation of society during the Communist period. The large number of losers under reform, i.e., the landless or nearly landless still associated with the former collective farms, can be found in countries that had a skewed land distribution in the pre-Communist period and now have large employment in agriculture.

The ability of winners and losers to organize themselves differs. All losers are still living within the former collective farms and are thus relatively concentrated. Preexisting labor unions of agricultural workers may also serve to organize opposition to privatization and the restructuring of collective farms. Members of the former nomenklatura may rely on their past organizational contacts. Some winners still live on collective farms. Many others have left (or were forced to leave) and are now urban dwellers, which makes it more difficult for them to form an organization and increases cost of collective action. Former Baltic citizens who at present are citizens of western countries may be found among the former landowners. This group can be decisive for articulating political positions and may also be able to invest resources in the political struggle, that domestic landowners lack.

Lithuania

Political development since the First World War

This section highlights some aspects of Lithuania's history, in particular, past agrarian reforms that are relevant for understanding the current privatization process. The description is based on Zetterberg (1993).

Lithuania reemerged as an independent nation after the First World War after being a part of Poland and later of Russia. At the outset Lithuania numbered approximately 2 million people, with ethnic Lithuanians constituting 84 percent of the population. Ethnic composition was affected by the Polish occupation of the historical capital of Vilnius, which had a sizable Polish population. The country was predominantly agrarian and rural, with a very small industrial sector of primarily food processing. The majority of Lithuanians were Catholic (85 percent), which together with the rural nature of the society contributed to the success of Christian Democrats. This party dominated Parliament in the 1920s. Social Democrats and 'people socialists' constituted other major parties. Political development starting in 1926 went in the direction of a one-party dictatorship. All parties except the right-wing Nationalist Party, called Tautininkai, were forbidden in 1934. The new constitution of 1936 increased the power of the president (Smetona), who was also the leader of the Nationalist Party.

Landownership in Lithuania was, for historical reasons, dominated by Polish and Russian nobility. In spite of that, Lithuanian land reform in the 1920s and 1930s was not very radical. Landowners were allowed to keep sizable properties and were compensated for the land they lost. The agrarian reforms (between 1919-1938) affected 717,962 hectares of arable land, of which 165,079 hectares were left with the landowners. Most of the land, (450,000 hectares) was allocated to new settlers and to smallholders.

Lithuania (as well as the other two Baltic countries, Latvia and Estonia) lost independence and became a Soviet Republic in July 1941. All the Baltic countries applied to be included among the Soviet Republics, but the applications were made by Communists, who won elections in which the participation of other parties was obstructed and the results by all accounts were manipulated. The Baltic countries were at the time of the elections forced to accept the presence of the Soviet military. (Similar Soviet demands or pressure against Finland resulted in the Finnish Winter War). The process of collectivization of agriculture started at that time and resumed when the Soviet Union regained control over the Baltic territory. In Lithuania the first kolchozes were established in 1947. The process of collectivization was speeded up by brutal and massive deportations of the rural population. In particular, larger landowners and large farmers (kulaks) were targeted. More than 200,000 persons were deported from Lithuania during 1947-1949 (Zetterberg, 1993).

Lithuania's farmstead system was destroyed during the Soviet period. Fewer than half of the original 300,000 farmsteads remain at the present time, many in bad condition (Poviliunas, 1993). Their deterioration was a result of both deliberate action and a lack of maintenance. Creation of new settlements where living conveniences, health centers, schools, etc., were provided contributed to the latter as old settlements were abandoned.

The process of regaining of independence in Lithuania was closely linked to political developments in the Soviet Union. During the Gorbatchev era popular movements organized and demands for independence became frequent. In particular, changes within the Communist Party in Lithuania should be noted. The Party split into two over the issue of independence. The majority, under the leadership of Brasauskas, endorsed the idea of an independent Lithuania while the minority constituted their own party faithful to the Soviet Communist Party. In the spring of 1990 the residents of Lithuania as well as the residents of other Baltic Soviet Socialist Republics elected deputies to the Republics' Supreme Soviets. The elections could be described as the most democratic to have been held since the countries were incorporated into the Soviet Union. Candidates representing various political parties ran for office. The political parties were, however, still small and at a developmental stage. Much greater influence in the elections was wielded by popular movements – in the case of Lithuania, by Sajudis (Lithuanian Restructuring Movement) (Bungs, 1993). The result of the elections was an overwhelming victory for Sajudis and defeat for the Communists. More than two thirds of the elected deputies were endorsed by Sajudis. One reason for the defeat of the Communists was their split into two competing parties. Lithuania declared independence from the Soviet Union on 11 March 1991 but was internationally only recognized (together with the other Baltic states) after the failed coup in the Soviet Union in August 1991. The victorious Sajudis consisted of a chaotic coalition of disparate political groups and individuals with little in common but a commitment to Lithuanian independence. Once that goal was achieved, internal peace gave way to bitter political quarrels that eventually paralyzed parliamentary work (Girnius, 1992b). Recognizing that a further deadlock was intolerable, the Supreme Court decided on new elections in the fall of 1992.

The result of the 1992 elections was a stunning reversal of the 1990 elections. Sajudis was defeated by a descendant of the Lithuanian Communist Party, the Lithuanian Democratic Labor Party (LDLP) still led by Brasauskas. The LDLP won 73 of 141 seats in Parliament. Sajudis gained only thirty deputies while the remaining seats were divided among nine parties and groups.[2] Several reasons for the defeat of Sajudis and the victory of LDLP can be found: the personal popularity of Brasauskas, the efficient organization of the LDLP in a country which by and large lacked normal political parties at the time, and discontent with the performance of Sajudis due to both political chaos and rapidly deteriorating economic conditions (Girnius, 1992b). The LDLP was strongly supported in rural areas. Victorious candidates of the party included the chairman of the Union of Agricultural Workers of Lithuania and his deputy and seven directors of agricultural companies that had replaced the collective farms.

The LDLP was also able to gain support from minorities who were allowed to participate in the elections due to liberal citizenship laws. The Law of November 1989 allowed all who were residents to acquire citizenship, reflecting relatively limited ethnic tensions in the country. A new law, passed in December 1991, was less liberal. Its impact, however, was limited, because the vast majority of those eligible for Lithuanian citizenship under the 1989 citizenship law had already chosen to become Lithuanian citizens (Bungs et al., 1992).

The process of privatization - main legislation

The process of privatization of agriculture in Lithuania, as well as in the other Baltic countries, began during the Soviet period, in 1989 with the Law of Peasant Farming. This law created private farms on a usufruct basis. After independence the collectivization of agriculture was declared illegal. The next step in land reform was taken in the summer of 1990, when personal subsidiary plots were allowed to increase from 0.5 hectare to 2-3 hectares. Several laws related to privatization of agriculture were passed in 1991. In April 1991 Parliament passed a law stating that collective and state farms could eventually be converted into agricultural companies and their capital privatized in accordance with Lithuanian law. Following the Law on Privatization of

Private Property, which was adopted on 30 July 1991, all kolkhozes and sovkhozes were declared enterprises under liquidation (on 1 November 1991).

The Law On Land Reform passed on 25 July established the right to own land which could be acquired either by buying or by having confiscated land returned. The right to restitutions was given to former landowners, their children, and grandchildren. Top priority was given to people who had worked for at least five years in the agricultural establishment who owned the land and to former political prisoners and deportees living in the area (Girnius, 1992a). The law recognized only two types of ownership, state and private. The Law On the Privatization of Property of Agricultural Enterprises (July 1991) stipulated that people wishing to obtain equipment could use funds in their investments accounts (investment vouchers received by all citizens), agricultural compensations received exclusively by people who were working in agricultural establishments, and cash. The value of special vouchers (called 'green checks') was dependent either on a person's age or length of work, without any consideration of qualifications. Property was sold at auctions or by share subscriptions. According to amendments adopted on 23 January 1992, at least 5 percent of the value was to be paid in cash. The Law On Restoration of Citizen's Rights on Survived Real Estates regulated restitution of nationalized property in-kind to citizens of Lithuania if that property was in the disposition of the state enterprises or collective farms. Compensations were paid if restitutions were not possible, and the Law on Agricultural Enterprises determined the organization of enterprises. Enterprises (or companies) have legal status as private limited liability companies, but under current legislation cannot acquire ownership title to the land they operate.

The Law on Land Reform was amended several times, most notably in July 1993. The amendments included additional methods of compensating former landowners (such as allotting plots of land in town or rural areas for construction of housing, allotting plots of forest or peatery, and giving state payments to acquire privatizable assets) and some restrictions regarding restitutions to former owners who were living in towns and lacked agricultural skills and education as well as equipment. Moreover, the new laws established a priority more favorable to villagers willing to acquire land, as follows: persons with rights to acquire land of personal households, persons residing in the country and returning land in the same locality; persons who where granted land for use according to the Law on Peasant Farms where the provision of the land had not been enregistered in due time. According to the government decision of March 1994 personal plots of 2-3 hectares could be purchased from the state, i.e., privatized. A complaint about this decision was made to the Constitutional Court. The verdict of the Court, passed on 8 May 1995 stated that the decision to privatize plots for investment vouchers did not contradict the Constitution, even if the land belonged to former owners. According to the amendment to the Land Law (26 April 1994), the landowners are given the right to sell the land. Thereby a land market, which previously had been lacking in Lithuania, was created. (Only owners having proper land titles can sell their land). Several changes in the legislation occurred or were underway by 1995. The compensation in cash for land to be returned was stopped in mid-1995. The level of compensation was very attractive compared with the profitability of farming. Thus, the demand was high, and, the money earmarked for compensation in cash quickly ran out. All functions related to land reform were passed to district governors (see next section).

Implementation of the privatization process

About 5,500 farms have been allotted land in accordance with the Law on Peasant Farms of 1989. Average size of such farms is 16 hectares, with about 90,000 total hectares allotted. The number of applications for restitutions of landownership amounted to 518,000, claiming a total area of 3.6 million hectares. Most claims (455,700) were for restitutions in-kind; 62,300 preferred compensation. Two thirds of applicants were rural inhabitants. (There existed, however, a large group of rural inhabitants, 150,000, without any claims to land.) Difficulties in obtaining documents to verify ownership (due to changes of borders) made the process of restitution difficult. Only one fifth of new holdings by established farmers had received proper title to the land by 1994. The situation improved by 1995, according to data from the Department of Land Survey and Geodesy (OECD, 1995). The total number of family farms was 134,500, including the 54,200 with proper land titles. Kazlauskiene and Meyers (1995) put the number at 56,700, including 5,000 farms created according to the Law on Peasant Farming from 1989. In addition, there existed almost 400,000 household plots, of, on average, 2.1 hectares but together occupying almost 28 percent of agricultural land. The total share of private farms, including plots in arable land, was almost 60 percent in 1995. Agricultural companies use 31.7 percent of land which is rented from the state. The contribution to production varies depending on the product, with the highest share for vegetables (94 percent) and the lowest for flax (45 percent). In 1991, household plots, contributed to 49.1 percent of production, family farms accounted for 20.2 percent and companies for the remaining 30.7 percent.

The process of returning land generated many problems due to conflicting land claims. In several cases conflicting claims originated from members of the same family. Even conflicts were not unimportant, since they contributed to delays in the process. However, they are hardly relevant for understanding the political economy of privatization. What is important in this context is the nature of conflicts between different categories of claimants. In general, the claims of former landowners were in conflict with:

1 Private farmers established on an usufruct basis (1989 legislation), since not all such farmers were former owners (90,000 hectares were allocated to such farms);

2 Smallholders (of 2-3 hectare plots) who received a large share of land. In some regions such plots occupied 30 percent of agricultural land and in suburban areas up to 50 percent (Kuodys, 1993). Moreover, such plots occupied land in the vicinity of settlements, i.e., near roads, infrastructure, etc. Smallholders received the right to *use* the land during the breakup of collective farms by the Sajudis government. The Communists privatized the land, giving the smallholders the opportunity to buy it;

3 Agricultural companies, in particular those specializing in milk and beef production and therefore in need of grazing land. Such companies were granted the right to use 0.6 hectare per cow during the Sajudis government. The LDLP-government increased the allotment and extended the rights to use the land as long as the company existed.

The legislation on privatization of collective and state farms envisaged dividing assets under privatization into technological units, and 12,000 such units were formed, ranging from whole collective or state farms to individual livestock units, grain stores, etc. 'There was a desire on the part of the government to fragmentize the former farms as much as possible, aiming at to increase the number of owners and limit the establishment of larger units which could be difficult to divide in the future' (Kuodys, 1993). The division had to be made before the end of 1991, the year when state and collective farms were formally abolished in Lithuania. The process was heavily regulated 'seeking to prevent the restoration of collective farm system as well as plundering. In fact, plunders only increased since the assets were devoid of owners for some time' (Kuodys, 1993). Similar views are held by Girnius (1994): 'The break-up of the farms was carried in a disorganised manner, and the heads of farms often stole equipments or sold it off to friends and relatives for prices far below market value'.

As a result of the restructuring, 1,160 state and collective farms were transformed to 6,000 new operational units, of which 4,400 were agricultural companies. The process of restructuring state and collective farms is by and large finished. By mid-1993, 83.2 percent of assets designated for privatization were already privatized. The rest has been offered at a 95 percent discount. The assets were privatized mainly by signing shares (66 percent, according to Kuodys, 1993).   At the beginning of 1994 the value of nonprivatized assets was less than one percent.

It can be argued that the resulting companies do not constitute a fundamentally different form of farming. On the contrary, their resemblance to former collective farming is striking. The main differences are that company units are smaller and appear to be assembled in a more chaotic manner. 'Some units were formed regardless of any logic...' (Kuodys, 1994).   One consequence has been several reported shortages of some categories of workers and redundancies of other specialists (Aleksiene and Zalimiene, 1993). Many companies were left without proper means of harvesting their crops (Girnius, 1994). Trade and specialization across companies are rare. All try to produce livestock and plant products and sell the surplus to the government. The most fundamental problem of former collective farming – low productivity of labor due to the persistence of free-riding – has not been resolved by the new farms. Albeit smaller, the companies are still too large to create a direct link between individual effort and individual reward. The problem of free-riding has been, furthermore, exacerbated by the fact that almost 50 percent of companies' assets belong to people of retirement age who are not active in production.[3] Conflicts over the provision of services, which were previously produced by collective farms and are demanded by retired people, abound (Druzinskas, 1994, personal communcation). According to Kuodys (1994), shareholders in partnerships do not feel like true owners, and care and maintenance of property is even worse than in the prereform period. An additional explanation for inadequate care of commonly owned property can probably be found in members' pessimistic assessment of the companies' future. People seldom invest time and effort into a venture with bleak future prospects. According to an investigation by Aleksiene and Zalimene (1993), only 9 percent of company members were optimistic about future prospects, 37 percent were uncertain, and a full 50 percent expected a worsening situation. Uncertainty about the future, in particular uncertainty due to unsettled land claims, makes it possible if not probable that companies will cease to exist if restituted land creates incentives for exploitation of common assets for future private benefits.

The number of companies decreased by 33 percent between 1992 and 1994. The number of employees decreased by 35 percent during the same time. Several went bankrupt. In the region of Kaunas 172 of 640 companies collapsed in recent years (OECD, 1995). At the same time an amalgamation of companies can be observed. The strongest, which are members of the Association of Enterprises, have even managed to find foreign markets for their products. At the end of 1995, 2,340 such companies were in existence (OECD, 1996). About onefifth of these are financially insolvent and will be liquidated, while 20-25 percent are in the process of being transformed into agro-service companies.

The implementation of privatization and restructuring requires a system of appropriate institutions. The following institutional structures were established to carry out agrarian reform in Lithuania (Kuzlis, 1992):

1 Municipal Agrarian Reform Services (MARS). These were the smallest administrative units, in charge of 3-4 farms at the level of local municipalities. MARS were involved both in collecting applications for land and for privatizing assets of agricultural enterprises (by organizing auctions or share subscriptions, etc.).

2 District Privatization Commissions to supervise the activities of MARS and investigate complaints against MARS decisions.

3 The Commission for Agrarian Reform, a provisional institution under the Government of the Republic of Lithuania.

4 The Central Privatization Commission, to coordinate the activities of all the privatization institutions.

The composition of MARS has been a point of contention (Druzinskas, personal communication), particularly regarding the involvement of agricultural specialists in the process. A process as complicated as the restructuring of agricultural enterprises could be argued to require a reliance on highly qualified personnel. However, considerable involvement of specialists would most likely give an advantage to the nomenklatura. The decision was made not to involve specialists.

The regional administration in Lithuania changed in 1994. According to the Law on Administrative Units of the Teritory of Lithuania (19 July 1994) the past structure was replaced by ten districts headed by a governor appointed by the government. Among other duties, the governor was responsible according to the Law on Management of the Districts (15 December 1994), for the implementation of land reform, state land cadastre, state regulation, and control of land use.

The food processing industry in Lithuania has been infamous for its inefficiency. In spite of the decrease in livestock production and the resulting lower deliveries to the processing plants, the employment in processing has not been adjusted accordingly and wages have been raised, resulting in a dramatic increase in processing costs (Girnius, 1994). Farmers upset over processing industry's inefficiency stopped delivering their goods to the industry and attempted to sell directly to consumers on the streets (Baltic Observer, 10 February 1994). The action was unsuccessful, however. Farmers and companies also attempted to establish their own small-scale processing facilities.

During the first stage of privatizing upstream and downstream industries, privileges were granted to producers of agricultural products in proportion to their deliveries or purchases. Payment could be made by vouchers and cash (not less than 5 percent). Only 18 percent of shares were bought by agricultural companies and farmers (OECD, 1995). Employees in enterprises designated for privatization were given special preferences and could acquire up to 30 percent of the company's capital. During the second stage (based on the resolution of 8 April 1994) agricultural producers could buy shares at 2.5 percent of their nominal value if paying in cash. The process of privatization was speeded up considerably: 261 of 283 state companies in upstream and downstream sectors were privatized by January 1995.

Looking at privatization as a whole, it can be observed that the process began earlier and developed more rapidly in Lithuania than in Estonia and Latvia. In Lithuania a strategy of an early and broad giveaway privatization was followed. The Law on Initial Privatization of State Property, passed on 28 February 1991, provided for the sale of industrial, transportation, construction, energy, trade, and other state enterprises as well as land and apartment buildings. The law granted the citizens of Lithuania investment vouchers that could be used for such purchases. Enterprises were privatized by three methods: auctions, sale of shares, and sales for hard currency. Lithuanians have mainly used their vouchers to acquire private apartments. This privatization, as well as other forms of small privatization, has been successful (Girnius, 1994).

In general, Lithuanian privatization has been described as 'more humane' than privatization programs in other Baltic countries. Employees have been given privileged access and employment guarantees. (This was, for instance, the case when Suchard purchased Kaunas Confectionery Plant in October 1993. The employees purchased 33 percent of the shares.)

Political competition and privatization

The first stages of agrarian reform in Lithuania were conducted by anti-Communist forces, namely by Sajudis, a popular front movement which transformed itself into a conservative party in December 1993 (Baltic Independent, 1993). It can be argued that Sajudis was guided by two objectives: the ambition to destroy the former collective system beyond the point of no return and the desire to put the interests of former landowners in the forefront. (The two objectives are, of course, closely related.) There is considerable evidence to support the first point. As argued by Poviliunas (1994), 'the hasty and ill-considered concept of agrarian reform' was 'mainly seeking political not economic goals'. Units were formed 'without any logic' or 'in disorganized manner'. Speed was clearly preferred over efficiency as the time allowed for the formation of new units was very short. Moreover, Kuodys (1993) argues that the goal was to divide the farms as much as possible and to prevent reversal. The generous allotment of land to smallholders (on a temporary basis) was also intended to contribute to the process of dismantling the former collective farms. 'The main reason for allotting every rural inhabitant an increased plot (up to 3 ha) of personal smallholding was the wish to promote farmers' independence from former collective farms' (Kuodys, 1994). The outcome of the process supports these intentions. Units have been reported as 'ill-designed', shortages amid redundancies can be found (Aleksiene and Zalimiene, 1993). Widespread bankruptcies among the companies also indicate that many of these were not viable.

The design of the restructuring process exhibited a number of strong anti-nomenklatura features, removal of which can be seen as essential to destroying the old system. In particular,

1 Egalitarian distribution of assets, based on a principle of homogenous labor input,

2 Reliance on laymen rather than on specialists in the process of reform implemention, and

3 The number of chairmen of collective farms replaced before the process started (Girnius, 1992a).

can be noted.

It could be argued that the speed and the design of the reform, together with the emphasis on restitutions, were aimed at the destruction of the power base of the Communist Party, in particular, of the rural nomenklatura. But this picture is somewhat contradictory because the collective farms were restructured, not dismantled. A speedy dismantling of collective farms and the transfer of assets to emerging private farms could have been expected to accompany restitutions in original boundaries, but this kind of policy was not followed. Instead, collective farms were reorganized as alternative business farms created from unsettled land and compensation claim contentions and uncertainty. A speedy dismantling and transformation of collective farms into private ones was probably not feasible under conditions in post-Soviet Lithuania due to lack of farmsteads, etc.

The desire for speed can be explained by the fact that Communists, in particular their leader Brasauskas, enjoyed considerable popularity due to pro-independence policy and personal charisma. The Lithuanian case illustrates that radical restructuring is not a foolproof method for eliminating or diminishing Communist influence. On the contrary, radical privatization under the Lithuanian conditions contributed to strengthening the Communist power base in rural regions by creating well identified and quite numerous losers. Rural votes contributed to the victory of LDLP.

The issue of the distribution of assets and its relation to party competition is another important factor in the analysis of political competition in Lithuania, where ethnic tensions were less pronounced than in Latvia and conflicts between interest groups sharing the same ethnicity played a major role. This was particularly the case after independence had been reached. The fact that the Communist Party took a clear pro-independence position at an early stage of the political development contributed to the removal of independence-related issues from the country's political agenda.

Restitution of land, and restitution within original boundaries in particular, generate well identified winners and losers. The former are persons with large land claims who possess farming skills. The latter are to be found among nomenklatura of state and collective farms and unskilled workers with no or limited claims on land.[4] Both *losing groups* are likely to be affiliated with a Communist Party or a successor to such a party. This has been the case in Lithuania. The LDLP opposed the Law On Land Reform, which recognized only private and state ownership, and advocated a third type of ownership: collective ownership. They asserted that Lithuanian agriculture was not prepared for the abolition of the collective farms (Girnius, 1992b). During the election campaign, the LDLP made promises to slow the pace of land reform (or even to roll it back) and offered support to collective ventures. The LDLP also received considerable support from the rural areas, and several of its politicians were associated with collective farms. It should be pointed out, however, that the LDLP appealed successfully to other groups as well, including businessmen who reaped the profits of nomenklatura privatization, and intellectuals. This resulted in antagonism between party intellectuals, or 'professors', and deputies from rural areas, or 'agriculturalists' (Girnius, 1992b).

After regaining power through the LDLP, the ex-Communists introduced several changes in favor of partnerships and against the interests of former owners. Most significant were the July 1993 amendments to the Land Law introducing restitution restrictions for former owners who were city dwellers and establishing a new order of priority in favor of villagers willing to acquire land, discussed above. 'Government commitment to restoring ownership to private farmers in the short run is decreasing', was the judgement of a World Bank mission (May 1993). Allotments of land increased for companies with livestock production, and smallholders' plots of 2-3 hectares, which had been created by Sajudis to speed the process of dismantling collective farms, were privatized by sales by ex-Communists, giving priority to the smallholders in any ensuing conflicts over the land use. It could be argued that collective ventures in agriculture were not really supported, since only the state and private persons could own land. Collective ownership was not allowed, depriving the companies of a legal base of landownership. Of course, cooperatives of individual owners of land were allowed. Amendments to the Constitution to allow legal persons to own land are currently under discussion. Otherwise, Lithuanian policy has not changed dramatically since the change to an ex-Communist government.

The *winners of reform*, particularly through restitutions, are most likely to be associated with a conservative party, a pattern of party competition that follows what can be observed in Western democracies. This has been the case in Lithuania. While in power, Sajudis supported the interests of landowners. In the political conflicts and debates surrounding the above-mentioned land distribution issues the conservatives endorsed the claims of landowners. (Sajudis took the question of 2-3 hectare plots to the Constitutional Court, requesting that priority be given to former owners (OECD, 1995). The Court, as mentioned before, decided in favor of the smallholders.

Looking at the organizational achievements of the pressure groups involved, three organized groups can be distinguished: landowners, private farmers, and companies. An organization of landowners emerged relatively shortly after Lithuania regained independence. The organization is small but has been described as influential, in particular during the Sajudis regime (Druzinskas, personal communcation). Another organization to be mentioned in this context is the Union of Agricultural Workers of Lithuania, which has been affiliated with the LDLP. The union has played a leading role in the establishment in June 1992 of the Lithuanian Association of Agricultural Enterprises. Activities of the union constitute a clear example of privatization losers being able to use preexisting organizations for their purposes. The interests of smaller farmers are represented by the Lithuanian Union of Farmers.

Thus, the pattern of pressure group competition and the pattern of political competition coincide very well in Lithuania. Landowners have relied on the support of Sajudis/Conservative party, while the losers in privatization and decollectivization have been supported by the LDLP or ex-Communists. Smallholders also have been supported by the Communists. (The decollectivization policy can also be seen as an attempt to create a new power base for ex-Communists among rural constituency.) Lithuanian political competition follows the Western pattern of political competition, which is related to socioeconomic cleavages. Such a pattern of competition is consistent with the prediction of Evans and Whitefield (1993) that in Lithuania 'social structure rather than ethnicity should emerge as a basis of party competition'. Our analysis has demonstrated that in the process of privatization in agriculture socioeconomic cleavages are decisive for party affiliation and are akin to those of Western countries. However, the same cannot be said about the process of political competition as a whole. Established parties or political blocks exhibit contradictory features. As pointed out above, the LDLP attracted not only 'traditional' left-of-center voters such as unskilled workers but also intellectuals and new capitalists. While in power, Sajudis, who generally can be placed right of center, to some extent applied the social democratic policy of rising wages and pensions (and fueling inflation).

Moreover, as remarked in The Baltic Observer (25 May 1994), party labels in Lithuania are no guide to party programs and politics: 'On several broad economic, social and foreign issues Lithuania's two major parties often echo each other's rhetorics'.

Latvia

Political development

Latvia, like Lithuania, emerged as an independent state after World War I. Latvia, or the region of Livland, had, however, never before existed as an independent state. The statehood of the new country could thus be claimed to be less established. The population of Latvia was slightly less than that of Lithuania but much more heterogeneous. Latvians constituted only 73 percent of the population and the majority of the population were Protestants. Latvia was somewhat more industrialized and urban than Lithuania. In politics, Latvia's Farmers Federation was an influential right-wing party having as many as twelve of the country's eighteen prime ministers between 1929-1934, in spite of its falling share of the votes. Social Democrats were the strongest force on the left side of the political spectrum and the largest party immediately after the independence. The Democratic Center represented the urban middle classes and played a median role between the left and the right. In the 1930s Latvia's political development went in the same direction as Lithuania's. Prime Minister Ulmanis (Farmers Federation) banned other political parties, starting with Communists and national socialists in 1934. Two years later he even overtook the presidency.

Latvia was, early on, a typical country of big estates. Landownership was dominated by large estates belonging to Baltic-Germans. Of the total area of land, the peasants, who were freed from serfdom only in the middle of the nineteenth century, owned 2.5 million hectares, or 39 percent. Owners of private estates held 48 percent of the land, and the rest belonged to the state, churches, and municipalities. The average area of private estates exceeded

2,000 hectares (League of Nations, 1939). After the agrarian reform of 1920, which is considered to be among the most radical reforms in Eastern Europe, the landownership structure changed completely. Landed estates were confiscated by the state, but landowners were allowed to keep 50 hectares of previously owned land. (The Agrarian Reform Law made it illegal from then on to own more than 50 hectares as a single property. It also forbade the division of land into plots under 10 hectares without the permission of the government.) No compensation was paid for confiscated land. Newly established farmers were allotted at most 22 hectares (Zetterberg, 1993). As a result of the reform, the agrarian structure of Latvia compared favorably with that of Western Europe. The number of smallholdings, which were not sufficient to provide owners with a livelihood, was small by comparison. 'By creating some 100,000 new farms owned by the peasants with full hereditary rights, the agrarian reform consolidated the base of the State', according to the League of Nations (1939). Table 4.1 illustrates the structure of landownership in 1935.

Table 4.1
Landownership in Latvia: Farm size and number in 1935

Size in ha	Number	%	Area	%	Average in ha
up to 1	44,078	16.0	13,669	0.3	0.3
1 - 2	11,611	4.2	17,668	0.4	1.5
2 - 5	22,878	8.3	79,450	1.8	3.5
5 - 10	44,089	16.0	336,203	7.5	7.6
10 - 15	39,689	14.4	495,448	11.0	12.5
15 - 20	38,167	13.8	667,085	14.9	17.5
20 - 30	35,448	12.9	844,406	18.8	23.8
30 - 50	24,302	8.8	948,469	21.1	39.0
50 - 100	14,365	5.2	936,797	20.9	65.2
over 100	1,071	0.4	147,769	3.3	138.0
Total	275,698	100.0	4,486,964	100.0	16.3

Source: Ministry of Agriculture of the Republic of Latvia, 1992.

Several similarities in the early political development of Latvia and Lithuania can be observed. Both countries experienced a brief period of democracy that ended in their becoming one-party states. Furthermore, even during the period when democracy prevailed, the political situation was highly unstable, with short-lived governments. The style of agrarian reform was, however, different in each country resulting in very different agrarian structures in the postreform period. In Latvia, an agrarian party managed to establish itself, while in Lithuania the farmers' votes went to the Christian Democrats. Political development in the Baltic countries seems to confirm an observation by Lipset and Rokkan (1967) that agrarian parties tend to emerge in countries where the influence of the Catholic Church is weak and independent farmers (rather than large estates) dominate farming.

Latvia lost its independence on 17 June 1940 under circumstances similar to those of Lithuania. The process of collectivization started in 1946. All land became nationalized, as in the rest of Soviet Union. The process of collectivization involved the deportation of 50,000 persons in 1948.

The Baltic countries, in particular Latvia, went through a process of fast industrialization and urbanization. At the same time, and closely related to the process of industrialization, the ethnic composition of the population changed. This change was due to the inflow of Russians, mainly for work within industry. Few of them learned indigenous languages or became integrated into the local communities. The share of Russians varies in the two countries. In Latvia where Latvians make up only slightly more than half of the population (54 percent), the Russians constitute 34 percent.[5] These Russians are concentrated in the cities. In Riga the share of Latvians in the population is only 30 percent (Mattson, 1993).

Political development in Latvia during the late Soviet period and early days of independence exhibited strong similarities to developments in Lithuania. The hard-line Soviet regime prevented an emergence of alternative political elites until the beginning of the Gorbatchev era, when popular movements started to organize. The Latvian counterpart to Sajudis, the Peoples' Front of Latvia (PFL), won in the elections to the Supreme Soviets in the spring of 1990. The Communists were defeated. Latvia declared its independence on 4 May 1991. The issue of independence was, however, more contentious than in Lithuania. The reason was the position of the Communists. In Lithuania, the majority of Communists took a clear stance in favor of independence, but only a minority of Latvian Communists endorsed the idea of an independent Latvia. The majority, which after a split formed a new party faithful to the Soviets, opposed Latvia's independence. (It should be remembered that Western democracies were not prepared to recognize the Baltics at that time.)

New elections were held in Latvia for the same underlying reasons that elections were held in Lithuania – the declining popularity of the pro-independence movement after its main goal had been achieved. Latvian elections were held in June 1993. The results turned out very differently from those in Lithuania. One reason was the differences in legislation on citizenship and naturalization, which in turn determined who was eligible to vote in the elections. Lithuanian citizenship laws were by far the most liberal of the Baltic countries. In Latvia, on the other hand, the requirements of long residency, and knowledge of the language (which is very limited among non-Latvians) resulted in a situation where most of the sizable non-Latvian minority was not allowed to participate in the elections. Latvian Way, with 36 of the 100 seats in Parliament (Sacima), was the most successful party among twenty-three competitors in the Latvian elections (only eight won representation). Latvian Way is a broad coalition of politicians and professionals, formed in January 1993. The candidates included known activists either in Latvia or in Latvian exile communities in the West. Their collective political orientation is right of center (Bungs, 1993). Latvia's Farmer's Union (LFU), representing agricultural interests, received 12 seats. (The LFU was founded in 1918 and restored in 1990.) Voters generally showed preferences for right-of-center candidates. From a broader perspective, it can be noted that Latvia (together with Estonia) seems to be an exception to the general pattern of political development in former Soviet republics. In nearly all of these, Communists retained power, even if under a new name.

The National Independence Movement of Latvia (LNNK), a party to the right of Latvian Way received 15 seats. Latvia's Democratic Labor Party (LDLP), stemming directly from Latvia's Communist Party (LCP), received less than 1 percent of votes and did not make it to Parliament. It should be remembered, however, that many potential voters for the LDLP were not allowed to participate in the elections. (The largest party on the left was Concord for Latvia-Rebirth of Economy, an election coalition with 13 seats.) The PFL, which won about twothirds of the seats in the first free elections, received less than the required 4 percent, so many well-known politicians such as Prime Minister Godmanis, did not get into Parliament. As a result of the election, a coalition was formed by Latvian Way and the FLU. The ruling coalition occupied only 48 seats. The post of Minister of Agriculture went, not surprisingly, to the LFU and Jannis Kinna.

The political situation continued to be unstable in Latvia. In the municipal election on 29 May 1994, the victory went to the Nationalist Bloc. Latvian Way received only 3.4 percent of the votes, to occupy only 2 seats in Riga City Council.

Conflict over the issue of agricultural policy within the government coalition began building during the spring of 1994. The Latvian farmers demanded a ban on imports of agricultural products also produced domestically, to remain in effect until 'appropriate customs unions can be adapted'. A newly elected chairman of LFU, Andris Rosendals, stated in the congress of the party on 26 March that the LFU will leave the ruling coalition if Latvian Way did not fulfill the above demand. The LFU currently has 2,300 members and is the largest party in Latvia (Baltic Observer, 31 March 1994). This threat materialized during the summer of 1994. The Latvian Way and LFU government was dissolved on 14 July. The LFU abruptly suspended all its activities in the government and its three ministers resigned to protest Latvian Way's rejection of its demand for higher tariffs on imported food and farm products. The two factions had from the start found themselves in an uneasy alliance. The source of division has been fundamentally different economic policy, with the conservative Farmers Union urging protectionist policies and the centrist-right Latvian Way being more free-market oriented (Baltic Observer, 28 July 1994).

The issue of citizenship and underlying ethnic conflict has continued to top Latvia's political agenda since independence, with conflicts between the president and the Seima during the spring of 1994. New citizenship laws were signed by the president on 10 August 1994. The new law allowed for naturalization of persons born in Latvia beginning in 1996. Those born outside Latvia have to wait until 2003. Under previous drafts of the law a quota of only 2,000 per year (i.e., 0.1 percent of the number of Latvian citizens) would be allowed. Protests from abroad, in particular from international organizations such as the Council of Europe and Conference on Security and Cooperation in Europe (CSCE), which would not admit Latvia until the quotas were deleted, were decisive in changing the drafts. It is not likely, however, that this issue has been completely removed from the political agenda.

The process of privatization - main legislation

The Law on Peasant Farming, 1989, was the starting point for the privatization process in Latvia, as it was in Lithuania. Several laws related to privatization were passed, starting in the pre-independence period with the Law on Land Reform in Rural Areas of Latvia (November 1990) defining provisions for submitting land claims and creating regulations for restoring landowner rights. The land reform was divided into two phases: the first takes place in years 1990-1996; the second, over a period of ten to fifteen years, starting 1 January 1993. In the first phase, land was allocated with the use rights only. In the second phase, proper ownership of the land can be received. Claimants and their heirs, as well as existing land users and any new applicants for the land (with use rights), had to make their claims before June 1991. In the Law on Land Privatization in Rural Regions (July 1992), priorities for satisfying land petitions were determined. The former owners (those who could verify ownership on 21 July 1940, regardless their citizenship) were given first priority for claiming land – their previously owned parcel if available, equivalent land in another location, or compensation. Excluded areas included land already containing developed farms, orchards, individual plots, etc. Second in line for land claims would be present users or new petitioners with plans for the following, in order of priority: expanding existing individual farms, constructing individual homes for present land users, expanding towns, and adding land to state and collective farms (World Bank,1993).

Another important step in the privatization process was to privatize the collectively held property as capital shares owned by individual workers (regulated by the Law on Privatization of Agricultural Enterprises and Collective Fisheries, June 1991). According to the law all state and collective farms were to be converted into shareholding companies and registered by 15 March 1992. The value of the property of the privatizable collective farms and of the state enterprises, which had been treated equally, was estimated using following principles: fixed assets were assessed according to the remaining value of the balance, other assets according to the data of book keeping. The total sum of the value of these assets had to be equal to the sum of privatization certificates in the enterprises (Zile, 1992). The allocation of shares to individual shareholders was mainly based on labor input. Some shares were allocated as compensation for nonland assets expropriated during collectivization. Most farms assigned about onethird of their property value to such compensations. Once all nonland assets had been sold to private individuals, the corporate farms were liquidated. In an attempt to stop the breakup of large farms, the law on privatization of nonland assets was amended in May 1995 to give these corporate farms the right to retain nonland assets needed for their continued operation.

The work toward privatization was, until 1993, conducted by a governmental organization (Zemesprojects), which already existed in the Soviet period. (Privatization of land in cities was handled by the Ministry of Architecture and Buildings.) Since the beginning of 1993, a new organization, the State Land Service, has had overall responsibility for privatization and land surveys.

Implementation of the reform

The total acreage requested by the claimants was 8 millions hectares, 27 percent more than the 6.3 million total acreage subject to land reform (3.9 million was agricultural land). Land was overclaimed in all regions of the country to varying degrees. Collective and state farms petitioned for 2.7 million hectares, individual farms reserved 1.8 million hectares,[6] 100,000 subsidiary plots were requested with a total acreage of 616,000 hectares, and 100,000 plots for home workshops with an average size of 2.4 hectares. The former landowners or their heirs numbered 100,000, or 36 percent of all the land petitioners. Of these, 29 percent were city dwellers, and 2 percent (or 1,400) were living abroad. Former owners have claimed 2.7 million hectares (Zile, 1992).

Conflicts between farms established on the basis of user rights and claims of former landowners and their heirs, as well as conflicts involving land claims and privatization of farm enterprises, have been frequent. The courts have not been able to resolve such conflicts (Zile, 1993). Moreover, there have been several instances of the local government and authorities disobeying court decisions, thus violating the law, and there have been no consequences (Zile, 1993).

By 1995 (the year of this writing), the process of privatization in agriculture has almost been completed. Individual farms are operating on 81 percent of the arable land. At the end of 1995 some 650 coorporate farms had been newly created by individuals using privatized assets and by successors of collective and state farms. The farms were operating 62,600 hectares, representing 17 percent of all agricultural land in Latvia (OECD, 1996). They produce 80 percent of Latvia's milk, 74 percent of its meat, and 31 percent of eggs. Corporate farms still produce 46 percent of pigs and 67 percent of poultry.

In privatization of processing industries, preferential treatment has been offered to associations of primary producers. According to the law passed in December 1992, which regulated privatization of the ten largest dairy plants, not less than 70 percent of the stocks were reserved for dairy producers. Employees were allowed no more than 10 percent. Small, local dairies were given free of charge to farmers' cooperative associations. A somewhat different approach was used for meat processing, where farmers were offered 25 to 35 percent of company stocks. In grain processing, the law stipulated that at least 51 percent should be offered to cooperatives or associations of agricultural producers. Privatization in food processing was almost finished by 1995.

The process of privatization in Latvia as a whole has been very slow. Even in small privatizations, which generally have been successful in all countries, Latvia is lagging behind. Voucher privatization started only in mid-1993, and a privatization agency was created in November 1993. The first 60,000 privatization vouchers were given to citizens who were 'politically repressed' or exiled during the occupation of the country. Those citizens received extra vouchers in proportion to the time they spent in exile or in jail. Every holder of a Latvian residence permit who lived in the country before 1992 was entitled to one voucher for each year of residence up to that date. In addition, every Latvian citizen was entitled to an additional allocation of fifteen vouchers. It should be observed that Latvia recognizes double citizenship (Baltic Independent, 1993). Privatization of flats, which has been very successful in Lithuania (almost all flats were privately owned by 1994), began in Latvia only in the autumn of 1995, except for houses built before the war. Such houses were restituted to the former owners, many of whom, especially owners of houses in old parts of Riga, were Latvian exiles. The present occupants have been given the right to stay for seven years; one flat per house has to be reserved for the former owner.[7]

Politics of privatization

To properly understand the politics of privatization in Latvian agriculture, the entire process must be placed in a wider context. This wider context involves the ethnic tensions or ethnic competition between Latvians and non-Latvian minorities living in the country. The establishment of an independent state can be expected to be the first priority of an ethnic majority. Closely related to this is the institutional issue of citizenship. To achieve such an objective may, however, be difficult if the majority is small, as in the case of Latvia. With ethnic Latvians constituting only slightly more than half of the population, statehood of the new country is only weakly established especially since the country also lacks a long tradition of independence. A fundamental issue underlying ethnic tensions is that of *control of national assets*. All the distributional conflicts are centered around this, as will be demonstrated below.

Underlying ethnic issues have been one reason for the differences in privatization of agriculture and of industry. The process of privatizing land has been *early* and decisive, compared with the slow and reluctant process of privatization in the rest of the economy. The first laws on privatization in agriculture were passed in 1990, while privatization in industry began several years later. In industry, where most (63 percent) of the labor force was non-Latvian (mainly Russian) and where management was Russian, privatization has been very cautious (Bungs, 1992). Latvians were afraid that if the Slavic or mainly Russian labor force were issued vouchers, they would use them to preserve the Soviet system, albeit under a different label, to safeguard their own positions and to impede economic reforms (Bungs, 1992). What motivated the speedy and decisive start of agricultural privatization in Latvia was that its main asset, the land, could be restituted, while in industry almost all assets had been created during the Communist era. Any privatization in industry would run into problems of eligibility and citizenship. Privatization of flats, which has not been implemented yet, faces similar problems, aggravated by the concentration of Russians in cities, particularly members of the former nomenklatura in Riga. LNNK, a party belonging to the nationalist bloc that was successful in Latvia's municipal elections, in 1994 announced 'plans for social justice' starting with the privatization of apartments in Riga (Baltic Observer, June 1994).

Another difference between agriculture and industry related to underlying ethnic conflicts is the principles applied in the distribution of assets. Privatization of the assets of former collective farms was based on restitution to former owners and on distributing assets to employees through vouchers.

Labor input was not the only basis for distributing assets in the process of privatizing collective and state farms, but most assets (76 percent) were allocated to labor shares (Zile, 1993). The principle behind such distribution recognized that the assets were created through the efforts of labor. The same principle was not applied in industry. On the contrary, most industrial workers will have limited possibilities of reaping the fruits of their work. Instead, preferential treatment has been given to former citizens of Latvia, even if they have not been living in the country.

A unique feature of Latvian reform was restitution to former owners who were not citizens. (For proper ownership, i.e., in the second stage of the reform, citizenship is required. However, double citizenship is recognized. Thus, Latvian exiles can claim property back and have been doing so. Several Latvians in Sweden have received back land and farmsteads, or what is left of them.) This generosity depends on the fact that former owners are ethnic Latvians. In other CEECs, former landowners living outside the country were as a rule of different nationalities. For Latvia, restitutions to Latvian exiles help increase the Latvian presence in the country.

It could be argued that the restitution policy towards Latvians living outside the country is also a response to strong pressure from this group. Latvian emigration after the war involved mainly well-educated, well-to-do people who had reason to fear Russian occupation. Successful emigrants possess at present both the means and the skill to influence Latvian politics. The largest of Latvian parties in the elections in 1993, the Latvian Way, consisted of members of old nomenklatura and exiled Latvians as well.

It can be argued that privatization in agriculture has not been central to political competition in Latvia. While ethnic tensions dominated the political struggle, agricultural privatization has mainly been a matter between fellow Latvians, including those living in exile. The peculiarities of the process, such as giving the right to restitution even to noncitizens and the choice of a gradual privatization strategy, can be explained thereby. The Communists have been only marginally involved in the agricultural privatization process, because their power base is in the industrial labor force dominated by non-Latvians rather than in agriculture. Furthermore, the major threat to independence was not Communists as such but Latvia's Russian population which supported the preservation of Soviet power in the past and whose future loyalty to the new Latvian state was questionable – particularly in light of the activities of such organizations as Interfront and the International Front of Workers of Latvian SSR (Bungs, 1992). This power base has been eliminated by changing the rules of the political game, leaving the majority of would-be voters for Communists and opponents to the independent Latvia out of the electoral process. A possible implication of this development for agriculture is that the unskilled workers who were losers of the land reform were left without support. As a result Latvian agriculture has increasingly become a sector dominated by private farming.

Latvia's Farmers' Union (LFU) did emerge as a strong political force in 1993-1994. The party has been representing already established private farmers and concentrating on issues similar to those addressed by agrarian parties in other countries – namely, protection and support. Their influence on privatization appears to be limited. The LFU caused a government crisis by leaving the ruling coalition in the summer of 1994.

Summary and conclusions

The Baltic countries exhibit several features different from these of other CEECs in this study. The most important difference – that both the Baltic countries in our study have been Soviet republics and not independent states (albeit with restricted sovereignty) – has been decisive for the whole process of privatization. Furthermore, the Baltic countries lack a long tradition of independence. Prior to the First World War, Latvia never existed as an independent state. Lithuania was a powerful nation only in the very distant past. Regaining independence has been the overriding priority of these countries, and this focus is consistent with the interests of their majority ethnic pressure groups, as argued earlier. Independence has, however, not been regained in one step. Independence should be seen as a process closely related to the weakening influence and power base of pro-Russian forces, in particular of Communist parties faithful to Soviet and Russian interests, especially in Latvia. The independence of the Baltic countries, recognized first after the failed coup in August 1991, has remained fragile. It has taken considerable political energy to achieve the removal of Russian troops. The Russian policy towards 'near abroad' constitutes a constant threat for the Baltic countries. Communist-nationalist forces in Russia (in particular, those of Mr. Zirinowsky) made repeated claims for Baltic territory. This was particularly threatening for Latvia, where its large Russian minority population represents potential support for such Russian claims.

The strong preference for restitution as a mean of privatization in the Baltic countries is related to the issue of regaining independence, in particular to the need to establish the illegality of collectivization and occupation of the Baltic countries. It should be remembered that the Baltic countries, at least from a formal point of view and according to official ideology in the past, decided to become republics of the Soviet Union. The decision, of course, was made under threat, and the applications to join the USSR were made by Communist parties. Nevertheless, the illegality of this past decision needed to be established. (As pointed out above, international support for Baltic independence was quite weak at the early stages.) Furthermore, undoing social injustice, a goal often argued in cases of restitution, can be seen as more pertinent in the Baltic countries than in other CEECs, because of the level of brutality and deportations involved in collectivization in the Baltics.

An important connection between the objective of regaining independence and privatization strategy relates to national control of assets. If property is restituted to the rightful owners, only those who were residents before the occupation are eligible. Moreover, if restitutions are offered regardless of present citizenship or based on recognition of double citizenship, as in Latvia, the numerical preeminence of the ethnic majority can be strengthened. This privatization strategy benefits the indiginous population and is clearly disadvantageous for the Russians who are recent immigrants. Other minorities with long roots in the Baltic countries are not discriminated against. If, as argued in this chapter, the issue of regaining independence is the Baltic countries' overriding priority, the power of the Russian minority is decisive, since Russians may show a preference for changing the status of the Baltic countries from independent nations to members of the Russian Federation. Other minorities are primarily interested in not being discriminated against.[8] Furthermore, territorial claims against the Baltic countries have not been made by politicians in other neighboring countries.

The ethnic issue has not been equally important in the two Baltic states. Distributional conflicts between ethnic pressure groups have been much less pronounced in Lithuania, due to the numerical preeminence of ethnic Lithuanians and the resulting more strongly established statehood. In Latvia, on the other hand, statehood was (and to some extent still is) less established, and the stakes were higher. Vital parts of the economy of the newly established state, namely the industrial sectors, were from the outset in the hands of 'aliens', many of them hostile to the idea of an independent Latvia. *These differences are clearly reflected in the choice of privatization strategy in the two countries.* Early, broad giveaway privatization in Lithuania provided every citizen with vouchers, while Latvia took a late and reluctant approach. Lithuania's choice clearly indicates less ethnic conflict and a lack of fear that national assets might end up in the hands of aliens. Moreover, given the Lithuanian majority, not much could be gained from discriminatory policies, especially considering the costs of such policies.[9] Latvians, on the other hand, have been very selective in issuing vouchers.

Because of lesser ethnic tensions in Lithuania, agricultural privatization was mainly driven by distributional conflicts between the winners of restitutions (the landowners), and the losers (the nomenklatura and the landless). The landless were numerous due to Lithuania's skewed land distribution in the prewar period. The resulting socioeconomic cleavages were clearly reflected in party affiliations, with competition between ex-Communists on the side of smallholders and collective farming and conservatives defending the landowners.

In Latvia the ethnic issue has dominated its politics. Even through distributional conflicts similar to those in Lithuania exist to some extent, a similar relationship between socioeconomic cleavages and party affiliation cannot be found. Land was more equally distributed in Latvia in the prewar period, and so the number of rural people without any claims to land was smaller in Latvia. The differences in prewar land distribution has, therefore, created a different balance of power between winners and losers in the two countries.

In Lithuania, affiliations between the losers of restitutions and restructuring in agriculture and the ex-Communists has had a strong influence on the continuation of the process of privatization. The pro-independence coalition, which won the first free elections, was not able to govern the country due to internal conflicts, which in turn resulted in new elections and the return to power of ex-Communists. The Communist revival altered the speed and the direction of privatization. The left-wing government has not rolled back privatization in agriculture, but has altered the process in ways that benefit smallholders and collective farms at the expense of landowners. Moreover, support to farm companies, for example, with sales to the agricultural processing industry on preferential terms, the government signals and supports its expectation that the companies will survive as permanent, alternative forms of operation rather than as transitory structures. What possibly contradicts this picture is that collective ownership of land is not allowed according to the Lithuanian Constitution (although discussions about such changes in the Constitution are taking place). Political development in Lithuania seems to conform with this chapter's theory that changes in policies can clearly be linked to changes in government. Moreover, the direction of change follows a predictable fashion.

In Latvia the political orientation of the government remained right of center after the second elections, and policy has not been revised. The government remains committed to 'real privatization', i.e., a farm sector dominated by small farms. Thus, the process of privatization developed in Latvia seems to confirm a link between the government's political orientation and the direction of privatization in agriculture. Privatization in agriculture has, however, not been a central political issue in Latvia, and socioeconomic cleavages in party formation are less clear than in Lithuania. For example, reform was never an issue in the electoral campaign of 1993. (Distributional conflicts between former owners and present users of land, which were less severe in Latvia, instead ended in the courts.)

The two Baltic countries differ in the timing of their privatizations as well. The reason is, again, indirectly related to ethnic issues. Lithuania's approach can be described as radical. Its goal of destroying the system of the past was very clear. State and collective farms were declared to be enterprises under liquidation on 1 November 1991. Latvians, on the other hand, preferred a very gradual approach. The reason the Lithuanian conservative government opted for a radical approach appears to be the presence of a Communists power base with rural nomenklatura as an important element. In contrast, the power base of Latvian Communists was in industry, among non-Latvian labor. Thus, Latvians 'could afford' gradualism in agriculture, because radical reform was not needed in the struggle for power with Communists. To eliminate the power base of Latvian Communists, electoral rules regarding citizenship were simply changed.

It has been argued in the theoretical introduction to this chapter that constitutional rules are decisive for the structure of political competition and that changing those rules results in political competition at two levels. The political competition observed in the Baltic countries involved both competition over the future structure of political institutions and over redistribution of assets within the present set of rules. In the case of Latvia, the competition over the structure of political institutions has turned out to be decisive for the redistribution of assets, directly and indirectly. Rules of citizenship discriminated against non-Latvians in the distribution of assets and in their participation as voters. The same rules also resulted in the elimination of the power base of the Communist Party, a possible ally to the losers of the agrarian privatization.

Privatization's impacts relate to efficiency, liquidity, and equity. The equity or distributional aspects of the process have been emphasised here as a driving force in this process. With regards to liquidity, the privatization process appears by and large not to be restricted by concerns for the financial position of the state. Assets have been restituted and not sold. Privatization of 2-3 hectare plots in Lithuania is, however, based on sales of the land. Moreover, for budgetary reasons, the Lithuanian government has shown a preference for compensations with alternative land rather than with money (World Bank, 1992).

Questions about efficiency concern both the process of restructuring and the outcome of the process up to now. The process of privatization can hardly be described as efficiently managed. This is particularly true in Lithuania, where collective farms were forced into liquidation and subjected to temporary management. The result of this approach was mismanagement and theft (Girnius, 1992; Povilunas, 1994). In both countries restructuring of former collective farms into alternative organizational forms was combined with restitutions of land in original boundaries. Privatization of bank assets took place separately from land restitutions. As argued in chapter one, a lack of complementarity between privatization strategies is hardly efficient, as it results in land that is privatized without needed resources such as machinery. The majority of family farms established in Lithuania lacked even basic machinery. In general, restitutions within original boundaries have turned out to be highly disruptive. The process of establishing the proper titles to the land, which is fundamental for the functioning of the land market, has been slow.

Questions about efficiency of the outcome of the privatization and restructuring process can be raised as well. Three forms have resulted from the process: private farms, small plots, and new collective farming structures such as farm companies/limited liability companies. The new collective structures resemble the old collective farms, in particular in Lithuania, and efficiency has not been improved. Restitutions and allocation of land to small plots has resulted in a highly fragmented farm structure with obvious implications for efficiency in farming. It could be argued that the average size of a private farm in the Baltic countries is not exceptionally low when compared with some Western countries (for example, Finland or Norway). The average size is now 9 hectares in Lithuania and 13.6 hectares in Latvia. However, in discussing land fragmentation one should also consider household plots. These small plots of 2 to 4 hectares, account for a large proportion of both agricultural production and arable land. In Lithuania such plots occupy in total about one million hectares; in some regions up to 50 percent of the land. Efficiency in agricultural production will obviously be impaired by such extreme fragmentation. It could be claimed that the plots should instead be evaluated in terms of social policy as a substitute for or complement to the social security system. Farm employment has been increasing (OECD, 1995) and urban people have been returning to the countryside in response to deteriorating economic conditions. Western experiences in this field are, however, not encouraging.

Efficiency in the privatization of upstream and downstream industries can be questioned as well. Allocating shares under preferential schemes to farmers is likely to limit the inflow of capital and technical and marketing skills to the industries concerned.

Finally, some comments can be made with respect to the application of a rational choice model to the analysis of the economies in transition. With respect to the situation in Lithuania, development has been erratic. The present state of affairs appears to be a result of a complicated political process in which several consequences appear not to have been fully anticipated in advance by those involved. Lithuania's radical approach to privatization was, as argued before, motivated by the desire to undermine the power base of the rural nomenklatura. However, the design and implementation of the process facilitated the return of the ex-Communists to power due to discontent among the rural population regarding the chaotic conditions that resulted from the process. Furthermore, the nomenklatura managed to enrich itself. These can hardly be described as the intended results. The Sajudis government most probably underestimated the difficulties involved. The opposition to privatization, in a situation with many losers, was probably underestimated as well.

Notes

1 I gratefully acknowledge comments by Olaf Bolin (Swedish University of Agricultural Sciences, Department of Economics) on earlier versions of the paper.

2 Twenty-five parties participated in the elections, and a threshold of 4 percent was applied. The electoral system used was a mixture of proportional elections and a single seat system. As a concession to national minorities, the two groups formally recognized as representing the minorities – Lithuanian Union of Poles and Concord for Lithuania – were not required to meet 4 percent threshold.

3 This fact is a direct consequence of the design of the privatization of former collective farm assets. Green vouchers were based on the number of years worked in agricultural enterprises, favoring older members. Because of the population's reluctance to use general privatization vouchers, mainly the green ones were used.

4 The study of agrarian reform in Latvia by Paloma and Segré (1992) indicates that skilled salaried employees of former collective and state farms, such as agronomists, livestock breeders, veterinarians, etc., are well represented among new private farmers. According to the same study, unskilled workers participate only marginally under privatization. The same appears to hold for these groups in Lithuania (Druzinskas, 1994).

5 In Lithuania, which is less industrialized, the share of Russians is 9 percent of the population, closely followed by Poles, at 7 percent. Lithuanians account for 80 percent.

6 The 1.8 figure is for 1996. For 1992, 607,000 hectares were requested by 35,000 farms.

7 This information is based on an interview with A. Salts, a Latvian exile living in Sweden who was active in Latvian politics (Nationalist Party). Salts has also received back land which belonged to his family.

8 Fear of such discrimination may, however, result in support for Communist or ex-Communist parties, as can be seen in the Baltics.

9 Good and friendly relations with Poland and Russia are probably more gainful to ethnic Lithuanians (as long as their independence is not

threatened) than any benefits gained from the unequal treatment of Polish or Russian minorities.

References

Abrams, B. and Lewis, K., (1987), 'A Median-Voter Model of Economic Regulation', *Public Choice*, Vol. 52, pp. 125-142.

Aleksiene, A. and Zalimiene, L. (1993), 'Sociological Researches of Employment in Agricultural Partnerships', unpublished manuscript.

Alesina, A. and Roubini, N., (1992), 'Political Cycles in OECD Economies', *Review of Economics and Statistics*, Vol. 59, pp. 663-688.

Baltic Independent, Various issues.

Baltic Observer, Various issues.

Becker, G. (1958), 'Competition and Democracy', *Journal of Law and Economics*, Vol. 1, pp.105-109.

Becker, G. (1983), 'A Theory of Competition Among Pressure Groups for Political Influence', *Quarterly Journal of Economics*, Vol. 68, No. 3, pp. 371-400.

Bolton, P. and Roland, G. (1992), 'Privatization policies in Central and Eastern Europe', *Economic policy - European forum*, 15 October, pp. 276-309.

Bolton, P. and Roland, G. (1994), 'The Break-Up of Countries: A Political Economy Analysis', unpublished manuscript.

Bungs, D. (1992), 'Latvia: New Legislation Opens Door to Reform', *RFE/RL Research Report*, Vol. 1, No. 17, pp. 73-79.

Bungs, D. (1993), 'Moderates Win Parliamentary Elections in Latvia', *RFE/RL Research Report*, Vol. 2, No. 28, pp. 1-6.

Bungs, D., Saulius, G., and Kionka, R. (1992), 'Citizenship Legislation in the Baltic States', *RFE/RL Research Report*, Vol. 1, No. 50, pp. 38-40.

Downs, A. (1957), *An Economic Theory of Democracy*, Harper and Row: New York.

Druzinskas, R. (1994), Personal communication.

Evans, G., and Whitefield, S. (1993), 'Identifying the Bases of Party Competition in Eastern Europe', *British Journal of Political Sciences*, Vol. 23, pp. 521-548.

Girnius, S. (1992a), 'Lithuania Sets Ambitious Goals', *RFE/RL Research Report*, Vol. 1, No. 17, pp. 67-72.

Girnius, S. (1992b), 'The Parliamentary Elections in Lithuania', *RFE/RL Research Report*, Vol. 1, No. 48, pp. 6-12.

Girnius, S. (1994) 'The Economies of the Baltic States in 1993', *RFE/RL Research Report*, Vol. 3, No. 20, pp. 1-14.

Hibbs, D. A. (1977), 'Political Parties and Macroeconomic Policy', *American Political Science Review*, Vol. 71, pp. 1467-87.

Hibbs, D. A. (1982), 'Economic Outcomes and Political Support for British Government Among Occupational Classes: A Dynamic Analysis', *American Political Science Review*, Vol. 76, pp. 259-79.

Hillman, A., (1989), *The Political Economy of Protection*, Harwood Academic Publishers: New York.

Kazslauskiene, N., and Meyers, W. (1995), 'Agricultural Privatization in Lithuania', *Baltic Report,* BR 20, Center for Agricultural and Rural Development (CARD), Iowa State University: Ames.

Kitschelt, H. (1992), 'The Formation of Party System in East and Central Europe', *Politics and Society*, Vol. 20, pp. 7-50.

Kuodys, A. (1993), 'Agrarian Reform in Lithuania', Finnish-Baltic Joint Seminar, Saku Estonia, Agricultural Economics Research Institute, Finland, Research Publications 72.

Kuodys, A. (1994), 'Agrarian Reform: Results and Prospects', Workshop on Agrarian Reform in Central and Eastern Europe, 10-12 March 1994, Latvia, Jurmala.

Kuzlis, B. (1992), 'Lithuanian Agrarian Reform: Legal and Organizational Aspects', Finnish-Baltic Joint Seminar, Vilnius, Lithuania, Agricultural Economics Research Institute, Finland, Research Publications 68.

Lipset, S. M. and Rokkan, S. (eds.) (1967), *Party-Systems and Voter Alignments: Cross-National Perspectives*, Free Press: New York.

League of Nations (1939), *European Conference on Rural Life 1939*, National Monographs drawn up by Governments, Latvia.

Lingle, L. (1992), 'Ethnic Nationalism and Post-Communist Transition Problems' in Somogyi, L. (ed.), *The Political Economy of the Transition Process in Eastern Europe*, Edvard Elgar Publishing: Aldershot.

Lindahl, B. (1995), 'Intresseorganisationer, Agrarpartier och Jordbundes-politik. En Nordisk Jämpövelse', unpublished dissertation, Institutionen för Ekonomi, Swedish University of Agricultural Sciences: Uppsala.

Mattson, S.-A. (1993), 'Swedsurvey i Lettland', *Svensk Lantmäteritidskrift*, Vol. 4, No. 93.

Ministry of Agriculture of the Republic of Latvia (1992), 'Agrifacts About Latvia (Agroinformacija)', Latvian State Institute of Agrarian Economics: Riga.

Olson, M. (1965), *The Logic of Collective Action*, Harvard University Press: Cambridge.

OECD (1995), 'Agricultural and Price Policy Development in Lithuania', Ad hoc group on East/West economic relations in agriculture, OECD: Paris.

OECD (1996), 'Review of Agricultural Policies: Lativa', Working Party, Agricultural Policies and Markets of the Committee for Agriculture, Joint

Working Party on the Committee for Agricultural and Trade Committee, OECD: Paris.

Paloma, S. and Segré, A. (1992), 'Latvia: Agrarian Reform and Production Systems in the Transition from a Command to Market Economy', Research Report N. 4/1992, Centre for Southern European and Mediterranean Studies: Roskilde, Denmark.

Peltzman, S. (1976), 'Towards a More General Theory of Regulation', *Journal of Law and Economics*, Vol. 19, pp. 211-240.

Poviliunas, A. (1993), 'Economic and Social Factors Influencing Linthuanian Agricultural Development', Finnish-Baltic Joint Seminar, Saku Estonia, Agricultural Economics Research Institute, Finland, Research Publications 72.

Poviliunas, A. (1994), 'Agricultural Decline in Lithuania: Reasons and Ways of Stabilization', Workshop on Agrarian Reform in Central and Eastern Europe, 10-12 March 1994, Latvia, Jurmala.

Rabinowicz, E. (1996), 'Swedish Agricultural Policy: A Case for Radical Reform', in Spanish translation in *Revista Española de Economía Agraria*.

Roland, G. (1992), *Issues in the Political Economy of Transition. The Economic Consequences of the East*, Centre for Economic Policy Research: London.

Stigler, G. J. (1971), 'The Theory of Regulation', *Bell Journal of Economics and Management Sciences*, Vol. 2, pp. 3-21.

Ström, K. and Leipart J. (1993), '1945-1990. Policy, Institutions and Coalition Avoidance: Norwegian Government', *American Political Science Review*, Vol. 87, No. 4, pp. 870-887.

Strömberg, D. (1994), *Demographic Political Interests Groups*, IIES, Stockholm University.

World Bank (1993), *Latvia: The Transition to a Market Economy*, The World Bank: Washington, D.C.

Zetterberg, S. (1993), 'Det Nationella Uppvaknandet och Vägen mot Självständighet', in Jokipii, M. (ed.), *Baltisk Kultur och Historia*, Bonniers.

Zile, R. (1992), 'The Basic Principles of Agrarian Reform in the Republic of Latvia', Finnish-Baltic Joint Seminar, Vilnius, Lithuania, Agricultural Economics Research Institute, Finland, Research Publications 68.

Zile, R. (1993), 'The Development of Privatization in Latvian Agriculture', Report 93-BR 14, Latvian State Institute of Agrarian Economics: Riga.

5 On liquidation councils, flying troikas and Orsov cooperatives: The political economy of agricultural reform in Bulgaria

Johan F. M. Swinnen

Introduction

Bulgaria has chosen to restitute agricultural land to its former owners. The Communists, who maintained power until 1991, first obstructed this legislation and then its execution. When radical reformers took over the government in 1991, the property rights restoration process in both legislation and implementation became radical, even by Central and East European standards. Subsequent governments, under increasing influence of the former Communists, have reduced support for the reform process and have attempted to limit the transfer of effective property rights from former collective farms to previous owners outside the collectives.

This chapter analyzes the interaction of political and economic factors in agricultural privatization and land reform legislation in Bulgaria between 1989 and 1995.[1] Property restoration is discussed in the framework of the ongoing political battle between former Communists and the anti-Communist reformers. The manner in which the restoration of property rights takes place affects the future distribution of assets and endowments in the country; the economic, social, and political organizational structure; and the ability of the nomenklatura to block the reforms. All three factors have important impacts on preferences and political alignment, especially of the rural electorate. Future political constraints have been a crucial issue in the choice of a property rights restoration process.

Policy and structural reform is not new to Bulgarian agriculture. Programs to centralize and decentralize have come and gone since forced collectivization in the 1940s. For example, in the first half of the 1970s cooperative farms, state farms, and units of the food processing industry were organized into huge agro-industrial complexes. Gross inefficiencies led to stagnating output and declining exports. By the second half of the 1980s, even the Communist leadership was forced to admit the effort had failed (Jackson, 1991a). Since then, several reform measures have been implemented to reduce inefficiencies in agriculture by decentralizing decisionmaking and increasing incentives to labor (Davidova, 1994). The critical difference in the changes since 1989 is the simultaneity of massive changes in the economy and the new political environment.

Compared with other CEECs, political change in Bulgaria has been lethargic. Until 1989 political opposition was barely visible (Penev, 1991). Bulgarian dissidents were silenced before the public learned about them, and then they disappeared altogether (Pirgova, 1991). However, the pace, intensity, and depth of changes since late 1989 have been extraordinary. According to Dimitrov (1991a),

> To most Bulgarians Gorbachev's 'perestroika' looked like an unattainable dream until the autumn of 1989; later on, it already seemed a left-behind utopia ... [and by 1991] ... no one now calls into question the irreversibility of the democratic process in Bulgaria.

Despite such optimism about democracy, former Communists, organized in the Bulgarian Socialist Party (BSP), had been relatively successful in maintaining their stake in power. Only after the October 1991 election could a government be formed that did not have to rely on the BSP for political support and for approval and implementation of land reform and privatization (table 5.1).

The BSP's relative success in holding its power and preventing effective reforms backfired. The prolonged inaction and the unexpected elective performance of the BSP stimulated a radical reaction as soon as reformers in the Union of Democratic Forces (UDF) came to power. This included regulations to speed up land reform and the installation of 'liquidation councils' to effectively liquidate the collective farms. This radical action was intended to make the reform measures irreversible and land a lasting blow to the political organizational strength of the BSP. The radical program was actually made possible by polarization at the executive level, because of the lack of a political center in Parliament following the 1991 elections. The program's outcome was the gradual reemergence of an effective political center, resulting in the fall of the UDF government in November of 1992. The governments that followed again relied on BSP support, slowed down implementation of reforms, and replaced many people in charge of the liquidation councils in order to influence the process.

After the BSP won a parliamentary majority in the 1994 elections, the new BSP government abolished the liquidation councils and replaced them with 'flying troikas', i.e., three-person committees elected by the members of the collective farms under liquidation.[2] At the same time, new legislation was submitted to limit the transfer of property rights from collective farm members to former owners.

Table 5.1
Important political events 1989-1993

1989	November	Zhivkov is replaced as Communist party leader
	December	UDF is formed
1990	January	The political monopoly of the BCP is revoked.
	April	Round Table Agreement announces elections for Grand National Assembly, which is to change the Constitution
	10 June	Parliamentary elections (see table 5.2)
	June	BSP - Government of Lukanov
	July	Zhelyu Zhelev is elected president by the National Assembly
	November	Lukanov government falls
	20 December	Coalition government of Dimitar Popov
1991	October	Parliamentary elections (see table 5.2)
	8 November	UDF government of Filip Dimitrov
1992	12-19 January	Presidential elections (5-year term) Zhelev (UDF) reelected in two rounds with 53.5% over V. Vulkanov (BSP - 46.3%)
	May	Shake-up of Dimitrov's government
	28 November	Fall of Dimitrov government
	December	Coalition government of Ljuben Berov, supported by BSP-MRF and a UDF faction.
1994	August	Caretaker cabinet of Reneta. Indjova takes over in preparation for general elections
	December	Parliamentary elections (see table 5.2)
1995	January	Zhan Videnov leads BSP-government

Ownership disputes continue after the reforms. Besides individual farms, two groups of producer cooperatives have emerged: 'blue' and 'red' (or so-called Orsov) cooperatives. The color refers to their political association: blue for the UDF and red for the BSP. The main distinction lays in the recognition of ownership of individuals. The 'red' cooperatives continue the practice from the former system when members were owners on paper, but were deprived the benefits of ownership (Davidova et al., 1997).

Part 2 of this chapter gives an overview of political changes in Bulgaria, followed by a brief discussion of the reform strategies of the various political groups. The next section uses a political economy framework to interpret the legislation and implementation of land reform and agricultural privatization.

Transition politics and economic reform in Bulgaria

A brief overview of political reforms

In November 1989, Thodor Zhivkov, the Bulgarian Communist Party (BCP) leader, was replaced, after thirtyfive years in office, by Petar Mladenov, the former foreign minister. One month later, nine independent groups formed an opposition coalition called the Union of Democratic Forces (UDF). Zhelyu Zhelev, a prominent Bulgarian philosopher exiled in the 1960s, became chairman of the UDF. Discussions between the main opposition groups and the Bulgarian Socialist Party (BSP - the new name for the BCP) yielded the Round Table Agreement of April 1990, stating that a Grand National Assembly be elected and given up to eighteen months to draft and vote on a new constitution (with a two-thirds majority), after which new parliamentary elections would be held (Engelbrekt, 1991a).

The first free elections in fiftythree years are held on 10 June 1990. The BSP won 211 of 400 seats (with 47 percent of the votes) of the Grand National Assembly, the UDF garnered 144 seats, the Movement for Rights and Freedom (MRF - a party deriving its support almost uniquely from the ethnic Turkish minority)[3] won 23 seats and the Bulgarian Agricultural National Union (BANU), 16 seats (table 5.2).[4] After the election, the disappointed UDF refused to cooperate with the BSP in forming a coalition government. Andrey Lukanov, the previous prime minister, formed a new BSP government. Consequent student sit-ins and street actions by the Civil Disobedience Movement with the backing of the Podkrepa Labor Union forced the resignation of BSP president Mladenov. On 1 August, 1990, the Grand National Assembly elected UDF chairman Zhelev as president of Bulgaria.[5] Pressure from the opposition continued in and outside Parliament, leading to the fall of the Lukanov's BSP government in November after a major wave of strikes.

As economic conditions worsened, a new government under the politically unaffiliated jurist Popov took effect on 19 December 1990. BSP, UDF, BANU, and politically unaffiliated members of Parliament supported the coalition government. The reformers received the ministries most important for them: finance, industry, trade, and services. BANU member Spirov became the minister of agriculture (Engelbrekt, 1991f). Popov announced on 23 December 1990 that economic austerity measures as part of an economic stabilization plan to be introduced on 1 February 1991 would include lifting controls on prices and drastically increasing interest rates. This induced producers and shops to stash away goods in expectation of price hikes and led to long queus in front of shops in January 1991 (Wyzan, 1992; Davidova, 1994). In July 1991, after months of stalemate in Parliament, a new constitution was approved by a coalition of the BSP and some members of the UDF coalition, chiefly the Bulgarian Social Democratic Party (BSDP) and the Bulgarian Agrarian National Union-Nikola Petkov (BANU-Nikola Petkov)[6], which together constituted a majority in the UDF parliamentary faction.

Table 5.2
Election results[a]

	1990		*1991*			*1994*
	Seats		Votes	Seat		Seats
BSP	211	BSP	33%	106	BSP	124
UDF	144	UDF	35%	111	UDF	69
MRF	23	MRF	7%	23	MRF	15
BANU	16	Other	25%	0	PU[b]	18
					BBB[c]	13
Total	400	Total	100%	240	Total	240

a   1991 and 1994 elections are based on proportional representation with 4% threshold (single-chamber), five-year Parliament.
b   Popular Union (PU) was a coalition of the Agrarian Union (formerly BANU) and the Democratic Party (formerly part of UDF).
c   Bulgarian Business Bloc.

In October 1991, general elections were held. The outcome was disappointing for the opposition, which, without the support of the MRF (see table 5.2), did not succeed in obtaining a majority in Parliament. The election was particularly disastrous for the centrist parties – BANU, as well as all the parties that had left the UDF coalition in the months before the elections did not reach the 4 percent threshold. The result was a stalemate in Parliament between two radically opposing parties: the UDF, with 111 seats, and the BSP, with 106 seats. The balance was held by the MRF with 23 seats.

After the election, a UDF minority government, headed by UDF chairman Filip Dimitrov and supported by the MRF,[7] started a radical approach to privatization policies while at the same time stressing the importance of economic austerity to achieve financial stabilization and curb the budget deficit (Engelbrekt, 1992a). The honeymoon period of this reform-minded government was short. Bulgaria's dependence on Soviet markets was high. The collapse of that market resulted in a steep drop in demand and in economic decline. By mid-1992, all hopes of a relatively speedy recovery had been dashed, and public discontent was growing. The UDF government's insistence on strict fiscal austerity and macroeconomic reform yielded praise from the West and from international financial institutions. However, increased domestic criticism that these policies aggravated the country's financial crisis led to conflicts within and outside the UDF coalition. Moderate UDF members, the labor unions (including Podkrepa, a UDF ally), and the MRF increasingly insisted on a change in policy to reduce the radical stance of the UDF government in both its economic reform program and anti-Communist actions (Engelbrekt, 1992c). President Zhelev joined critics of the government by warning UDF politicians against the extreme positions by which he claimed the UDF was alienating potential supporters and losing its own voters' support. Zhelev, by far the most popular politician in Bulgaria, was reelected in January 1992 on a UDF ticket, although he belonged to the moderate wing of the original coalition. The conflict led to a first political crisis in May 1992, ending in a reshuffling of the cabinet. Instead of improving, relations between the UDF and the MRF continued to worsen.[8] Impatience with the steadily deteriorating economic and social situation (unemployment was 15 percent at the end of 1992) and the government's inability to meet the public's high expectations led to its fall in October 1992. Lack of popular support resulted in a vote of no-confidence on 28 October 1992, in which the MRF joined the opposition BSP to defeat the government.

After two months of debate, Lyuben Berov, former economic advisor to the president, formed a new government on 30 December 1992. Berov's government, a combination of technocrats and politicians supported by a coalition of BSP, MRF, and the left wing of the UDF, promised to take a 'socially oriented' approach and to engineer a 'smooth' transition toward a market economy.[9] The implication was that the social costs of radical reforms would become lower for Bulgarians in general. Nevertheless, Berov claimed to continue the reforms started under the previous government, while correcting some 'mistakes' of his predecessor, and named (large-scale) privatization top priority (BBN; Engelbrekt, 1993a).

In the fall of 1994 Berov's government resigned and Renata Indjova led a temporary 'caretaker' government until the December 1994 elections. The elections were a convincing victory for the BSP, which captured an outright majority with 124 of 240 seats (table 5.2). As a result, Zhan Videnov formed a homogeneous BSP government in January 1995.

What has motivated the BSP since the fall of the totalitarian regime in November 1989? Several authors paint an uncompromising picture of the BSP's objectives, indicating that its ultimate goal has been to secure the interests of the ex-Communist nomenklatura. Ideology was a means to achieve this goal and was abandoned as soon as it no longer came in useful. The BSP exchanged its socialist image for nationalist ideology in the 1980s, and since 1989 has positioned itself as the guardian of 'a smooth transition, stability, and social security' during the reforms. Its prime strategies for securing the nomenklatura's interests under changing political institutions have been (1) the 'transformation of political influence into economic clout' and (2) covering up political and financial crimes (Pirgova, 1991; Penev, 1991, 1992; Genchev, 1991; Minchev et al., 1991).

Penev (1991) paints the BSP as a totalitarian-type party with a modern leftist program, whose members include adherents of ideologies cutting across the political spectrum. What brings those people together, Penev writes, are 'crimes committed under the Communist regime, a reluctance to change their status, concealed nationalism, a delusion and, in some of them, an earnest intention to implement social reform'.[10] At the beginning of the 1980s, technocratically minded politicians within the BCP anticipated the imminent breakup of the Soviet empire and the collapse of the economic system of socialism and called for market reforms in the economy. These technocrats made the first steps toward converting state property into state-regulated private property. In 1986-87 the BCP under Zhivkov proclaimed the beginning of antitotalitarian reforms: a drive toward political pluralism and a market economy and the establishment of state-owned companies. Pirgova (1991) argues that Todor Zhivkov approved the projects, showing no ideological scruples, because his only goal was to stay in power by protecting himself from changes in the USSR and by preparing for the transition to a market economy.[11]

Both authors agree that the BSP's strategy after the reforms was to cover up their crimes and use privatizaton to move into key positions in the emerging market economy. In this, there was little consideration for the national interest and no ideological constraint. According to Pirgova, most high-ranking BSP functionaries assumed that an election victory would allow them to enact their scenario: to remain in power, privatize the state property, and secure top positions for party apparatchiks-turned-capitalist, and finally to cover up political and financial crimes.[12] Genchev (1991) gives an equally scathing view of the BSP's post-1989 strategy: 'In the course of political manoeuvres after the elections the way was paved for an economic operation aimed at robbing the national wealth. The economic and political bureaucracy was quick to part with the Communist utopias of public property and quite unscrupulously threw itself into private business, diverting a substantial amount of state funds to its own benefit'.

It is too simplistic to reduce the objective of the BSP and its members to the goal of securing the nomenklatura's interests. However, the evidence suggests that this objective (and associated strategies) seem to have been an important motive underlying nomenklatura actions and BSP policy preferences vis-à-vis economic reform policies (see, e.g., Bogetic and Hillman, 1995a,b; Jackson, 1991a,b).

Objectives and strategies of the reformers

Determining the objective of the opposition since 1989 is more difficult because the opposition has been a more heterogeneous group. Initially the entire opposition, with the exceptions of the MRF and BANU (an old Communist ally), was united in the Union of Democratic Forces (UDF), a coalition initially of 9 parties and some affiliated groups with observer status. This early UDF was a 'markedly artificial formation of parties covering the entire political gamut, united by a single idea – fighting the BSP', according to Dimitrov (1991a). The UDF coalition included restored former (pre-1940) social democratic political parties such as the Nikola Petkov Bulgarian Agrarian National Union (BANU-Nikola Petkov)[13] and the Bulgarian Social Democratic Party (BSDP). Other parties were rapidly emerging as fragile and ideologically vague political formations: (1) the Glasnost and Democracy clubs, composed mainly of dissident intellectuals, most of them former Party members, at the liberal center of the Union; (2) the Ecoglasnost Movement, bringing together intellectuals and young people with a network of branches across the country; (3) the right-wing Democratic Party and Radical Democratic Party. Until November 1990 the Podkrepa Labor Confederation, an anti-Communist trade union group, was also affiliated with the UDF (Pirgova, 1991; Genchev, 1991).

As soon as the UDF participated in a major policy discussion (formulated of a new Bulgarian constitution), divisions within the UDF appeared.[14] The radical anti-Communist opposition refused to support the constitutional bill because it consolidated the Communist elite's identity with the democratic system. The moderate opposition, grouped around president Zhelyu Zhelev and motivated by the necessity of stabilizing the democratic process and creating institutional guarantees for its irreversibility supported the bill despite ideas imposed by the socialist majority.

The radical anti-Communists derived most of their support from those urban groups most affected by the crisis and from the pre-Communist economic elite of the country. The goal of the UDF's right wing was to remove the BSP from

136

power and create of a middle class of property owners reflecting the pre-Communist hierarchy. To attain this goal, the UDF attempted to bring the nomenklatura to court and to prison for their alleged crimes and supported the claim of one million former owners for the full and, if possible, physical restitution of property taken away by the Communist regime.

After the new constitution of 1991 legalized the BSP, the UDF realized that it had underestimated the BSP's electoral support (Dimitrov, 1991b), it focused on destroying the support base of the BSP by breaking up the existing organizational structures that formed the core of the BSP's organizational strength. The UDF also attempted to block (and cancel) any privatization procedures that allowed the nomenklatura to use their privileged position and financial strength to build up power in the emerging market economy.

The UDF maintained a staunch anti-Communist stance, both in its economic reform program and in its insistence on decommunization of society. While these were originally the goals of all reformers, they increasingly became the goal of the right wing of the UDF. A larger group of opposition politicians moved away from this radical stance, often separating itself from the UDF and claiming a political center movement. The goal of the 'center' was to proceed with privatization while reducing the negative social impacts of the reform. Also, the center increasingly retreated from the position of decommunization of the country (Engelbrekt, 1992b, c). However, because of internal division, this center lost its representation in Parliament in the October 1991 elections, and this contributed to the polarization of politics and radical shifts in policies in Bulgaria. The new center, organized around Zhelev, reemerged with the Berov government, which removed several UDF members from key positions (Engelbrekt, 1993a, b). Further splits from the UDF and reorganization of the political center (e.g., the creation of the centrist Popular Union) continued in 1993 and 1994. The 1994 elections brought the Popular Union into Parliament (see table 5.2).

A political economy interpretation of agricultural reform

The law for agricultural landownership and land use

In February 1991 the Grand National Assembly approved the Law for Agricultural Landownership and Land Use (LALOLU).[15] The stated goal of the law was to return farmland to those who owned it prior to collectivization. The opposition accused the BSP and the nomenklatura of blocking the law's implementation. After the October 1991 election, the UDF government made land reform and privatization a priority issue. The LALOLU was substantially amended by the UDF government in March 1992, with several restrictions removed from the original version and the introduction of new guidelines for execution of the law. The amended law specified that where possible the former boundaries of farmland be identified and the land restored to its former owners or their heirs in its original form. The law also stipulated how to make restitutions in cases where the original land could be returned. Municipal land councils (MLCs) became responsible for issuing ownership certificates following the evaluation of property claims. The law further stipulated that all existing cooperatives, agrofirms, and other collective farm structures be terminated, along with the activities of the managing and controlling boards of those organizations. The regional governors appointed liquidation councils (LCs) to manage the agricultural units until termination of their activities and to take all necessary steps pertaining to liquidation (Davidova, 1994). LCs also regulated the distribution of the farms' nonland assets. The government made immediate implementation of the law a priority of its general reforms. The law was strongly criticized (1) for introducing enormous complexities in the privatization program and (2) for destroying the existing 'efficient' large-scale farm structure to create an overly dispersed landownership structure with important negative impacts on efficiency.

Under the Berov government, many of the LC chairmen were replaced, a move which suggests a general strategy to influence the property rights process by changing the preferences and incentives of the implementing institutions. The 1995 BSP government pushed this strategy to the extreme by liquidating the liquidation councils and replacing them with three-person councils (the flying troikas) representing the involved parties. Furthermore, the government proposed a series of laws intended to restrict the effective property rights of new (former) owners and to increase the property rights of current users of the land. Some of these proposals were judged unconstitutional by Bulgaria's Supreme Court.

In the rest of this section, I interpret changes in regulations and government reform strategies within a political economy framework, beginning with June of 1990.

Inaction under the Lukanov Government (first half of 1990)

Before the June 1990 elections the BSP believed that it could stabilize the economy without substantial reform, and it blocked and opposed reform proposals as much as possible. Penev (1991) claims that the first Lukanov government did its best to prevent an escalation of social tensions by suspending the foreign debt servicing and by spending the country's last remaining convertible currency. The Bulgarian economy reached its lowest point, and the foreign debt skyrocketed. The state apparatus broke down as those actively involved with the old regime sought chances for political survival. At a lower level, the former nomenklatura hastened to transform its political influence into economic clout by seizing key positions in newly established companies.

However, Lukanov's inaction and the resulting economic decline contributed to the BSP electorate's realization that reforms were necessary (Dimitrov, 1991a). Faced with the imminent danger of losing its power, the BSP stalled for time to carry out its original plans by using its majority to block the efficiency of Parliament. The few reforms it allowed fit into its overall strategy of using the reforms it could not prevent for its own advantage. It used its powers to prepare itself for the 'post-reform' situation, i.e., by designing the policy reform procedures (privatizations) so that the nomenklatura would best be able to benefit, via widespread and strategic post-reform positions.

One of the Lukanov government's first moves in February 1990 was to issue a decree allowing private farmers to lease up to 30 hectares of farmland. According to Jackson (1991b), only 138.000 hectares had been taken up, suggesting either a lack of incentives administrative barriers, possibly from local officials who controlled land use. Bulgaria already had a law that permitted the conversion of state enterprises into 'firms', which could be joint-stock companies. Jackson further reports that:

> there was active founding of additional 'socialist' units, possibly indicating entrepreneurial activity on the part of the nomenklatura. However, the biggest increase was in the number of private firms. Of course, some of the private firms could also have been formed by the illegal conversion of public property by managers and other members of the nomenklatura (Jackson, 1991b).

The first thing the UDF did as soon as it was in position to influence government policies was try to prevent this from happening. Therefore, soon after his election as president in August 1990, UDF chairman Zhelyu Zhelev suspended privatization.

Legal land reform and executive inaction under the Popov Government

On 22 February 1991, the LALOLU was approved. The law provided for the return of collectivized land to former owners or their heirs. Under the law, a household could own up to 30 hectares of land, or up to 20 hectares in intensive agricultural areas. This version of the privatization process, i.e., restitution to former owners, followed the UDF's position and was vigorously opposed by the BSP, which wanted to give the land to those who currently farmed it. The law, however, did not specify in detail the process of restitution. Another proposal by the BSP – that private land, if not used for agricultural purposes over a period of three years, be expropriated – also failed to win the necessary support. Instead, a law was passed to tax such specified land (Nikolaev, 1991). BSP representatives consistently opposed restitution, arguing it would have serious negative effects on economic performance. Engelbrekt notes (1991d) that:

> company managers, many of whom are affiliated with the BSP, stand to lose most if the state returns property to its former owners. Moreover, managers have benefitted from the so-called privatization process, a largely uncontrolled process whereby resources are often transferred from state enterprises to private firms.

The main problem with the land law was its lack of effectiveness. One could argue that the BSP allowed it to pass because they understood it could not be effective without their cooperation. As such, the process resembled land reform attempts that have failed elsewhere (e.g., Colombia and the Philippines), where ineffective legal reforms were implemented by the ruling party, reducing the pressure for effective reforms without actually contributing real changes (Hayami, 1991; Junguito, 1991; de Janvry, 1981).

In Bulgaria, obstacles occurred both at the government level and at the local level where the reform and restitution was to be implemented. The legislative problems occured because the law included unclear passages and did not specify the details of its implementation, and therefore needed to be supplemented by regulations specifying details and explaining unclear passages. However, supplemental regulations were several times delayed. At the local level, the nomenklatura were still in charge of both the collective farm and the local administration, which controlled the municipal land commissions (MLCs). Nikolaev (1991) discusses several press reports that give examples of interference in the process by local managers and individuals who wanted to claim their land.

The spring and summer of 1991: frustration and radicalization of the UDF

The spring of 1991 witnessed debate over the new constitution and a growing division within the UDF. The UDF's leaders tried to keep their fragile coalition together, but their efforts failed to avert a serious split between the UDF's National Coordinating Council (NCC) and its parliamentary caucus, dominated by Bulgarian Socialist Democratic Party (BSDP) leader Petar Dertliev. The UDF-NCC called on UDF member organizations not to approve the new constitution. Nine member organizations supported the NCC's position, while the BSDP, the Federation of Clubs for Democracy, and the

140

Green Party did not. BANU-Nikola Petkov abstained. While everybody agreed that the new constitution had flaws, supporters approved it because it finally cleared the way to get on with legislation stimulating economic reforms. This position was summarized by President Zhelev, who described the constitution as 'a reliable basis for the implementation of democratic change', for which amendmends might be necessary, which could be introduced in the course of reform (Engelbrekt, 1991c).[16]

On 10 April, 1991 the BANU-Nikola Petkov and the BDSP issued a joint statement announcing that they were establishing 'UDF-Center' within the movement. One fundamental reason behind this move was that both parties were clearly to the left of the other member organizations and were critical of some aspects of the economic reforms implemented under the Popov government. The UDF-Center preferred to see the establishment of a 'social state', which would include more egalitarian income and tax policies, and it would raise no objection to a greater degree of state intervention in order to realize these aims (Engelbrekt, 1991b). Both parties of the UDF-Center were also by far the largest in membership (roughly 100,000 members each in the spring of 1991) and felt that they did not have a corresponding voice in the UDF. An additional factor in forming the UDF-Center was the establishment of local UDF citizens' committees in the countryside, which often seemed to compete for membership with the local BDSP and BANU-Nikola Petkov chapters. Finally, both parties were republican, while several of the liberal and conservative parties within the UDF supported a return to a monarchy.

The UDF leadership succeeded for a while in preventing a split in the UDF. However, as the October 1991 elections came nearer, several parties left the UDF coalition to campaign on their own in the elections. Their insistence on using the UDF name to increase their recognition led to increasing confusion: such parties as the UDF-Liberals, UDF-Center, and BANU-Nikola Petkov participated as independent parties in the election next to the UDF (with the remaining coalition parties). Clearly, the exit of the moderate or left-wing parties from the UDF coalition (such as the BDSP and most of the BANU-Nikola Petkov) left the UDF more radical than ever, just before the elections.

In the meantime, disappointment and frustration outside Parliament grew quickly in the summer as implementation of the LALOLU created problems and delays. While the complexity of the process caused troubles, it also served as a welcome excuse for introducing further delays by those who opposed the law. In April President Zhelev had already accused the government of being scandalously slow in handling the land reform (Nikolaev, 1991) and in late June, Finance Minister Kostov accused the nomenklatura of blocking the reform (Engelbrekt, 1991d).

Compared with most northern CEECs, the impact of the BSP on the land reform process in Bulgaria was remarkable: it had taken part in the discussions and the writing of the law, and was now able to control (block) its execution. If it was the BSP's intention to approve the law in Parliament and consequently block the law to show its inefficiency – as we have argued above – the strategy worked well. It might have worked too well.

The October 1991 elections

Growing frustration with implementation of the land law and with the inability of Parliament to deal with other urgent problems seems to have radicalized the electorate in the summer of 1991. While many polls indicated between 5 and 9 percent of the votes went to several of the centrist parties, the actual vote showed that none of these parties received more than the 4 percent minimum required vote.[17] This left 25 percent of the electorate unrepresented in Parliament and created a stalemate between two radically opposing parties, with the MRF on the side holding the necessary seats to form a majority. The radicalized UDF, which without its two largest blocks captured 35 percent of the votes, came out strongly in the elections. However, the BSP was also surprisingly strong, holding on to 33 percent of the vote, deriving large parts of its support from the rural areas (Engelbrekt and Perry, 1991; Davidova, 1994).

The results of the elections changed two critical factors. First, the disappearance of the political center left the way open for the UDF to pursue its radical policy if it could gain the MRF's support which was likely, since the MRF was very much opposed to the BSP, because the BSP had stirred up nationalist tendencies in regions with mixed ethnic groups. Second, the UDF realized that (a) unless it succeeded in developing a widespread support base beyond the urban centers it could never obtain the majority, and (b) maybe even worse, unless somehow the support base of the BSP (through its hold on the rural areas) could be substantially reduced, the BSP would continue to threaten the reform measures. The UDF realized that the choice of agricultural privatization program could play an important role in this. Even if it would not provide the UDF with a 'natural support base' outside the main urban center, a radical land reform program, if well implemented, would have a reasonable chance of breaking the existing social and economic structure, which formed the backbone of the BSP's organizational strength in the rural areas, and, thus, of securing democratic and economic reforms.

Asset distribution, organization, and social classes. Since 1989, the BSP's support base had gradually retreated to areas of ethnic tension and outlying provinces. However, in the 1991 elections the erosion of BSP support was relatively limited even in most rural areas, including rich agricultural regions where an alliance existed between the relatively affluent population and well-organized socialist structures opposed to restitution of land to private owners (Dainov, 1992). The previous indicates the importance of developing of such a support base and organizational structure for political parties. The process of land reform could affects this in two ways. First, the process of privatization affects the distribution of asset endowments in society. As such, it affects the distribution of economic interests throughout society and will determine social classes, based on endowment ownership and, hence, future political alignments. Second, it affects the main organizational structure of the rural areas, which was the base for the BSP's organizational advantage. The impact of this discrepancy was reflected in the way the electorate could be mobilized and influenced.

The development of a middle class. The UDF's normal support base has been the middle class. However, as Dimitrov (1991a) claims,

> In Bulgaria the civil revolution preceeded the civil evolution. The change was inititated and is still represented by a political movement for civil rights, which, however, does not have the natural power base of such a movement: the middle class of citizens. The middle class is a reference group extrinsic to Bulgarian society. Its values are taken over by strata living around the poverty line. These values are convincingly defensible only in name of future interests: on the condition that the reforms work and the strata get richer.

The logical beneficiaries of market reforms, i.e., the emerging business class, did not provide a guaranteed support base for the UDF. To the contrary, during the Dimitrov government, UDF relations not only with the trade unions, but also with company directors and the slowly rising number of private businessmen, worsened. Since many emerging managers and businessmen had nomenklatura backgrounds, the anti-Communist UDF was generally suspicious of this group and its demands. Viewing businessmen as natural allies of the BSP, the UDF alienated many of them by calling for the reinforcement of taxation authorities and for an offensive against illegal and black-market operations (Engelbrekt, 1992c). Therefore, it seems logical that the UDF was focusing on the restoration of the pre-Communist property owners as its 'natural' long-term support base. Pre-Communist distribution of land was very egalitarian (Lampe and Jackson, 1982). The restoration of property rights in real boundaries would create a large class of small-to-middle-size property owners (Buckwell et al., 1994), a class that could become a reliable support base for the UDF.

In many cases, however, division among heirs of the previous owners might make the property too small to encourage an aspiring 'middle class'.[18] Still, even if it took time to develop a middle class, the UDF might consider it a safe base in the long-term for preserving the anti-Communist stance of the government. This would be consistent with Hungtington's (1968) claim, 'No social group is more conservative than a landowning peasantry' (see also Prosterman and Riedinger, 1987). The emerging unified agrarian party under the leadership of Anastasia Moser seemed to be close to this position: 'The middle class is the basis of democracy worldwide and there can be no democracy in Bulgaria without it. That is why land restitution and privatization are so vital. It is the farming sector that will allow the emergence of a solid middle class: people owning private property which makes them independent' (Radeva, 1993).

Political organization. The overwhelming influence of the Communist organization for the past forty years has left the BSP with well-organized structures throughout the country, while the UDF and other parties are still searching to establish such structures, especially in the countryside. Unlike other CECs, in Bulgaria alternative structures were nonexistent because the opposition lacked connections in the economy, or in cultural and political life.[19] Opposition figures lacked the experience of inter-institutional confrontation because they often came from structures loyal to the party-state (Dimitrov, 1991a). The process of privatization would affect the post-reform economic, social, and political institutions and organizational arrangements. For example, the social and political organization in Bulgaria's rural areas used to rely on the economic organization. The manager of the farm unit was part of the political leadership of the area and important in the social structure, if only because of the farm's near monopoly in regional employment. While the opposition parties have tried and succeeded in setting up local chapters of their parties, the relative success of the BSP in maintaining political support in most of the rural areas must partly be attributed to the maintainance of the old organizational structure. Economic organization plays a key role in rural political organization.[20] Therefore, one of the keys to reducing the support base of the BSP was to destroy a crucial part of the political organization, i.e., the collective farm organization, as the main economic and social structure in the rural areas.

A radical land reform attacks three key strategies of the radical UDF factions. It seriously damages the organizational structure from which the BSP has derived its remarkable electoral strength. It creates a long-term political support base for the reformers and for the reforms. Finally, it removes the nomenklatura from positions key to blocking implementation of the reforms and so ensures a succesful reform.

Soon after the October 1991 elections, the UDF determined to transform the political and economic scene, formed a new government with the silent support of the MRF. The absence of a political center allowed the UDF to pursue its radical program. One of their priorities was breaking the deadlock in the land reform process and pushing the land restitution process through in its most radical form. The LALOLU was substantially amended in March 1992, to remove many of the original restrictions included in the first version. The amended law stipulated that reinstatement of property be done within the real boundaries where these still existed or could be easily reestablished. Where boundaries of land no longer existed, reinstatement of ownership was to be done within real boundaries of farmland of equivalent area in compliance with a plan of farmland division. The law specified that all farm structures under the former system be removed by liquidating all collective farm units. Of great importance, the amended law included detailed specifications on how to implement the law. The amended LALOLU further stipulated that transactions for transfer of assets concluded by the collective farms after 1 January, 1990 be declared null and void and that outsiders manage the collective and its liquidation until this process was completed (Davidova, 1994).[21]

Once the amendments were approved, the BSP shifted its attention to the rural areas, where it tried to prevent the liquidation councils from taking office, the administration from handling the claims, and potential farmers from leaving the collective farm (Nikolaev, 1992b).

Insistence on implementation of the UDF's radical economic program increasingly created tension within and outside the UDF, eventually contributing to the fall of the Dimitrov government. A crucial factor was that the Turkish minority in Bulgaria was overwhelmingly agricultural in occupation. The Turkish people in rural areas had little to expect in terms of land titles, as they were not to receive any land and were among the hardest hit. In great part because of this, it became increasingly difficult for the MRF leadership to support the UDF's policies.[22]

The Berov government: a shift to the center

Because of it relied on BSP support, the Berov government did not stimulate land reform with the same eagerness as the previous UDF government. This was reflected in two amendments to the land law, intended to stimulate credit supply for the agricultural sector, including for collective farms under liquidation. This move was a clear departure from the Dimitrov government, which had refused to provide credit subsidies for farms under liquidation (Swinnen, 1994).

In addition, many members of the liquidation councils installed under the UDF government were replaced (according to one source, more than 75 percent of the LC chairpersons). While some replacements might have been for technical reasons, the scale of this change reflects the political importance of the LCs, which were responsible for division of the collective farm assets and for farm liquidations. The liquidation council's role in the reform process is further confirmed by the fact that after the 1994 elections, when the BSP obtained a majority, the Videnov government abolished the LCs.

The Videnov government: Orsov cooperatives and flying troikas

After obtaining a majority in the December 1994 elections, the BSP government introduced several amendments to the LALOLU (see appendix 5.1). In May 1995 substantial amendments were passed through the National Assembly. In fact, some 50 percent of the LALOLU regulations were amended (BBN). In general these amendments ruled out most of the Dimitrov government's March 1992 amendments and returned to the spirit of the original 1991 law. The reasons given for the amendment proposals stressed the disruptive character of the reforms: the fragmentation of land and rapid decrease in the value of nonland assets of organizations under liquidation due to lack of incentives for the liquidation councils to preserve them.

The amendments were passed by the National Assembly, but rejected by the Bulgarian president on legal grounds and returned for an additional reading to the National Assembly. Despite the president's reaction, the National Assembly passed the amended land law again, with only minor changes. In June 1995 the Constitutional Court rejected several texts of the amendments as anticonstitutional.

Three amendments were not ruled out by the Constitutional Court that are particularly relevant to the farming structures and the future of agricultural reform (Davidova, 1995; Davidova et al., 1997).[23]

One adopted amendment introduced an administrative procedure for the removal of farms under liquidation from the court registers. The liquidation councils were also to be removed. This amendment made it up to the eligible owners to identify physical or legal persons to determine the share of each owner and allocate the assets. This to some extent was intended to restart the process, thereby impeding the move from unrestored property to effective and full private property rights.

There could be complications with the indebtedness of farms under liquidation that could increase problems in agriculture. The law did not provide for the collection of debts, but only stated that for the next three years creditors could decrease their taxable profit by the amounts due by the farms under liquidation. This provision seemed unlikely to satisfy the creditors,

146

mainly commercial banks, and could further undermine their willingness to give loans to agriculture.

The liquidation of the liquidation councils apparently served three purposes. First, it got rid of this UDF-created institution and its role, which was defined by law. Second, it cleared the debts of farms under liquidation. Third, it allowed the cooperatives under liquidation to register as private cooperatives, and to distribute assets to them. For these reasons, the UDF parliamentary group (1995) objected that

> on the one hand the existing property will be transferred to the management of the new cooperatives as representatives of the majority of those present at the 'general assembly'. On the other hand the immediate termination of the liquidation councils will result in easy disappearance of all assets, funds, and documentation and, what is more important, to the termination and disappearance of the legal body, subject to sanctions from the creditors of the cooperative. The chaos created by this act will undoubtedly lead finally to the necessity of the state to pardon the debts of the cooperatives (as it has done before).

The second important amendment opened the door for the municipal land commissions to initiate revisions of their decision to recognize the ownership when they saw errors. The danger posed by this amendment was that a large reviewing process would start. It could also lock the bulk of property rights to agriculture assets in uncertainty.

The third amendment concerned the land market by introducing legal requirements for prioritizing purchasers. The seller of land would not be free to sell to whomever offered the highest price. He would have to offer the land, in the following order, to: the neighbors, agricultural producers in the same settlement, the municipality, the State, all others. In settlements whith a shortage of land for landless producers or for compensation of owners, the State is obliged by this amendment to buy the land offered. These amendments obviously will impede the development of the land market, which is a difficult process anyway given the slow pace of the issue of notarial deeds.

These and other amendments (see appendix 5.1) clearly restricted the transfer of property rights from the state and collective farms under liquidation to former owners. Property rights were defined imperfectly, and co-ownership was introduced. The major beneficiaries of these amendments would be former collective farm managers and landless rural workers, both important in the BSP constituency. Not surprisingly, the amendments were heavily opposed by the UDF, who argued that they would limit private ownership, impose severe restrictions on ownership, use, and exchange of agricultural land, and that they were in conflict with the Bulgarian constitution.

The introduction of these laws created legal uncertainty regarding the status of the former collective farms under liquidation, run by a three-member committee elected by the cooperative members, the so-called flying troika. These committees took over the cooperative management and transformation work.

Ownership disputes have continued after the privatization, partly due to the new amendmends. Besides individual farms, two groups of new producer cooperatives have emerged: 'blue' and 'red' cooperatives. The color refers to their political association: blue for the UDF and red for the BSP. The red cooperatives are also referred to as 'Orsov cooperatives', after Zlatko Orsov, the BSP member of the National Assembly who played a key role in the 1995 BSP amendmends.

The main distinction between blue and red cooperatives is their attitude towards individual onwership (Davidova et al., 1997). The blue cooperatives use well-identified privately owned assets and try to give a fair return to land, labour and capital. In contrast, Orsov cooperatives continue the practice of the former collectives where members were owners on paper, but were deprvived of most effictive property rights.

Orsov cooperatives work on land in 'ideal' boundaries, meaning that the land is privately owned, but that property rights are not defined on a specifically determined piece of land. The advantage of this approach is that it may allow for some land consolidation when members want to leave. However, the system has an inherent incentive for the management of the farms to maintain the system based on ideal boundaries, for its effect on property rights distribution, and because it increases exit costs and therefore discourages members wanting to leave the cooperative.

Conclusion

This chapter explains agricultural reform legislation and, more specifically, property rights restitution and collective farm transformation policies as the outcome of a political bargaining game between radical reformers (politically represented in the UDF) and people opposed to land restitution and radical decollectivization (mainly represented by the BSP). The interaction between reform choice and political strength has gone two ways: reform impacts have affected political preferences, and thus parliamentary equilibria, while vote distribution has affected policies.

The hold on power by the BSP until 1991 postponed any substantial reform. The results of the October 1991 elections (including the disappearance of the political center from Parliament) allowed radical reformers in the UDF to push through very radical reform legislation, including the removal of collective farm management from the reform-implementing institutions. A radical land reform addressed three key strategies of the radical UDF factions: (a) it damaged the organizational structure from which the BSP had been deriving its remarkable electoral strength; (b) it created a long-term political support base for the reforms; and (c) it removed the existing management from key positions to block the implementation of the reforms.

This radical policy contributed to a reduction in support for the UDF government, leading to its fall in 1992. Since then, the BSP has gradually recovered government control. By 1994, the recovery of the BSP has allowed this party to weaken many of the reform effects and to change property rights redistribution to an approach more favorable for BSP constituents, i.e., former collective farm management and landless rural workers.

Notes

1. For a general review of agricultural policy reform in Bulgaria, see Schmitz et al. (1994). For a general review of political economy issues in economic reform in Bulgaria, see Bogetic and Hillman (1995a). For an excellent formal model of the interaction of political and economic factors in Bulgarian agrarian reform, see Lyons et al. (1994).

2. The concept of 'flying' toikas refers to the shaky legal basis of the committees. Orsov is the main agent behind the new legislation and policies, a BSP member of Parliament.

3. The ethnic Turks make up around 10 percent of the approximately 8.6 million Bulgarians and are overwhelmingly located in the rural areas, largely depending on agricultural production. Until recently Turks lived and worked in tightly knit ethnic communites. Economically Turks generally did well until recently, when their traditional agricultural economy began breaking down. In the Kardzhali region, for example, where Turks constituted about 70 percent of the population in mid-1992 (which may have since declined because of emigration), tobacco growing, the region's main agricultural activity, is on the verge of collapse. The quality of life is plummeting and the rate of unemployment is among the highest in the country. Because of its economic downturn, Turks have begun migrating from rural to urban areas and from there to cities in Turkey.

   In addition, 600,000 to 800,000 Gypsies (Roma) and 250,000 to 300,000 Pomaks live in Bulgaria. The social and economic problems of the Roma have always been more severe than those of any other group. Since the fall of communism, their conditions have further deteriorated. Barred from registering as an ethnic-based party and thwarted by internal division, the

Roma have not been able to organize polically and have mostly supported the BSP. Pomaks are descendants of Bulgarian Slavs whose forebears converted to Islam under Turkish occupation. They speak Bulgarian and live mostly in the Rhodope Mountains and the Lovech area. They are typically agriculturalists who constitute a religious rather than an ethnic group. The Pomaks in the Rhodope region depend chiefly on tobacco growing for their livelihood (Engelbrekt, 1991e; Ilchev and Perry, 1993; Troxel, 1993).

4   Two agrarian parties emerged in the post-1989 political landscape. Both claimed to be the rightful heir to the Bulgarian Agricultural National Union (BANU), founded in 1899 and experiencing its 'finest hour' under the leadership of Alexander Stamboliyski, who was assassinated in 1923. After the Communist takeover in 1944, part of BANU joined the Communist-led Fatherland Front and remained a faithful ally of the BCP for the next 45 years. They were rewarded with parliamentary seats and ministerial posts. In 1989, this faction dismissed its long-time leader and tried to shed its Communist past. It participated in the June 1990 elections as the independent party BANU and gaining 16 seats.

Some of the BANU leaders who opposed the Communist takeover in 1944 escaped in exile. At home, a remaining BANU faction under Nikola Petkov emerged as the main opposition force to the BCP and the Fatherland Front after 1944. However, the movement was crushed in the following years, and Petkov was executed in 1947. Several of the BANU leaders who had been persecuted reemerged in 1989 and created the BANU-Nikola Petkov Party. By April 1990 it claimed to have 120,000 members. Like many of its leading personalities, leader Milan Drenchev had spent several years in concentration camps. Any attempts to unite this party with the official BANU party to create a large agrarian party strong enough to present an alternative to the BSP and the UDF were blocked by those with old ties to the BSP. In the meantime, BANU-Nikola Petkov joined the UDF and won 34 seats in the UDF caucus in 1990 (Nikolaev, 1992a, 1993; Penev, 1992; Radeva, 1993).

5   Zhelev was unanimously elected. On the motivation of the BSP to elect Zhelev, while being in the majority, see Grigorova (1991).

6   See note 4.

7   The MRF had no ministers, a very sensitive issue in Bulgaria. The BSP campaigned heavily on anti-Turkish sentiments, aligning itself with small nationalist parties. The UDF, afraid to lose support on nationalist grounds, anted to avoid any indication that the MRF wielded too much influence in the government.

8 On 24 September, 1992 the MRF joined the BSP in removing Stefan Savov, the hard-line UDF member of Parliament as chairman of Parliament.

9 Of 110 UDF representatives, 23 voted in favor of Berov's government. Late March 1993, 19 of them set up their own caucus in the National Assembly: the New Union for Democracy. Several conservative BSP members voted against the government to protest the participation of MRF members in the government. Radical UDF members called the BSP-MRF alliance an 'unholy coalition' because of the earlier aggressive nationalist stance of the BSP, e.g., attempting to ban the MRF from participating in the elections (Engelbrekt, 1993a).

10 On divisions within the BSP, including the fight between reformers and conservatives, see Engelbrekt and Nikolaev (1992).

11 Pirgova (1991) further argues that the doctrinaires within the BCP found themselves in the position of dissidents under the old regime. The authorities were as intolerant of them as they were of advocates for the Western way of life. She claims that that is why doctrinaires who enjoyed the reputation of dissidents have fit into political life since 1989.

12 The BCP members who took part in the 1984-85 forced assimilation of ethnic Turks have been the fiercest opponents of the democratization process. They also tried to infiltrate nationalist parties that could provide a cover-up for their crimes, while at the same time inciting ethnic unrest in mixed population regions to stir nationalist sentiments (Pirgova, 1991).

13 See note 4.

14 Representatives of the UDF often emphasized that it was only a temporary coalition, to be dissolved as soon as communism lost its grip on Bulgarian society. Others said the UDF had become more like one party. Initially, the official UDF position, repeated by all its leading representatives was that the different political and ideological outlooks it embraced did not hamper close cooperation and need not be concealed from the voters (Engelbrekt, 1991b). For an overview and discussion of the different member groups, see Penev (1992) and Dimitrov (1991a).

15 For more details on the LALOLU, see Buckwell et al. (1994). For a more recent discussion, see Davidova et al. (1997).

16 Among the most controversial items in the new constitution was the prohibition of political parties with a primary ethnic or religious agenda, a statement clearly focused at blocking the MRF from participating in elections. While the MRF was originally prevented (by court) from participating in the October 1991 elections, pressure from the West seems to have induced Bulgaria's Supreme Court to allow the MRF to participate (Engelbrekt, 1991e).

17 The election results also had a dramatic impact on the agrarian parties. Efforts to unite the two agrarian parties (BANU and BANU-Nikola Petkov) gained momentum in the spring of 1991 when general elections were announced. First, a returned emigrant from France, Tsenko Barev, succeeded in capturing the leadership of BANU and in convincing some members of BANU-Nikola Petkov to join his party, now called BANU-United. Disagreement on substantial issues and on the distribution of the election slots with the right-wing parties within the UDF coalition induced most remaining BANU-Nikola Petkov members to go into the October 1991 election as an independent party. However, both parties failed to make the 4 percent election required to be represented in Parliament. This was a surprising result, as polls had forecasted 8.5 percent for BANU-United and 4.7 percent for BANU-Nikola Petkov (Engelbrekt and Perrry, 1991).

The electoral disaster strengthened the unionist forces. However, the personal ambitions of the main leaders blocked unification. It was only after Andriana Dimitrova-Moser, daughter of one of the main exiled BANU leaders, returned from exile that Drenchev was removed as BANU-Nikola Petkov leader and Barev was ousted from the BANU-United leadership. Under Dimitrova-Moser's leadership both parties united as BANU in late 1992. Although most of BANU's support was in the countryside, it hoped to become a rallying place for all those dissatisfied with the two chief antagonists on the Bulgarian political scene (Nikolaev, 1993; Radeva 1993). Ultimately, BANU joined forces with the Democratic Party, a centrist group that split from the UDF to create the Popular Union, gaining 18 seats in the 1994 elections (table 5.2).

18 The 'traditional conservative tendency of rural voters seems to work against the UDF now. However the reason is not entirely clear. Conservatism is usually attributed to landownership, which is not the case here. There might be some general conservatism; one factor for which might be that there is a majority of elderly people and women in rural areas, people who might be relatively hard hit by reforms and rely strongly on the existing social security system.

19 The use of existing social or cultural organizations to politically organize rural areas was also important in Western Europe at the turn of the century. For example, in Belgium and France, the existing organization of the Catholic Church played a crucial role in helping right-wing political parties capture the rural electorate. It is remarkable how former Communist parties won the first free elections only in the parts of Eastern Europe with a predominant Eastern Orthodox culture. Penev (1991) argues that while the pervasive influence of the Communist party in social, economic, and political life was overwhelming everywhere in the CECs, those CECs not

influenced by Eastern Orthodox churches went through more dramatic political destabilization, because of their traditionally close links to Europe and independent religions. The public opinion in Catholic or Protestant countries regarded the ruling Communist Party as national traitors. In contrast, the prevailing religion in Bulgaria is Eastern Orthodox Christianity, and religion in Bulgaria has been a part of ideology tightly controlled by politics. In Bulgaria, religious destabilization was just as unlikely as political destabilization because religion had a low social standing and the governing institutions of the church were bound up with the Communist state (Dimitrov, 1991a).

20 There is an analogy here with Olson's (1965) 'social byproduct theory' on the importance of economic incentives to hold political organization (of, e.g., farmers) together (see also de Gorter and Swinnen, 1995).

21 According to Nikolaev (1992b) one of the articles most hotly disputed by the socialist opposition was one obliging citizens to give up land that the Communist regime had placed at their disposal even though it was not officially their property. (The original LALOLU explicitly stated that these people would be allowed to keep such land.) Although this issue concerned less than 1 percent of Bulgaria's total arable land, the BSP was particularly sensitive about it, since a large number of plots were handed out to members of the former nomenklatura, who had built houses on them. The amended version of the law included detailed specifications for how to determine property rights in cases where buildings have been erected on such land.

22 Davidova also indicates that 'despite the fact that until the autumn of 1992 the MRF tended to support the UDF and afterwards has been in a silent coalition with BSP, there have been several ad hoc coalitions formed on the basis of different proposals for reform process'.

23 One amendment that was rejected provided for former owners to be restituted only up to the area they had pooled into collective farms and state farms, and any state-cooperative organizations formed on the basis of those farms. During the forced collectivization, people tried to declare less than they owned in order to keep some land out of the collective farms. The amendment proposed that even if they had documents for the total land area, only what was recorded as land contributed to collective farms would be recognized for restitution.

References

BBN (Bulgarian Business News), various issues.

Bogetic, Z. and Hillman, A. (eds.) (1995a), *Financing Government in the Transition: Bulgaria. The Political Economy of Tax Policies, Tax Bases, and Tax Evasion*, World Bank Regional and Sectoral Studies, The World Bank: Washington DC.

Bogetic, Z. and Hillman, A. (1995b), 'Privatizing Profits of Bulgaria's State Enterprises', *Transition*, March, pp. 4-7.

Buckwell, A., Davidova, S. and Trendafilov, R. (1994), 'Land Reform: How Will the Future Look?', in Schmitz, A., Moulton, K., Buckwell, A. and Davidova, S. (eds.), *Privatization of Agriculture in New Market Economies: Lessons from Bulgaria*, Kluwer Academic Publishers: Boston, London, and Dordrecht.

Dainov, E. (1992), 'Bulgaria: Politics after the October 1991 Elections', *RFE/RL Research Report*, 10 January, Vol. 1, No. 3, pp. 12-16.

Davidova, S. (1994), 'Changes in Agricultural Policies and Restructuring of Bulgarian Agriculture', in Swinnen, J. (ed.), *Policy and Institutional Changes in Central European Agriculture*, Avebury: Aldershot

Davidova, S. (1995), 'Review of Agricultural Policy and Trade Developments in Bulgaria in 1995', paper presented at the OECD Ad Hoc Group of Experts on East-West Agriculture, Paris, 4 October 1995.

Davidova, S., Buckwell, A. and Kopeva, D. (1997), 'Bulgaria: Economics and Politics of Post-Reform Farm Structures', in Swinnen, J., Buckwell, A. and Mathijs, E. (eds.), *Agricultural Privatization, Land Reform and Farm Restructuring in Central and Eastern Europe*, Avebury: Aldershot.

de Gorter, H. and Swinnen, J. (1995), 'The Economic Polity of Farm Policy: Reply', *Journal of Agricultural Economics*, Vol. 46, No. 3, pp. 403-414.

de Janvry, A. (1981), 'The Role of Land Reform in Economic Development: Policies and Politics', *American Journal of Agricultural Economics*, May, Vol. 63, pp. 384-392.

Dimitrov, R. (1991a), 'Formation of the Bulgarian Opposition 1989-1991', *Bulgarian Quarterly*, No. 1, pp. 53-65.

Dimitrov, R. (1991b), 'Formation of the Bulgarian Opposition 1989-1991 (Continued)', *Bulgarian Quarterly*, No. 2, pp. 43-52.

Engelbrekt, K. (1991a), 'The Grand National Assembly to Adopt a New Constitution', *Report on Eastern Europe*, 19 April, pp. 5-9.

Engelbrekt, K. (1991b), 'Cracks in the Union of Democratic Forces', *Report on Eastern Europe*, 17 May, pp. 1-5.

Engelbrekt, K. (1991c), 'Constitution Adopted, Elections Set', *Report on Eastern Europe*, 16 August, pp. 1-5.

Engelbrekt, K. (1991d), 'Economic Reform: Results and Prospects', *Report on Eastern Europe*, 23 August, pp. 1-7.

Engelbrekt, K. (1991e), 'The Movement for Rights and Freedom to Compete in Elections', *Report on Eastern Europe*, 4 October, pp. 1-5.

Engelbrekt, K. (1991f), 'Opposition Narrowly Defeats Socialists in National Elections', *Report on Eastern Europe*, 25 October, pp. 1-5.

Engelbrekt, K. (1992a), 'New Bulgarian Government Hopes to End Delays', *RFE/RL Research Report*, Vol. 1, No. 17, 24 April, pp. 80-84.

Engelbrekt, K. (1992b), 'Bulgaria's Communist Legacy: Settling Old Scores', *RFE/RL Research Report*, Vol. 1, No. 28, 10 July, pp. 6-10.

Engelbrekt, K. (1992c), 'The Fall of Bulgaria's First non-Communist Government, *RFE/RL Research Report*, Vol. 1, No. 45, 13 November, pp. 1-6.

Engelbrekt, K. (1993a), 'Technocrats Dominate New Bulgarian Government', *RFE/RL Research Report*, Vol. 2, No. 4, 22 January, pp. 1-5.

Engelbrekt, K. (1993b), Bulgaria's Communists: Coming or Going?, *RFE/RL Research Report*, Vol. 2, No. 21, 21 May, pp. 37-41.

Engelbrekt, K. and Nikolaev, R. (1992), 'Bulgaria: Socialist Party Elects New Leader', *Report on Eastern Europe*, 17 January, pp. 27-31.

Engelbrekt K. and Perry, D. M. (1991), 'The Run-up to the National Elections: Politics and Parties', *Report on Eastern Europe*, 11 October, pp. 4-8.

Genchev, N. (1991), 'The Liberal Alternative of the Post-Totalitarian Society', *Bulgarian Quarterly*, No. 3, pp. 44-56.

Grigorova, L. (1991), 'Political Institutions and Stability', *Bulgarian Quarterly*, No. 1, pp. 66-77.

Hayami, Y. (1991), 'Land Reform', in Meier, G. (ed.), *Politics and Policy Making in Developing Countries. Perspectives on the New Political Economy*, ICS Press: San Francisco.

Hungtington, S. (1968), *Political Order in Changing Societies*, Yale University Press: New Haven.

Ilchev, I. and Perry, D. M. (1993), 'Bulgarian Ethnic Groups: Politics And Perception', *RFE/RL Research Report*, Vol. 2, No. 12, pp. 35-41.

Jackson, M. (1991a) 'The Rise and Decay of the Socialist Economy in Bulgaria', *Journal of Economic Perspectives*, Vol. 5, No. 4, pp. 203-209.

Jackson, M. (1991b), 'The Dangers of Procrastination in the Transition from Socialism to Capitalism', *Report on Eastern Europe*, 12 April, pp. 1-7.

Junguito, R. (1991), 'Comment', in Meier, G. (ed.), *Politics and Policy Making in Developing Countries. Perspectives on the New Political Economy*, ICS Press: San Francisco.

Lampe, J. R. and Jackson, M. R. (1982), *Balkan Economic History 1550-1950*, Indiana University Press: Bloomington.

Lyons, R., Rausser, G. and Simon, L. (1994), 'Disruption and Continuity in Bulgaria's Agrarian Reform', in Schmitz, A., Moulton, K., Buckwell, A., and Davidova, S. (eds.), *Privatization of Agriculture in New Market Economies: Lessons from Bulgaria*, Kluwer Academic Publishers: Boston, London, and Dordrecht.

Minchev, O., Young, D. and Prigorova, M. (1991), 'Editorial Comment', *Bulgarian Quarterly*, No. 2, pp. 5-10.

Nikolaev, R. (1991), 'The New Law on Farmland, *Report on Eastern Europe*, 3 May, pp. 1-4.

Nikolaev, R. (1992a), 'Union and Disunion among Bulgaria's Agrarian Parties', *RFE/RL Research Report*, Vol. 1, No. 12, 20 March, pp. 1-6.

Nikolaev, R. (1992b), 'Bulgarian Farmland Law Seeks to Hasten Privatization', *RFE/RL Research Report*, Vol. 1, No. 21, 22 May, p.30-33.

Nikolaev, R. (1993), 'Bulgaria and Its Emigrants: Past and Present', *RFE/RL Research Report*, Vol. 2, No. 27, 2 July, pp. 51-56.

Olson, M. (1965), *The Logic of Collective Action,* Harvard University Press: Cambridge.

Penev, V. (1991), 'Chances of Political Stability', *Bulgarian Quarterly*, No. 1, pp. 44-52.

Penev, V. (1992), 'Platforms of Political Centre Parties and Coalitions in the 1991 Election Campaign', *The Bulgarian Watcher*, pp. 45-47.

Perry, D. M. (1991), 'Minorities and Bulgarian Nationalism', *Report on Eastern Europe*, 13 December, pp. 5-9.

Pirgova, M. (1991), 'Political Forces' Motivation and Conduct', *Bulgarian Quarterly*, No. 1, pp. 32-43.

Prosterman, R. L. and Riedinger, J. M. (1987), *Land Reform and Democratic Development*, The Johns Hopkins University Press: Baltimore and London.

Radeva, N. (1993), 'Market Economy Starts from Farming: Interview with Agrarian Leader Anastasia Moser', *Bulgarian Economic Review*, 4-17 June, p 5.

Schmitz, A., Moulton, K., Buckwell, A. and Davidova, S. (1994), *Privatization of Agriculture in New Market Economies: Lessons from Bulgaria*, Kluwer Academic Publishers: Boston, London, and Dordrecht.

Swinnen, J. (1994), 'Political Economy of Reform in Bulgarian Agriculture', in Schmitz, A., Moulton, K., Buckwell, A. and Davidova, S. (eds.), *Privatization of Agriculture in New Market Economies: Lessons from Bulgaria*, Kluwer Academic Publishers: Boston, London, and Dordrecht.

Swinnen, J. (1996), 'On Policy Induced Transfers in the Bulgarian Agro-Food Chain: The Case of the Wheat-Flour-Bread Chain', unpublished manuscript, Department of Agricultural Economics, K.U.Leuven.

Troxel, L. (1993), 'Bulgaria's Gypsies: Numerically Strong, Politically Weak', *RFE/RL Research Report*, Vol. 2, No. 27, pp. 58-60.

Wyzan, M. L. (1992), 'Bulgaria: Shock Therapy Followed by a Steep Recession', *RFE/RL Research Report*, Vol. 1, No. 45, pp. 46-53.

Appendix 5.1
Some of the amendments to the Land Law, May 1995

Land market

The owners can sell land to the state at prices fixed by the Council of Ministers. The Minister of Agriculture announces in the State Gazette the names of settlements in which there is a need for land for allocation to landless people, for compensation to landowners for lost land, or for other purposes. When an owner offers land to the state in these settlements, the state cannot decline to buy it. If the owner would like to sell the land at other than regulated prices, he has to prioritize buyers in the following way: neighboring landowners, agricultural producers in the same settlement, other buyers.

Compensation

Compensation of owners for lost land from the state or municipal land reserves is prioritized in the following order: agriculturalists and other people under 35 who make a commitment to be agricultural producers for 10 years; people engaged in agriculture in the settlement in which land for compensation is given; members of cooperatives or farming companies in the same settlement; others who are eligible for compensation.

Liquidation of former collectives

With enforcement of the amended law, all liquidation committees terminate their activity and farms under liquidation are removed from the regional court registers. People having rights to share the assets of the farms under liquidation are co-owners of these assets. They can transfer these rights to the cooperative or the company they are involved with, which will act on their behalf. The other option is that the general assembly of the co-owners chooses a physical or legal entity which will divide the assets among eligible owners. For a period of three years the banks, other legal entities, and sole traders can decrease the amount of taxable profit by the amount they have to collect from the former farms under liquidation.

MLC decisions

The Municipal Land Commission (MLC) can amend its decision for the recognition of ownership in case of factual mistakes. The revision of the decision could be required by the owner or could be initiated by the MLC.

Permanent crops

For areas under permanent crops, rice, and irrigation facilities, separate land reallocation plans have to be developed. The owners must not destroy them before their full depreciation.

Landownership by foreigners

The possibility of joint ventures with over 50 percent Bulgarian participation in owning agricultural land is abolished. Agricultural land cannot be jointly owned.

Source: Davidova, 1995.

6 Process and politics of agricultural privatization in the Czech and Slovak republics

Isabelle Lindemans[1]

Introduction

This chapter discusses the political economy of land reform and agricultural privatization in former Czechoslovakia. More specifically, it focuses on how the political debate and the agricultural reform process was influenced by post-1989 political and economic developments, by Czechoslovakian history, and by pre-Communist distribution of landownership.

Although in 1993 Czechoslovakia split into the Czech Republic and the Slovak Republic, this study considers the agricultural restitution and transformation policies for Czechoslovakia as a whole, for three reasons:

1 The most important legislation on agricultural reform was passed before the split of the country.

2 After the split this legislation remained in the two republics.

3 As a consequence, although political developments were fairly different in the Slovak and the Czech republics, agricultural reform in both was characterized by an extensive restitution program and an agricultural transformation strategy more disruptive than in Hungary, but probably less disruptive than in countries such as Bulgaria and Romania.

The reform-minded Czech and Slovak governments could not resist the political demand for land restitution for historical reasons. At the same time, they were concerned about the disruptive effects of agricultural reform, which they tried to minimize. The more radical proposals for agricultural transformation and restitution were supported by the Christian democratic parties, who attempted to create a social and economic structure closer to

Church ideology because this would change the future political alignment of the rural electorate. A stronger Church organization in rural areas would facilitate the political organization of the Christian democratic parties. This was attempted in two ways: (1) by demanding restitution for the Church and (2) by supporting a more radical transformation of agricultural entreprises, which remained strong Communist support bases after November 1989.

This chapter is organized as follows. The first section describes the different land reforms after World War I. The second section gives an overview of political changes after November 1989 (see also appendix 6.1). The last section discusses the agricultural reform in relation to Czechoslovakian postwar agricultural and political history and more recent political and economic developments.

Historical perspective of agricultural reforms

The state of Czechoslovakia was formed in 1919 following the division of the Austro-Hungarian Empire after World War I. Unlike the Czech lands (Moravia and Bohemia), Slovakia had been under Hungarian governance for centuries. Like other East European nations emerging from the Austro-Hungarian and Ottoman empires, Czechoslovakia was governed by a democratic regime, comparable to Western democracies. Contrary to most other CEECs, however, Czechoslovakia had a relatively stable democracy. Except for the years 1926-1929, the coalition governments during the interwar period were formed of the same five largest parties (*Petka*). According to Okey (1986), one of the factors that helped Czechoslovakia maintain a democracy was the Agrarian Party's mediation between right and left parties. The Agrarian Party was the largest party in interwar politics. While their original constituency was the Czech and Slovak peasantry, they had support as well from the middle classes.

Czechoslovakia was characterized by very unequal land distribution. Immediately after its independence, the Petka government started land reform. The government had two objectives: (1) breaking the power of the former foreign elite who dominated the Czechoslovakian economy (most of the large estates were owned by German landlords in the Czech lands and by Hungarian landlords in Slovakia), and (2) winning the support of the peasantry for democratic ideology (Okey, 1986; Rotschild, 1992: Wolchik, 1992). The Confiscation Act of 1919 prohibited ownership of more than 150 hectares of agricultural land or more than 250 hectares of nonagricultural land. Land exceeding this limit had to be distributed among Czech and Slovak landless peasants or smallholders. It was estimated that this act concerned approximately 34 percent of Czechoslovakia's agricultural land.

Implementation of the reform was legislated by the Distribution Act and Compensation Act of 1920. However, the government spread the implementation of the land reform out over thirty years. By 1931 only 300,000 hectares (of the more than 5 million hectares in estates larger than 100 hectares) had been transferred. Table 6.1 shows that 0.5 percent of the estates still occupied 40 percent of the total area in 1931. In the 1930s, the implementation of the laws of 1919 and 1920 gained momentum. By 1937, 4 million hectares (about 30 percent of the total area), 1.3 million of which were agricultural land (about 16 percent of total agricultural land), were transferred from large estates to landless peasants or smallholders (Kaser and Radice, 1985a; Skully, 1992; Thompson, 1993). By 1939, about 15 percent of agricultural land remained in large estates of more than 100 hectares. More than 70 percent of the agricultural land was in estates smaller than 30 hectares, both in the Czech lands and in Slovakia (see table 6.1).

After World War II, an agreement between the Soviets and Czechoslovakia banned a number of parties, based on the argument that they had collaborated with the Germans. This limited the number of parties to four in Bohemia-Moravia and two in Slovakia. All right-wing parties, including the Agrarian Party, were eliminated. The parties allowed to continue were part of the government coalition; there was no true opposition. Beginning in mid-1945, important services such as police and the armed forces were under Communist control (Wolchik, 1992).

After World War II, several changes in landownership occurred, mainly induced by the Communist Party. Immediately after the war, land confiscated under German occupation was returned to its 1939 owners. In 1945 nearly 2 million Sudeten Germans living in Czech border regions were forced to emigrate under an international agreement with the Allied Forces. Their land, together with land of other collaborators, was confiscated by the state and given to Czech peasants, many of whom had migrated from other Czech regions to the borderlands. In Slovakia, land from expelled Hungarians was given to Slovak peasants, but the 1945 land redistribution was less important in Slovakia than in the Czech lands. Approximately 1.4 million hectare agricultural land was redistributed in the Czech border lands; 100,000 hectares in the Bohemian interior, and 275,000 hectares in Slovakia. Land was distributed with a maximum of 13 hectares per recipient (Kaser and Radice, 1985b).

Migrants to the borderlands were mainly Communist supporters who received preferential treatment when land was redistributed. The result was increased support from the Czech rural population in the border regions for the Communist Party which was in charge of the Ministry of Agriculture. Strong support in these regions was one of the factors in the Communist Party's victory in the first elections after the war, held in 1946. The Communist Party gained nearly 40 percent of the Czech vote and became the largest party in the Czech lands. In Slovakia, in contrast, the Communists won only 30 percent of the vote. The Democratic Party, representing the agricultural population and the Catholic clergy, became the largest party, with 62 percent of the Slovak vote (Korbel, 1959).

Table 6.1
Land distribution in Czechoslovakia 1931-1948

Year	Holdings size (ha)	Holdings thousand	Holdings %	Acreage thousand ha	Acreage %
1931	<2	422.7	26.3	212.5	1.6
	2-5	704.0	43.8	1,869.0	13.9
	5-50	464.3	29.0	5,535.0	41.2
	50-100	7.3	0.4	505.0	3.7
	>100	8.8	0.5	5,333.8	39.6
	Total	1,607.1	100.0	13,455.3	100
1938	0.1-30				71.6 (Bohemia)
					73.5 (Moravia)
					76.4 (Slovakia)
	>30				28.4 (Bohemia)
					26.5 (Moravia)
					23.6 (Slovakia)
1939	>100				15
1948	>50		60-75		

Source: Kaser and Radice, 1985a; Statistická rocenka Republiky Ceskoslovenské - rocník, 1938; Korbel, 1977.

A law of July 1947 started another land reform, intended to fully apply the previously unsuccessful land reform of the interwar period to the larger landowners. The upper limits of 150 hectares for agricultural land and 250 hectares for nonagricultural lands were reintroduced.

In February 1948, a government crisis regarding control over the police led to the resignation of the non-Communist parties. The Communist Party formed a new government with only members of the Communist Party or

162

sympathizers selected from other parties. In March 1948, a new land reform was directed against large landholders, reducing the upper limit of holdings to 50 hectares for private ownership. The State was allowed to confiscate any land exceeding this amount (Wolchik, 1992; Kaser and Radice, 1985b).

The total area transferred under the land reforms between 1945 and 1948 was about 4.2 million hectares (agricultural and nonagricultural). Of these transferred lands, 3 million hectares belonged to Sudeten Germans and to the Hungarian minority in Slovakia, representing 36.5 percent of the total acreage of the Czech lands and 11.4 percent of the total acreage of the Slovak lands. Approximately 1.7 million hectares of agricultural land (almost a quarter of all agricultural land) was distributed among 350,000 families, most of whom were landless. The state obtained 2.5 million hectares of land, of which 0.5 million were agricultural. The land reform of 1948 particularly favored the state: 200,000 hectares of agricultural land went to private farmers, 70,000 hectares to cooperatives, and 130,000 hectares to the state. The agrarian structures emerging from these land reforms were too rapidly overturned by new agricultural reforms to allow for exact and detailed data on their respective effects. It is estimated that the share of farms between 5 and 50 hectares increased from 30 percent in 1931 to 60-75 percent in 1948, at the expense of holdings larger than 50 hectares.

However, the resulting property rights were incomplete.[2] Farmers were allowed to cultivate the newly acquired land, but they were not allowed to sell or rent it. Furthermore, the Communist Party pursued the policy of delaying the legal registration of land transfers in order to make the farmer more dependent on the Ministry of Agriculture (Korbel, 1959, 1977; Kaser and Radice, 1985a,b).

Up to this time, land reform had been directed at breaking the power of large landholders and winning rural support for Communism. The second stage of Communist agricultural reform started with the law of 1949 regulating the collectivization of agriculture. Several methods were used to push farmers into cooperatives. Individual farmers were discriminated against in the allocation of machinery. Compulsory deliveries at unfavorable prices forced many small farmers to enter the cooperative farms 'voluntary' in order to survive. Often, collectivization was achieved *manu militari*. Usually, the largest farmer in the village was expropriated or forced to sign papers giving land to the state.

Legally, land in Czechoslovakia has never been nationalized. For the most part, land was moved into cooperatives or the state farms, without a change in formal ownership, but with abolition of the right to execute effective private property rights. Initially the collectivization law of 1949 included the possibility of dividing the cooperative's income among its members, partly according to the volume and quality of work done by a member and partly according the amount of land each had brought into the cooperative. In practice, however, compensation for land brought into the cooperative was often not paid and the practice was finally abolished. In 1955 a government decree stated that all agricultural land leased by the owners to other peasants could be, by government order, put in use of a cooperative.[3] Those peasants who entered a cooperative brought with them all land they farmed, including the land they did not own. The cooperatives also employed agricultural workers who brought no land into the cooperative. As a result, a growing amount of land in the cooperatives was not owned by the cooperative members. A law of 1975 stated that the right to use agricultural land by socialist agricultural organizations was free of charge and unlimited in time and that a socialist organization was authorized to use the land to the same extent as a legal owner (Karlik, 1993).[4]

In 1956 approximately 37 percent of agricultural land was in cooperative farms, 10 percent in state farms. A remarkable expansion of the socialist agricultural sector occurred in the late 1950s. In 1960, more than 80 percent of agricultural land was in cooperatives, less than 5 percent in state farms (Kaser and Radice, 1985a). In 1989 about 68 percent of agricultural land was in cooperatives. The state farms had become more important, holding 28 percent of agricultural land. A large part of the land in state farms came from cooperative farms taken over by the state farms (Doucha, 1993; OECD, 1994).

Political changes

The November 1989 revolution

After the mass demonstrations of students in Prague and the national strike in November 1989, a new government was formed under the Communist Marian Calfa on 10 December. For the first time since 1948 the dominance of the Communist Party (CP) was broken: more than half of the members of the new government were not Communists. On 29 December 1989, Vaclav Havel was assigned president by the Federal Assembly. On 23 January 1990, the Federal Assembly passed a law which made it possible to remove deputies considered unsupportive of democratic reform. Under this law, 100 Communist deputies were replaced with deputies nominated by the opposition (Civic Forum and Public Against Violence). As a result, the Communist Party lost its majority in the Federal Assembly. In February 1990, the Federal Assembly decided to hold elections on 8 and 9 June 1990 and adopted a new electoral law (Ramkema, 1990; Pehe, 1990, 1991a).[5]

In June 1990, the Federal Assembly and the Czech and Slovak republics' National Councils were elected. An overview of the results is given in table 6.2. The political forces that had led the democratic revolution in 1989, the Czech Civic Forum (CF) and the Slovak Public Against Violence (PAV), were the decisive winners of the elections with together a majority of 170 of the 300 seats in the Federal Assembly. The CF was the largest faction with 112 seats in the Federal Assembly. The CF also gained a majority in the Czech National Council. The PAV did not get a majority in the Slovak National Council, but became the largest faction. The Communist Party received 13.6 percent of the votes and became the second largest party in the Federal Assembly and in the Czech National Council. In the Slovak National Council, the Communist Party received fewer votes than the PAV, the Christian Democratic Movement (ChDM), and the separatist Slovak National Party (SNP).

The Slovak ChDM went into the federal election in a coalition called the Christian Democratic Union (ChDU), with two Czech Christian democratic parties – the People's Party (PP) and the Christian Democratic Party (ChDP). Their political program included the transformation of Czechoslovakia as a democratic country with a free market economy. However, in contrast to the CF and PAV, the Christian democrats' program stressed the role of the Catholic Church and moral values in society. In the elections for the Federal Assembly the ChDU ended third. In the Slovak National Council the ChDM became the second strongest party, but in the Czech National Council the Christian democrats were less well represented. The difference between the two republics can be explained by the stronger Catholic tradition in Slovakia. The ChDM left the coalition immediately after the election.[6]

The consequence of these election results was that the CF and PAV held a secure position in federal and Czech politics, and that the Communists were left with little political influence. In the Slovak Republic, the position of the PAV was not as strong, but its main political rival was not the Communist Party but the ChDM. The federal government was a coalition of the CF (10 members), PAV (3 members), and the ChDM (1 member). Calfa (unaffiliated) was named prime minister. The Czech government was also dominated by the CF (16 of the 19 members), and Petr Pithart (CF) became Czech prime minister. The Slovak government was dominated by PAV. Vladimir Meciar (PAV) became Slovak prime minister. Havel was reelected president (Pehe, 1991a; Orbis, 1991a).

Table 6.2
Election results 1990

Party	Seats
a. Czech National Council	(total number of seats: 200)
CF	123
CP of Czechoslovakia	32
Society for Moravia and Silesia	22
ChDU	19
Liberal Democratic Party	4
b. Slovak National Council	(total number of seats: 150)
PAV	48
CP for Czechoslovakia	22
ChDM	31
Slovak National Party	22
Coexistence	14
Democratic Party	7
Green Party	6
c. Federal Assembly	(total number of seats: 300)
CF-PAV	170
CP of Slovakia	47
ChDU	40
Slovak National Party	15
Coexistence	12

Source: Kusin, 1990.

Party disintegration

After the elections, Czechoslovakian politics was characterized by the disintegration of the leading political movements (table 6.3). The CF and PAV were two umbrella groups for movements and individuals with a variety of political views. They had no coherent party program or internal hierarchical structures.   They were united in their opposition to the previous regime. However, soon after these parties came to power, disputes regarding party organization and the implementation of economic reforms made their disintegration unavoidable.

166

Table 6.3
Disintegration of the major parties in 1991-1992

Initial party	Date of split	Emerging parties
CF	February 1991	CDP
		CDA
		CM
PAV	March 1991	MDS
		CDU
CP	December 1991	PDL
		CPBS
		DPL
ChDM	March 1992	ChDMS
		SChDM

Disintegration of the Czech anti-Communist movement. Shortly after the elections, a small faction broke with the CF and renamed itself the Liberal Democratic Party. Stronger division of the CF occurred after the assignment of Vaclav Klaus as chairman. In February 1991, the CF split into the Civic Democratic Party (CDP) of Klaus, the Civic Movement (CM), the Civic Democratic Alliance (CDA), and some smaller groups like the more leftist Social Democrats. The CDP and the CDA had similar political agendas calling for rapid privatization and minimal state intervention in the economy. The CM supported economic reform, accompanied by social welfare measures (Pehe, 1991b). The split of the CF did not result in a strong reorganization of the federal or Czech governments. In the federal government, 8 of the 10 CF members became affiliated with the CM, 1 with the CDA and 1 with the CDP. In the Czech government, 8 of the 16 CF members associated with the CM, 2 with the CDA, 4 with the CDP, and 2 became unaffiliated (Orbis, 1991a).

Disintegration of the Slovak anti-Communist movement. The PAV split was also influenced by different views on economic reform. Most disagreement concerned the question of how much emphasis the party should place on Slovak national concerns. An important factor in the PAV's split was the increasing rivalry between the PAV and the ChDM. In November 1990, the PAV lost to the ChDM in local government elections (Pehe, 1991a). The ChDM's propaganda for a looser form of coexistence with the Czechs contributed to its victory. In reaction, Vladimir Meciar and his followers insisted on a more radical nationalist platform for the PAV. In March 1991, Meciar founded a new party: PAV-For a Democratic Slovakia, later renamed Movement for a Democratic Slovakia (MDS). The MDS emphasized national concerns and a slowing down of economic reforms. Meciar argued that the economic reforms formulated at the federal level were not suitable for Slovakia. Remaining members of the PAV renamed their party the Civic Democratic Union (CDU) and took a more moderate view of Slovak nationalism (Pehe, 1991c; Obrman, 1992b). This split made the ChDM the strongest political party in the Slovak National Council. In April 1991, Meciar was dismissed as Prime Minister by the Slovak National Council.[7] The former PAV was replaced by the ChDM as ruling party in the Slovak Government with 10 of the 22 members, and Jan Carnogursky (ChDM) was appointed prime minister. The CDU kept 10 members in the Slovak government, and the Democratic Party, 2. The MDS joined the opposition (Pehe, 1991e, Orbis, 1991b).

Slovak nationalism caused a second split: in March 1992 the ChDM split into the strongly nationalist Slovak Christian Democratic Movement (SChDM) with chairman Klepac and the Christian Democratic Movement for Slovakia (ChDMS) with chairman Carnogursky (Pehe, 1992b).

Disintegration of the Communist Party. The falling apart of the most important political parties had important implications for the political equilibrium and stability. The Communist Party became the party with the largest number of seats in the Federal Assembly (see table 6.4). Initially, parties emerging from the split of the CF and the PAV agreed to cooperate until the next elections. However, the differences between the new parties were too great for successful cooperation. This should have increased the Communist Party's relative influence on politics, but the Communists became increasingly internally divided as well. Division in the (federal) Communist Party emerged on two levels. First, the Slovak Communists and the Communist Party for Bohemia and Moravia (CPBS), the two constituent members of the Party, did not agree on the future image of the Party. The former took a more social democratic direction and renamed itself the Party of Democratic Left (PDL). The latter was dominated by diehard Stalinists, who blocked party reforms (Pehe, 1991g). Second, internal disagreement in the Communist Party for Bohemia and Moravia caused a split in December 1991, when a reformist group broke away and established the Democratic Party of Labor (DPL) (Pehe, 1992a). The overall result of the political parties' disintegration was an unclear realignment of political power in the Federal Assembly.

Table 6.4
Composition of Federal Assembly in April 1991

Party	Seats (total: 300)
CP of Slovakia	47
Civic Movement	40
Civic Democratic Party	40
PAV	32
ChDM	26
Association for Moravia and Silesia	16
Slovak National Party	15
ChDU	14
PAV-for a Democratic Slovakia	14
Coexistence	12
Liberal Democratic Party	2
Others	34

Source: Pehe, 1991d.

The elections of 1992

The first election campaign was dominated by general anti-Communist political platforms, a range of political views, especially regarding issues of nationalism, and implementation of economic reform. By the eve of the elections of 1992, a wide range of political parties with more distinctive platforms had emerged.[8] According to Pehe (1992c) the campaign was dominated by four issues: (1) Czechoslovakia's future status, (2) the pace and extent of economic reform, (3) screening of government officials for links with the former secret police, and (4) Czech-German relations.[9] The election results are given in table 6.5. In contrast to the 1990 elections, which were a great success for the anti-Communist movement in both republics, the results of the 1992 elections reflected two very different political trends in the Czech and the Slovak Republic.

The 300 seats of the Federal Assembly were divided among 12 parties, as follows (Pehe, 1992d): 113 seats for the 'radical' reformers (of which the Czech coalition CDP-ChDP had 85 seats)[10] proposing radical liberalization and a continued federation of Czech and Slovak republics; 147 seats for 'smooth' reformers (of which the MDS had 57 seats), advocating the introduction of more welfare measures and a stronger role for the state in the economy and

169

often emphasizing Slovak national interests; 57 seats for the Communists; and 40 seats for parties representing ethnic or extreme-right interests.[11] The federal government was formed as a coalition of CDP-ChDP with the MDS and the PP. Jan Strasky (CDP) became prime minister and Vaclav Havel was reelected president.

Table 6.5
Election results in 1992

Party	Seats
a. Czech National Council	(total number of seats: 200)
Civic Democratic Party-ChDU	76
Left Bloc (Communists)	35
Czechoslovak Social Democracy	16
Republican Party	14
ChDU	15
Liberal Social Union	16
CDA	14
Association for Moravia and Silesia	14
b. Slovak National Council	(total number of seats: 150)
MDS	74
Party of Democratic Left (Communists)	29
Slovak National Party	15
ChDMS	18
Coexistence	14
c. Federal Assembly	(total number of seats: 300)
Civic Democratic Party-ChDP	85
Left Bloc	34
Czechoslovak Social Democracy	16
Republican Party	14
ChDU	13
Liberal Social Union	12
MDS	57
Party of Democratic Left	23
Slovak National Party	15
ChDM	14
Coexistence	12
Social Democratic Party in Slovakia	5

Source: Pehe, 1992d.

Although the Czech elections were not an enormous success for the radical reformers, the results showed approval of the reforms by a large part of the Czech population. In the Czech National Council, parties supporting radical economic reforms won a slight majority with 105 of the 200 seats (of which 76 were CDP-ChDP seats).[12] The Communist Party's popularity, with 7.5 percent of the seats, was comparable to its reception in the first elections.[13] Parties advocating smoother reforms gained 16 percent of the searts. Parties with no distinct economic program gained 14 percent of the seats (Obrman, 1992b).[14] A coalition government with the CDP, the ChDP, the CDA, and the PP was formed with prime minister Klaus.

In contrast with the Czech Republic, Slovak election results showed a strong disapproval of the course of reforms and reflected deep nationalistic feelings. In the Slovak National Council, political power was highly concentrated in parties supporting smoother reforms and with a nationalist agenda: 118 seats of the 150 went to the MDS, the SNP, and the PDL (Obrman, 1992b). The more reform-minded parties (the ChDM and the ethnic Hungarian Coexistence Party) were left with little influence over legislation. Vladimir Meciar was named prime minister of the Slovak government, in which only 2 seats were not occupied by members of the MDS (Pehe, 1992e).

The split of Czechoslovakia

Beginning in 1968 the Czech and Slovak republics coexisted as a federation. In addition to sharing the Federal Assembly and the federal government, the republics each had their own governments and parliaments. On 12 December 1990, growing Slovak demands for more independence resulted in a constitutional amendment. This amendment consisted of a power-sharing agreement that transferred some federal powers to the republics.[15] In 1991, new federal, Czech, and Slovak constitutions had to be adopted. Disputes about this constitutional arrangement ended in a deadlock, further aggravating Slovak nationalist feelings.[16] After the elections of 1992, which were a success for Slovak nationalist parties, the Slovak National Council declared the Slovak Republic's sovereignty on 17 July 1992. Three days later, president Havel announced his resignation (Obrman, 1992d). On 22 July 1992, Czech and Slovak prime ministers Klaus and Meciar agreed to dissolve the Czechoslovakian Federation on 1 January 1993 (Pehe, 1992f).

The politics of the agricultural privatization laws

General privatization legislation

After the Communist Party lost its majority, the Federal Assembly passed a series of important reform laws in April 1990. For example, all citizens were given the right to establish private businesses, without limits on private property or number of employees. However, these laws had little effect on the growth of private business or on the privatization of the Czechoslovakian state sector. The foundations of Czechoslovakian economic privatization were laid by the coalition government of Marian Calfa, after the first democratic elections. In September 1990, the federal government adopted the Scenario for Economic Reform, a program for economic reforms in Czechoslovakia (Martin, 1991a).

A general legal framework for privatization was laid out in law no. 171/1991 for the Czech Republic and law no. 253/1991 for the Slovak Republic, which passed on 23 April 1991 and 24 May 1991 respectively. These laws can be summarized as follows: on the republic level, the most important privatization institutes were the Republic Ministries of Privatization and the National Asset Funds. On the federal level, the Federal Asset Funds and the Federal Minister of Finance played the same role as the National Ministers of Privatization. On both levels the ministers in charge of the different economic sectors (e.g., minister of industry, minister of agriculture) assisted the ministers of privatization and the minister of finance. Republican assets were to be privatized by republican institutions, federal assets by federal institutions. Most assets were in the hands of the republics, which made the federal institutions less important in implementing economic reform (Drabek, 1993). However, the legislation of privatization remained a federal issue. Privatization proposals were usually prepared by the concerning enterprise, reviewed by the minister of industry or the minister of agriculture, and approved (or disapproved) by the minister of privatization (or of finance, in case of federal assets). The Asset Funds took over administrative control in two stages. First, they transformed the enterprise into a joint stock company and transfered its shares to the Asset Fund. Afterwards, they disposed these shares (Drabek, 1993).

On 2 October 1990, law no. 403/1990, known as the Restitution Law, was approved by the Federal Assembly. This law provided that about 70,000 properties expropriated under the Communist regime be returned to the original owners (Pehe, 1991a). On 21 February 1991, a second restitution law was adopted: the Law on Extrajudicial Rehabilitation. It provided the legal basis for restitution of expropriated industries and businesses. The law specified that restitution would only apply to individuals (not to churches or organizations such as political parties) and that it would only cover property confiscated between 25 February 1948 and 1 January 1990. On 25 October 1990, the Small Privatization Law (no. 427/1990) was passed, permitting privatization of more than 100,000 small state-owned businesses by auction (Pehe, 1991a). Law no. 92/1992 of February 1992, the Large Privatization Law, provided for the privatization of most large state-owned firms, mainly by a voucher scheme. Each citizen received at a low fee a number of investment points to exchange for vouchers. Private investment funds, specialized in the handling of vouchers emerged (Havel and Kukla, 1992). A first wave of large privatization was realized in 1992. A second wave started in 1993.

The debate on agricultural reform legislation

Already in April 1990, before the first elections, law no. 114/1990 was adopted. This law granted farmers the right to reclaim their property rights (right of use) to agricultural property that had been forcibly collectivized after 1948. The law concerned only a small amount of agricultural property and did not include a detailed implementation plan. As a result, the law was only of marginal importance in the agricultural reform process (Lundell, 1990; Martin, 1990; Kraus et al., 1994).

The Scenario for Economic Reform of the CF-PAV-ChDM coalition government of September 1990 was not as comprehensive regarding agricultural reform as it was on other economic reform. The scenario only stated that most state farms had to be privatized and that members of a cooperative farm could decide for themselves their farm's future business (e.g., as a joint stock company or a firm with a cooperative status). Economic reforms in agriculture were to be regulated by a separate set of laws on restitution, privatization, and transformation (Martin, 1990).

Adoption of the basic laws on agricultural reform was preceded by a heated debate in the Federal Assembly. The initial attempt was to pass a law that included both restitution of agricultural assets and the transformation of the cooperatives. In March 1991, two draft laws on agricultural reform were submitted to the Federal Assembly. The first draft was initiated on 28 March by the Calfa government, half constituted by members of the CM and with the other half of its members from the CDP, CDA, ChDM, and CDU. The second draft law, best known as the 3T initiative[17], was supported by the ChDP.[18]

The government proposed to return land to its original owners, but only land that had been transferred to cooperatives or state farms after February 1948. As a consequence, land confiscated under the law of March 1948 would not be returned. This law put a limit of 50 hectares on private ownership (see before). The government wanted to avoid large distortions in the existing structures of cooperatives and state farms and so proposed compensation for those people who had joined a cooperative without having owned any land. The government's draft law emphasized minimizing the negative effect of agricultural privatization on consumers and on the members and management of cooperative farms. The government faced strong resistance for decollectivization. As in other CEECs, managers of the collective and state farms were strongly opposed to decollectivization. Members and workers of the collective and state farms showed little enthusiasm for returning to individual farming. Lack of entrepreneurship, no tradition in private farming, and severe macroeconomic conditions are often mentioned as the major reasons for this lack of enthusiasm (Csaki, 1991; Pryor 1992). Workers often performed activities with very limited specialization and therefore lacked comprehensive practical experience. Moreover, unlike private farmers, cooperative and state farmers profited from social security and stable wages, independent of agricultural market conditions. Therefore, members and workers of collective and state farms were opposed to decollectivization (Divila and Socol, 1993).[19] Consumers were opposed to decollectivization because they feared disruptions in food supply caused by the decollectivization process. A less disruptive transition to more efficient private-property-based enterprises had the advantage that agricultural production would not fall dramatically during the transition period.

As explained earlier, Czechoslovakian landownership was transformed several times as a result of different land reforms before the Communist takeover in February 1948. As a consequence, the date chosen as a reference for land restitution was very important. Several reasons can be given for the government's 1948 reference date. In February 1948, the first Communist government was formed. Despite the Communist Party's influence since 1945, it was argued that the laws before February 1948 were adopted by a democratic government. Second, the general privatization laws of 1990 stipulated that restitution was only possible for property confiscated after February 1948. Extending restitution to property confiscated before 1948 would create a precedent for restitution of Church property, which was mainly confiscated before 1948. Third, the number of Czechoslovakian citizens whose land was expropriated before February 1948 was relatively small, thereby limiting domestic opposition to this proposal. The 1948 time limit for restitution primarily excluded former large landowners hurt by the land reform of 1947, expelled Germans and Hungarians expropriated in 1945, and the Catholic Church (Wädekin, 1993).[20] About 70 percent of the land redistributed between 1945 and 1948 belonged to Germans and Hungarians.

Agricultural enterprises remained strong bastions of local Communist support after November 1989 (Martin, 1990). Agricultural enterprises under the Communist regime were the backbone of rural political organization. Farm management was generally in the hands of political supporters. A more radical transformation of the agricultural production structure could help the anti-Communist government to break down the rural organizational structure and, as a consequence, to damage rural Communist support.[21] The 1990 elections, however, were successful for the CF, PAV, and ChDM, while results for the Communist Party were only moderate. Hence, the governing parties could 'afford' to place more importance on the efficiency of the transition than on destroying Communist power bases. Apparently, the division of the major parties during the first months of 1991, which temporarily gave the Communist Party the largest number of seats in the Federal Assembly, did not induce a more radical stance on decollectivization by the government. Although the Communist Party became the largest faction, the party did not increase in popularity and in December 1991 split up. Hence, it did not increase its influence on Czechoslovakian political and economic developments.

In contrast with the government draft, the 3T initiative draft law reflected a much stronger anti-Communist attitude.[22] The ChDP criticized the government's draft law for being in favor of the former Communists and against former landowners. The ChDP argued that the existing cooperatives were not legitimate structures but Communist organizations. The party proposed a radical transformation of agricultural production structures, with the establishment of new cooperatives in which only landowners could participate. Family farms had to receive preferential treatment. The 3T initiative draft included two exceptions to the general privatization laws of 1990 and 1991 for restitution in agriculture.

First, land restitution would not be limited to individuals but would include religious communities, such as the Catholic Church, and also cooperatives. Different processing, service, and financial cooperatives had operated before the Communist regime in Czechoslovakia. Restitution of cooperatives' property nationalized after 1948 was supposed to give original owners linkage to the processing industry and make the start of private farming easier.

Second, not only land and other agricultural property confiscated after February 1948 would be returned to its former owners, but those whose property was expropriated before February 1948 would also have the right to claim their property back (Martin, 1991b). Since most of the property of the Catholic Church was expropriated between 1945 and 1948, an extension of the 1948 time limit was crucial for the Catholic Church.

Unlike the government parties, the ChDP did not do well in the first free elections. Unlike the Comminist Party, the ChDP lacked both organizational structures and a national constituency in rural areas. This reduced its chance for electoral success. Agricultural reform affects the development of economic and social organizations, which, in turn, affects political activities and preferences. Typically, the organization of agricultural production into 'new' cooperatives, compared with family farms, affects the political preferences and choices of the rural electorate. In addition to the organization of the production structures, the existence (and use) of social and cultural organizations, such as the Catholic Church, strongly influence a party's electoral success. For instance, use of the rural organization of the Catholic Church played a crucial role for right-wing parties in capturing the rural electorate in Belgium and France early in the twentieth century (Lindemans, 1992). In the same way, the use of religious organizations in CEECs can help in the political organization of new parties. Successful Christian democratic parties also ensure political representation of church interests and of church opinions on political and social issues. This reciprocal relationship between political parties and the Catholic Church also played a role in Czechoslovakia.

The Catholic Church was ruthlessly repressed after the Communist takeover in 1948. Expropriated and without any income, the Church became fully dependent on, and hence influenced by, the state. Since 1948 the state paid the wages of the priests. After the November 1989 Revolution, becoming more independent from the state financially became a priority for the Catholic Church. It was important for the Church to have good political representation by the Christian democratic parties (Martin, 1992). In turn, larger influence by the Catholic Church would help the Christian democratic parties strengthen their political influence in rural areas. It appears that with their proposals for agricultural reform and restitution, Czech Christian democrats attempted to strengthen the position of the Catholic Church in order to influence the future political alignment of the rural electorate in their favor.

This was attempted in two ways. First, restitution of Church property would make the Church economically less dependent on the state and better able to extend its activities. After 1989, churches remained financial dependent on the state because they still had no proper revenues to maintain their buildings and finance their charitable activities.[23] For example, in Slovakia, where the Catholic Church traditionally had a very strong position, under a hundred Catholic schools remained in 1993 (Fisher, 1993). Second, as long as agriculture remained organized as it was during the Communist regime, the pervasive Communist influence in economic, political, and social life hampered the Catholic Church efforts in rural society.[24] By supporting a radical transformation of collective farms into family farms, the ChDP aimed to break up the Communist organization and remove Communist nomenklatura from important economic and social functions, thereby reducing Communist influence on the rural population.

The Land Law

On 21 May 1991, the Federal Assembly adopted the Law on the Revision of Ownership Relations of Land and Other Agricultural Property, better known as the Land Law.[25] The main principles of the law were as follows (Svitek, 1992):

1 The law covered land, buildings, and other agricultural property confiscated between 25 February 1948 and 1 January 1990.

2 Foreigners could not own land.

3 Assets could only be restituted to citizens with permanent residence in Czechoslovakia.

4 The claimant had to be the original owner or a rightful heir.

5 The claimant could only be an individual. The restitutions to organizations or religious communities were not covered.

6 If the assets could not be returned in-kind, the owner would receive compensation. The government would pay compensation for unreturned land, the cooperatives would pay for other unreturned assets.

7 The deadline for claims was 31 December 1992.

8 Former owners could not claim more than 150 hectares of agricultural land or more than 250 hectares of both agricultural and nonagricultural land.

Although the Land Law adopted the principle of restitution in historical boundaries, claimants were not always given the land they formerly owned. The law specified that it was possible to give a comparable piece of land if the new owners wanted to exercise their right to privately farm the land. Many landowners of 1948 had several small scattered plots. In such cases, a single plot at the periphery of the cooperative could be given (Skully, 1992). No distinction was made between the restitution of land used in state farms and land from cooperative farms.

When the Federal Assembly passed the Land Law, it postponed the legislation of several controversial issues in order to avoid further delay of land restitution (Martin, 1991b). These issues included (1) the restitution of land to churches, (2) the transformation of agricultural production units, and (3) the restitution of land exceeding the limit of 150 hectares agricultural land and 250 hectares of land in general (we will discuss this legislation later). In this way, the Land Law was acceptable to both the government and the opposition parties. Although the government did not give in to the demands of the Christian democratic parties, these parties were given a second chance in separate legislation. The government parties could agree with the Land Law because it included options to minimize excessive (additional) disruption in the production structure, given the fact that land restitution would be disruptive in itself. There was much more support for restitution of land than for decollectivization of the production structures. It was hoped that the law would provide 'historical justice' and at the same time limit any negative impact on efficiency caused by production structure disruptions.

The Transformation Law: the transformation of cooperative farms

On 21 December 1991, the Transformation Law dealing with the transformation of the cooperatives was passed.[26] This law can be summarized as follows (Mladek, 1992; Doucha, 1993; Lamser, 1993):

1 The law covers all the assets of the cooperatives, after deduction of the assets restituted according to the Land Law and used for debt payments to banks and the State.

2 Of the assets, 25 percent were to be sold for money to provide some capital for the transformed cooperative. The remaining assets would be divided in-kind or in cash as follows: 50 percent divided among the former owners of the land according to the amount of land used by the cooperative; 20 percent divided among the employees according to years worked in the cooperative; 30 percent divided among the former owners of assets other than land, according to the amount of these assets used by the cooperative.

3 The former owners of assets and employees of the cooperative were to be represented in the General Assembly of owners and employees. Each cooperative was to establish a Transformation Council. This council would be elected by the General Assembly and have representatives of both asset owners and employees.

4 The Transformation Council would prepare and execute the transformation according to the 50/30/20-principle explained above. The General Assembly would determine the future structure of the cooperative: it could remain a cooperative, split into several cooperatives, become a joint stock company, or be liquidated.

5 The new owners of the assets could use their property shares (1) as starting capital for new private farms, established on the basis of the Land Law, (2) as a membership investment in a transformed cooperative, or, if neither of the first two options was chosen, (3) as 'dead capital'. In this case,

repayment would take place seven years following the beginning of the transformation.

6 The deadline for transformation was set on 28 January 1993. After that date, the cooperative would be liquidated.

In this transformation procedure, both the owners of assets and current members would be compensated and have equal influence on the future status of the cooperative, since each member of the General Assembly would have one vote. This was more in favor of the cooperative than was the initial proposal of the ChDP, which included only representation for landowners. Cooperative farms were generally favored because there was supposed to be an agreement between 'entitled' and 'obliged' persons in the kind and structure of property released when new owners (the 'entitled' person) decided to start private farming. However, the collective farm management, or very often the courts, made the final decision about what to release and to whom. Those who wanted to start private farming had the right to ask a collective farm for release of property according to the value of their restitution and transformation claims. The problem was that collective farmers were usually not willing to release the claimed production assets, unless the assets were less useful or for an overvalued price. Many of these cases ended in court proceedings. Often, members of collective farms would establish new enterprises. The members, or often only the managers, of the collective farms transferred attractive property from the collective farm to these newly established farms at favorable prices, or to those people who promised to add the property to the newly established enterprise. The original collective farms, which were supposed to be the source of assets and livestock for private farmers, were often left with old and useless property unless the transfer of the most attractive property went to an enterprise owned by (former) collective farm members (Sedlacek, 1995).

The privatization of state farms

As already mentioned, the Land Law of May 1991 included the restitution of land and agricultural property used in state farms. Land and other assets not reclaimed were to be privatized under law no. 92/1992 of 26 February 1992 concerning 'large privatization' in general. This meant that the state farms were to be privatized by vouchers accessible to all Czechoslovakian citizens. However, a few state farms were privatized by large-scale vouchers privatization. Most state farms were privatized on the basis of privatization projects submitted by the Minsitry of Agriculture. Contrary to the transformation law for cooperative farms, the transformation program for state farms did not favor former owners or present state farm workers.

179

The reform implementation started slowly. The initiative for restitution of land had to come from the former landowners themselves. By the end of 1992, only 180,000 of the potential 3.5 million former landowners had submitted the necessary papers. Of those, only 20,000 had actually retrieved their land according to the Land Law (OECD, 1993). In May 1993, still only 7 percent of the land covered by the Land Law (150,000 hectares) had actually been returned to previous owners. However, much progress was made in 1994, so that nearly 80 percent of total agricultural land was in 'private' hands by 1995 (Ratinger and Rabinowicz, 1997).

The transformation of the cooperatives in accordance with the Transformation Law was completed in January 1993. However, no fundamental changes occurred in the farm structure. In the Czech Republic, the transformation of 1,197 cooperatives resulted in 1,233 new cooperatives, 39 shareholdings companies, 59 other companies, and 24 companies facing liquidation proceedings. In mid-1993, the Czech cooperative sector still occupied about 50 percent of the agricultural land. Since that time, land has continued to be withdrawn from the cooperatives (Ratinger and Rabinowicz, 1997). In the Slovak Republic, the transformation of 929 cooperatives resulted in 965 new cooperatives, 12 shareholding companies, and 9 limited liability companies. In the Slovak Republic, 70 percent of the agricultural enterprises were still cooperatives in 1993. Transformation only concerned property of the cooperative, without the assets claimed under the Land Law. An important problem was lack of documentation of former ownership. Problems with restitutions caused delays in the transformation of cooperatives. Amendment of the Land Law (no. 565/1992) extended the deadline for submissions of landownership proof in cooperatives until the end of 1995, when the cooperatives (including those already transformed) would be obligated to reserve property shares (OECD, 1994).

The resulting ownership structure

In discussions on land reform, neither the government nor the Christian democrats of the opposition emphasized the fact that a fairly unegalitarian landownership would result from restitution based on pre-Communist ownership. The Land Law only limited the size of a claim to 150 hectares of agricultural land and 250 hectares of land in general.[27] In 1992, an amendment of the Land Law canceled the upper limits.[28] As a consequence, in both the Czech and the Slovak republics, the resulting private landownership was unegalitarian. In the Czech Republic approximately 8,000 of the 38,000 private farms owned more than 10 hectares and 735 private farms owned more than 100 hectares. The small group of private farms larger than 100 hectares together owned 55 percent of the privately farmed land. As a result of restitution to previous big landowners, some of these farms have developed on the basis of 'landlord-non operator'. In the Slovak Republic, 3 percent of private farmers own more than 50 hectares (with an average of 100 hectares), or approximately 35 percent of privately farmed land. About 20 percent of the private farms are between 10 to 50 hectares and occupy about 42 percent of all privately farmed land. Of the private farmers, 39 percent own fewer than 2 hectares (OECD, 1994).

Some comments need to be made about these data. First, comparing 1993 data with data from 1939 indicates that the present land distribution is even more unegalitarian than that in 1939. While the 1993 data only concern land that is privately farmed, large landowners might be more inclined to take their land. Land can be privately owned and rented out by the owner to a cooperative or a state farm.[29] Further, large landowners would be more motivated than small landowners to reclaim their property. This may partly explain the increase in the share of private land in large estates. Second, private farms of more than 100 hectares are more important in the Czech Republic than in the Slovak Republic and the restitution of very small plots (under 2 hectares) is more important in the Slovak Republic than in the Czech Republic. One reason is the difference in land inheritance rules. Before 1948, Slovakia followed the Napoleonic inheritance code in which land was divided among all their heirs, while in the Czech Republic land was usually passed on to a single heir (the eldest son). Kabat and Hagedorn (1997) report that, as a consequence of this, before 1945 the typical family farm in Bohemia and Moravia (the Czech part) cultivated 20 to 50 hectares of arable land, while a typical Slovakian family farm used only 2 to 5 hectares.

As explained in section 2, a large part of the cooperatives' land did not come from its members or workers. This is well reflected in the ownership structure after the transformation of the cooperatives: in the Slovak Republic only 28.4 percent of land used in cooperatives belonged to the members of those cooperative (see table 6.6).

An explanation of the government's restitution and decollectivization policies

From a rational choice-revealed preference perspective, one can conclude the following about the Czechoslovak government's policy choice of agrarian reform: restitution in-kind was chosen because the political demand for land restitution was very strong among domestic citizens.

Table 6.6
Ownership structure of land used in cooperatives
in the Slovak Republic in 1993

Owners	Percentage
Individuals:	67.18
members	28.43
non-members	38.75
State	6.16
Churches	1.67
Municipalities	1.73
Municipial associations	3.62
Others (mainly nonidentified)	19.64

Source: OECD, 1994.

Why did the Czechoslovakian government choose a more general restitution policy than for example Poland and Hungary? First, in Czechoslovakia, land confiscated after 1948 mostly belonged to Czech and Slovak citizens. In Poland, in contrast, most state lands had formerly belonged to emigrated Germans. Second, both Hungary and Czechoslovakia had several land reforms after the Second World War. This made restitution in-kind more difficult because one piece of land could be claimed by several former owners. In Hungary, this problem was solved by giving compensation in vouchers instead of restitution in-kind. In Czechoslovakia, the choice of a restitution reference date was easier, because most of the land redistributed before 1948 belonged to Sudeten Germans or Hungarians. Third, most of the land in Czechoslovakia was (formally) still privately owned, although the property rights had been given to the cooperatives,[30] whereas in Hungary, only about 35 percent of the land was, formally, still privately owned. Owners of these lands were restituted their property rights.

There was much less demand for decollectivization in Czechoslovakia than elsewhere. The Czech and Slovak government had little to gain politically from a radical decollectivization policy. The number of potential extra voters who would benefit was relatively small, and their votes were likely to be captured by other parties, such as the Christian democratic parties, which were pushing for a radical decollectivization policy. However, the Christian democrats did not have enough political power to push through a more radical agricultural reform. In addition, production disruptions from a radical decollectivization process raised food consumers' concerns and opposition. If accompanied by a series of appropriate measures, restitution in-kind would not necessarily force the existing production structures to break up into small units. This, in turn, would provide some protection to former management and the employees of the collective farms. While Czechoslovakian agricultural reform legislation included the privatization of agricultural land (and other assets) by restitution, its voucher schemes or distribution under the Transformation Law left room for a cooperative production structure, adapted to a free market economy. Although the final decisions regarding transformation projects were in the hands of the government, reform in Czechoslovakian agriculture was highly decentralized. The transformation of cooperatives depended mainly on the willingness of the farm management to cooperate and on choices made by cooperative members and owners regarding assets that could determine the future status of the farm. As discussed above, this left much room for managers of the collective farms to manipulate the reform process, shifting its benefits in their favor more than would have been possible had the reform implementation been stronger or controlled by outsiders (as in the attempted Bulgarian reforms).

Restitution to churches

A hotly debated issue in the privatization debate was restitution of church property, including land. When the Land Law was approved in May 1991, it left restitution to churches and religious communities to separate legislation. In March 1992, the People's Party initiated a draft law on restitution of Church property.[31] The Calfa coalition government did not support the draft law, arguing that it would slow down the privatization process and that it was inconsistent with the privatization laws of 1990 and 1991 which allowed only restitution to individuals. The Federal Assembly voted down the draft law on 15 April 1992. The most important argument used by both Communist and reform-minded representatives who voted against the draft was that restitution to churches implied that the collective farms would lose much of their land, which might lead to a decline in agricultural production. However, a statement by the Catholic bishops on 25 March 1992 made it clear that in most cases the Church would rent its property to the current tenants in state and collective farms (Martin, 1992). Moreover, since the Land Law already covered about 80 percent of the land, the argument that restitution of land formerly owned by the Church would break up the farms seems to have been only rhetorical.

The real reason for opposing restitution was political. The main consequence of restitution to churches would be an increase in their assets and income, which would be used, among other things, to support Christian democratic political parties. As a reaction to this refusal for Church restitution, the Catholic Church made its support for the Christian democrats very clear. In May 1992, a month before the second elections, Slovak Catholic bishops issued a letter that was read in churches throughout Slovakia. This letter explicitly backed candidates and parties 'supporting human and religious rights' and demanded that Catholic Church members not vote for a party or movement that vetoed the adoption of the law on restitution of Church property (Martin, 1992).

Agricultural reform after the split of Czechoslovakia[32]

Soon after the elections of 1992, agricultural reform was overshadowed by discussion about the split of Czechoslovakia. After division of the federal state, agricultural reform developed separately in the two republics. The basic laws on agricultural reform had been passed in 1991 and 1992 as federal legislation, and these laws remained in place. Differences between the policies of the Czech and the Slovak republics mostly concerned amendments to speed up the process or make minor adjustments.

Agricultural reform in the Czech Republic. In the Czech Republic, the rural and urban areas displayed important differences in their choice of parties in the elections of 1992. Parties supporting radical liberalization and fast reform received more support in urban than in rural areas. The CDP-ChDP coalition and the CDA gained respectively 27 and 3 percent of the votes in rural Southern Moravia, compared with 48 and 12 percent in Prague. Parties supporting more moderate economic reforms and more state intervention received more votes in rural areas than in urban areas. These regional differences can partly be explained by the fact that rural regions were more affected by unemployment and other social problems. However, the Communist Left Bloc had even results in all regions (Obrman, 1992b). Unlike some other CEECs, in the Czech and Slovak republics election results showed a shift of political support in rural areas from radical reformers to moderate reformers, and not to the Communists.

In the CDP-CDA-ChDP-PP coalition government of Klaus, the post of minister of agriculture went to Josef Lux, member of the PP, which has been politically more successful in some traditional Catholic rural regions of Moravia than in Prague. The political importance of this post is illustrated by the fact that Klaus insisted on a member of his party for the post of deputy minister of agriculture. The CDP's need to keep the coalition with the two Catholic parties (PP and ChDM) and the limited electoral support in rural areas for the CDP and the CDA suggest that the way was open for concessions on agricultural reform by the CDP and the CDA. However, while the CDP and CDA supported measures to speed up agricultural reform, they still emphasized the negative side effects of a more disruptive agricultural reform process on the country's economy. By speeding up the agricultural reform process, the CDP and the CDA hoped to reduce any negative effects caused by uncertainty, for both agricultural producers and consumers. For example, it was thought that the negative effects of a slow agricultural transformation on agricultural production, would increase people's discontent toward economic reforms in general. By speeding up the agricultural reform process, the CDP and the CDA also hoped to reduce growing rural support for those parties that propagandized a more gradual approach to economic reforms and more state intervention.

The Czech CDP-CDA-PP-ChDP government announced its new Agrarian Policy Program on 30 October 1992. The general trend was clear: to accelerate the process of agricultural reform as much as possible. The state farms were to be privatized in a second wave of large privatization, which was to begin in the summer of 1993. By the end of 1994 all state farms were to be privatized. The restitution of property rights to land belonging to state farms was complicated by the fact that about half of the state farms' property had been taken over from former collectives, not from individual owners. Although the transfer of land from cooperative farms to state farms did not change ownership rights, poor information on the transfer and administrative problems made restitution more difficult in practice. Therefore, these lands were not immediately privatized, but were rented until 1995, to avoid further delay in the privatization of state farms (OECD, 1994). However, because of technical difficulties and administrative undercapacity, by August 1993 only 127 of the 1,306 privatization projects had been approved. Therefore, state farms were removed from the second large privatization wave which had to start in October 1993 (Agra Europe).

Amendments to the Land Law of 1 June 1993 aimed at speeding up the restitution procedure. Claimants were then able to go to court to get their land back immediately or to get compensation in cash. The amendments also introduced 'internal auction', to be used in case of disagreement among those seeking restitution of property to go with the land, for example, tractors (Agra Europe).

No new laws or amendments forcing the cooperatives to a more fundamental restructuring were introduced. It was supposed that some cooperatives transformed under the Transformation Law of 1991 would undergo a *second transformation* under the more general Commercial Code of 1991.[33] However, this second transformation would only occur after the approval of the general assembly of the cooperative and would never be ordered or controlled by the state. It mainly concerned the transformation into other types of enterprises for example, a joint stock company or a limited liability company.

In November 1992, the ChDP submitted a proposal to penalize heads of cooperatives who slowed down the privatization or who did not sufficiently cooperate in land restitution. The proposal aimed at speeding up the implementation of the Land Law and also provided for penalties on the sales of returned property in order to make short-term profits. The Liberal Social Union criticized the proposal, saying that it intimidated cooperative officials and that the government was attempting to get rid of them while the farmers were in favor of the present officials. In December 1992, the Sanction Law was passed, which regulated penalties for nonobservance of the Land Law and the Transformation Law.[34] However, sanctions could only be applied if retarding the restitution or transformation process was willful, which could rarely be proved.

The political debate on restitution of property to churches was still ongoing in 1994. The ChDP and PP demanded restitution of property to churches confiscated after February 1948. However, the CDP and the CDA remained strongly opposed to restitution to the Church. This debate, which caused a government crisis in the summer of 1993, threatened the cohesion of the coalition (Agra Europe; Pehe, 1994a).

Agricultural reform in the Slovak Republic. One of Meciar's major arguments for the division of Czechoslovakia was that the economic results of the reforms were significantly more negative for Slovakia than for the Czech Republic. Although Meciar promised gentler reforms in his election campaign of 1992, soon after Slovakia's independence he was pressed by the deteriorating economy and by loan requirements of the World Bank to impose strict monetary and fiscal rules at the expense of social programs. This, in turn, led to a dramatic fall in popularity for Meciar and the MDS. In March 1993, foreign minister Milan Knazko left the MDS and formed his own party, the Alliance of Democrats. As a result, the parliamentary seats of the MDS decreased from 74 to 66 of the total 150 seats. In addition, Ludovit Cernak, the Slovak National Party member of the government, resigned, and the SNP withdrew its support from the government. The MDS was left with a minority government and had to find new coalition parties. No solution appeared until the SNP agreed in November 1993 to form a coalition government with the MDS (Fisher, 1994). This government, however, fell by March 1994.

The political turmoil and the economic problems in Slovakia did not result in major changes in agricultural reform. No further transformation of cooperatives was planned. The privatization of state farms was delayed by landownership problems. Law no. 17/1993 was passed to accelerate the process, enabling privatization while guaranteeing the future rights of those receiving restitution. Land with no clear ownership would not be privatized, but leased on a long-term basis (OECD, 1994).

As in the Czech Republic, there was a strong discussion in Slovakia regarding restitution to the Church. Before the elections of 1992, the MDS was strongly opposed to Church restitution. However, on 20 July 1993 the MDS initiated a law supporting Church restitution. One explanation is that the MDS agreed to the proposal in exchange for support to its minority government by the Christian democrats. Fisher (1993) argues that the change of MDS strategy was to increase its popularity, which had declined since the elections.[35] Except for the PDL, all parties in the Slovak National Council supported the law proposal. On 29 September 1993, the Slovak National Council passed a law, restituting all property of churches and religious communities that had been confiscated after World War II.[36] Of the 106 deputies present, 76 voted in favor of the law, 20 voted against, and 10 abstained. However, Slovak president Michal Kovac vetoed the bill, arguing that it was contrary to the protection of ownership rights anchored in the Slovak Constitution. His main criticism was that the Church Restitution Law included restitution of property currently owned by individuals or collective farms. These owners would receive no compensation for the property, even if they had purchased it. On 27 October, an amended Church Restitution Law was adopted. This amended law excluded cooperative farms from the obligation of returning property to the Church without compensation (Fisher, 1993).

Conclusion

This study indicates that political considerations, as well as historical factors such as postwar politics, the expulsion of Sudeten Germans and Hungarians, and precollectivization land reforms all influenced the Czechoslovakian government's decisions regarding agricultural privatization. The Land Law returned land to the 1948 owners. The private landownership that emerged was fairly unegalitarian. Minimizing economic disruption was an important consideration of the Czechoslovakian ruling parties in their decisions reading agricultural reform. Less weight was given to the potential long-term effects that decollectivization might have on the political alignment of the rural electorate because of the overwhelming success of anti-Communist political forces in the first free elections of 1990. Political calculations regarding agricultural privatization and transformation were mainly determined by considering the potential gain in support from new private landowners and the potential loss in support from consumers and from management and employees of agricultural production enterprises. The combination of a minimally disruptive agricultural transformation program with an extensive restitution program was the optimal scenario.

The demand for a more radical agricultural reform was mainly voiced by the Czech Christian democratic parties in the opposition. Their proposals for restitution to Churches and for agricultural reform were an attempt to change the rural social organization and power structure more radically, in order to influence the future political alignment. With their support for church restitution, Christian democratic parties tried to strengthen the role of the Church in society because this would facilitate the parties' political organization in the long run. Further, decollectivization would break up the Communist political organization and weaken the Communist influence on social, political, and economic life in rural areas. However, the Christian democratic parties did not perform well in the 1990 elections and did not have enough political power to obtain Church restitution or a more radical agricultural reform.

After the division of Czechoslovakia, the Czech government parties, which supported radical liberalization, faced the growing success of parties propagandizing for slowed reforms and more state intervention. The government's policy to accelerate agricultural reform can be understood as an attempt to reduce the negative effect of uncertainty for consumers and agricultural producers in order to avoid a further loss of political support. Unlike the Czech Republic, the Slovak Republic (under the minority government of Meciar) passed legislation providing for Church restitution in exchange for political support from the Christian democratic parties.

Notes

1   The author thanks LICOS, Almanij Antwerpen, and the National Foundation for Scientific Research (NFWO) through an FKFO grant for financial support for this research project. I further thank Jo Swinnen, Ladislav Kabat, Josef Kraus, and participants at a workshop in Leuven for critical comments on earlier versions of this paper.
2   See Rabinowicz and Swinnen (1997) for a definition and discussion of property rights.
3   Law no. 50/1955 on land for securing agricultural production. This law also specified that all land of small farmers and kulaks not properly farmed could be used by an enterprise of the socialist sector (Karlik, 1993).
4   Law no. 123/1975.
5   Only registered parties able to prove a support base of more than 10,000 people were allowed to run in the elections (Pehe, 1991a). To win representation in the Federal Assembly, the Czech National Council, or the Slovak National Council, a minimum of respectively 5, 5, and 3 percent of the votes was required.
6   The remaining elected parties had mainly ethnic, regional, or ecological agendas (Kusin, 1990; Pehe, 1991a).

7   In March 1991, Meciar received a vote of no confidence of PAV, that argued that he had misused secret police files and that his popular statements had endangered democracy (Pehe, 1991e).

8   An overview of the parties registered for the elections of 1992 is given in Pehe (1992c).

9   Shortly before the elections of 1992, a Czechoslovak-German treaty stated that the expulsion of Germans from Czechoslovakia after World War II was unjust.   Also, leftist parties were opposed to extensive German investment in Czechoslovakia.

10 The Civic Democratic Party and the Christian Democratic Party formed a temporary coalition before the 1992 elections. This coalition increased the tiny ChDP's chances to win representation, given the election law of 1990, which disfavored small parties. Immediately after the elections, the two parties loosened their cooperation.

11 Other 'radical' reformers were the People's Party and the Christian Democratic Movement. Other 'smooth' reformers were the Czechoslovak Social Democrats, the Social Democratic Party in Slovakia, and the Liberal Social Union. Nationalist parties included the Slovak National Party and, the Republican Party.   'Ethnic' parties refers to the Coexistence (Hungarian ethnic) Party (Pehe, 1992d).

12 Other parties were the Civic Democratic Alliance and the Christian Democratic Union-People's Party (Obrman, 1992b).

13 Czech Social Democrats, Liberal Social Union (Obrman, 1992b).

14 Republican Party, Party for Moravia and Silesia.

15 The constitutional amendment of 1990 stated that the Federal government had to keep control over defense, foreign affairs, foreign trade, the central bank, taxation, customs, and price reforms.

16 The Christian Democratic Movement insisted on a state treaty between the Czech and Slovak republics. By this treaty the republics would formulate their intention to coexist in a federation. Further, it would explain which of the republics' rights and powers were to be transferred to federal institutions. The Christian Democratic Movement also emphasized that the republics' constitutions had to be established before the federal constitution. Most Czech and federal politicians reacted against the state treaty because the signing of such a treaty would require a temporary sovereignty for the republics (Pehe, 1991f).

17 3T refers to the first letters of the authors of the alternative draft. Mr. Tyl, a member of the Federal Assembly and vice-chairman of ChDP, Mr. Tlusty as a member of CDP and member of Czech Parliament, and Mr. Tomaszek, a lecturer without political membership.

18 The 3T initiative was not fully accepted by the PP. This party existed during forty years as te National Front, led by the Communist Party.

19 In fall of 1990 an opinion poll among farm workers by the Research Institute for Agricultural Economy in Prague showed a strong resistance to private farming.   Only 7 percent polled intended to become private farmers, 75 percent preferred to continue working in state-run enterprises. For 75 percent of the farm workers, financial problems were the largest barrier to beginning a private farm.   A large, 74.8, percent did not know how to find consumers for their products, and 46.8 percent feared the risks involved in private farming.   More than a third of the respondents said that they would not be prepared to work longer hours with less leisure time (Martin, 1990).

20 Discussion of the reference date was influenced by international politics. At the same time that the Land Law was to be approved by the Federal Assembly, negotiations were held between Czechoslovakia and Germany for a new interstate treaty in an attempt to 'draw a line under the past'.   In these negotiations, restitution to Sudeten Germans became a very sensitive issue.

21 For further and more general discussion of this issue, see chapter 2 and chapter 13 of this volume.

22 Church restitution was also demanded by the Slovak ChDM.   The viewpoint of the ChDM on agricultural reform might have been different from the other governmental parties.   However, because the ChDM only had one member in government, its impact on the government's draft must have been slight.

23 Buildings used for religious purposes were restituted to the Catholic Church in 1990.   The debate on Church restitution concerned buildings not used for religious purposes, and land (Pehe, 1994b).   Since there are no official records on land confiscated from the churches, it was difficult to estimate how much land should be returned to the Catholic Church.   In the Slovak Republic, it is estimated that between 60,000 hectares and 150,00 hectares were confiscated, of which 50,000 hectares or more were farmland (about 1.5 percent of Slovak farmland).   In the Czech Republic, it is estimated that the Catholic Church formerly owned 220,000 hectares of land (Fisher, 1993; Pehe, 1994b).

24 A 1990 poll by the Public Opninion Research indicated that in the Czech Republic only 20 percent of Czechs believed in God, 50 percent were atheist, 30 percent agnostic.   A public opinion survey of 1946 showed nearly the opposite trend: only 12 percent of the people questioned were atheist, two thirds were believers.   Tomás Rubácek, the vice-chairman of the Czech Coalition Party ChDU, argued that the most important reason for this change was that forty years of Communist propaganda had resulted in an antireligious attitude and this attitude was hard to change (Knox, 1993).

25 Law no. 229/1991.

26 Law no. 42/1992.

27 In most cases the limits on claims under the Land Law were not relevant, because the 1947 land reform imposed a limit on private ownership of 150 hectares of agricultural land and 250 hectares of land in general.

28 Amendment no. 313/1992. This amendment further made it possible for persons who lost property under the land reform of 1945 because of alleged cooperation with the enemy during the second World War to claim their property back if (1) they could prove that they had not collaborated, (2) if they had Czechoslovak citizenship, and (3) if they had permanent residence in Czechoslovakia. Although it concerned only a small group, the amendment became very controversial because in some cases it enabled descendants of former German and Hungarian nobility to claim huge amounts of property (Pehe, 1994b).

29 According to a 1991 poll conducted by the Public Opinion Research, of respondents who wanted to claim their land back, only 23 percent assumed that they would use it themselves. Of the others, 41 percent wanted to lease the land, 10 percent wanted to sell it (Martin, 1991b).

30 When a cooperative farm was taken over by a state farm, the property rights were transferred to the state farm.

31 An earlier draft on restitution to churches was proposed by 68 deputies from various parties in June 1991. However, the Federal Assembly refused to discuss the draft law (Martin, 1992).

32 For more details and recent information on farm restructuring, ownership distribution and reform effects, see Ratinger and Rabinowicz (1997), Kabat and Hagedorn (1997), and OECD (1996).

33 Law no. 513/1991.

34 Law no. 39/1993.

35 Since it is estimated that 60 to 70 percent of the Slovak people are Catholic, the dramatic decline in support for the ChDMS in the elections of 1992 implied that the Catholics were not well represented in Slovak politics. As a consequence, there existed a large group of potential Catholic voters for the MDS. On the other hand, the resistance of the MDS before the elections of 1992 might be explained by the fact that those individuals who would base their voting behavior on Catholic issues would vote for the ChDM.

36 For the Christian churches, the law covered property confiscated between May 1945 and January 1990. For Jewish organizations, the law covered property confiscated since November 1938.

References

Agra Europe, various issues.

Csaki, C. (1991), 'Socialist' Agriculture Transformed Perspectives on Food Trade', *Transition* (The World Bank), Vol. 2, No. 10, pp. 1-3.

Doucha, T. (1993), 'Agricultural Policy and Trade Developments in the Czech Republic', paper presented on the OECD Seminar *East/West Economic Relations in Agriculture*, OECD: Paris.

Drabek, Z. (1993), 'Institutional Structure, Supervision and the Main Contested Areas in the Czech and Slovak Privatization Process', *Trends and Policies in Privatization*, CCEET, OECD, Vol. 1, No. 2, special feature, pp. 108-126.

Divila, E. and Socol, Z. (1993), 'The Conception Questions of Forming New Entrepreneurial Subjects in the Czech Agriculture', *Prague Economic Papers*, No. 4, pp. 358-369.

Fisher, S. (1993), 'Church Restitution Law Passed in Slovakia', *RFE/RL Research Report*, 19 November, pp. 51-55.

Fisher, S. (1994), 'Slovakia: The First Year of Independence', *RFE/RL Research Report,* 7 January, pp. 87-91.

Havel, J. and Kukla, E. (1992), 'Privatization and Investment Funds in Czechoslovakia', *RFE/RL Research Report*, 24 April, pp. 37-41.

Kabat, L. and Hagedorn, K. (1997), 'Privatisation and Decollectivisation Policies and Resulting Structural Changes of Agriculture in Slovakia', in Swinnen, J., Buckwell, A. and Mathijs, E. (eds.), *Agricultural Privatisation, Land Reform and Farm Restructuring in Central and Eastern Europe*, Avebury: Aldershot.

Karlik, J. (1993), 'Questions of Ownership and Use of Land and Other Agricultural Means (in Agricultural Cooperatives)', *Prague Economic Papers*, No. 3, pp. 265-283.

Kaser, M. C. and Radice, E. A. (1985a), *The Economic History of Eastern Europe, 1919-1975, vol. I*, Clarendon Press: Oxford.

Kaser, M. C. and Radice, E. A. (1985b), *The Economic History of Eastern Europe, 1919-1975, vol. II*, Clarendon Press: Oxford.

Knox, K. (1993), 'Losing Their Religion', *The Prague Post*, Vol. 3, No. 34.

Korbel, J. (1959), *The Communist Subversion of Czechoslovakia,* Princeton University press: Princeton.

Korbel, J. (1977), *Twentieth-Century Czechoslovakia, the Meaning of History*, Columbia University Press: New York.

Kraus, J., Doucha, T., Sokol, Z. and Prouza, B. (1994), 'Agricultural Reform and Transformation in the Czech Republic', in Swinnen, J. (ed.), *Policy and Institutional Reform in Central European Agriculture*, Avebury: Aldershot.

Kusin, V. V. (1990), 'The Elections Compared and Assessed', *Report on Eastern Europe*, 13 July, pp. 38-47.

Lamser, Z. (1993), 'L'Agriculture Tchèque et Slovaque en Transformation'. *Économie Rurale*, No. 214/215, pp. 45-48.

Lindemans, I. (1992), *De Politieke Economie van Landbouwprotectie in Frankrijk en het Verenigd Koninkrijk, 1880-1960*, unpublished Master's thesis, Faculty of Agricultural Sciences, K.U.Leuven.

Lundell, M. R (1990), 'Privatization and Land Reform in Romania, Hungary, and Czechoslovakia', *CPE Agricultural Report*, Vol. III, No. 6, pp. 24-32.

Martin, P. (1990), 'Agricultural Reform', *Report on Eastern Europe*, 16 November, pp. 5-8.

Martin, P. (1991a), 'A Balance Sheet', *Report on Eastern Europe*, 1 February, pp. 7-10.

Martin, P. (1991b), 'New Law on Land Privatization Passed', *Report on Eastern Europe,* 19 July, pp. 10-14.

Martin, P. (1992), 'Major Issues Confront the Churches in Czechoslovakia', *RFE/RL Research Report*, 17 July, pp. 61-65.

Mladek, J. (1992), 'Transformation, Restitution and Privatization in Agriculture', *Privatization Newsletter of Czechoslovakia*, No. 9, October, pp. 1-3.

Obrman, J. (1992a), 'The Czechoslovak Elections', *RFE/RL Research Report*, 26 June, pp. 12-19.

Obrman, J. (1992b), 'Slovakia Declares Sovereignty; President Havel Resigns', *RFE/RL Research Report*, 31 July, pp. 25-29.

OECD (1993), *Agricultural Policies, Markets and Trade, in the Central and Eastern Europeans Countries, the New Independent States and China, Monitoring and Outlook 1993*, OECD: Paris.

OECD (1994), *Agricultural Policies, Markets and Trade, in the Central and Eastern Europeans Countries, the New Independent States and China, Monitoring and Outlook 1994*, OECD: Paris.

Okey, R. (1986), *Eastern Europe 1740-1985, Feudalism to Communism*, Harper Collins Academic: London.

Orbis (1991a), 'The Czechoslovak Federal Government', *Czechoslovak Economic Digest*, No. 4/91, p. 3.

Orbis (1991b), 'The Governments of the Slovak Republic and the Czech Republic', *Czechoslovak Economic Digest*, No. 5/91, pp. 2-3.

Pehe, J. (1990), 'An Overview of the Democratic Revolution', *Report on Eastern Europe*, 9 March, pp. 4-11.

Pehe, J. (1991a), 'The Instability of Transition', *Report on Eastern Europe*, 4 January, pp. 11-16.

Pehe, J. (1991b), 'The Civic Forum Splits into Two Groups', *Report on Eastern Europe*, 8 March, pp. 11-14.

Pehe, J. (1991c), 'Growing Slovak Demands Seen as Threat to Federation', *Report on Eastern Europe*, 22 March, pp. 1-10.

Pehe, J. (1991d), 'The Changing Configuration of Political Forces in the Federal Assembly', *Report on Eastern Europe*, 19 April, pp. 9-13.

Pehe, J. (1991e), 'Political Conflict in Slovakia', *Report on Eastern Europe*, 10 May, pp. 1-6.

Pehe, J. (1991f), 'The State Treaty between the Czech and the Slovak Republics', *Report on Eastern Europe*, 7 June, pp. 11-15.

Pehe, J. (1991g), 'Divisions in the Communist Party of Czechoslovakia', *Report on Eastern Europe*, 26 July, pp. 10-13.

Pehe, J. (1992a), 'Czechoslovakia's Changing Political Spectrum', *RFE/RL Research Report*, 31 January, pp. 1-31.

Pehe, J. (1992b), 'Slovak Nationalism Splits Christian Democratic Ranks', *RFE/RL Research Report*, 27 March, pp. 13-16.

Pehe, J. (1992c), 'Czechoslovakia: Parties Register for Elections', *RFE/RL Research Report*, 1 May, pp. 20-25.

Pehe, J. (1992d), 'Czechoslovakia's Political Balance Sheet, 1990 to 1992', *RFE/RL Research Report*, 19 June, pp. 24-31.

Pehe, J. (1992e), 'The New Slovak Government and Parliament', *RFE/RL Research Report*, 10 July, pp. 32-36.

Pehe, J. (1992f), 'Czechs and Slovaks Prepare to Part', *RFE/RL Research Report*, 18 September, pp. 19-28.

Pehe, J. (1994a), 'Czech Government Coalition: Striving for Stability', *RFE/RL Research Report*, 11 February, pp. 15-21.

Pehe, J. (1994b), 'Legal Difficulties Beset the Czech Restitution Process', *RFE/RL Research Report*, 15 July, pp. 6-13.

Pryor, F. L. (1992), *The Red and the Green. The Rise and Fall of Collectivized Regimes*, Princeton University Press: Princeton.

Rabinowicz, E. and Swinnen, J. (1997), 'Political economy of privatization and decollectivization of Central and East European agriculture: Definitions, issues and methodology', chapter 1 in this volume.

Ramkema, H. (1990), 'The November Revolutie van 1989', in Mercks, K. and Ramkema, H. (eds.), *Republiek aan de Moldau: de Tsjechoslowaakse Erfenis*, Werkgroep Oost-Europa projekten: Utrecht.

Ratinger, T. and Rabinowicz, E. (1997), 'Changes in Farming Structures in the Czech Republic as a Result of Land Reform and Privatisation', in Swinnen, J., Buckwell, A. and Mathijs, E. (eds.), *Agricultural Privatisation, Land Reform and Farm Restructuring in Central and Eastern Europe*, Avebury: Aldershot.

Rotschild, J. (1992), *East Central Europe between the Two World Wars*, University of Washington Press: Washington DC.

Sedlacek, M. (1995), 'What is the Political Economy of Agriculture in the Czech Republic?', unpublished manuscript, Wye College, University of London: Wye.

Skully, D. W. (1992), 'Privatization and the Size Distribution of Farms in the CSFR?', 27th EAAE Seminar, *Eastern European Agriculture: Problems, Goals and Perspectives*, 18-20 March, pp. 168-172.

Svitek, I. (1992), 'Reprivatization in Czechoslovakia', *Reprivatization in Central & Eastern Europe*, C.E.E.P.N., pp. 56-60.

Thompson, S. (1993), 'Agrarian Reform in Eastern Europe Following World War I: Motives and Outcomes', *American Journal of Agricultural Economics*, Vol. 75, pp. 740-744.

Wädekin, K. E. (1993), 'Bulgaria, Czechoslovakia and the GDR', in Braverman, A., Brooks, M. and Csaki, C. (eds.), *The Agricultural Transition in Central and Eastern Europe and the Former U.S.S.R.*, The World Bank: Washington DC, pp. 244-264.

Wolchik, S. L. (1992), 'Czechoslovakia', in Held, J. (ed.), *The Columbia History of Eastern Europe in the Twentieth Century*, Columbia University Press: New York.

Appendix 6.1
Important political events: 1989-1993

1989	November	Fall of Communist Regime
	December	Formation of temporary coalition government
		Havel assigned President
1990	January	Communists form a loose majority in Federal Assembly
	June	Elections:

Results: see table 6.3

President: Havel

New governments:
- a. Federal
  - Pr.Min.: Calfa
  - coalition: CF-PAV-ChDM
- b. Czech Republic
  - Pr. Min.: Pithart
  - coalition under CF
- c. Slovak Republic
  - Pr.Min.: Meciar
  - coalition under PAV

	November	Local Government Elections
1991	March	PAV splits in MDS and CDU
	April	Fall of Meciar's government
		CDM Slovak government with Prime Minister Carnogursky
	June	CF splits in CDP and CM:
	December	Democratic Party of Labor breaks with CP for Bohemia and Moravia
1992	March	ChDMs splits in SChDM and ChDMS
	June	Elections:

Results: see table 6.4

President: Havel

New governments:
- a. Federal
  - Pr.Min.: Pithart
  - coalition CDP-ChDP-PP-MDS
- b. Czech Republic
  - Pr.Min.: Klaus
  - coalition CDP-CDA-ChDP-PP
- c. Slovak Republic
  - Pr.Min.: Meciar
  - government of MDS

1993	January	Split of Czechoslovakian Federal Republic

7 The politics and policies of privatization of nationalized land in Eastern Germany

Konrad Hagedorn

Introduction: privatization and variants of institutional change

Institutional economics describes institutional change in a way that often suggests a sort of *intellectual polarization*. 'Pure' institutional change is supposed to occur by means of self-organization (i.e., by collective action in which all individuals participate in a fair way). We are used to associating this type of institutional change with *positive value judgements*: the system of rules arising through self-organization is supposed to be efficient in economic terms, (by saving transaction costs) and, since this approach provides the people concerned with opportunities to participate, it also corresponds with our notions of justice. On the other hand, institutional change driven by political decisions is associated with a tendency towards inefficiency and a lack of justice, first, because of the high cost of political consensus building and decisionmaking; and second, because of opportunistic behavior that arises to influence the political process when the decisions on institutional rules are made.

Theoretical background: the evolutionary theory of constitutions

The differentiation between endogenous and exogénous determinants of institutional change has been adopted in the evolutionary theory of constitutions (see Leipold, 1981, 1985, 1988, 1989a, 1989b; Schmidtchen, 1989; Schüller, 1988), which takes into account the evolutionary character of constitutional order, as well as the fact that it is shaped by politics.

Exogenous influences are abstracted in the first phase, that is, the emergence of institutions is considered to be a process of self-organization affected only by endogenous driving forces. The evolutionary theory of constitutions is based primarily on the theoretical approaches of the 'new institutional economics' (see Elsner, 1987), including public choice theory, property rights theory, economic theory of law, and transaction cost economics. These theories systematically transfer the cost-benefit calculations of neoclassical economics to the realm of institutions: since it is the central goal of economic behavior to use limited resources sparingly, humans behaving economically will not only attempt to reduce the cost of production, but also the cost of transaction involved in their economic decisions. Therefore, institutions[1] are formed that minimize the total cost of production and transaction.

In the second phase, the evolutionary theory of constitutions explicitly considers the possibilities and motives of influential politicians in establishing the economic order, for example, by referring to corresponding concepts of institutional choice developed by Schenk (1981, 1982, 1983). This theory takes into account the *dynamic character* of all processes of institutional change using adequate theoretical approaches, e.g., in the economic sphere by referring to the concept outlined by Heuss (1965) in his dynamic theory of market competition, and in the political sphere by following the framework given by Olson's (1982) theory of collective action. In principle, there may be many approaches to explaining the behavior of political actors in processes of institutional change that can be used in the evolutionary theory of constitutions (e.g., components of public choice theory), but approaches from neighboring disciplines such as policy analysis can also be called up.

The above outline of two basic categories of determinants of institutional change can be extended by relating them to two corresponding categories of institutional innovation. This is expressed through:

> the distinction originally developed by Lachmann (1963) between inner institutions of the market economy, which develop from markets and competition, and intentionally designed external institutions. It has been demonstrated that only *internal institutions* develop according to relative transaction costs with institutional competition being a decisive process for discovery. A requirement for the functioning of this process, however, is the existence of basic rights, i.e., *external institutions* which must be set and safeguarded by the government in order to firmly establish a market economy (Leipold, 1985, p. 49).

Such a distinction is also made by Schüller (1991) and by Bohnet and Reichardt (1993). This distinction is aimed at the question, for which *type* of institutions can such an explanation, namely one based *exclusively* on transaction cost economics, claim validity? The answer, of course, is internal institutions for which, at the least, there is in principle the possibility of their arising without political manipulation. They are to be distinguished from the external institutions of the market economy, which represent the necessary framework for a market economy and, consequently, are also the prerequisite for it. Because external institutions are consciously designed to last for a long time, the peculiarities of the political sphere (e.g., in parliamentary democracies, the conditions of the voters' market) must be taken into account in an analysis of those institutions. By treating the two institutional levels separately, the fact that transaction costs play a different role and are not equally important in each category becomes clear. For example, we may suggest that external institutions are relatively detached from economic efficiency and cost considerations (Leipold, 1985).

With the recommendation that we treat the two levels of institutions separately, it must be said that internal institutions *can*, theoretically, develop free of political interference and in the sense of transaction cost economics, but there is no guarantee of its *actually* happening that way. An abstinence of political actors from designing such institutions assumes that they see no possibility of serving their own interests (whether selfish or altruistic) through manipulation of the process of institutional innovation.

Furthermore, from a more fundamental perspective, it appears that the above statement is rather important. If we consider that the main purpose, or at least the result, of designing and redesigning institutions for the citizens is to establish rights, then *internal institutions exclusive of the state are inconceivable and undeniable*, because the holder of rights has to be able to make his claim on the state for the enforcement and use of those rights. 'A right is the capacity to call upon the collective power to stand behind one's claim to a benefit stream' (Bromley, 1991). 'A rights holder has the capacity *to command* the state to act in a certain way. The effective protection from this authority is nothing more than a correlated duty or obligation for all others' (Bromley, 1995, p. 40, emphasis in original). Certainly, if the state, along with its political actors and organizations, is needed to protect the individual's property rights concerning conditions between the rights holder and others who may also be interested in the object of the rights, then, strictly speaking, an explanation of institutions based exclusively on transaction cost economics is unimaginable.

Obviously, we have to accept that institutional change cannot take place without participation of the state to some extent, and along with it, corresponding political influence. Nevertheless, different levels and ways of political determination of institutions are imaginable, ranging from the restriction of state participation as a truly protective representative of property rights that have come about through processes of self-organization to the detailed political regulation of institutional change.

The latter case applies to the political decisionmaking process regarding privatization of nationalized land in Eastern Germany, which is strongly influenced by bureaucratic procedures. In contrast, there is more scope for self-organization in the area of collectivized land, where the process of transforming collective farms is to a large extent left to decentralized mechanisms regulated by a legal framework of rules and supported by various forms of government assistance. These observations lead us to certain questions (see Hagedorn, 1996; Hagedorn and Klages, 1994):

1 What differences exist between institutional change produced by political regulations and institutional change based on self-organization? What are the advantages and the disadvantages? It seems to be an adequate interpretation of 'self-organization' to assume that institutions are predominantly shaped by market mechanisms and competitive procedures so that the outcome of institutional change is to a large extent determined by transaction costs.

2 If the institutional innovations desired can only be achieved by political coordination – as in the case of privatizing of nationalized land[2] – the question arises whether (and how) certain deficits of politically organized institutional choice can be compensated for. In the East German case, this could happen if the privatization policies were in part connected with market mechanisms (e.g., land auctions) or opportunities for participation (e.g., mediation procedures).

3 In addition, we have to make sure that such modifications or complements of the privatization policies are not only rational in economic terms; they must also be acceptable on the political level (i.e., for the actors in the political process). For this reason, the special political economy of decisionmaking processes has to be taken into account. This means that additional questions arise, such as whether the decisionmakers who coordinate the process of institutional choice can actually arrange the consensus, depending again on the political actors involved, on the policy networks in which they are included, and their political interests and strategies.

To get closer to an answer to these questions, we first have to look for the problem's theoretical structure, which may be based on adequate approaches of institutional economics, political economics, and policy analysis. This is the first step of our analysis (section 2). These theoretical considerations will then be discussed on an empirical basis by analyzing two episodes from the political process towards compensation and privatization in which considerable changes to the 'privatization regime' were on the political agenda (see also Hagedorn 1993a, 1994a, 1995; Hagedorn and Klages, 1994; Klages and Hagedorn, 1993; Klages, 1994; Klages and Klare, 1994, 1995a,b,c): the replacement of the

Gerster proposal through the Bohl Paper and the submission of the Gattermann proposal as an alternative to the government's plan for an Indemnification and Compensation Bill, and its dismissal through a Bonds Model of the German Federal Government (sections 3 and 4). At the end, a compromise concerning the assessment of compensation payments and the design of a Land Acquisition Program through which the political decisionmaking process on indemnification and compensation could find a provisional end will be outlined (section 5). To begin, we will briefly outline the situation in East German agriculture which prevailed before decollectivization and privatization began.

The initial situation of privatization: structure of agriculture in Eastern Germany

To understand the initial situation of East German agriculture, we first have to look at those agricultural policies of the German Democratic Republic (GDR) by which ownership structures and organization of agricultural production were fundamentally changed after World War II. Two major political decisions affected the ownership structures and organization of agricultural production in a fundamental way:

1 *Land Reform (1945-49)*: The nationalized agricultural land which has to be privatized originated from two sources – from the so-called land reform, which took place in the Soviet Occupied Territory from 1945-1949, and, to a minor extent, from expropriations during the first phase of collectivization of agriculture in 1952 and 1953 (for details, see Klages, 1994). In the process of the land reform, which actually consisted of *confiscation procedures*, 7,160 farm and forest operations whose owners were classified as 'big landlords' and 'squires' and which were larger than 100 hectares (average size: 350 hectares) were expropriated without any compensation. In addition, 4,537 farm operators lost their property (average size: 30 hectares) because they were said to be Nazi-leaders and war criminals. From the land acquired through these confiscations, together with agricultural land and forests that belonged to the state before the end of World War II, a land reserve with a total area of 3.3 million hectares was established. From this land reserve, 2.2 million hectares were (preliminarily) reprivatized to so-called new settlers (i.e., farmers who were refugees from the eastern provinces of Germany now belonging to Poland and Russia, peasants with small farms, and farm workers who received this land (average size: 8 hectares) as 'working property'. The rest of the expropriated land remained nationalized property and was mainly used to establish state-owned estates (Volkseigene Güter - VEGs).

201

2 *Enforced Collectivization (1952-60)*: Collectivization had little impact on the (formal) ownership structure of land. During this period of collectivization, another significantly large area of land was expropriated, but only part of this became registered state property. During the first wave of collectivization in 1952 and 1953 24,200 farms were expropriated. Up to 700,000 hectares were confiscated and held in trust by the county councils. In most cases county councils handed the land over to the agricultural production cooperatives (Landwirtschaftliche Produktionsgenossenschaften, or LPGs) founded in those years, without charging them rent. Collectivization did change the organization of agriculture by establishing and expanding the LPGs. Formally, the land still belonged to the individual owners, but the LPGs were endowed with unrestricted rights to use the land, including the right to set up buildings. The LPGs' assets were considered collective property, so there was no private claim upon collective assets when members were dismissed.

The initial situation regarding the ownership structure and organization of production prior to decollectivization and privatization can be characterized as follows:

1 About 70 percent of agricultural land was privately owned, 30 percent was state property or state-governed private property. The main physical assets in agriculture were considered collective property.

2 Organization of agriculture was dominated by LPGs. In 1989, 4,530 LPGs cultivated 82.2 percent of the agricultural land. State farms were only of marginal importance: 580 state farms cultivated 7.5 percent of the agricultural land. Collective and state farms specialized in either animal or plant production. Even in 1989 only 5.4 percent of the agricultural land[3] was used for small-scale private farming.

Accordingly, collective farms prevailed in the initial stage of the transformation process. Most problems arose with decollectivization (i.e., the restructuring of the LPGs). Privatization of nationalized land seemed to be far less important for the restructuring of the agricultural sector. In spite of this, the political economy of restructuring agriculture in Eastern Germany was predominantly shaped by debate about the issues of privatizing nationalized land. This may be because problems of indemnification and privatization could only be solved through extensive political and administrative procedures and involved legal questions requiring extensive legislation and administration.

As privatization in Eastern Germany has been guided by the principle, 'restitution deserves priority over indemnification', only a part of the expropriated land could be included within the privatization schemes. According to Klages (1994), the area of agricultural land available for privatization could be calculated as follows: In 1993-'94, the area leased out by the Land Administration and Utilization Company (the Bodenverwaltungs- und -verwertungsgesellschaft - BVVG, to which the Treuhandanstalt - THA, i.e., the German privatization agency, assigned the task of privatizing agricultural land) amounted to approximately 1.14 million hectares. Furthermore, the privatization agency (Treuhandanstalt - THA) possessed approximately 245,000 hectares of nationalized land which formerly belonged to the state-owned estates. In total, the agricultural area to be restituted to former owners can be estimated at approximately 500,000 - 600,000 hectares, of which already 200,000 hectares have been returned. Only the remaining 1.0 to 1.1 million hectares of agricultural land were expected to be available for privatization schemes. This amounts to approximately 18-20 percent of the total agricultural area in Eastern Germany.

Towards a conceptual structure of the problem

Differences between institutional innovation by political regulation and institutional change based on self-organization

The main differences between institutional change through political coordination and institutional change based on self-organization are due to the influence of *external determination* on the people concerned instead of there being more *self-determination,* and to the differences regarding the *speed* with which decisions rearding the institutional changes are made and actually implemented.

In particular, the following factors influence institutional change.

1 If institutions are reshaped step by step, and if this is done by the people themselves, the revision of rules and organizational structures is simultaneously accompanied by a consensus; or, at least, more insight is probably given to the necessity of the changes. In contrast, institutional change demanded by the state encounters more disagreement and resistance.

2 If reconstruction of institutions is based on large-scale political programs, there are always people who suffer huge losses in income or property. These losses occur suddenly, not gradually, and are clearly noticeable for the losers. Landowners who lost their property by expropriation during land reform in Eastern Germany after World War II may be a good example. Another example is the right granted to production cooperatives (LPGs) to

operate nationalized land that they did not own and for which they did not pay rent. This type of institutional change always raises the political question whether the losers should receive compensation.

3   The reason political conflicts become a part of the game lies not only with the losers but also with the winners. If gains from new institutional arrangements happen within a very short period of time and are produced by single political decisions, there are very strong incentives for rent-seeking behavior favoring the interests of clientele groups. For example, politicians in Germany had to decide whether former owners should receive payment or – to some extent – land as compensation was a major issue for the interest groups involved.

4   Institutional change by self-organization usually proceeds in small steps and therefore limits the cost of errors. Proceeding with large steps which is typical in the political approach to institution building, increases the cost of decisions when they prove to be wrong. Furthermore, inadequate decision-making is more likely to occur, because collective action often provides opportunities to externalize the cost of such decisions, by putting the burden on other groups.

5   Sometimes political concepts of institutional change may be well elaborated and reliable so that they protect people from taking wrong routes or detours. But it is also possible for well-known institutional arrangements to merely be copied and transferred as in the present case, from Western to Eastern Germany. It is questionable whether such transferred arrangements will prove adequate for coping with Eastern Germany's future requirements. Traditional notions of the size and organization of a family farm can serve as an example.

Finally, we have to recognize that in a pluralistic society with a mixed economy, political construction of economic institutions can only happen very insufficiently, that is, with drawn-out bureaucratic procedures. This is a fundamental problem (see Schulz, 1992). Politicians may introduce some basic institutional structures such as private property, but the main process of institutional innovation will begin after such introductions. In other words, it is easier for state agencies to build up a system of central planning, because the real economic order is part of the political concept. In contrast, if a market economy is supposed to work, an evolutionary process of selection regarding economic and institutional solutions must take place. This is also true for the question of what types of farm enterprises and other agrarian institutions will result from the transformation process. Government can make and implement decisions regarding the economic constitution, but it cannot prescribe the final economic structure, which can and only will develop in a polycentric and evolutionary way.

Basic possibilities to compensate for the deficits of institutional innovation through political coordination

Starting from the premise that problems of indemnification and privatization can only be solved by extensive political and administrative procedures (for example, legal questions which require extensive legislation and administration), we can then ask whether decisions and procedures could be improved by excluding some areas or tasks from the administrative system and leaving them to other institutional arrangements (with a network of bureaucratic and other mechanisms for their coordination). In principle, two such possibilities can be imagined:

1 Compensation for the deficits of politically regulated institutional change, which is oriented towards the objective of not predetermining the evolution of the systems of agrarian institutions, and which integrates all groups concerned (i.e., expropriated farmers and successor farms of the LPGs, owners, and tenants). For this purpose, market mechanisms might be introduced to support selection processes leading to an efficient agrarian structure (e.g., land auctions, voucher systems), perhaps complemented by a program of agricultural structure policies to provide the farmers with a basic amount of owned land.

2 Compensation for the deficits of politically regulated institutional change by introducing methods of participation and consensus building to get away from the narrow focus on the materialistic aspects of privatization. A more balanced approach could include procedures of alternative dispute resolution (ADR) (e.g., mediation).

We will only return to the first of these variants of institutional improvements later.

Political conditions for improving the results of the privatization process of politically regulated institutional change

Could such complementary elements be accepted under real political conditions? This depends on whether (and to what extent) the political actors involved want to keep those decisions by which institutions such as landownership are shaped in their own hands or at least to maintain direct control over these decisions, and to what extent they are open to more pluralistic coordination mechanisms which they could only influence indirectly. This question has already been formulated in a similar way by Schenk (1981, 1982, 1983) for systems comparison in comparative economics. The approach used by Schenk is based on transaction-cost economics in the tradition of Coase, and above all, on Williamson's (1975) concept of 'markets and hierarchies' as two main institutional choices. Schenk not only discusses the determinants of choice between markets and hierarchies (i.e., the amount of investments particular to transaction costs, insecurity regarding the process and success of transactions, and frequency of transactions), but introduces additional differentiations within the category of *hierarchy*.

Starting from the market and hierarchy typology, Schenk differentiates between hierarchies according to those procedures by which the decision makers in office coordinate processes on subordinated levels (see Schenk, 1982). Regarding such coordination mechanism, Schenk distinguishes between the 'price supported regime', 'budget regime', and 'planning regime'. The competencies of the decisionmakers, for example, and of the owners of private enterprises – or of government agencies in the case of the public administration – are assumed to be weak in the case of price-supported regimes, to be stronger in the case of budget regimes, and to be strongest in the case of planning regimes. The opposite is true in the case of the subordinated management agencies. By choosing among these regimes simultaneously, the scope for market mechanisms is determined.

On the macroeconomic level Schenk also distinguishes between institutional arrangements which are imaginable (i.e., the 'commercial regime' versus the 'regulating regime') and the 'regime based on direct state control'. The choice among these institutional alternatives is left to the politicians, and is also the reason why their motives and decisionmaking criteria have to be considered as dominating determinants of institutional choice. As a consequence, in Schenk's approach, the criterion of efficiency he acknowledges as valid for the commercial regime is accompanied by the criterion of political opportunism. For individual politicians it is supposed to be opportunistic to choose in such a way as to secure an important proportion of competencies for themselves. This interest tends to oust the principle of institutional choice based on economic efficiency (Leipold, 1985). If we go a step further, we could think of a *continuous scale of governance structures* on which the competencies of the governing agencies change from 'very strong' on the one side, to 'very weak' on the other, to which the scope for market mechanisms and pluralistic and polycentric coordination mechanisms would correspond.

It is up to the political economy of the privatization process to allow for modifications that act against a regime of direct bureaucratic control and in favor of one with more markets and participation. This determines whether, and to what extent, such modifications can make their way into political decisions and up into administrative implementation. Strictly speaking, this can only be understood if we analyze all potential channels of influence politicians can make use of. These first apply to those actors and interactions within the 'protected policy network of agricultural policy' (Hagedorn, 1993c, 1994, 1996; Hagedorn and Schmitt, 1985), where interest groups, bureaucracies, parliamentary committees, etc., participate in established systems of information and negotiation. Moreover, influences on this subsystem from outside have to be taken into account, above all those deriving from electoral behavior and party competition. Also to be anticipated are external influences on internal decisionmaking processes if the policy network of agricultural policies is opened, because in this case conflicts with the interest of actors of other policy networks (for example, of financial policies) become virulent.

In other words, whether reasonable combinations of economic and political coordination mechanisms are feasible crucially depends on the particular circumstances which prevail before the transformation process. Therefore, the political situation at the starting point of the transformation process plays a considerable role.

Policy networks in the decisionmaking process toward privatization

In Germany we find a specific political situation in the forces relevant to policies of indemnification and privatization. Traditionally, issues of agricultural policy have been negotiated and determined within one political subsystem which protects itself against outside influences (see Hagedorn and Schmitt, 1985; Hagedorn 1996; Mehl, 1995). In the case of privatization, however, several systems are involved:

1 The *traditional policy network of agriculture*, which is located mostly in Bonn, still represents the decisionmaking center in the area of agricultural policies for Eastern Germany. It has been shaped by patterns of negotiation and decisionmaking that were institutionalized during the old Federal Republic, and consequently is oriented towards the West.

2 The *financial policy network*, also located in Bonn, is also supposedly oriented towards the West. The Ministry of Finance is responsible for the policies of indemnification, and since expropriation of agricultural and forest property in quantitative terms goes beyond the limits of one sector, this ministry must coordinate decisions with processes in the agricultural policies network (and vice versa). Such overlapping relations are also necessary to respond to questions from the Ministry of Agriculture and

farmers unions regarding restitution and indemnification, with adequate considerations given to agricultural and forest policy objectives. Above all, agricultural politicians demand that indemnification will at least partly be provided by offering land to the former owners, and that the procedures of compensation will be linked with a land acquisition program for former owners.

3 In addition to the two networks in Bonn, there is the *policy network of agriculture in the New Bundesländer*, which consists of the agricultural ministries of the Länder and the agricultural administration and interest groups on different levels. Due to historical background and the geographic distance, this network is dominated by other interests and relationships.

To show the differences in political influence between these networks, we must consider two main clientele groups with contradicting interests in the process of privatization: former owners of land from West Germany, and large-scale agricultural enterprises in East Germany, (particularly the successors of the former agricultural production cooperatives, or LPGs). Their differences can be described as follows:

1 *Imbalances or asymmetries of information.* The advocates of the former owners who live in West Germany know how to use the channels of information and communication within the systems of government, bureaucracy, and associations in Bonn. Those actors who work for large farm enterprises in East German agriculture are quite familiar with the administrative, personal, and social circumstances in the rural areas in the New Bundesländer.

2 *Different methods of influence.* The lobbyists of the former owners are able to make use of those political mechanisms (cooperative relations, mutual obligations, logrolling agreements) which work within the political networks. Those which represent the interests of the large farms in East Germany can exploit other sources of power. For example, they can enact pressure by influencing the polls and create disturbances by organizing farmer demonstrations, etc.

3 *Unequal impact on implementation.* The former owners from West Germany are in a good position during the first phase of a policy process, which is finished when a law has been passed. But during the phase of implementation, those who want to help the successors of the East German production cooperatives are stronger, because they can modify or even determine the criteria and procedures that are ultimately applied. Politicians

tend to exclude those problems from decisionmaking in Parliament that cause major conflicts and could be detrimental to gaining a consensus and prefer to leave such problems to the administration. Therefore, access to implementation presents a considerable source of influence. In the case of privatization of agricultural land, for example, the criteria applied to lease or sales contracts are established in this phase of the process.

If we assume rational behavior, political actors will try to make use of the strong elements of their position, and try to compensate for the weaknesses they have in the policymaking process. They will try to achieve a privatization regime that provides them with opportunities to mobilize their specific potential to exert influence and to prevent their weaknesses from becoming relevant. Whether these hypotheses can be empirically substantiated will be analyzed in the following sections. We will describe several episodes of political decisionmaking on the privatization issue (see also Hagedorn 1993a, 1994a, 1996; Hagedorn and Klages, 1994; Klages and Hagedorn 1993; Klages 1994; Klages and Klare, 1994, 1995a,b,c). First to be discussed is the decision for a bureaucratic concept of privatization when the so-called 'Gerster Proposal' was replaced by the 'Bohl Paper'. Second, we will point out that an attempt to move towards greater market orientation by means of a voucher concept, as suggested by the Gattermann Proposal, failed due to the political economy of privatization and instead led to a Bonds Model preferred (and accepted) by the federal government. Third, we will briefly point out the status of privatization, which refers to a land acquisition program for selling nationalized land at favorable terms, and which also has been approved by Parliament but is still to be implemented by the administration.

The decision for a bureaucratic concept of privatization - from the Gerster Proposal to the Bohl Paper

The Treuhand Guideline from May 1992

The first rules for privatizing nationalized agricultural land were laid down by the Treuhand Guideline of 3 March 1992, which was modified and finally implemented on 29 May 1992 (see Top-Agrar-Spezial, 1992a; Agra Europe, 1992a,b). In particular, the procedure used by the THA and the BVVG to lease and sell the Treuhand land was set out as follows:

1 The prices for leasing and buying Treuhand land should correspond to *market prices*. The evaluation is supposed to be based on comparisons with other cases in the land market. If local comparable values are not available,

the land may be sold for 150 DM per soil point. Any deviation from this procedure is to be made only when circumstances require so (quality of site location, for example).

2 If there exist several applications to lease or purchase the same piece of land, then aside from the price offered, the decision should be based on the 'farm development concept'. The intended production program, planned investments, as well as the number of future employees should all be included in this farm development concept.

3 In addition to the amount of rent or price offered and the farm development concept, the choice of competing applicants has to take into account the following criteria:
  - the qualifications of the management;
  - the already existing basis for the farm;
  - the agricultural area purchased or leased from others;
  - the consequences upon the region put into effect by the plans;
  - the effects upon the development concept of neighboring businesses; and
  - utilization possibilities of the surrounding Treuhand properties.

4 When the qualifications for the different examining criteria are approximately equal, then distribution of land will proceed in accordance with the following priority list:
  - re-establishers of farms or their inheritors provided that they will operate the farm themselves;
  - new establishers who were local residents by 10 March 1990;
  - succeeding farmers of former LPGs (legal persons);
  - persons who establish a new private farm and become local residents and/or cooperate with local farmers.

5 As a precautionary measure against an excessive concentration of rented or owned land, permission has to be obtained from the THA for infringement of the following property allowances:
  - 300 hectares to one buyer;
  - 500 hectares to the leaser (legal persons: 1,500 hectares);
  - for buyers of more than 100 hectares: 1,800 hectares overall size of farm (legal persons: 2,500 hectares).

The Gerster Paper from June 1992

These rules of a basic concept for land privatization were complemented by those of a working group from the coalition of the Christian and Free

Democrats chaired by a member of Parliament named Gerster. When the Gerster Paper was published, the main conflicts related to the privatization issue were revealed for the first time. The reason the paper caused controversial discussions was that it tried to combine privatization procedures with aspects of compensation for former expropriation. Due to an agreement between Germany and Russia which had been confirmed by the German Constitutional Court ('Bundesverfassungsgericht'), those persons whose property had been expropriated during the so-called land reform, from 1945-1949, were not eligible for restitution, but could receive compensation within certain limits. Such an element of compensation was included in the Gerster Paper in its proposed 're-establisher program' giving special privileges to former owners regarding their access to nationalized land. Three groups were supposed to be consciously preferred over others if they wanted to buy land:

1 Former landowners whose land had been expropriated during the so-called land reform from 1945 to 1949, provided that they were ready to move to their farms in Eastern Germany;

2 Other former owners who were eligible for restitution;

3 And landowners from Eastern Germany who had extracted their land from an LPG, had in the meanwhile re-established their farm, and wanted to enlarge their holding by buying or renting additional land from the THA.

Correspondingly, the following groups were supposed to be *excluded* from the program:

1 Residents of Eastern Germany who did not own any land before, but wanted to establish a new farm of their own;

2 Agricultural enterprises originating from the reorganization of LPGs, provided that it was necessary for the LPG successors to buy or rent the land in order to fulfill the requirements of a restructuring and development plan, confirmed by local authorities;

3 Persons who wished to establish a new private farm and become local residents and/or cooperate with local farmers in Eastern Germany, but did not yet reside in Eastern Germany.

If the land was not sold but leased on a long-term contract, persons who re-established their old farms (re-establishers) and those who established a new farm (establishers) were supposed to be treated equally (see Agra Europe,

1992d). An additional stipulation suggested by the Gerster Committee was a differentiation in priorities, i.e., that first only the re-establishers could buy land, then – after a deadline had elapsed – the establishers would be permitted to buy land. In contrast, the THA and the agricultural ministers of the New Bundesländer in Eastern Germany insisted on equal treatment of the two groups. In addition, certain upper limits to the amount of land bought or rented by one person, company, or cooperative were determined.

According to the Gerster Proposal, applicants had to submit a farm development concept. Land prices and rents were to be set in accordance with market values, to be determined by a special evaluation method based on comparable sale or lease contracts in the region. If this was not feasible due to a lack of transactions on the regional land market, 150 DM per soil point was to be taken as a guideline. In addition, persons entitled to a so-called settlement model were supposed to obtain land at very low credit cost. The Gerster Committee demanded expressly that the THA should hold aside enough land for the re-establishment program, and not block it by making long-term lease contracts exclusively with other farmers.

For the allocation of land made reasonable through financial support, certain ceilings were to apply: a maximum of 160 hectares or 8,000 soil points for acquisition, and acquisition exceeding allowances were also to be possible but no longer promotable under the guidelines of the re-establishment program. The capital costs for land acquisition were thus to be reduced, so that, excluding any settlement made within the first five years free of liquidation, it would amount to 3.50 DM per soil point, with a maximum allowance of 5.20 DM per soil point (3.50 DM as interest payment in the amount of the regular cost of leasing and an additional 1.70 DM as a settlement). The subvention of this land was to be for a running term of twenty years. Five years after the expiration of the reduced interest rate (twenty-five years after the original purchase) the buyers or inheritors were to be permitted to sell the land.

Criticism of the Gerster Paper

Opposition to the Gerster Paper came mainly from the New Bundesländer[4] and the Social Democrats, but above all from Brandenburg, where the Social Democrats were in office. But the Bundesrat[5] as well published a conclusion in November of 1992 which disagreed with the Gerster Paper's concept. The main points of criticism were[6] (see Agra Europe, 1992c) the following:

1 At a special conference a few days before the Gerster paper was complete, the agricultural ministers of all Bundesländer and the Federal Ministry of Agriculture reached an agreement to lease the land with long-term contracts,

and not to sell it, i.e., to sell it later (in the sense of 'preprivatization'). In spite of this, the Ministry of Finance obviously supported a program which again gave priority to selling the land instead of leasing it first. East German politicians felt deceived.

2 Local farmers – both people who had established a new family farm and members of cooperatives or companies, e.g., of the LPG successors – were discriminated against in comparison with the re-establishers. Only the re-establishers were supposed to be allowed to apply for the re-establishment program, and would have had to have been served with land in advance. This meant – in the eyes of East German politicians – treating some (wealthy) West German investors better than the (poor) East German farmers (see also Bundesrat, 1992). This action also contradicted the above mentioned special conference of agriculture ministers, in which they had consented and agreed to the creation of a settlement model to be made with the Bundesländer giving equal opportunities for the local re-establishers and the local new establishers.

3 Furthermore, equal opportunities regarding access to land were not provided, because a certain area of land should have been put into a land reserve to be used exclusively for the re-establishment program. This land would no longer be available for leasing to East German farmers on a long-term basis, i.e., twelve-year contracts, but first had to be offered to the re-establishers. Moreover, it was argued that the survival of farms that were already operating the land on short-term lease contracts was endangered, if portions of that farmland were to be taken away and used for the re-establishment program (see Bauern-Zeitung, 1993).

Obviously, the Gerster Paper mobilized the East-West conflict in Germany. Special opposition and critique arose because of its exclusion of new establishers from the acquisition of reasonably priced land. In East Germany, no one could expect any understanding for the proposal that only those already possessing property would benefit from of a highly subsidized program, while landless farmers would come away empty-handed. This partly included people who had been active in the agricultural sector during the past forty years in second and even third generations but who – despite their farming history – under GDR governance had not had any chance at all to establish their own farms.

In this situation the government had to react very quickly. A working group chaired by Bohl – the minister in the Chancellor's Office – soon presented a new model for privatization of land which was mainly oriented towards two objectives: to reduce the time pressure for privatization (see Ernährungsdienst, 1992b,c) and to disarm the conflicts between the groups involved. A three-phase model was proposed (see Grund, 1992; Agra Europe, 1992e, 1993d). In the first phase all land was to be leased for twelve years by means of a bureaucratic procedure. Applicants for land had to present a farm development concept, and have sufficient qualifications to run the farm. If there happened to be more than one applicant, and if those applicants were equally qualified, then the BVVG was to proceed according to a priority list:

1 Re-establishers – both those eligible for restitution and those who not – the heirs of these groups, and local farmers who established a new farm. Unfortunately, conflicting groups were put together here: former owners from West Germany and new farmers in East Germany. As a consequence, another regulation was added: in case of rivalry between applicants from two subgroups, the 'victims of the land reform' were to be taken into account in the sense of a 'balance of interests', i.e., this group was supposed to obtain some land regardless of the outcome of the application process. This guideline was termed the 'interest harmonization clause'.

2 Successors of LPGs.

3 Persons wanting to establish a new farm, but not residents of East Germany.

A 'survival clause' specified that if land leased by twelve-year contracts was taken away from other farms, this should not endanger the economic existence of those farms. The tenants were to promise that they would operate the land independently and by themselves. They would also receive an option to buy the land later (the 'purchasing option'). The lease contract could be seized before the twelve years expired, if there were former owners eligible for restitution. These contracts contained what was termed a 'cancellation clause'.

In the second stage proposed by the Bohl Paper, a Land Acquisition and Settlement Program was planned to offer land at favorable conditions to certain groups. The first component, the Land Acquisition Program, focused on former owners eligible for indemnification, i.e., for compensation for losses they suffered by confiscation or expropriation of their land and other properties. Within certain limits, they could choose compensation by payments or in land. The program restricted the amount of land one former

214

owner could buy, and if the land was sold again by that former owner within twenty years, the profits had to be transferred to the THA budget.

The second component of the program, the Settlement Program, was open only to 'natural persons', i.e., re-establishers or new establishers who were local residents. Companies and registered cooperatives which were the successors of the LPGs and the individual members of these farm firms were to have no access to this program (a restriction that was waved in the final version). Other farmers who operated family farms or belonged to civil partnerships did have access to the program; they could buy land until 50 percent of their farm consisted of owned land.

However, the applicants were only able to buy that land which they had *already have rented* in the first phase of the program, provided that they would still operate it. Other persons were excluded – there was a 'closed shop' – market mechanisms and/or any sort of competition was abandoned. Only if some lease contracts were to be terminated before the twelve years expired (when, for example, the farms on rented land were given up) could applicants without lease contracts have a chance to buy land, provided that they fulfill the resulting conditions of the program. In addition, expropriated former owners who did not receive land in the first phase, and therefore could not be compensated by means of land in the Land Acquisition Program, were allowed to buy land in the Settlement Program, but were required to lease it to the former operator, who had rented it before on a long-term basis.

In the third phase of privatization, after the first two programs had been carried out, the rest of the land would be sold on the land market without any restrictions and without financial support from the government.

Criticism of the three-phase model of the Bohl Paper

When this model was presented to the public by the Bohl Paper, another wave of criticism came in response, predominately from the New Bundesländer. It can be summarized as follows:

1 Again, the special treatment of former landowners, this time by means of the 'interest harmonization clause', was regarded as a privilege for this group and was neither accepted by Brandenburg nor by the Social Democrats in Parliament.

2 Sufficient protection of those farms which were expected to give up land having been leased to other farms in the first phase outlined above would have to be guaranteed according to the 'survival clause'. This claim was difficult to fulfill, especially for the agencies involved. For example, if 500 hectares were taken from a farm with 3,000 hectares, would this

'endanger' the economic survival basis of the farm? It would be nearly impossible for a bureaucracy like the BVVG to make reasonable decisions on such issues.

3 The long-term lease agreements offered by the BVVG to their tenants demanded adherence to the declaration made in the presented farm development concept, and in the case of deviation put the expiration of the lease contract in sight, as long as the deviation was not on grounds of compelling circumstances (see Agra Europe, 1993a). This restriction, barely controllable within reason, certainly contradicted the responsibility of the business person or entrepreneur to adapt to unforeseeable changes in economic conditions, whether internal or external.

4 The lease contract suggested by the BVVG allowed for a renegotiation of the amount of rent to be paid after the first three years. This could cause 'waves of negotiations' over time, and in this way decision on rents would be institutionalized as a matter of political negotiations. The land markets which still worked properly in Germany could suffer from such increasing intervention.

5 If successor enterprises of LPGs changed the structure of their group of members such that only less than 50 percent of the shares were held by former LPG members, then the lease contract was to be canceled immediately. This restriction was made to avoid situations in which outsider lease-interested parties could buy their way into a farm enterprise, thus bypassing the priority list for access to nationalized land.

6 The restriction that only natural persons could buy land on favorable conditions was, of course, not accepted in the New Bundesländer especially not by those farmers on farms organized as legal entities, which still represented the majority of the East German farms. The additional reservation, that even the individual members of those farms organized as legal entities were supposed to be excluded, met with incomprehension.

7 Placing the purchase limit at the equivalent of 50 percent of a farmer's land, under phase two (the Settlement Program), appeared less useful as objective criterion. The operator of a farm in the early stages of development (young farmers who had not stocked up as much leased property as more mature businesses), would be at a disadvantage. Taking into account that small operations need to expand just in order to survive, it was argued that a set-limit applying equally to all subsidized land purchases be established.

8 Market access and competition were completely suppressed in the Bohl Paper, as nobody but the tenant was allowed to buy rented land. The functions of coordination normally fulfilled by the land market, i.e., allocation of land and price setting, were replaced by bureaucratic decisions. For example, the land acquisition program for former landowners was supposed to be extended to leased land, as already mentioned. This meant that former owners could acquire land operated by East German farmers, but that they had to accept (and even extend) the existing lease contract. However, purchase prices of leased land were lower than those of vacant land. In Germany, however, there is no real market for selling or buying leased land, i.e., there is no empirical basis for the BVVG to estimate prices for this land.

The program was developed first for nationalized land not part of the nationalized estates operated as state-owned farms (Volkseigene Güter - VEG). But in October 1993, the program was transferred to the VEGs which are to be privatized in a similar way by the BVVG. The estates are to be divided into reasonable subunits and either sold immediately or leased on a trial basis (see Agra Europe, 1993b,c).

Conclusions from the first episode of decisionmaking

The Gerster Proposal originated from political activities within the Western policy network in Bonn.   This proposal tried to make the privatization procedure more flexible by introducing small market components. However, it also tried to build up strong market restrictions by implementing priorities for one particular group (former landowners). A counterreaction from the East German policy network arose immediately.   In this case, the mechanisms mentioned in section 2 were employed by mobilizing public protest, which finally resulted – along with the presentation of the Bohl Paper – in the near abolishment of market mechanisms and an introduction of bureaucratic procedures. Only the first component of the three-phase concept has been implemented to date. The BVVG has so far only made long-term lease contracts with tenants.   The main task of privatization, privatization of landownership, has been postponed.

An attempt towards a market-oriented revision: the voucher concept of the Gattermann Proposal

In November 1993, a working group of the coalition of the Christian and Free Democrats, whose chairman was member of Parliament Gattermann, proposed to use vouchers as a means of compensation for those formerly expropriated. This concept had first been promoted by an interest group of former landowners supported by members of Parliament who also acted as lobbyists for 'victims of the land reform'. In substance, the Gattermann Proposal was a response to the draft bill of the Indemnification and Compensation Law – EALG of 5 May 1995. According to the EALG, compensation payments for expropriations were to be partially financed by a levy on property in East Germany that was (or would be) returned to its original owners.[7] This became a major source of conflict, because these owners, who already had to finance investments, would be additionally burdened by the levy. This and other points of criticism were brought to a hearing for the EALG before the Finance and Law Committee of the Bundestag on 15-16 September 1993 (see Agra Europe, 1993e). The Gattermann Proposal was aimed first at eliminating the property levy. Second, it proposed offering the former owners compensation by means of real property. Third, as an organizational tool to implement this method of indemnification, a voucher model was presented.

The voucher model from Gattermann and the commission for indemnification and compensation from November 1993

The basic idea behind the Gattermann Proposal was first to eliminate the financing of indemnification (the property levy) and to offer victims of former expropriations compensation through real property, using the voucher model.

1 The proposed vouchers were to be used in three ways:
   a Trade the vouchers: on the market for certificates
   b Buy public property: in this case, buying directly or by means of associations especially founded for the purchase of public property
   c Return to the state: after January 2004, to receive a money payment of 25-47 percent of the voucher's nominal value, depending on the year of issue

2 Public property was to be offered in auctions which would allow certain groups to use a right of preemption:
   a Owners of vouchers belonging to persons who offered the highest price would obtain a right of preemption if their vouchers covered at least one quarter of the price of the land
   b If several persons offered the highest price (or were within the upper price margin), a priority list would be applied:
      - former owners of the property would be preferred to other owners of vouchers

- with more than one former owner involved, the person with the highest percentage of old property rights in relation to the auctioned piece of property would be preferred
- with no former owner involved, priority would be given to the person with the greatest number of vouchers

3 During the auctions the former owners could make use of a special right: they could join the group of persons offering the highest prices, even if their own first bid was lower.

4 Upper limits to the purchase of vouchers were proposed: owners of vouchers who received them directly as a compensation for expropriated property would be allowed to buy additional vouchers up to three times the number they originally possessed. In some cases, this limit would go up to 3 million DM. Other persons buying vouchers would generally be bound to the limit of 1 million DM.

5 Finally, a modification of the three-phases concept of the Bohl Paper was proposed. First, the length of the lease contracts would be extended from twelve to eighteen years. Second, the interest harmonization clause – which favored former owners if they competed with others for leased land – was to be eliminated. Obviously, the conditions for tenants were promised to be improved in order to provide compensation for the extended opportunity given former owners to buy the land.

The certificate model as a basic approach for solving the indemnification issue as well as the privatization problems

After listing the main points of the proposal, we may ask what advantages and what disadvantages could be expected if such an instrument were actually implemented.

1 Advantages include that the state would be relieved from several burdens and tasks:
- from a large proportion of the financial burden for compensation payments, because indemnification was mostly to be provided by the distribution of vouchers good for real estate
- from the distribution of land and other property, because this would take place by means of the voucher market and real estate auctions
- from fixing prices, because this also would occur on the voucher market and through auctions of public property

- from other problems of coordination, because these problems were no longer to be solved solely by politicians and administrators (many decentralized actors were to be part of the game – banks, brokers, investors, etc.)

2 The privatization process would become more flexible due to
  - an extended period of time for privatization
  - mobilization of the variety of actors involved
  - improved participation by buyers of small property

3 We could also expect that privatization of public property would, in many cases, increase efficiency.

On the other hand we must also take into account some disadvantages of the vouchers concept. Among the many arguments against this approach, it has been said that vouchers would not be feasible in political terms, because politicians might be accused of selling out East Germany to West Germans.

Problematic consequences of basic relevance

Aside from the above problems in the Gattermann Proposal, there exist other implications (see, in detail, Klages and Hagedorn, 1993; see also Doll et al., 1993). The Gattermann Proposal implies a separation between ownership of land and operation of land, and this separation tends to be too extreme and could lead to a specific polarization. The property rights are divided – one group 'poor East German farmers' gets the right to use the land and the other group 'wealthy West German landlords' the right to own it. Admittedly, this is an exaggeration, but clearly, a distribution of rights would be institutionalized thereby leading to social imbalance. Ownership rights are always a source of independence and power, and if farmers only have the right to use the land, there will always be a certain degree of dependence. Thus, the privatization procedure should aim at a better balance and more variety regarding the resulting distribution of rights. This is difficult to achieve due to the political economy of the privatization issue, which has produced a type of conflict resolution that works according to an exchange of group favors: some ownership rights for the former landowners in exchange for long-term lease contracts for the farm operators. To correct this imbalance, the certificate model could be complemented by a landownership program that would provide as many agricultural operations as possible with the advantages of a certain amount of owned land.

To do historical justice to the idea of reparation, certain priorities in favor of former owners are integrated into the competitive model of the Gattermann

Proposal, as was similarly done with the Gerster Paper. In the Gatterman Proposal, however, these priorities are granted by a double preferential treatment. If a former owner can cover a quarter of the price by means of vouchers, he/she can join the group of bidders who have offered the highest prices, even if this owner's initial offer was very low. He/she can claim the right of preemption. However, a right of preemption which is arranged in this way and combined with an ex post-access to the highest bid is incompatible with the principles of auctions. Auctions are intended to cause the participants to reveal their preferences during the first bid, and they aim to sell to the participants who can make the best use of their resources. If some privileged participants are allowed to present a second bid, their first bid will be based on strategic considerations and will not reveal their preferences. A reliable comparison of willingness to pay and, along with it, the bidder's expectation of success is not possible by means of such modified auctions.

Problems of privatization based on tenure with and without a government lessor

The Bohl Paper proposed selling the land to the tenants who operate the farm so that they could become landowners. In contrast, the Gattermann Proposal supported a farming system based more on leased land. More nonfarmers would have access to land and could lease it to farm operators. As a compensation for the above-mentioned special rights at the auctions for old owners, the tenants would receive an increased term on their lease contracts. However, if tenancy plays a too large role in agriculture, and if the proportion and distribution of owned land is inadequate, then certain economic and political problems are likely to arise (see, for details, Hagedorn, 1993a). Some arise independent of whether or not the lease contract is made with the state as lessor or with a private owner. Others correspond typically to when the state is lessor.

1 The land cannot be used as collateral by the farm operator if he/she wants to obtain loans for investments, because he/she does not own the land.

2 Whether a farm based on rented land can develop continuously depends on the extension of the lease contracts. From the tenant's point of view this means a strong dependence upon the lessor. In the case of the state as lessor, this may result in an inclination towards exploitation of the tenant's weak position or an obligation towards social objectives protecting the tenant's interest. Which of those alternatives will actually be chosen depends on the characteristics of the political system.

3 In democratic societies an agricultural system designed in this way leads to regulatory measures in the land market that will make allowances for the security of the tenants so that the status of a 'pseudo owner' is attainable. It seems more responsible to strive for an agricultural system touching on 'real' ownership from the very beginning, because then the aforementioned political incentives to move towards an increase in the intensity of political intervention do not arise.

4 If it is a question of the lessor being in the position of having a partial monopoly – as is the case with the BVVG, whose decisionmaking processes are implemented no differently from those of a large bureaucratic organization – special problems arise regarding the costs and typical inadequacies of such a coordination mechanism. The lease agreements, for instance, must be carried out under considerable administrative expenditures. In contrast, if the land is broadly distributed among many owners such decisions on leasing and renting are made by the many economic actors involved without causing high administrative costs.

5 The concentration of power associated with centralized landownership in the hands of government agencies may not be noteworthy, provided that democratic control of politics is working well. However, in the development of each society, there can be phases in which democratic principles and constitutional rights carry little weight and the possible arbitrariness of decisions concerning farmers regarding to land distribution, expropriation, and setting of rents, etc., should be approached cautiously. An agricultural system based on broadly distributed landownership offers better security against arbitrary treatment.

6 Even if situations such as those mentioned above do not occur, the problem that large bureaucracies do not disappear still remains. Although the agency established for leasing the land (the BVVG) is supposed to be in effect only until all the nationalized land is sold, the question arises whether this will actually happen, given the interests of the various bureaucracies involved.

7 Finally, bureaucratic control through government of the lease market can hardly be expected to be efficient, especially when it leads to incompatibilities with the interests of the economic actors concerned. Illegal lease markets will emerge, because formless leasing agreements among farmers and landowners will be produced, resulting in an undesirable lack of security concerning rights and planning.

Because the average share of rented land is very high in East German agriculture, the farmers in the New Bundesländer are extremely dependent on the continuity of lease contracts and on the level of rent. This dependency could lead to situations in which political pressure is exerted upon those political actors responsible for agricultural policies to change the land lease laws in a way that creates more security and greater political protection for the tenants. This indicates an important reason why the land should be sold as quickly as possible to the present farmers or former landowners. Experiences from other countries show that it is reasonable to avoid further interventions in the lease market. In the Netherlands, for example, the effects of tenants' protection have been analyzed in detail, especially by van den Noort (1993). He reports that the share of leased land in the Netherlands has dropped by nearly 20 percent from 53 to 35 percent of the total area of agricultural land. The number of tenants has decreased by a yearly average of 2 percent. In West Germany, in contrast, the percentage of leased land has increased in the course of the structural transition.

If a leased farm is to be sold in the Netherlands, the lessee holds the right of preemption as long as he/she is willing to pay market prices. If the lessee does not make use of this opportunity, he/she still has the right to continue to keep the land for another six years. Van den Noort (1993) shows that the accrued loss in market value resulting from a decision to lease a farm, and the opposite, the increase in market value that accrues to those who can decide that the lease comes to term (i.e., the premium for vacant possession), represent an exact reflection of the tenants' political protection. These empirical results illustrate a special type of irony in the legislation concerning tenant protection. Originally, such a policy was supposed to reinforce the weak economic position of the lessees. The real effects, however, by responding to economic incentives, go in the opposite direction: young farmers who want to rent a farm or try to enlarge their holding by renting additional land do not find a sufficient supply of land on the lease market.

Conclusion from the second episode of the decisionmaking process

The Gattermann Proposal, like the Gerster Proposal, was a Western initiative originating from the political network in Bonn. The dominant strategy was also to open the bureaucratic privatization scheme in a market-oriented way in order to allow access to former landowners. Targeted priorities of this group were again included in the competitive model. This was the main cause of a strong political reaction from East German agriculture.

As a consequence, a political consensus based on the Gattermann Proposal could not be achieved, mainly because of the strong protest from the East German politicians and farmers' associations (see Agra Europe, 1993f).

Therefore, representatives of the coalition parties, such as the Christian Democrats and the Free Democrats who participated in the working group mentioned above, agreed upon an alternative model on 23 November 1993 (see Klages and Klare, 1994). The new proposal was based partly on the draft bill of the EALG of 10 May 1993, but also integrated some elements of the Gattermann Proposal (see Grund, 1993; Ernährungsdienst, 1993a,b): the levy on restituted property proposed in the previous version to finance the indemnification payments was cancelled; the assessment basis for the indemnification payments was raised considerably; and the regressive scale applied to the relationship between the amount of compensation paid and the area of land formerly expropriated was reinforced to counteract the raising of the assessment basis and to keep the resulting budgetary burden within the constraints agreed upon beforehand. Simultaneously, the deadline for payments was postponed by suggesting a model according to which indemnification claims could only be made by mortgage bonds due in year 2004 and not yielding any interest in the meantime.

All market elements of the Gattermann Proposal were deleted from the records with the new Bond Model, leaving only the (fiscal-politically motivated) issuing of budget certificates effective far into the future – but without their being related to any property, and used only as a transformer for indemnities. These certificates were designed to be marketable; however, they are only equal to the comparable market value under realization of the loss of interest when claimed before the maturity date (2004).

The provisional conclusion of the decisionmaking process of September 1994: a Bond Model and a Land Acquisition Program

Based on the above-outlined alternative model, a consensus could be achieved for passing the Indemnification and Compensation Act (EALG) from 24 September 1994. The Bundesrat refused at first to accept the draft of the new bill, because the interests of the New Bundesländer came into play. A settlement was finally achieved after the joint mediation committee from the Bundesrat and Bundestag presented a compromise proposal during a second attempt at mediation, in which equal treatment of legal persons (essentially representing the successors of the LPGs) compared with the previous owners, new establishers, and re-establishers concerning their opportunity to buy nationalized land and forest property was ensured (see Agra Europe, 1994a).

As far as the passed law and its conception of indemnification as applied to the privatization of agricultural land, there are two components of special interest: the assessment of compensatory payments for former expropriations and the simultaneously passed Land Acquisition Program (see Indemnification and Compensation Act - EALG, 1994; Agra Europe, 1994b; Klages, 1994; Klages and Klare 1994, 1995a,b,c). The assessment of the indemnification and compensatory payments is derived from the threefold ratable value of the expropriated operations, based on those values from 1935. However, the amount of indemnification will be graded regressively, the increases of the compensatory payments being decreased proportional to the growing amount of the ratable value of the property. Former compensations which the recipient has obtained in the past are to be credited to the newly calculated indemnification. In addition, the amount of compensation decreases through the loss of interest arising from the fact that the indemnification is issued in the form of bonds which first mature in 2004.

Both programs of the second phase of the Bohl Paper (Land Acquisition and Settlement Program) were summed up in one Land Acquisition Program. All buyers of nationalized land participating in this program are to pay the triple amount of the ratable value from 1935 for the purchased land and forest property. This amount, on average, translates to 3,000 DM per ha, corresponding to approximately half of the market value. If the land is sold again within twenty years, profits must be transferred to the state budget. The Land Acquisition Program represents a special area of the Indemnification and Compensation Act, because farmers who can make no claim for indemnification nor compensation also belong to the entitled category of persons. As a matter of fact, all active farmers may take part in the program if they fulfill the following requirements:

1 They have to be new establishers in the locality, re-establishers, legal persons or with respect to the latter but of less importance, members of farms organized as legal persons.

2 The land they wish to purchase has to already have been leased by them over a long period of time, at least twelve years.

3 The purchase of land is subject to specific restrictions which are based first on the overall amount of soil points to be acquired (maximum of 6,000) and second, from the restriction that the share of property, including that newly acquired, not exceed 50 percent of the overall size of the existing farm.

What is remarkable is that the original predominant objective of the Land Acquisition Program – that of providing those previous owners having no claim for restitution with an option to buy back their properties – lost considerable influence in the course of the political decisionmaking process and ended up playing a rather insignificant role. 'The privileges described above are certainly available to previous owners who have leased Treuhand land for long terms. Those previous owners no longer active as farmers, however, may only purchase land under additional restrictions to be derived from their claim upon indemnification and compensation payments as follows:

1 A purchase claim for agricultural properties amounting to half the amount of indemnification.

2 Further *restrictions* to be taken into consideration are:
   - the second-place status of the previous owners (without lease contracts) in comparison with an equally interested buyer, who, being a leaseholder of the property at hand, is more entitled
   - the obligation to extend the lease contract for a total of eighteen years to the present leaseholder, independent from his economic situation and expiration of the existing lease contract
   - a reduction of the soil point ceiling restriction (see above) to 3,000 instead of 6,000' (Klages, 1994, p. 113)

A complete cancellation of competition between interested buyers is characteristic of this Land Acquisition Program. The tenants of the land already belonging to the privileged declared in the three-phase model of the Bohl Paper now receive absolute priority in comparison with their sole competitors, who are the previous owners having no claim for restitution. Not only the development of the Land Acquisition Program accompanied by the compromise arranged by the mediation committee, but more importantly, the prospective effects of this program – as analyzed by Klages and Klare – make it very clear that in the course of the political process East German agriculture showed a growing ability to succeed and that the previous owners from West Germany continually had to revise and reduce their originally high objectives. As a result of a quantitative analysis, Klages (1994, p. 118) emphasizes that 'from the purchasing possibilities provided by the EALG, it is not so much the previous owners having no claim for restitution who can greatly benefit here, but very much the BVVG leaseholders, and above all, the legal persons'. The Land Acquisition Program is arranged first according to the interests of the active agricultural businesses already holding a lease agreement. 'All other competitors, especially the previous owners not entitled to restitution, are to be characterized as the 'losers' of the political arena in respect to the original concept of privatization' (Klages, 1994, p. 119; see also Klages and Klare, 1994, 1995a,b,c).

Conclusions

In conclusion, let us come back to our question of whether it might be possible to modify the governance structure of privatization in a way that leads to a compensation for the deficiencies of institutional change based on political decisions.

If we look at the development from the Gerster Proposal to the Bohl Paper, competition is nearly completely abolished and the market for nationalized land is completely restricted. Within this *closed shop*, prices have to be fixed by the land administration, and interest groups participate in this implementation process. Bureaucratic criteria which are really questionable have to be applied, and difficult conflicts of interest have to be resolved by bureaucratic procedures, as demonstrated by the terms 'interest harmonization clause' and 'protection of existing farms'.

If we consider how the federal government responded to the Gattermann Proposal, we must conclude that this attempt reinforced the governance structure of privatization to be oriented towards state control. This can be seen from the fact that the Land Acquisition Program, which initially was based on guidelines at the ministerial level, became a part of the indemnification act. The property levy was eliminated, but the main market-oriented element of the proposal (compensation for expropriations by traded vouchers) was not accepted.

This idea was reduced to state bonds (debt certificates) given to the former owners as a means of indemnification, to be returned for money in the year 2004, or to be sold in the meantime. The former owners can use their indemnification claims to buy nationalized land according to the rules and restrictions laid down in the Bohl Paper (see section 4), which were modified in minor points by the final version of the Indemnification and Compensation Act. However, the Land Acquisition Program still has to be implemented (for a discussion of the impact of this program see Klages and Klare, 1994, 1995a,b,c).

The concluding phase of the political decisionmaking process finally made it clear that only through the compromise made in the last steps of the legislative procedure, which administratively secured priority interests for those farmers active in East Germany, was a conclusion of the process attainable. Moreover, this points to the rather fast learning process of the East German farmers and their interest representatives in using the political system of the Bundes-republik to enforce their priorities. The design of the Land Acquisition Program reveals, in the end, that even the remaining residue of competition between tenants and previous owners was cancelled.

Two main reasons are openly responsible for the rejection of the market-oriented opening of the procedure and complete shutdown of competition (see

Top-Agrar-Spezial, 1993). First, the East German farmers were afraid of disadvantages. They hoped to receive land by the Land Acquisition Program, and this land would – if the Gattermann Proposal had been accepted – no longer have been available but instead sold in auctions. Second, the political actors were afraid that they would no longer be able to control the conflicts caused by privatization if more market mechanisms were introduced. This is easy to understand and to explain, because public opinion and movements of protest in Eastern Germany are very important for politicians, particularly in years like 1994 when there was a series of elections.

Notes

1   In this context we understand institutions to be those 'public systems of coordination' which define mandatory patterns of behavior for social interactions. Institutions can be conceived of as a result of economizing societal interaction processes. By standardizing actions and reactions, as well as expectations and the fulfillment thereof to a certain degree, resources (especially time) which are otherwise used for the casuistic exploration of agreements can be used for other purposes. The welfare-increasing effect of institutions is mainly founded in the their assuming the function of a guarantee. They give to the respective decisionmaker a high degree of certainty about what the behavior of others will be if he himself makes a certain decision. This eases and accelerates decisionmaking processes and is therefore an essential source of economic efficiency.

2   At this point we have to take into account that the process of transforming agriculture in Eastern Germany is only *partly* determined by the privatization of nationalized land, because most of the land in the former German Democratic Republic had not been expropriated but only collectivized, and this land has already been returned to private owners. Fundamental questions of transformation of centrally planned agricultural systems are discussed by, Hagedorn (1991a,b, 1992a,b,c), Swinnen (1992, 1993a,b, 1994a,b) and Pryor (1992).

3   In addition, there were about 357,000 small household plots with an average size of 0.75 hectares. If we take these into account, 10.2 percent of cultivated agricultural land was in private use.

4   Bundesländer are the federal states of Germany. The New Bundesländer were established on the territory of the former GDR.

5   Germany has two houses of Parliament. The members of the Bundestag are elected in general elections, the members of the Bundesrat are determined by the Bundesländer.

6   See Agra Europe (1992c,d); Ernährungsdienst (1992a); Top Agrar Spezial (1992b,c,d) and a letter written by Brandenburg's Agricultural Minister Zimmermann to Federal Agricultural Minister Kiechle from 6 October 1992; see also a motion proposed by the Social Democrats in the Bundestag from 19 October 1992, and of the Bundesland Brandenburg in the Bundesrat from 28 October 1992, as well as corresponding recommendations made by parliament committees from 11 November 1992.

7   The following description of the Gattermann Proposal is based on the following sources of information: letter from member of Parliament Gattermann to the Secretary of State in the Federal Ministry of Finance, Joachim Grünewald, member of Parliament, from 19 September 1993, and to members of the Committee from 24 September 1993; summary description of the 'compensating certificates model' for the EALG, presented by Hans H. Gattermann and Wilhelm Rawe, member of Parliament, of 14 October 1993 (paper for a hearing within the coalition of coordination group Indemnification and Compensation Law concerning an alternative concept for the Indemnification and Compensation Law of 10 October 1993); note of Dr. Rüdiger Sannwald, planning group, for Mr. Wilhelm Rawe concerning proposals of the AfA (v. Wangenheim) (this refers to an interest group of the former owners, K.H.) compared with the proposals of Mr. Gattermann from 28 September 1993; comments from the Federal Ministry of Finance on the proposal of the member of Parliament Gattermann for the Bohl meeting of 9 September 1993, Grund (1993).

References

Agra Europe (1992a), 'Treuhandverwaltungsrat stimmt Verwertungskonzept zu', *Länderberichte*, Vol. 33, No. 13, pp. 4-6.
Agra Europe (1992b), 'Richtlinie für die Verwertung volkseigener Flächen', *Länderberichte*, Vol. 33, No. 26, Sonderbeilage, pp. 1-8.
Agra Europe (1992c), 'Wiedereinrichterprogramm noch in diesem Jahr?', *Länderberichte*, Vol. 33, No. 28, pp. 26-28.
Agra Europe (1992d), 'Ostdeutsche Landwirtschaftsminister kritisieren Bonner Agrarpolitik', *Länderberichte*, Vol. 33, No. 38, p. 40f.
Agra Europe (1992e), 'Langfristige Verpachtung als Einstieg in die Flächenverwertung', *Länderberichte*, Vol. 33, No. 50, pp. 13-17.
Agra Europe (1993a), 'BVVG legt Mustervertrag für langfristige Verpachtung vor', *Länderberichte*, Vol. 34, No. 11, pp. 10-13.

Agra Europe (1993b), 'Bundesfinanzministerium legt Konzeption für die Verwertung der Güter vor', *Länderberichte*, Vol. 34, No. 27, p. 1f.

Agra Europe (1993c), 'BVVG erhält zusätzliche Aufgaben', *Länderberichte*, Vol. 34, No. 27, p. 42f.

Agra Europe (1993d), 'Treuhandflächen in „vorsichtigen Schritten' privatisieren', *Länderberichte*, Vol. 34, No. 38, p. 12f.

Agra Europe (1993e), 'Entwurf des Entschädigungsgesetzes stößt auf breite Ablehnung', *Länderberichte*, Vol. 34, No. 38, pp. 13-15.

Agra Europe (1993f), 'Koalition erzielt Kompromiß für Entschädigungs- und Ausgleichsregelung). *Länderberichte*, Vol. 34, No. 48, p. 1f.

Agra Europe (1994a), 'Neuer Kompromißvorschlag zum Entschädigungsgesetz', *Länderberichte*, Vol. 35, No. 36, pp. 22-25.

Agra Europe (1994b), 'Gesetz über die Entschädigung nach dem Gesetz zur Regelung offener Vermögensfragen und über staatliche Ausgleichsleistungen für Enteignungen auf besatzungsrechtlicher oder besatzungshoheitlicher Grundlage (Entschädigungs- und Ausgleichsleistungsgesetz - EALG vom 27 September 1994)', *Länderberichte*, Vol. 35, No. 42, Dokumentation, pp. 1-16.

Antrag der Abgeordneten Horst Sielaff et al. und der Fraktion der SPD, 'Struktur- und sozialverträgliche Verwertung volkseigener land- und forstwirtschaftlicher Flächen in den neuen Ländern durchführen', Bundestags-Drucksache 12/3476 v. 19.10.1992.

Antrag des Landes Brandenburg, 'Entschließung des Bundesrates zur Verwertung landwirtschaftlicher Flächen durch die Treuhandanstalt in den neuen Bundesländern', Bundesrats-Drucksache 736/92 v. 28.10.1992.

Antrag des Landes Brandenburg, 'Empfehlungen der Ausschüsse zur Entschließung des Bundesrates zur Verwertung landwirtschaftlicher Flächen durch die Treuhandanstalt in den neuen Bundesländern', Bundesrats-Drucksache 736/1/92 v. 16.11.1992.

Bauern-Zeitung (1993), 'Bauernprotest gegen Bodenentzug. Demonstrationen vor den BVVG-Niederlassungen in Neubrandenburg, Schwerin und Rostock', No. 36, p. 8.

Beschluß des Bundesrates, 'Entschließung des Bundesrates zur Verwertung landwirtschaftlicher Flächen durch die Treuhandanstalt in den neuen Ländern', Bundesrats-Drucksache 736/92 (Beschluß) v. 27.11.1992.

Bohnet, A. and Reichhardt, M. (1993), 'Der Beitrag der Transaktionskostenökonomik zu einer Theorie der Transformation von Wirtschaftsordnungen', *Jahrbücher für Nationalökonomie und Statistik*, Vol. 213, No. 3-4, pp. 204-226.

Brief des Landwirtschaftsministers des Landes Brandenburg, Edwin Zimmermann, an Bundesernährungsminister Kiechle vom 29.06.1992.

Brief des MdB Gattermann an den Parlamentarischen Staatssekretär im Bundesministerium der Finanzen, Joachim Grünewald, MdB, vom 19.09.1993.

Brief des MdB Gattermann an die Mitglieder der Rawe-Kommission v. 24.09.1993.

Bromley, D. W. (1991), *Environment and Economy: Property Rights and Public Policy*, Blackwell: Oxford.

Bromley, D. W. (1995), 'The Social Construction of Land', in Hagedorn, K. (ed.), *Institutioneller Wandel und Politische Ökonomie von Landwirtschaft und Agrarpolitik, Festschrift zum fünfundsechzigsten Geburtstag von Prof. Dr. Günther Schmitt*, Campus Verlag: Frankfurt.

Doll, H., Hagedorn, K., Klages, B. and Klare, K. (1993), 'Überlegungen zur gesetzlichen Verankerung und praktischen Umsetzung des Landerwerbsprogramms', Unveröffentlichte Stellungnahme für das Bundesministerium für Ernährung, Landwirtschaft und Forsten: Braunschweig.

Elsner, W. (1987), 'Institutionen und ökonomische Institutionentheorie', *Wirtschaftswissenschaftliches Studium - WIST*, Vol. 16, pp. 5-14.

Entwurf eines Entschädigungs- und Ausgleichsgesetzes - EALG - vom 12.05.1993. Bundestags-Drucksache 12/4887.

Ernährungsdienst (1992a), 'Siedlungskaufmodell bleibt umstritten', No. 36, 26 March, p. 1.

Ernährungsdienst (1992b), 'Flächenverkauf soll zurückgestellt werden', No. 127, 7 November, p. 1.

Ernährungsdienst (1992c), 'Weichen für Flächenerwerb gestellt', No. 135, 28 November, p. 1.

Ernährungsdienst (1993a), 'Vermögensabgabe soll entfallen. Zukunft des Entschädigungsgesetzes weiter unklar. Uneinigkeit in Bonn', 28 October, p. 2.

Ernährungsdienst (1993b), 'Einig über Entschädigung. Schuldverschreibungen statt Vermögensabgabe', 25 November, p. 1.

Gattermann, H. H. and Rawe, W. (1993), 'Zusammenfassende Darstellung des Ausgleichzertifikatmodells zum EALG, vorgelegt am 14. Oktober 1993', Grundlage für eine koalitionsinterne Anhörung der Koordinierungsgruppe Entschädigungs- und Ausgleichsleistungsgesetz zum Alternativmodell zum Entschädigungs- und Ausgleichsleistungsgesetz vom 19.10.1993.

Gesetz über die Entschädigung nach dem Gesetz zur Regelung offener Vermögensfragen und über staatliche Ausgleichsleistungen für Enteignungen auf besatzungsrechtlicher oder besatzungshoheitlicher Grundlage (Entschädigungs- und Ausgleichsleistungsgesetz - EALG), Bundesgesetzblatt, Teil II, 1994, pp. 2624-2639.

Grund, M. (1992), 'Landverwertung. Neues Programm - neue Hoffnung', *Top-Agrar-Spezial*, 19 December, pp. 8-10.

Grund, M. (1993), 'Entschädigung: Doch noch Coupons für den Landerwerb?', *Top-Agrar-Spezial*, 18 December, pp. 12-14.

Hagedorn, K. (1991a), 'Konzeptionelle Überlegungen zur Transformation der Landwirtschaft in den neuen Bundesländern', in Merl, S. and Schinke, E. (eds.), *Agrarwirtschaft und Agrarpolitik in der ehemaligen DDR im Umbruch. Giessener Abhandlungen zur Agrar- und Wirtschaftsforschung des Europäischen Ostens*, Vol. 178, Duncker und Humblot: Berlin.

Hagedorn, K. (1991b), 'Gedanken zur Transformation einer sozialistischen Agrarverfassung', *Agrarwirtschaft*, Vol. 40, No. 5, pp. 138-148.

Hagedorn, K. (1992a), 'Wirtschaftliche und politische Triebkräfte der Umformung einer sozialistischen Agrarverfassung', in Boettcher, E., Herder-Dorneich, P., Schenk, K.-E. and Schmidtchen, D. (eds.), *Ökonomische Systeme und ihre Dynamik. Jahrbuch für Neue Politische Ökonomie*, Vol. 11, J.C.B. Mohr (Paul Siebeck): Tübingen.

Hagedorn, K. (1992b), 'Zukunftsvorstellungen und Übergangsprobleme der Landwirtschaft in der ehemaligen DDR aus der Sicht der Evolutionären Ordnungstheorie', in Schmitt, G. and Tangermann, S. (eds.), *Internationale Agrarpolitik und Entwicklung der Weltagrarwirtschaft*, Schriften der Gesellschaft für Wirtschafts- und Sozialwissenschaften des Landbaues e.V., Bd. 28, Landwirtschaftsverlag: Münster-Hiltrup.

Hagedorn, K. (1992c), 'Transformation of Socialist Agricultural Systems', *Journal of International and Comparative Economics*, Vol. 1, pp. 103-124.

Hagedorn, K. (1993a), 'Bodenmärkte und Bodenmarktpolitik in den neuen Bundesländern', in v. Alvensleben, R., Langbehn, C. and Schinke, E. (eds.), *Strukturanpassungen der Land- und Ernährungswirtschaft in Mittel- und Osteuropa*, Schriften der Gesellschaft für Wirtschafts- und Sozialwissenschaften des Landbaues e.V., Vol. 29, Landwirtschaftsverlag: Münster-Hiltrup.

Hagedorn, K. (1993b), 'Transforming Socialist Agriculture: An Institutional Perspective', in Kabat, L., Fandel, P., Batkova, D., Bartova, L. and Kapustik, P. (eds.), *Eastern European Agriculture - Problems, Goals and Perspectives*, Proceedings of the 27th Seminar of the European Association of Agricultural Economists (EAAE), 18-20 March 1992, Nitra, Vysoke Tatry, Czechoslovakia.

Hagedorn, K. (1993c), 'Institutions and Agricultural Economics', *Journal of Economic Issues*, Vol. 27, No. 3, pp. 849-886.

Hagedorn, K. (1994a), 'Die Privatisierung volkseigenen landwirtschaftlichen Bodens in den neuen Bundesländern', *Kühn-Archiv*, Vol. 88, No. 2, pp. 226-224.

Hagedorn, K. (1994b), 'Interest Groups', in Hodgson, G., Tool, M. and Samuels, W. J. (eds.), *Handbook of Institutional and Evolutionary Economics*, Edward Elgar: Cheltenham.

Hagedorn, K. (1995), 'Politisch dirigierter institutioneller Wandel: Das Beispiel der Privatisierung volkseigenen Bodens', in: Hagedorn, K. (ed.), *Institutioneller Wandel und Politische Ökonomie von Landwirtschaft und Agrarpolitik, Festschrift zum fünfundsechzigsten Geburtstag von Prof. Dr. Günther Schmitt*, Campus Verlag: Frankfurt.

Hagedorn, K. (1996), 'Das Institutionenproblem in der agrarökonomischen Politikforschung', in v. Böventer, E., Gahlen, B. and Hesse, H. (eds.), *Schriften zur angewandten Wirtschaftsforschung*, Vol. 72, J.C.B. Mohr (Paul Siebeck): Tübingen.

Hagedorn, K. and Schmitt, G. (1985), 'Die politischen Gründe für eine wirtschaftspolitische Vorzugsbehandlung der Landwirtschaft', in Boettcher, E., Herder-Dorneich, P. and Schenk, K.-E. (eds.), *Jahrbuch für Neue Politische Ökonomie*, Bd. 4., J.C.B. Mohr (Paul Siebeck): Tübingen.

Hagedorn, K. and Klages, B. (1994), 'Konzepte zur Privatisierung volkseigenen landwirtschaftlichen Bodens und Entwürfe zum Entschädigungs- und Ausgleichsleistungsgesetz: Analyse und Alternativen', *Landbauforschung Völkenrode*, Vol. 44, No. 1, pp. 44-53.

Heuss, E. (1965), *Allgemeine Markttheorie*, J.C.B. Mohr (Paul Siebeck): Tübingen.

Klages, B. (1994), 'Privatisierung der Treuhandflächen', in Klare, K. (ed.), *Entwicklung der ländlichen Räume und der Agrarwirtschaft in den Neuen Bundesländern, Landbauforschung Völkenrode*, No. 152, Bundesforschungsanstalt für Landwirtschaft (FAL): Braunschweig.

Klages, B. and Hagedorn, K. (1993), 'Konzepte zur Privatisierung volkseigenen land- und forstwirtschaftlichen Bodens und Entwürfe zum Entschädigungs- und Ausgleichsgesetz. Eine Untersuchung unter besonderer Berücksichtigung des Zertifikatmodells', Unveröffentlichte Stellungnahme für das Bundesministerium für Ernährung, Landwirtschaft und Forsten, Bundesforschungsanstalt für Landwirtschaft (FAL): Braunschweig.

Klages, B. and Klare, K. (1994), 'Der neue Entwurf des Entschädigungs- und Ausgleichsleistungsgesetzes - Analyse und Bewertung', *Agra Europe*, Vol. 35, No. 23, Länderberichte, Sonderbeilage, pp. 1-11.

Klages, B. and Klare, K. (1995a), 'BVVG-Flächen: kaufen oder langfristig pachten?', *Top-Agrar-Spezial*, 21 January, No. 1, pp. 8-11.

Klages, B. and Klare, K. (1995b), 'So werden Alteigentümer jetzt entschädigt', *Top Agrar* (1995b), No. 5, pp. 44-46.

Klages, B. and Klare, K. (1995c), 'Lohnt sich der Flächenkauf zum dreifachen Einheitswert?', *Top Agrar*, No. 5, pp. 46-47.

Lachmann, L. M. (1963), 'Wirtschaftsordnung and wirtschaftliche Institutionen', *ORDO - Jahrbuch für die Ordnung von Wirtschaft and Gesellschaft*, Vol. 14, pp. 63-77.

Leipold, H. (1985), 'Ordnungspolitische Implikationen der Transaktionskostenökonomie', *ORDO - Jahrbuch für die Ordnung von Wirtschaft and Gesellschaft*, Vol. 36, pp. 31-50.

Leipold, H. (1988), *Wirtschafts- and Gesellschaftssysteme im Vergleich*, Stuttgart.

Leipold, H. (1989a), 'Das Ordnungsproblem in der ökonomischen Institutionentheorie', *ORDO - Jahrbuch für die Ordnung von Wirtschaft und Gesellschaft*, Vol. 40, pp. 129-146.

Leipold, H. (1989b), 'Neuere Ansätze zur Weiterentwicklung der Ordnungstheorie', in Boettcher, E., Herder-Dorneich, P. and Schenk, K.-E. (eds.), *Jahrbuch für Neue Politische Ökonomie*, Vol. 8, J.C.B. Mohr (Paul Siebeck): Tübingen.

Mehl, P. (1995), *Reformansätze und Reformwiderstände in der Agrarsozialpolitik der Bundesrepublik Deutschland. Politikinhalte und ihre Bestimmungsgründe von 1976 bis 1990*, Dissertation, Braunschweig.

Mehl, P. and Hagedorn, K. (1994), 'Die Übertragung des landwirtschaftlichen Alterssischerungssystems auf die neuen Bundesländer im Gesetzentwurf der Bundesregierung zur Reform des agrarsozialen Sicherungssytems', *Landbauforschung Völkenrode*, Vol. 44, pp. 77-90.

Olson, M. (1982), *The Rise and Decline of Nations: Economic Growth, Stagflation and Rigidities*, New Haven.

Pryor, F. L. (1992), *The Red and the Green. The Rise and Fall of Collectivized Agriculture in Marxist Regimes*, Princeton Unviersity Press: Princeton.

Schenk, K.-E. (1981), *Märkte, Hierarchien und Wettbewerb: Elemente einer Theorie der Wirtschaftsordnung*, München.

Schenk, K.-E. (1982) '„Institutional Choice" und Ordnungstheorie', Walter Eucken-Institut, Vorträge und Aufsätze, Vol. 82., J.C.B. Mohr (Paul Siebeck): Tübingen.

Schenk, K.-E. (1983), 'Institutional Choice und Ordnungstheorie', in Boettcher, E., Herder-Dorneich, P. and Schenk, K.-E. (eds.), *Jahrbuch für Neue Politische Ökonomie*, Vol. 2, J.C.B. Mohr (Paul Siebeck): Tübingen.

Schmidtchen, D. (1989), 'Evolutionäre Ordnungstheorie oder: Die Transaktionskosten und das Unternehmertum', *ORDO - Zeitschrift für die Ordnung in Wirtschaft und Gesellschaft*, Vol. 40, pp. 161-182.

Schüller, A. (1991), 'Eigentumsrechte. Ökonomische Anreiz- und Kontrollwirkungen im Prozeß der marktwirtschaftlichen Systementfaltung', in *Transformation der Eigentumsordnung im östlichen Mitteleuropa*, *Wirtschafts- und sozialwissenschaftliche Ostmitteleuropa-Studien*, Vol. 17. Johann-Gottfried-Herder-Institut: Marburg an der Lahn.

Schüller, A. (1988), 'Ökonomik der Eigentumsrechte in ordnungstheoretischer Sicht', in Cassel, D., Ramb, B.-T. and Thieme, H.-J. (eds.), *Ordnungspolitik*, München.

Schulz, J. (1992), 'Zu transformationstheoretischen Ansätzen der ordoliberalen Schule und der amerikanischen Institutoneökonomik', *Zeitschrift für Wirtschaftspolitik*, Vol. 41, pp. 231-256.

Stellungnahme des Bundesministeriums der Finanzen zum Vorschlag von MdB Gattermann für die Bohl-Runde am 28.09.1993.

Swinnen, J. (1992), 'The Development of Agricultural Policies in Eastern Europe. An Endogenous Policy Theory Perspective', *Discussion Papers on the Economic Transformation: Policy, Institutions and Structure*, Working Paper 2/1992, Leuven Institute for Central and East European Studies: Leuven.

Swinnen, J. (1993a), 'Policy and Institutional Reform in Central European Agriculture', *Discussion Papers on the Economic Transformation: Policy, Institutions and Structure*, Working Paper 18/1993, Leuven Institute for Central and East European Studies: Leuven.

Swinnen, J. (1993b), 'Development of Agricultural Policies in Central and Eastern Europe', *Food Policy*, Vol. 18, pp. 187-191.

Swinnen, J. (1994a), 'Political Economy of Transition Price and Trade Policy Changes in Central European Agriculture', unpublished manuscript, Department of Agricultural Economics, K.U.Leuven.

Swinnen, J. (1994b), 'Overview of Policy and Institutional Reform in Central European Agriculture', in Swinnen, J. (ed.), *Policy and Institutional Reform in Central European Agriculture*, Avebury: Aldershot.

Top Agrar-Spezial (1992a), 'Ab Juli wird langfristig verpachtet und verkauft. Interview mit dem Generalbevollmächtigten der Treuhand, H.-J. Rohr, in Berlin', 24 June, pp. 4-7.

Top Agrar-Spezial (1992b), 'Regierung contra Opposition beim Wiederein-richterprogramm', 19 September, p. 32.

Top Agrar-Spezial (1992c), 'Rohr mahnt: Neueinrichter einbeziehen!', 19 September, p. 33.

Top Agrar-Spezial (1992d), 'Mit dem Gerster-Plan das Thema verfehlt', 5 October, p. 25.

van den Noort, P. C. (1993), 'Reform of the Farm Tenancy System - The European Scene', in the 32nd EAAE-seminar, *Capital and Finance in West- and East-European Agriculture*, contributed papers, European Association of Agricultural Economists (EAAE): Wageningen.

Vermerk von Herrn Dr. Rüdiger Sannwald, Planungsgruppe, für Herrn PSt a. D. Wilhelm Rawe über Vorschläge der AfA (von Wangenheim) im Vergleich zu den Vorschlägen von Herrn Gattermann vom 28.09.1993.

Williamson, O. E. (1975), *Markets and Hierarchies: Analysis and Antitrust Implications*, Free Press: New York and London.

Williamson, O. E. (1985), *The Economic Institutions of Capitalism*, Free Press: New York and London.

8 Process and politics of agrarian reform in Hungary

Erik Mathijs[1]

Introduction

Up to the Second World War, Hungarian agriculture was dominated by large estates, while most of the rural population was landless. Interwar land reform had not changed this. Immediately after the Second World War, in 1945, a provisional government dominated by the Communists passed a land reform law that redistributed the bulk of the country's arable land. Collectivization started in 1948 and was more or less completed in 1962. From 1967 onwards, individuals no longer active in the cooperative farms were forced to sell their land to the cooperative. As a result, unlike most other Central and Eastern European countries (CEECs) in Hungary most of the land was collectively owned rather than privately or state owned. The New Economic Mechanism of 1968 introduced some free-market principles to increase the performance of the agricultural sector, and Hungary became a relative succes story in the Eastern Bloc. Agricultural exports were, and still are, very important for the Hungarian economy. Agricultural cooperatives have been the main producers of these exports goods.

The Hungarian agricultural reform debate was dominated by a concern for efficiency and historial justice. The chosen reform resulted both in a fragmentation of landownership and a consolidation of the cooperative structure. Discussion about the reforms started after the democratic elections in 1990, which were won by the most important opposition group, the Hungarian Democratic Forum (HDF). Its leader, Jozsef Antall, formed a right-wing coalition government with the agrarian Independent Smallholders' Party (ISP) and the Christian-Democratic People's Party (CDPP). The democratic government implemented privatization legislation for the whole of the economy. Legislation to privatize and transform the agricultural sector was

237

included in the Compensation Laws of 1991 and 1992, the Cooperative Laws of 1992, and the Land Law of 1994.

Reform legislation included both restitution of land and partial compensation. Under the Compensation Laws, former property owners and victims of the Nazis and the Communist regime were eligible for compensation in the form of vouchers. With these vouchers they could purchase land owned by the collectives or state farms in auctions. State farms were to be sold by the State Property Agency. Under the Cooperative Laws collectives were required to transform themselves into private cooperatives or joint stock companies and had to divide all assets in the form of business shares. Members who wanted to leave a collective were allowed to do so. Finally, the Land Law of 1994 concluded the reform legislation by setting limits to the amount of land a person or an organization could buy or lease.

We interpret the resulting legislation in Hungary as the outcome of a political bargaining process, with the parties and the interest groups they represented as the main actors. The framework used here is based on the analysis of Bulgarian reform by Lyons et al. (1994) and by Swinnen (1994). That analysis emphasised the distributional effects of land reform and its impact on the political alignment of the rural areas as key factors in the choice of an agrarian reform process. It also identified the importance of the distribution of political power following Bulgaria's 1989 political reform. More specifically, the strength of the political center and of the ex-Communist Party were important to understanding the government's choice.

Hungary's agricultural reform legislation was the result of intensive parliamentary debates in 1991. The main actors included the ISP, defending the interest of rural smallholders, the centrist HDF, with the consumers' interest in mind, and the workers and managers of the cooperatives organized in the National Federation of Agricultural Producers and politically represented by the Agrarian Alliance. The HDF had little incentive to pursue radical agrarian reform, as this would cause much disruption. Because of the HDF's strength in Parliament, it was possible to impose a moderate reform. An additional factor in this outcome was that in Hungary, a major part of the land was already primarily owned by collective farms. In this, Hungary difffered from most other CEECs, where most land was still formally privately owned. Hungary's Constitutional Court ruled against treating land differently from other assets in the privatization process.

Although private farming has increased enormously, lack of government commitment to individual or family farming and resistance on the local level by the collective farm management has resulted in a sector still dominated by huge farming units in joint ownership. Alongside these transformed cooperatives or companies, private plots are scattered throughout the country.

This chapter is organized as follows. Section 2 describes political reforms in Hungary since 1989. Section 3 discusses the economic factors underlying the reform process and gives an overview of the legislation on agricultural privatization and transformation. An interpretation of the agricultural reform is provided in section 4. The implementation and the results of Hungary's agrarian reform are discussed in the final section.

Political reform in Hungary: an overview[2]

The emergence of democracy and the first elections

The 'Hungarian compromise' designed by Party Secretary János Kádár in the 1960s survived for about twenty-five years, but failed in the changing environment of the 1980s and 1990s. Kádár's compromise had tried to please both the Soviets, by being loyal to Soviet foreign policy, and the people of Hungary, by improving living standards and relaxing the ideological climate. However, stagnation in the Hungarian economy and worsening living standards, caused this centrist model to be increasingly questioned in the 1980s. Discontent led to the removal of some Communist Party officials, including Party Secretary János Kádár, in the spring of 1988. Reform-minded Communists increasingly gained power in the Hungarian Socialist Workers' Party (HSWP). Opposition parties were allowed and many pre-Communist parties were refounded. Roundtable talks between the HSWP, the government, and opposition parties ended on 18 September 1989, with an agreement to introduce a multiparty system and democratic elections. On 23 October 1989, a symbolic end was made to Communist rule when the Republic of Hungary was proclaimed (Swain, 1991).

In the beginning it was difficult for the Hungarian electorate to locate the new political parties on the political spectrum.[3] Most of the parties more or less agreed on economic policies, and they all attacked the practices of the former Communist Party (Okolicsanyi, 1990a). The Hungarian Democratic Forum (HDF) emerged in 1987 from a movement calling for democracy and a multiparty system. It was supported by some reformers of the Hungarian Socialist Workers' Party. The HDF tried to unite a wide range of ideas: it had deep populist and national roots, but also included classical liberal and Christian-Democratic values (Reisch, 1990a). The HDF advocated a moderate approach of gradual, controlled privatization. The parties closest to the HDF were the Christian Democratic People's Party (CDPP) and the Independent Smallholders' Party (ISP). The ISP was refounded in November 1988. The main concern of this conservative, one-issue party was returning all land to its original owners (or their heirs), based on holdings in the summer of 1947. The

Alliance of Free Democrats (AFD) was founded in November of 1988 and profiled itself as a center-left party, although it advocated aggressive free-market principles. It was (and remains) the party of the urban intellectuals who played a major part in the Hungarian democratic opposition beginning in the late 1970s. Opponents often pictured the AFD as a party of former Marxists and Jewish intellectuals (Barany, 1990a). Closest to the AFD was the Alliance of Young Democrats (AYD), which was sometimes called the youth organization of the AFD. Together, the AYD and the AFD were the most radical defenders of complete privatization. Other political parties believed to play a major role in the 1990 election included the Social Democratic Party (SDP), the reform-minded Communists of the Hungarian Socialist Party (HSP), and the orthodox Communists of the resurrected Hungarian Socialist Workers' Party.

The first free elections in over forty years were held on 25 March and 8 April 1990 to elect the 386-member single chamber (which included 8 deputies coopted after voting to represent national minorities). Voters needed to elect representatives from three different lists: individual, regional, and national. Whereas almost 65 percent of the electorate participated in the first round of the elections, only 45.5 percent voted in the second round. Parties needed 4 percent of the vote to be represented in Parliament. Several parties, including the HSWP, the Social Democrats, and the Hungarian People's Party (successor to the postwar National Peasant Party), did not achieve this percentage. The Hungarian Democratic Forum emerged as a clear victor, with 24.7 percent of the vote yielding them 42.5 percent of the seats, while the HDF's main rival, the AFD, came in second with 23.8 percent of the seats (see Appendix 8.3). Several radical candidates failed to be elected (Barany, 1990b).

The Antall Government

After the 1990 elections, the two largest parties, the HDF and the ADF, signed a political agreement reducing the number of laws that required a two-thirds majority in Parliament, so that a future government could more easily tackle important problems. However, the HDF formed a coalition without the AFD because of important ideological differences. As compensation, the AFD was permitted to nominate the presidential candidate. This agreement resulted in a so-called *cohabitation* similar to that found in France and the USA.

The HDF represented Christian-Democratic values and Hungarian traditions, while the ADF included 'Jewish intellectual leaders among its leaders and is more urban in outlook' (Pataki, 1990). HDF Chairman Jozsef Antall opted to cooperate with the ISP and the CDPP. On 23 May 1990 the cabinet proposed by Antall was presented and consisted of sixteen ministers: eight members of the HDF, four of the ISP, one of the CDPP, and three independent specialists.

From the beginning, the ISP demanded the agricultural portfolio and so Ferenc Jozsef Nagy became Minister of Agriculture. The ISP also received the portfolio of labor and two ministerial posts without portfolio: one in charge of land reform (Jeno Gerbovits) and one dealing with minority and church affairs, Hungarian minorities abroad, and youth problems (Reisch, 1990b).

On 22 May 1990, Antall presented his program to Parliament. Its four guiding principles were 'freedom, compliance with the will of the people, economic transformation, and the return to Western Europe' (Okolicsanyi, 1990b). In September 1990, the government published 'The Program of National Renewal' in which it commited itself for the next three years to the transformation to a market economy (Okolicsanyi, 1990d). On 4 August 1990, Arpad Göncz was elected President of the Republic. Local elections were held in September and October of 1990. A large number of former Communist local council officials were reelected.

All major political decisions in the 1990 coalition were taken by the HDF (Pataki, 1992c). On 14 December 1990, Prime Minister Antall replaced some of his key ministers in response to increasing public criticism of his cabinet's performance. The criticism had culminated at the end of October 1990 in a three-day taxi and truck drivers' strike and road blockade which had almost paralyzed the country following an increase in gasoline prices. One of the most striking cabinet replacements was that of Gerbovits, the national secretary of the Hungarian Peasant Association who was responsible land reform, by the unknown Gergatz (Reisch, 1991).

Antall's refusal to support radical land reform led to increasing tensions between the HDF and the ISP. Discussion within the ISP about how to deal with this refusal led to a breakup of the ISP. During the spring of 1991, some ISP leaders threatened to withdraw from the coalition, but were not followed by their ministers and most of the deputies. On 21 February 1992, the presidium of the ISP decided to withdraw the party from the ruling coalition. However, 35 of the 45 parliamentary deputies, including the ministers in office (Gergatz and Kiss), continued to support the government as an independent caucus called the Historical Platform (later called the Group of 36), led by Gyula Pasztor. ISP president Torgyan expelled these caucus members from the ISP (Suskosd, 1992; Pataki, 1992a). The opposition to Torgyan further splintered into four new groups or parties, so that up to five 'smallholders' parties' claimed to represent the smallholders in Parliament. An attempt before the 1994 elections to reunite the four groups opposed to Torgyan into the United Historical Independent Smallholders' Party failed. Most members of the former ISP remained faithful to Torgyan's party, which was renamed the Independent Smallholders' and Civic Party, or ISCP (Pataki, 1994).

In February 1993, a second major reorganization of the government occurred. Antall replaced several ministers to improve the cabinet's teamwork and efficiency. Gergatz, who lost party support after the ISP breakup, was replaced by Janos Szabo, the parliamentary leader of the Group of 36 (Pataki, 1993). On 12 December 1993 Jozsef Antall died and was replaced by the independent Peter Boross, previously Minister of Internal Affairs.

The 1994 elections

A public opinion survey in June 1992 showed that a majority of the Hungarian people was disappointed with the political and economic changes. Polls showed that the two most important parties, the HFD in the government and the AFD in the opposition, had lost support from the electorate (Pataki, 1992b). Both represented more than one ideology, and both the AFD and the HFD had failed to keep unity within their parties. In August 1992, the nationalist Istvan Csurka, vice-president of the HDF, published a radical anti-Communist and anti-Semitic manuscript. He was expelled from the HDF for his anti-Semitic views. In February 1993 Csurka launched a 'National Movement' advocating a 'third way' for Hungary between the East and the West. Attempts to unite radical populist forces into the 'Hungarian Road Circles' by Csurka and into the 'Christian National Unity' by Torgyan failed. Both populist leaders went to the elections seperately, Csurka with his newly founded Hungarian Justice and Life Party and Torgyan with the ISCP.

The 1994 elections were held on 8 May and 29 May. Voter turnout was high (68.9 per cent in the first round and 55.1 in the second). The Hungarian Socialist Party (HSP) led by Gyula Horn gained the absolute majority with 54.1 percent of the seats. The HDF lost 32 percent of its seats and retained only 9.5 percent of the seats. The AFD won 18.1 percent of the seats and the reformed ISCP, 6.7 percent (see Appendix 8.4). The extremist parties that had emerged on the political spectrum, such as the Workers' Party on the left and Csurka's Hungarian Justice and Life Party on the right, did not achieve the necessary 5 percent. Neither did the Agrarian Alliance and a liberal bloc, although they did bring one candidate into Parliament through the individual lists. However, this Agrarian Alliance candidate joined the AFD faction. The HDF was especially punished for Hungary's economic problems. Voters hoped that the former Communists would ease the pain of transition by restoring the former social security system (Oltay, 1994). On 24 June 1994 the HSP and the AFD, together controlling 72 percent of the seats in Parliament, reached a coalition agreement. The new government was backed by a two-thirds majority in Parliament.

Privatization and transformation of Hungarian agriculture

Economic factors affecting the 1990 agrarian reform

Before going into the details of the reform legislation, we will first discuss some key economic factors that affected the choice of reform program: the importance of agriculture in the overall economy, the prereform structure, and the distributional effects of different policy options. Agriculture was, and still is, a key sector in the Hungarian economy. In 1989, agriculture employed 647,800 persons, or 15.9 percent of the active population. Gross domestic product in agriculture and forestry amounted to 600 billion HUF or 17.8 percent of Hungary's GDP (Hungarian Central Statistical Office, 1991). But the importance of the agricultural sector is primarily reflected in the importance of exports of food and agricultural products. OECD (1993) reports that food and agricultural exports amounted to 2.64 billion USD in 1991 and held at 2.65 billion USD in 1992. This meant a trade surplus in agriculture of 2 billion USD.

The strengths and weaknesses of Hungarian agriculture, which had resulted from policy directions taken between 1950 and 1988, formed the initial conditions for its transition (Csaki and Varga, 1993). Mihályi (1993) argues that although economic reforms under the Communist regime failed in many ways, they narrowed the spectrum of choice in 1990. He considers these reforms to have had three advantages at that time: increasing tolerance of entrepreneurship, an inflow of Western capital, and government imposition of monetary constraints (subsidy cuts and tax increases) on the banks and their clients, including the agricultural producer cooperatives. Let us discuss the prereform agrarian structure and the distributional effects in more detail.

Pre-Communist situation

After World War I, Hungarian agriculture was dominated by large estates, and most rural people were landless. Between the wars, several attempts were made to redistribute land among the many landless. However, the landowning class succeeded in preventing any kind of radical reform. Under the land reform of 1920 pursued by the Smallholders' Party, which had won the 1920 election, only 6 percent of all arable land (300,000 hectares) was redistributed to some 400,000 families. Many of these holdings were not viable, and between 1926 and 1938 some 67,000 of them were auctioned (Berend, 1985). As a result, Hungary maintained a semifeudal structure. At the end of the Second World War, almost half of Hungary's people earned their living in agriculture. Most of these were peasants who did not own their land or who possessed holdings under 2.8 hectares. In contrasts the 1,000 wealthiest families owned a quarter of all arable land, and the Catholic Church owned over half a million hectares (Hoensch, 1988).

Immediately after the Second World War, a provisonal national government consisting of Communists, Social-Democrats, and Smallholders was installed. Land reform was one of the main issues on their agenda. All parties agreed that some form of land reform was to be conducted (Brus, 1986). The National Peasants' Party, which was manipulated by the Communists, published its land reform plans on 14 January 1945. These plans were adopted by the Communist Party to tackle the rural poor's growing impatience and formed the basis of the decree issued on 15 March 1945. Large estates of more than 575 hectares, land owned by 'traitors of the fatherland' and 'Horthy fascists' and land owned by the Church was expropriated. Of these 3.222 million hectares of confiscated land, 1.874 million hectares were given to 642,000 people (most of them agricultural workers and smallholders). An upper limit for holdings was set at 50 hectares for the gentry and 115 hectares for peasants. The Communists succeeded in overturning the social structure in the countryside: 95 percent of the rural population now owned small plots. Despite the fact that the average farm size was under 3 hectares (Brus, 1986; Hoensch, 1988), many argue that a viable agricultural sector emerged in the next three years, a period they refer to as the 'golden age' of Hungarian agriculture. In fact, there was general agreement that a significant private farm structure was the best answer to Hungary's historic, social, and natural specificities (Juhász, 1991).

Pretransition situation

Hungarian agriculture was collectivized in three drives. Between each one, considerable decollectivization occurred (Pryor, 1992). The Communists assumed absolute power in 1948. The first campaign (1949 to 1953) only partially succeeded in forcing farmers into cooperative and state farms, mainly because it was not well planned (Juhász, 1991). Malenkov's 'New Course' after Stalin's death in 1953 was adopted by Party leader Imre Nagy. The system of compulsory deliveries was abandoned. In 1955 the hard-line Communists, headed by Rákosi, came back into control, and collectivization continued. However, as Krushchev no longer advocated Stalinist methods, he disapproved of Rákosi's policy, and Imre Nagy returned to power. In the summer of 1956, cooperative farms began to disband again (Swain, 1985). After the revolution of 1956, János Kádár came to power. The third campaign of collectivization (1957 to 1961) was more succesful, but that success was primarily due to the presence of Soviet troops (Pryor, 1992). Nevertheless, the government had a liberal policy towards private farming by members of the cooperatives, and they set agricultural prices to cover production costs. In

1964-65, farms could make their own input and output decisions to some degree. This approach resulted in a symbiosis of small- and large-scale farms (Juhász, 1991). In 1968 the New Economic Mechanism was introduced to reduce central planning and to allow market prices to influence production decisions (Cochrane, 1990).

As a result of these policies, a mixed farming system emerged. Large-scale farming was practiced by state farms and farming cooperatives and was integrated with private, small-scale farms on a part-time or full-time basis. All means of production of *state farms* were state owned. Their employees were wage earners, but nevertheless carried on small-scale agricultural production. The average state farm cultivated 7,500 hectares and employed 945 people. The dominant production organizations, however, were the various *agricultural producer cooperatives*. They had an average size of 4,400 hectares and employed 400 people on average. All members were obliged to contribute all means of production to the cooperative, but in the beginning the land still remained in the possession of the individual person, in legal terms. The Hungarian government created the possibility for cooperatives to actually own land by passing a law on land use in 1967 (Swain, 1993b). Individuals no longer active in agriculture were forced to sell the land to the cooperative for a low price. The proportion of member-owned land fell from more than 70 percent in 1968 to around one-third in 1989. Cooperatives also took over state land they had previously been renting. As a result, 35.1 percent of the land farmed by cooperatives was in private hands, 61.1 percent was collectively owned, and 3.8 percent state owned (see table 8.1).

Table 8.1
Distribution of ownership of land farmed by cooperative farms,
1968-1989 per cent

Year	State	Cooperative	Members *
1968	27.7	0.1	72.2
1975	4.4	44.7	50.9
1980	3.4	51.6	45.0
1985	4.0	56.7	39.3
1989	3.8	61.1	35.1

* and those having the same legal status: partners in matrimony, living together with a member, being the widow of a member, aged persons entitled to land rent, and persons with usufructuary right.

Source: Harcsa, 1991.

245

In *specialized agricultural cooperatives*, members individually cultivated their own land (mostly a vineyard or an orchard), but marketing, processing and certain services were organized collectively. In 1990, there were 62 such specialized cooperatives on a total area of 93,000 hectares. Finally, *private farming* was practiced, mostly on a part-time basis. There were about 1.5 million farms in Hungary altogether, of which only some 20,000 were full-time farms, cultivating only 1 percent of the country's total farmland (Juhász, 1991). However, especially in animal husbandry and the cultivation of fruit and vegetables, small-scale farming provided more than half of Hungary's production (see table 8.2). According to official statistics, 76.2 percent of agricultural land was in 1,246 agricultural producer cooperatives, 62 agricultural associations of cooperatives, and 80 specialized agricultural cooperatives, 13.4 percent in 136 state farms and 9.5 percent in approximately 1,435,000 small-scale farms in 1989 (Hungarian Central Statistical Office, 1990).

Table 8.2
Small-scale production as percentage of total production

	1988	*1991*
Wheat	1.3	6.4
Maize	18.8	25.2
Potatoes, vegetables	80.7	87.1
Fruit	63.8	61.8
Grapes	51.6	57.5
Cattle-breeding	20.7	23.6
Pig-breeding	53.7	48.0
Poultry-raising	45.4	56.2

Source: Hungarian Central Statistical Office, 1989 and 1991.

Distributional effects

To discuss the distributional effects of possible policy options, we refer to a study by Szelenyi and Szelenyi (1993), who calculated that, based on 1983 data, almost 40 percent of all Hungarian heads of households were descendants of families that owned land in 1948, the year in which collectivization began (see table 8.3). However, because many of these descendants migrated to the cities, one third of urban households became entitled to restitution. Szelenyi and Szelenyi also emphasized the 'under-urbanization' of Hungary which resulted in a large number of industrial workers living in the countryside. These workers retained household plots that evolved into real labor intensive, market-oriented mini-farms. Because the rural working class was less skilled than the urban, rural workers would be the first to be laid off in urban factories and would have great incentive to start up private family farms. They represented 5 to 10 percent of the rural population, and many were descendants of peasant families.

Table 8.3

Distribution of landholding in 1948 in Hungary by 1983 heads of household and distribution of landownership in 1948 by 1983 residence of household head

Size of landholding in 1948 (hectares)	Household head (percent)	1983 Residence of Urban (percent)	household head Rural (percent)
0	61.7	66.1	48.5
0 - 2.85	19.8	17.6	25.9
2.86 - 5.7	12.3	10.9	16.9
Over 5.7	6.1	5.4	8.8

Source: Szelenyi and Szelenyi, 1993.

About 500,000 people worked on collectivized farms, either as cooperative members, or as workers. Most would not receive land through restitution, so they preferred the status quo or privatization through means other than restitution. The agrarian technocrats also did not support restitution. However, they had more to gain from privatization of cooperative farms than from the status quo. In Hungary, the makeup of the managerial class drastically changed in the late 1960s. Before, management was in the hands of middle-class peasants, but in the late 1960s and early 1970s a young new agricultural technocracy emerged and eventually took over as managers in the 1980s. Szelenyi and Szelenyi state that 'the new technocratic elite was more open to Western ideas and did not have the ideological reservations of the old guard against markets or even private property or capitalism'. This new elite tried to use the breakdown of the Communist system to reinforce their positions in the transformed cooperatives and in the industrial enterprises where many of them held high managerial positions. These 'green barons' used their positions to manipulate the privatization process (Pryor, 1992). To defend this 'political capitalism', they formed their own political party, the Agrarian Alliance.

The agrarian reform laws

Agrarian reform includes both privatization of property rights and reorganization of the cooperative and state farms. These issues are related because privatization of collective property requires some transformation of the old production units. The government must give attention to economic, social, and political considerations when deciding on the process of privatization and transformation.

The transfer of property rights from the state to private persons can be done by restitution of property to its former owners or their heirs, or by selling or auctioning state property. Privatization in Central and Eastern Europe typically also implies some form of compensation for historical injustice by the Communists or even the Nazis. Compensation or restitution can be either full or partial, and direct (in-kind) or indirect (cash or vouchers). The government can further decide to force the old cooperatives and state farms to break up in order to create a smaller-scale, family-farm-type organization. This strategy can be referred to as *decollectivization* in the sense of Pryor's (1992) definition. In this sense, decollectivization does not occur when collective farms are transformed into private cooperatives which largely maintain the same economic organization.

In Hungary there was broad consensus about how to transform the cooperatives but not about how to privatize them. The agricultural reform debate was dominated by the issue of restitution and compensation. Three parts can be distinguished in the privatization and transformation of cooperative farms. (The privatization and transformation of state farms was regulated by separate legislation.) First, members of a cooperative farm who had always retained title to part of the land were permitted to withdraw their land freely from the cooperative. This was already achieved under the last Communist government in February 1990. A law was passed to allow members of cooperative farms who have retained title to their land to withdraw it from communal cultivation and farm it privately. At that time the law was of little significance, as only 1 to 3 percent of the members made use of this right, but the law was an important precondition for agricultural privatization. However, as in other CEECs, most of this privately owned land could not be restituted in historical boundaries. In some cases, lotteries were used to allocate the land among the members. Second, former landowners who had lost their land were compensated for their losses. Approximately half of the collectively owned land (which made up more than two thirds of all the land cultivated by cooperatives) was used for compensation. This was regulated by the Compensation Laws. Finally the Transitional Cooperative and Unified Cooperative Laws dealt with the transformation of cooperatives and the privatization of their remaining assets, which included about half of the collectively owned land. Both sets of laws will be discussed in more detail.

The Compensation Laws

Due to political and constitutional factors, which will be discussed in the next section, four compensation laws (or restitution acts) were needed to settle the reallocation of property. The first three compensation laws dealt with the criteria for giving compensations. Under the First Compensation Law (Law XXV of 1991) people who had lost property after 8 June 1949 received compensation. The Second Compensation Law (Law XXIV of 1992) redefined the criteria to address losses beginning from 1 May 1939 in order to include claims by Jews who had lost their property on 5 May 1939, when a law restricting property ownership by Jews had come into effect. The Third Compensation Law (Law XXXII of 1992) compensated persons deprived of freedom or life for political reasons between 11 March 1939 (date of the enactment of the second anti-Jewish law) and 23 October 1989 (proclamation of the Republic). Finally, the government decided to issue a Fourth Compensation Law (Law IL of 1992) to speed up the implementation of the previous laws. Each local authority had to establish a land administration committee to supervize auctions and to ensure that all land in its area was under cultivation (Swain, 1993b).

People had to file claims that they had lost property during the considered period. Only partial, monetary compensation was granted, that is for property up to the value of 200,000 HUF, former owners were compensated 100 percent, but with a degressive scale of compensation thereafter (see table 8.4).

Table 8.4
Amount of compensation under the First Compensation Law

Level of damages in HUF	Compensation percentage
up to 200,000	100
200,000 - 300,000	50
300,000 - 500,000	30
over 500,000	10

Source: OECD, 1994.

Former owners or their descendants who claimed compensation, received vouchers based on the estimated value of the lost property. These compensation vouchers could be used (1) to buy physical assets and shares in newly privatized companies, including state farms; (2) to buy, at auctions, land designated for compensation; (3) to buy apartments owned by the state or local authorities; (4) to claim a life annuity from the state (for elderly people); (5) to sell directly or through the stock exchange at a market-determined daily rate. Further, vouchers were interest-bearing securities for three years.

The face value of the compensation vouchers was based on the original valuation of the lost land, which was calculated on the basis of cadastral net income of the arable land, expressed in gold crown units. The average gold crown value of Hungarian land was 20 gold crowns per hectare. On the assumption that the average hectare of farmland was worth 20,000 HUF in 1991, one gold crown's worth of land would equal 1,000 HUF of compensation.

Land for compensation originated from two sources: part of collectively owned land in cooperative farms (see further), and state farms set aside for privatization. Land could be acquired through land auctions. Purchased land not cultivated for a minimum of five years could be confiscated. However, the land could be sold or leased to others to cultivate. The land had to be held for three years before it could be resold. Land could be bought using compensation vouchers only by the first bearer of vouchers. The deadline for the presentation of compensation requests to the County Compensation Offices was set at 16 December 1992. Land auctions began in August 1992.

The Transitional Cooperative and Unified Cooperative laws

Two laws dealing with the transformation and privatization of cooperatives were accepted in Parliament in January 1992: the Transitional Cooperative Law and the Unified Cooperative Law. These laws allowed the cooperatives to choose from three alternatives: (1) to transform the cooperative into a shareholding company and sell the shares to outsiders, (2) to divide the property of the cooperative among its members, or (3) to transform the cooperative farm into a free cooperative, in conformity with the principles adopted at the 1966 Vienna Congress. The activity of the new cooperatives was extended to purchasing and marketing in addition to production (Mészáros, 1994a). These laws also contained a schedule of transformation, including such steps as the distribution of all nonland property among members, creating a land bank for compensation, land auctions, etc.

All the collectively owned nonland assets were valued as they appeared in the accounts and divided as business shares. People eligible for these business shares were existing members, people who had been members for at least five years before the Transitional Law came into force, and their heirs. Business shares could also be given to employees and families of cooperative members by decision of the general assembly of the transformed cooperative. Because property was to be returned to those who had contributed to its accumulation, criteria for use by the general assembly were drawn. These included length of membership, level of salary, and the value of any collectivized property. Business shares could then be exchanged for physical assets by consensus or by auction. In the end, nonland assets could be owned by individuals, transformed cooperatives, or business organizations (OECD, 1994).

The distribution of land was treated differently. All the land of the cooperatives was divided into three land funds: (1) land still privately owned; (2) collectively owned land set aside for members and employees determined by law (30 gold crowns in value of land for each member and 20 gold crowns for each employee); (3) the residual collectively owned land set aside for compensation under the Compensation Laws. Table 8.5 indicates how land cultivated by the cooperatives was allocated in practice: over one third was already in private hands; almost one third (or half of the collectively owned land) was allocated for compensation; and a final one third was allocated to members and employees or remained cooperatively owned.

Table 8.5
Estimations for the future use of land within the cooperatives

Private property	36.2 %
Allocated for compensation	32.3 %
Allocated for members and employees	14.5 %
Allocated for future cooperative land use	13.7 %
State owned	2.8 %
Forseeable private use	0.5 %

Source: Mészáros, 1994b.

Members who wanted to leave the cooperative had to bear the cost of surveying their land themselves (OECD, 1994). They were also obliged to accept a share of the debts of the cooperative, proportional to the assets being taken out. Farm debts have been handled differently in the various CEECs. Debts were fully canceled in Bulgaria and Romania, but were not in Hungary and former Czechoslovakia (Pryor, 1992).

Even before the democratic revolution, the Communist government committed itself to privatization, albeit a controlled rather than a spontaneous privatization, mainly to attract foreign capital. In 1988, a law established new rules to regulate the creation, operation, merging and dissolution of companies. Law XIII of 1989 established the conditions and means of transformation from state-owned and directed enterprises to business entities.

The transformation and privatization of state farms was the responsibility of the State Property Agency and not the Ministry of Agriculture. People able to buy shares of state farms included existing workers and tenants, on-farm and outside owners of compensation vouchers, creditors (banks), and domestic and foreign investors. Not all of the 121 state farms were to be privatized. Twenty-four farms specializing in seed propagation, animal stock breeding, and research remained under state ownership. They were transformed into enterprises controlled to some degree by the State Asset Holding Company. Properties to remain in state ownership were listed in the government decree of August 1992, under Law LIII of 1992.

The other 97 state farms were broken up into viable farm units. Each state farm's commissioner had to submit a rationalization or decentralization plan by 30 June 1992. The transformed farms were then offered for sale at auction or by tender. Farms with assets (excluding land) under HUF 10 million could be sold at auction; farms with higher value, by tender (Privinfo, VIII/1, 1992, p. 20; IX/1 1992, p. 32).

The Land Law

The final step in the privatization process was the regulation of landownership and land rental. A new Land Law was passed in April 1994. The law states that Hungarian individuals can only buy land up to a maximum of 300 hectares. Foreigners and companies cannot buy farmland. Residents and foreigners can lease up to 300 hectares, and Hungarian companies or cooperatives up to 2500 hectares (Mészáros, 1994a).

Interpretation of the reform of Hungarian agriculture

Politics in the agricultural reform debate

A public opinion poll in May 1990 asked the question, What is the right solution to the land rights issue? Forty percent of the respondents answered that the members of the cooperatives should decide what to do. Another

23 percent said that cooperatives should stay as they were. Clearly, a majority wanted cooperatives to stay. Only 23.5 percent of those asked advocated restitution of land. The opinion of this last group was represented by the ISP, which received 12 percent of the votes in the 1990 elections. The ISP is the most rural of all political parties. It won 57 percent of its vote in the countryside (see table 8.6). In the land reform debate the ISP took the most radical position of all parties. It first advocated a radical land reform returning property to all previous owners based on the situation in 1947, that is, after the breakup of the large estates caused by the 1945 land reform but prior to the Communist collectivization. It considered this period a time of relative prosperity for the 642,000 Hungarian peasant families (Okolicsanyi, 1990a). After the elections, the ISP modified its program in response to severe pressure from both the opposition parties and its coalition partners. However, the ISP still wanted a privatization and reorganization of agriculture that favored the 'Hungarian peasant'. Its objective was to give back as much land as possible and to destroy the cooperative structure.

Table 8.6
Composition of the vote according to settlement, 1990 elections

	Nation	Budapest	Other cities	Villages
HDF	24.7	26	40	34
AFD	21.3	32	43	25
ISP	11.7	12	31	57
HSP	10.9	31	40	29
AYD	8.9	22	44	34
CDPP	6.5	13	36	51
Total	100.0	22	40	38

Source: Racz, 1991.

The HDF has a far more urban constituency than the ISP. Therefore, it was more concerned with the interests of the urban consumers that with those of the peasants or of an emerging middel class of family farmers. The position of the HDF on agricultural reform was to minimize disruption, and was therefore much more in favor of the cooperative structures. The gradual economic reforms since 1968 brought a relatively competitive agricultural sector. Under the so-called 'goulash Communism', Budapest set its own political and economic course relatively independent of Moscow. Therefore, appraisal of the former agricultural system was not as negative there as in many other CEECs. Many Hungarians had (and still have) strong beliefs in the feasibility of 'their' system based on the symbiosis of large- and small-scale farming. The major political parties, such as the AFD and the HDF, wanted to keep the cooperative structure as the backbone of Hungarian agriculture. Moreover, as Mihályi (1993) emphasizes, vested interests, deeply established forms of thinking, legal traditions, and informal connections do not disappear overnight.

The vested interests in agrarian reform are not always obvious. In general, the following interest groups can be identified. Cooperative directors and managers, agricultural engineers and experts, and local administrators could lose significantly from a decollectivization program because of a decline in their economic and political power and influence. However, they might at the same time be in an excellent position to benefit from 'moderate' reforms, which would not induce a major decollectivization or which would allow them to set up private farms. They might influence the transformation process with their preferential access to information during the transition period. Hungary's agriculture could not survive without these highly trained professionals. To the extent that the restitution program (or asset privatization program in general) tends to stimulate decollectivization and to distribute the basic production factors in agriculture to others, this group would oppose such programs.

Collective farm workers might be hurt most by decollectivization. They might lose their jobs and their social environments. Land and nonland asset restitution to former owners typically does not favor agricultural workers (in contrast to privatization procedures such as vouchers based on labor input in the collective farm). Managers, experts, and workers of cooperatives also have an interest in moderate reforms and in preventing asset restitution and decollectivization. In Hungary they have organized themselves into the National Federation of Agricultural Producers (MOSZ), a successor to the former Communist-controlled association of agricultural producer cooperatives, and are represented in Parliament by the Agrarian Alliance. The HDF, the AFD, and the HSP also take postion on agricultural reform that are close to this interest group's position. Of course, if some of these individuals are to be restituted important areas of land or are ideologically opposed to the collectivized system, they might favor the policies forwarded by the ISP.

Practical and economic constraints

The case against full restitution of landed property was supported by some *practical constraints*. Restituting not only the land to the victims of the Communist regime since 1948, but also to people harmed by the 1945 land reform and during the Second World War, could bring more than one claim to the same plot of land. Moreover, giving back land in historical boundaries would create an administrative nigthmare because the physical characteristics of former farms and plots have been lost. Capital improvements made over the forty years of collective ownership would be difficult to apportion among former owners (OECD, 1994). Finally, the lack of expertise and agricultural entrepreneurs outside the existing cooperatives would be an important factor to consider. As indicated before, many urban people were eligible for compensation. Some of them did not express interest in claiming their piece of land. Because many of the plots restituted were so small, claiming costs often outweighed the potential gains. Therefore, it was expected that most of these urbanites would not buy land with their vouchers or would sell or rent their land to cooperatives or companies.

Several *economic constraints* also restricted the policy choice set. As gross foreign debt rose to 65 percent of GDP (about 22 billion USD), Hungary had to meet very high debt servicing payments (OECD, 1994). This has limited the government's ability to provide funds to support the agricultural sector and its transition. More specifically, the debt has reduced the government's ability to settle the debts of the cooperatives or to give full monetary compensation. Compensation could only be partial. Moreover, the agricultural sector has been an important contributor to the surplus on the current account of the balance of payments. Therefore, efficiency considerations have called for disrupting production of export products as little as possible. Finally, as restitution would leave half of Hungary's people landless, it threatened employment in the countryside.

The HDF-ISP compromise and the role of the Constitutional Court

Restitution was the most heated and controversial issue in the agrarian reform debate. Because one third of the land cultivated by cooperatives was still in private hands, the key question was how to privatize the other twothirds – the collectively owned land. The privatization of this land could be handled in three ways. First, all of this land could be given back to its original 1947 owners. This was the initial radical ISP position. Second, part of the land could be given back to former owners for compensation, and part could be given to the members and workers of the cooperatives who were cultivating it. A third option was to give all the land to those cultivating it.

On 22 July 1990, the HDF and ISP coalition partners agreed on a compromise Land Privatization Law. Land would be given to former owners who intended to cultivate it. However, three months later, the Constitutional Court ruled that the bill was unconstitutional because it gave preferential treatment to land over other forms of property. Taking away land from the cooperative farms without compensating them was also ruled unconstitutional (Okolicsanyi, 1991a). Consequently, the Land Privatization Law was recast as a general compensation law, by which compensation would be given for the private property lost after 8 June 1949. During parliamentary committee debates the condition was dropped that only those former landowners who still lived in the area in which the land was located could receive land. After lengthy debates and several hundreds of modifications, the Compensation Law passed in Parliament on 24 April 1991. On 29 May 1991, the Constitutional Court ruled once again that major parts of the law were unconstitutional because the law differentiated between landowners and owners of other property, offering full compensation only for expropriated land (Pataki, 1991).

In the summer of 1991, an amended Compensation Law was finally approved (Okolicsanyi, 1991b). It specified that former owners of land would receive partial compensation (see previous section for details). In its answer, the Constitutional Court ordered that a second law be passed to compensate for property confiscated between 1 May 1939 and 8 June 1949. The date of 1 May 1939 was chosen because on 5 May 1939 a law restricting ownership of property by Jews had come into effect. The Second Compensation Law (April 1992) extended compensation not only to Hungarian Jews but also to former owners of large estates, ethnic Germans who had lost property or were deported during this period, and the Catholic Church. The Third Compensation Law (May 1992) compensated persons deprived of freedom or life for political reasons between 11 March 1939, date of the enactment of the second anti-Jewish law, and 23 October 1989.

In the spring of 1992, some 300,000 hectares of land were left idle (OECD, 1994). Officials of the Ministry of Agriculture as well as opposition politicians argued that something needed to be done to avoid production declines, and further uncertainty, both for the cooperatives and for future owners (Swain, 1993a). A Fourth Compensation Law was voted to give priority to claimants who committed themselves to farm the land they acquired without delay.

The Cooperative Transitional Law and the Unified Cooperative Law were supported by almost all parties, except the ISP. Cooperatives were not destroyed, but could choose their organizational structure. The HDF wanted to prevent the disruption of production with these measures. The HFD's aim was not to create a middle class of farmers, but to confirm the role of the former workers and managers. In this way, production relations would be disrupted to a minimum, the main concern of the ruling HDF (Swain, 1993b). The ISP reacted by proposing amendments to increase the number of people who had claims on cooperative farm property. However, the ISP did not achieve its goal of breaking up the cooperatives, partly because interest in private farming remained low. In conclusion the laws induced important changes in ownership relations in agriculture, but they left the organizational structures largely intact.

Swinnen (1994) and Lyons et al. (1994) explain the choice of the agricultural reform process in Bulgaria as the outcome of a political fight between various political parties and interest groups. Lyons et al. model the decision process as a multilateral bargaining game between (a) a reformist party in favor of total disruption of the old agrarian structure defending the agricultural producers, (b) (ex-)Communists in favor of a status quo defending the collective farm managers, and (c) a center party with the intermediate position of defending primarily consumers. They predict that the outcome of the game, in the form of a disruption factor, would be close to the policy option of the center party. As Swinnen and Lyons et al. show, the nonexistence of such a center party in Bulgaria led to the choice of radical privatization and radical transformation policies in Bulgarian agriculture and, therefore, maximal disruption.

Swinnen (1994) states that the absence of a political center in Bulgaria and the imminent threat of the (ex-)Communist opposition returning to power encouraged the reformist government to pursue a radical privatization and decollectivization. To ensure its chance for reelection in the long run, the government had an incentive to implement a policy that would make reform irreversible. Restituting the land in real boundaries and decollectivizing the cooperatives would change the political preferences of the rural electorate. It would also reduce the power of the collective farm managers and the organizational strength of (ex-)Communists in the rural areas.

Applying this framework to the case of agrarian reform in Hungary, the center party would be the HDF which took an intermediary stance between the HSP and the Agrarian Alliance defending collective farm managers interests and the ISP favoring the radical policies of restitution and decollectivization. The HDF did not have its constituency in the rural areas, among the agricultural establishment, or among former landowners. As the most important opposition movement against Communism, the HDF was supported in the 1990 elections mostly by an urban constituency. Therefore, in the debate about the transformation of agriculture, one could argue that the HDF defended the interest of the consumers. Hence, while it was heavily committed to privatization, economic considerations dominated its point of view on decollectivization, and the HDF opted for a moderate reform.

The Hungarian case differs in three important aspects from the Bulgarian case. First, the Communist parties were heavily defeated in the first democratic elections in Hungary. The HSWP did not even gain entry to the Parliamant, and the HSP won only 9 percent of the vote. Without the threat of a Communist return to power, the HDF had less incentive to remove the collective farm managers from their position. Instead, it could focus on using the skills of the collective farm managers for improving the efficiency of the economy. One could argue that this argument is inconsistent with the major victory of the HSP in the 1994 election. However, it must be noted that in the various CEECs the collective farm managers – the so-called 'nomenklatura' – are evaluated differently. In Hungary, as a result of the gradual reform process of the last decades, the management of cooperative farms changed drastically during the last decades and was based (relatively more when compared with other CEECs) on skills rather than on political links. In addition, when reform decisions were made in 1991, there was little indication of an HSP revival.

Second, the gain of more than 40 percent of the seats by the centrist HDF in 1990 put this party in a strong position to implement its moderate reform policies. However, because the ISP was in the coalition and the HSP or the Agrarian Alliance were not, the HDF had to indulge some ISP demands to keep the coaliton alive. Therefore, the government opted for a mix of restitution and partial compensation, and the transformation but not the breakup of cooperatives. The decision of how to achieve the cooperative transformation was left to the general assemblies of the cooperatives.

Finally, the fact that two thirds of the land used by the collective farms was no longer formally owned by individuals but by the collectives made land more like other (nonland) assets than was the case in Bulgaria and most other CEECs. This allowed the government to limit restitution to one third of the farmland used by the collectives.

Implementation and results of agricultural reform

The agrarian reform process was characterized by short deadlines and imperfect information. In many cases, the management of a cooperative provided farmers with incomplete and incorrect information by spreading false rumors about compensation and transformation. Another tactic was to postpone as long as possible the real estate auctions (Okolicsanyi, 1993b). The short deadline for the reform of cooperatives also slowed down the reform process. Members of the cooperative had to decide before December 1992 whether or not to leave their cooperative, a short time for such a radical decision. This led to the demand for an extension of the deadline for withdrawing assets-in-kind (OECD, 1994). A new law extending this deadline was heavily opposed by organizations representing the cooperatives' interest, particularly the National Federation of Agricultural Producers (MOSZ). However, this organization could not prevent passage of the law (Okolicsanyi, 1993). In the beginning most cooperatives remained cooperatives led by the same people with power and influence similar to that they had under the Communist regime (Pryor, 1992). Swain (1993b) reports that two thirds of the former management was re-elected. By early 1993 about 90 percent of members had not withdrawn their land from the cooperative. Csorba (1993) reported that as much as fourfifths of all land was owned by individuals who would not cultivate the land themselves. Of the land already in private hands, 80 percent belonged to elderly people no longer active. Moreover, 55 percent of the members and employees of the cooperative who received land were beyond their active working age. Most of these individuals lease their land to cooperatives or corporations.

However, more and more cooperatives went broke. In early 1993, onethird of the cooperatives declared bankruptcy. Most of them produced on marginal land not suited for commercial farming. The final deadline for the transformation of cooperatives was extended from 31 December 1992 to the end of September 1993 (OECD, 1994). The compensation process slowly progressed, and a multitude of organizational structures emerged out of the land reform. According to official statistics, shareholding and limited liability companies, and partnerships used 28 percent of the total agricultural land in 1995. Agricultural producer cooperatives used 24 percent and individual family farms 29 percent. However, the category of individual farmers includes both full-time farmers and land used as garden, as te lower limit to be included in the statistics is 400 square meters.

Finally, an important point is that the transformation and restructuring of cooperatives is determined by several factors. One factor we discussed extensively is the government's choice of transformation and privatization policies. Another key factor is the economic environment, including profitability and risk of agricultural production, access to credit and other inputs, and the reform of up- and downstream activities. All these factors affect the riskiness of agricultural production and, therefore, the attractiveness for individuals to set up their own farms. With an uncertain environment and low profitability in farming, as was typically the case in Hungarian agriculture during 1989-1994, the incentive for collective members and workers to leave the cooperative framework was strongly reduced. As a result of this uncertainty, it was not worthwhile for the workers of cooperatives to give up the possibility of assured income from the cooperative and additional small-scale farming to undertake a risky, individual adventure. Therefore, the chosen transformation policies were only one factor affecting the continuing domination of large-scale operations in Hungary.

Conclusion

The conflict between efficiency and historical justice in agricultural privatization dominated the reform debate in Hungary. The strongest advocate of full restitution was the ISP. In their first proposal the ISP wanted to return property to all previous owners based on conditions in 1947, before collectivization but after the 1945 land reform. However, the major parties opposed full restitution of property rights. The HDF feared such policy would disrupt Hungary's agricultural production system. Its main concern was to minimize disruptions in agricultural production. Hungary could not afford setbacks in the agricultural sector, since agricultural exports were one of the country's main sources of convertible currency. Moreover, the HDF argued that the Hungarian agricultural system had proved itself quite successful in the past. Therefore the HDF, and most other political parties, wanted an agricultural sector based on private property but with a large-scale farm structure similar to that already in existence. This was best achieved by a nondisruptive agricultural privatization and transformation policy in which only partial and monetary compensation would be granted to victims of the Communist regime.

Because of the political strength of the political center, represented by the HDF, which had clearly won the 1990 elections (and by the AFD), Hungarian agricultural reform was largely based on the HDF's moderate reform strategy. However, as in other CEECs, land still formally owned by individuals was restituted. Only the land owned by the collectives and part of the state-owned land was privatized through a less disruptive voucher privatization process and allocation of land to collective members and employees.

Given the intensity of the restitution debate, we believe that the main reason for not restituting other land was the nature of landownership before 1989. Unlike other CEECs, in Hungary twothirds of the land used by collective farms was owned by the collectives. This made an important difference, a difference that was emphasised by the Constitutional Court's ruling against restitution of this land. As the land was like other property assets of the collectives, there could be no distinction between collectively owned land and other assets in privatization procedures.

This special nature of pre-reform landownership combined with the strong position of the political center allowed the Hungarian government to choose a (relatively) less disruptive program.

Notes

1   The author gratefully acknowledges comments by Jo Swinnen and Sándor Mészáros on earlier versions of the paper.
2   Appendix 8.1 gives an overview of the most important political events between 1989 and 1994.
3   An overview of the most important political parties on the eve of the 1990 election is given in Appendix 8.2.

References

Barany, Z. D. (1990a), 'The Alliance of Free Democrats: From Underdog to Potential Victor', *Report on Eastern Europe*, Vol. 1, No. 14, 6 April, pp. 11-13.

Barany, Z. D. (1990b), 'The Hungarian Democratic Forum Wins National Elections Decisively', *Report on Eastern Europe*, Vol. 1, No. 17, 27 April, pp. 11-13.

Berend, I. T. (1985), 'Agriculture', in Kaser, M. C. and Radice, E. A. (eds.), *The Economic History of Eastern Europe 1919-1975. Volume I: Economic Structure and Performance Between the Two Wars*, Clarendon Press: Oxford.

Brus, W. (1986), 'Post-war Reconstruction and Socioeconomic Transformation', in Kaser, M. C. and Radice, E. A. (eds.), *The Economic History of Eastern Europe 1919-1975. Volume I: Economic Structure and Performance Between the Two Wars*, Clarendon Press: Oxford.

Cochrane, N. J. (1993), 'Central European Agrarian Reforms in a Historical Perspective', *American Journal of Agricultural Economics*, Vol. 75, pp. 851-856.

Csaki, C. and Varga, G. (1993), 'Hungary. Economic Dimensions', in Braverman, A., Brooks, K. and Csaki, C. (eds.), *The Agricultural Transition in Central and European Europe and the Former U.S.S.R.*, The World Bank: Washington D.C.

Csorba, J. (1993), 'The Spectacular Decrease of State Property II: 1992 - The Crisis Year of Agricultural Business?' *Privinfo*, Vol. 2, No. 18, September, pp. 43-47.

Harcsa, I. (1991), 'Privatization and Reprivatization in Hungarian agriculture', *Acta Oeconomica*, Vol. 43, No. 3-4, pp. 321-348.

Hoensch, J. K. (1988), *A History of Modern Hungary 1867-1986,* Longman: London and New York.

Hungarian Central Statistical Office (1990), *Statistical Pocket Book of Hungary 1989*, Statistical Publishing House: Budapest.

Hungarian Central Statistical Office (1991), *Statistical Yearbook 1989*, Statistical Publishing House: Budapest.

Hungarian Central Statistical Office (1994), *Hungarian Statistical Handbook 1993*, Statistical Publishing House: Budapest.

Juhász, J. (1991), 'Large-scale and Small-scale Farming in Hungarian Agriculture: Present Situation and Future Prospects', *European Review of Agricultural Economics*, Vol. 18, No. 3-4, pp. 399-415.

Lyons, R. F., Rausser, G. C., and Simon, L. K. (1994), 'Disruption and Continuity in Bulgaria's Agrarian Reform', in Schmitz, A., Moulton, K., Buckwell, A. and Davidova, S. (eds.), *Privatization of Agriculture in New*

Market Economies: Lessons from Bulgaria, Kluwer Academic Publishers: Boston, London and Dordrecht.

Mészáros, S. (1994a), 'The Reform Process in Hungarian Agriculture: An Overview', in Swinnen, J. (ed.), *Policy and Institutional Change in Central European Agriculture and its Likely Impacts on Domestic and International Markets*, Avebury: Aldershot.

Mészáros, S. (1994b), 'Short Survey of 1993/1994 Changes in Hungarian Agricultural Reform', Paper presented at the Initial Workshop of the COST Network on 'Policy and Institutional Change in Central European Agriculture and its Likely Impacts on Domestic and International Markets', Leuven, 9-11 June 1994.

Mihályi, P. (1993), 'Hungary: A Unique Approach to Privatization - Past, Present and Future', in Szekely, I. and Newbery, D. (eds.), *Hungary: A Country in Transition*, Cambridge University Press: Cambridge.

OECD (1993), *Agricultural Policies, Markets and Trade. Monitoring and Outlook 1993. In the Central and Eastern European Countries, the New Independent States and China*, OECD: Paris.

OECD (1994), *Review of Agricultural Policies: Hungary*, OECD: Paris.

Okolicsanyi, K. (1990a), 'The Economic Programs of the Major Hungarian Parties', *Report on Eastern Europe*, Vol. 1, No. 15, 13 April, pp. 10-13.

Okolicsanyi, K. (1990b), 'Prime Minister Presents New Government's Program', *Report on Eastern Europe*, Vol. 1, No. 23, 8 June, pp. 20-23.

Okolicsanyi, K. (1990c), 'The Economic Program for National Renewal'. *Report on Eastern Europe*, Vol. 1, No. 50, 14 December, pp. 9-11.

Okolicsanyi, K. (1991a), 'The Compensation Law: Attempting to Correct Past Mistakes'. *Report on Eastern Europe*, Vol. 2, No. 19, 10 May, pp. 7-11.

Okolicsanyi, K. (1991b), 'Compensation Law Finally Approved', *Report on Eastern Europe*, Vol. 2, No. 36, 6 September, pp. 22-25.

Okolicsanyi, K. (1993b), 'Hungarian Agricultural Production Declines', *RFE/RL Research Report*, Vol. 2, No. 44, 5 November, pp. 46-49.

Oltay, E. (1994), 'The Former Communists' Election Victory in Hungary', *RFE/RL Research Report*, Vol. 3, No. 25, 24 June, pp. 1-6.

Pataki, J. (1990), 'New Government Prefers Cautious Changes', *Report on Eastern Europe*, Vol. 1, No. 28, 13 July, pp. 20-24.

Pataki, J. (1991), 'The Constitutional Court's Search for Identity', *Report on Eastern Europe*, Vol. 2, No. 25, 21 June, pp. 5-9.

Pataki, J. (1992a), 'Role of Smallholders' Party in Hungary's Coalition Government', *RFE/RL Research Report*, Vol. 1, No. 14, 3 April, pp. 20-23.

Pataki, J. (1992b), 'Hungarians Dissatisfied with Political Changes', *RFE/RL Research Report*, Vol. 1, No. 44, 6 November, pp. 66-70.

Pataki, J. (1992c), 'Will the Governing Coalition Survive', *RFE/RL Research Report*, Vol. 1, No. 48, 4 December, pp. 36-39.

Pataki, J. (1993a), 'The Hungarian Cabinet Reshuffle', *RFE/RL Research Report*, Vol. 2, No. 12, 19 March, pp. 42-46.

Pataki, J. (1993b), 'Hungary's Smallholders Fail to Unite before National Elections', *RFE/RL Research Report*, Vol. 2, No. 10, 11 March, pp. 15-19.

Pryor, F. L. (1992), *The Red and the Green. The Rise and Fall of Collectivized Agriculture in Marxist Regimes*, Princeton University Press: Princeton.

Racz, B. (1991), 'Political Pluralisation in Hungary: the 1990 Elections', *Soviet Studies*, Vol. 43, No. 1, pp. 107-136.

Reisch, A. (1990a), 'The Democratic Forum at the Finish Line', *Report on Eastern Europe*, Vol.1, No. 14, 6 April, pp. 17-21.

Reisch, A. (1990b), 'New Government Combines Party Politicians with Professional Experts', *Report on Eastern Europe* No. 25, 1(22 June), pp. 17-22.

Reisch, A. (1991), 'Prime Minister Replaces Key Ministers', *Report on Eastern Europe*, Vol. 2, No. 6, 8 February, pp. 11-15.

Suskosd, M. (1992), 'Home and Away. Why History Doesn't Repeat Itself: The Saga of the Smallholders' Party', *East European Reporter*, Vol. 5, No. 4, pp. 52-55.

Swain, N. (1985), *Collective Farms Which Work?*, Cambridge University Press: Cambridge.

Swain, N. (1991), 'Hungary', in Szajkowski, B., Allcock, J. B., et al. (eds.) *New Political Parties of Eastern Europe and the Soviet Union*, Longman Harlow: Essex.

Swain, N. (1993a), 'Agricultural Transformation in Hungary: The Context', ESRC EWI Workshop, *Transitions to Family Farming in Post-Socialist Central Europe*, 25-28 March 1993: Budapest.

Swain, N. (1993b), 'The Smallholders Party versus the Green Barons: Class Relations in the Restructuring of Hungarian Agriculture', paper presented to Working Group Three, *Restructuring of Agriculture and Rural Society in Central and Eastern Europe*, of the XVth European Congress of Rural Sociology, 2-6 August 1993: Wageningen.

Swinnen, J. (1994), 'Political Economy of Reform in Bulgarian Agriculture', in Schmitz, A., Moulton, K., Buckwell, A. and Davidova, S. (eds.), *Privatization of Agriculture in New Market Economies: Lessons from Bulgaria*, Kluwer Academic Publishers: Boston, London, and Dordrecht.

Szelenyi, B. and Szelenyi, I. (1993), 'Hungary. The Social Effects of Agrarian Reform', in Braverman, A., Brooks, K. and Csaki, C. (eds.), *The Agricultural Transition in Central and European Europe and the Former U.S.S.R.*, The World Bank: Washington D.C.

Appendix 8.1
Important political events, 1989-1994

1989	June	Negotiations between the HSWP and the opposition (Roundtable Talks) start
	18 September	Agreement on Roundtable Talks
	23 October	Proclamation of the Republic of Hungary
1990	February	Government passes a law allowing cooperative members to withdraw their land
	March & April	Parliamentary elections
	29 April	Political Pact between HDF and AFD
	23 May	Antall Government
	22 July	Agreement within the coalition on a Land Privatization Law
	3 August	Arpad Goncz is elected President of the Republic
	18 September	First Privatization Law passed in Parliament regarding state-owned stores, restaurants, and services
	30 September	Local elections
	2 October	Constitutional Court rules drafted Land Privatization Law unconstitutional
1991	24 April	First Compensation Law passed in Parliament
	29 May	Constitutional Court rules First Compensation Law unconstitutional
	26 June	Amended First Compensation Law passed in Parliament
1992	January	Transitional Cooperative Law and Unified Cooperative Law passed in Parliament
	21 February	Torgyan decides to withdraw from the governing coalition resulting in the breakup of the ISP
	7 April	Second Compensation Law passed in Parliament
	12 May	Third Compensation Law passed in Parliament
1993	13 December	Jozsef Antall dies
1994	April	Land Law passed in Parliament
	8 and 29 May	Parliamentary elections
	24 June	Coalition agreement between HSP and AFD

Appendix 8.2
Overview of Hungary's major political parties
on the eve of the 1990 elections

Agrarian Alliance
Agrárszövetség (ASZ)
Founded: 3 December 1989
President: Tamás Nagy
Origins: merger between the Agrarian Reform Circles Movement and the
               Association of Agrarian Reform Circles which emerged within
               the HSWP
Elections: 3.13%, 1 seat

Alliance of Free Democrats (AFD), Free Democrats
Szabad Demokraták Szövetsége (SZDSZ), Szabad Demokraták
Founded: 13 November 1988
President: János Kis
Origins: urban opposition group
Elections: 21.39%, 91 seats

Christian Democratic People's Party (CDPP)
Kereszténydemokrata Néppárt (KDNP)
Founded: 17 March 1989
President: László Surján
Origins: continuation of the more progressive Barankovics branch of the
               Democratic People's Party, founded in October 1944
Elections: 6.46%, 21 seats

FIDESZ, Alliance of Young Democrats (AYD)
FIDESZ, Fiatal Demokraták Szövetsége
Founded: 30 March 1988
President: Viktor Orbán
Origins: opposition
Elections 8.95%, 22 seats

Hungarian Democratic Forum (HDF), Democratic Forum
Magyat Demokrata Fórum (MDF), Demokrata Fórum
Founded: 27 September 1987
President: József Antall
Origins: nationalist-Christian opposition group
Elections: 24.73%, 165 seats

Hungarian People's Party (HPP), Hungarian People's Party - National Peasant Party
Magyar Néppárt (MNP), Magyar Néppárt - Nemzeti Parasztpárt
Founded: 8 March 1989
President: Gyula Fekete
Origins: continuation of the National Peasant Party, established in December 1944
Elections: 0.75%

Hungarian Socialist Party (HSP)
Magyar Szocialista Párt (MSP)
Founded: 7 October 1989
President: Gyula Horn
Origins: direct descendant of the HSWP
Elections: 10.89%, 32 seats

Hungarian Socialist Workers' Party (HSWP)
Magyar Szocialista Munkáspárt (MSZMP)
Founded: 17 December 1989
President   Gyula Thürmer
Origins: refounded Communist Party
Elections: 3.68%

Hungary's Cooperative and Agrarian Party
Magyarországi Szövetkezeti Agrárpárt
Founded: 24 November 1989
President: János Nyilas
Origins: countryside
Elections: 0.10%

Hungary's Social Democratic Party (HSDP)
Magyarországi Szociáldemokrata Párt (MSZDP)
Founded: 9 January 1989
President: Anna Petrasovits
Origins: refounded HSDP, which was first formed in 1890
Elections: 3.55%

Independent Smallholder, Land Laborer and Citizens' Party (ISP),
Smallholders' Party
Független Kisgazda, Földmunkás és Polgári Párt (FKgP), Kisgazda Párt
Founded: 12 and 18 November 1988
President: Ferenc József Nagy
                József Torgyán
                leader in Parliament: Gyula Pásztor
Origins: refounded ISP
Elections: 11.73%, 44 seats

Source: Swain, 1991.

Appendix 8.3
Results of the 1990 elections in Hungary

Name of party (alliance)	Number of seats	Percentage
Hungarian Democratic Forum (HDF)	164	42.5
Alliance of Free Democrats (AFD)	92	23.8
Independent Smallholders' Party (ISP)	44	11.4
Hungarian Socialist Party (HSP)	33	8.5
Alliance of Young Democrats (AYD)	21	5.4
Christian Democratic Party (CDP)	21	5.4
Agrarian Alliance	1	0.3
Independents	6	1.6
Single candidates representing two parties	4	1.0
TOTAL	**386**	**100.0**

Source: Barany, 1990b.

Appendix 8.4
Results of the 1994 elections in Hungary

Name of party (alliance)	Number of seats	Percentage
Hungarian Socialist Party (HSP)	209	54.1
Alliance of Free Democrats (AFD)	70	18.1
Hungarian Democratic Forum (HDF)	38	9.5
Independent Smallholders' and Civic Party	26	6.7
(ISCP)	22	5.7
Christian Democratic People's Party (CDPP)	20	5.1
Alliance of Young Democrats (AYD)	1	0.3
Agrarian Alliance	1	0.3
Liberal bloc		
TOTAL	**386**	**100.0**

Source: Oltay, 1994.

9 Political economy aspects of Polish agrarian reform

Isabelle Lindemans and Johan F. M. Swinnen[1]

Introduction

This chapter relates agricultural reform in Poland after the fall of the Communist regime to Poland's political, economic, and institutional environment. It focuses on two questions. First, why in Poland was land not restituted as it was in many other Central and East European countries (CEECs)? Second, why has decollectivization of Polish state farms been relatively slow?[2] The Polish institutional environment was more favorable for decollectivization than were the environments of other CEECs, due to the importance of private family farming in Poland's prereform agricultural sector. Decollectivization was consistent with the dominant economic institutions. Further, decollectivization would have caused only relatively minor disruptions in the agri-food sector because private farming would have provided a food supply buffer during a transition period.

In this chapter we use a public choice framework and analyze the political market for privatization and decollectivization. The choice of agricultural reform policies implies a distribution of economic benefits and losses. Those economic effects translate into political gains and losses, affecting the political constraints of the decisionmakers in government. For example, privatization and decollectivization policies affect political support and opposition from new landowners, employees and management of state farms, and from consumers concerned with food security.

We argue that three characteristics of the Polish agricultural economy had an important impact on its chosen privatization policies and decollectivization. First, most of Poland's state-owned land is in regions which before World War II belonged to Germany. Land restitution would thus have involved returning most of this land to German former owners. This made restitution a nonissue in Poland. Second, agricultural privatization has an important regional

269

dimension. Most of the state farmland is in north and west Poland, while family farms on privately owned land dominate in the other regions. As a consequence, the demand for privatized assets, including land, was regionally separated from the supply. Together with the low demand for privatized assets because of low profitability and difficult access to credit, the latter explains the slow progress of state farm privatization. Finally, because only about 20 percent of Poland's land was state-owned and collectivized, the effect of privatization and/or decollectivization policy choice on the political alignment of the rural electorate was relatively minor. In combination with the importance of the already established Polish Peasant Party in the rural areas, this reduced incentives for political parties to use the decollectivization policies to affect the social structure of the rural areas.

The prereform agricultural production structure

About 26 percent of the active population in Poland was employed in agriculture in 1989, producing approximately 15 percent of the total GNP. Of the population working in agriculture 84.5 percent was employed in private farms, producing 75 percent of Polish agricultural production. Table 9.1 gives the pattern of landownership between 1950 and 1990. Polish landownership during the Communist regime was unique because of the predominance of private landownership. Enforced collectivization in the 1950s failed: only 10 percent of the land was collectivized and most of it was later reprivatized. Indirect pressure for collectivization – for example, by discrimination towards family farms in the upstream and downstream sector, obligatory deliveries, and land taxes – did not induce a substantial change in landownership. In 1990, 77 percent of the land was still in the hands of private farms. State farms occupied 19 percent of the land, agricultural cooperatives only 4 percent. Table 9.2 shows how Polish private farming was dominated by small production units in 1989. Nearly 50 percent of the family farms owned 5 hectares or less. Even if only holdings of more than 1 hectare are taken into consideration, the average size of a Polish private farm was 6 hectares in 1989. The average size of a state farm amounted to approximately 2,300 hectares in 1991.

There are important *regional differences* in Poland's agricultural structure. In central and east Poland (the regions which were already Polish territory before World War II) family farms dominate. In these regions family farms sometimes occupy more than 90 percent of the agricultural area. In north and west Poland, large areas (up to 50 percent of the agricultural area) are occupied by state farms (Rowinski, 1994; Kwiecinski and Leopold, 1991). Before World War II these regions belonged to Germany. In 1944, immediately after

270

the war, most Germans living in these regions emigrated, and the land (about a third of Poland's total surface) was confiscated by the Polish state. Although a part of the confiscated land was redistributed to peasant families, most of these lands came to constitute the basis of the state sector in farming (Kaser and Radice, 1985; see table 9.3).

Table 9.1
Polish landownership, 1950-1990

| | % of agricultural land | | | | | |
	1950	1955	1960	1970	1980	1990
State farms	9.6	13.5	11.9	15.4	19.5	18.9
Cooperatives	0.8	9.2	1.2	1.3	4.0	3.8
Private farms	89.5	77.3	86.9	81.0	74.5	77.0

Source: Kwiecinski and Leopold, 1991.

Table 9.2
Private farm structure in Poland in 1989

| size | number | | area | |
ha	1000	%	ha	%
1-5	1108	48.7	2.7	19.9
5-10	692	30.4	4.4	32.3
10-15	293	12.9	3.2	23.5
>15	183	8.0	3.3	24.3

Source: Kwiecinski and Leopold, 1991.

Privatization and decollectivization in Polish agriculture

In general little progress was made in privatizing Polish state farms from 1991 to 1993. The law of October 1991 established the Agency of the Agricultural Property of the State Treasury (AAPST), which had responsibility for the privatization of state farms. This body's task was to take over the assets of the state farms and to supervise their sale or lease (Rowinski, 1994). Officially, the privatization of state farms began on 1 January 1992. By the end of February 1993 1,010 state farms (67.6 percent of the 1,495 state farms) were under the control of the AAPST (Agra Europe). The total area to be taken over by the AAPST was approximately 3.1 million hectares. Aproximately 2.8 million hectares (90 percent) was bought up by the AAPST at the end of July 1993. However, due to the lack of credits and low profitability in agriculture, there was little interest in purchasing the available state land from the AAPST. Only 20 percent of the land under the supervision of the AAPST had been sold or leased in July 1993: 34,000 hectares had been sold and 474,000 hectares had been leased (Agra Europe).

Table 9.3
State farms in the various Polish regions in 1953

Region	% of arable land in state farms
Centralwest	16.0
Centraleast	3.2
Southeast	5.4
South	15.8
West	27.2
Northwest	48.3
North	37.5

Source: Sokolovsky, 1990.

In the meantime, the AAPST was responsible for managing the state farms, and no fundamental restructuring occurred. The initial description of the AAPST's task explicitly stated that it was responsible for the transfer of state farm assets to economic units securing better utilization of these resources and for the creation of economically viable production units (OECD, 1993b; Adamowicz, 1993). In September 1992, the government's agricultural program included a more detailed description of the goals of this transfer. In regions of dispersed private family farming, land was to be used primarily to increase the size of existing family farms. In regions with a considerable share of state farms, the land was to be used to establish new, economically strong family farms. The creation of extremely large farms was to be avoided (OECD, 1993a). However, the program did not include detailed specifications about how these goals were to be achieved. For instance, there were few restrictions of the Polish land market: there was no upper limit on farm size. Only the amount of land sold to foreigners is restricted (OECD, 1993b).

In summary, agrarian reform in Poland during the period 1989 to 1993 was characterized by a lack of restitution and a low degree of decollectivization of the state farms. We first explore why no restitution of land took place in

Poland. Then we discuss the economic and political aspects of Polish state farm decollectivization.

An explanation of the agricultural privatization program

Compared with other CEECs, the absence in Poland of an intense political debate on restitution in agriculture is striking. The main reason for this was the nature of former landownership. First, most of Polish land was already owned by private farmers during the Communist regime. Second, about three quarters of the land confiscated after World War II belonged to Germans who left the regions which became part of Poland after 1944. Therefore, land restitution would in many cases have involved giving land property rights to former German owners. The vast majority of the Polish population opposed such policy, and it never became a real issue in the privatization discussions. In addition, more than half of that land was and continues to be used by private farmers, increasing further resistance to the idea of restitution.

In May 1991, the government of Krzysztof Bielecki accepted a draft law on reprivatization. This draft law proposed restitution, but only for those assets which had been taken over by the state 'illegally'. The confiscation of land under the Decree on Agricultural Reform of 1944, which put a limit of 50 hectares on landownership, and the transfer of land property rights from Germans to the Polish state in 1946 were considered legal policies. Restitution only covered land that had been confiscated without any law as legal basis and under compulsory state control. About 8 million hectares of agricultural land became Polish state property during the period of 1944 to 1946, but only 1.2 million hectares were considered to have been taken 'illegally'. Of the land confiscated, 3.3 million hectares were given to state farms, and about 4.7 million hectares were given away or sold to peasants (Jedrzejczak, 1992). The draft law on restitution did not pass the Sejm before the elections of October 1991. Another draft law on restitution, which contained roughly the same proposals, was presented to the Sejm in August 1992, by the government of Suchocka (Agra Europe, 1992). However, even at the end of 1993, no legislation on reprivatization had been agreed to, either for agriculture or for the rest of the economy. Compared with other CEECs, the privatization of agricultural assets in Poland has lagged behind. Unlike other CEECs, Poland treats its agricultural land in roughly the same manner as its non agricultural assets.

273

Decollectivization of state farms: policies, determinants, and effects

A key factor contributing to the relatively slow privatization and decollectivization of Polish state farms was the low demand for state farm assets by private agricultural producers. There were two reasons for this. The first was low profitability in agriculture due to adverse developments in agricultural terms of trade. In addition, credit needed for investments was scarce and expensive, making it both difficult and risky for private farmers to invest in additional land. The second reason was regional differences in supply and demand. Because financial sources were scarce and profitability low, most private interest was in purchasing additional small parcels of land to extend existing farms. However, most of the state farmland is in north and west Poland, while family farms on privately owned land dominate in the other regions. As a consequence, the demand for land was regionally separated from the supply.

The impact of the prereform agrarian structure

The question of whether the Polish tradition of private family farming has had a positive impact on the decollectivization process is answered ambiguously in the literature. Some authors expected a relatively easy reform of Polish state agriculture (Adamowicz, 1993; Blanchi, 1990). The prevalence of private businesses in Polish agriculture created an initial economic institutional environment that was well adapted to individual farms emerging from decollectivization. Polish individual producers were expected to leave the state or cooperative farm to start a private family farm more easily than producers in other CEECs.

Arguments underlying this expectation, such as the tradition of decision making autonomy and experience of investment planning, often refer to Poland's existing human capital (Halamska, 1993, Rembisz and Rosati, 1993). Other arguments refer to Poland's unique pre-reform structure and its influence on the institutional environment (these include informal institutions, such as 'the attachment to the ground' and the social status of the landowner-occupier) (Halamska, 1993). The lack of human capital, together with informal institutions (customs, norms, and social taboos), generally forms the most conservative factor in the CEEC agrarian reform process (Swinnen, 1993).

The idea that the large private sector in Polish agriculture created favorable preconditions for decollectivization is often countered by the argument that Polish family farms had to operate in a state-controlled economy environment. It is argued that this environment induced nonmarket behavior in the farmers, characterized by an 'acquired helplessness and dependence on the state' rather than a profit-oriented risk-minimization strategy and thus encouraged a reluctance to privatize (Kwiecinski and Leopold, 1991). Over four decades, Polish family farms adapted themselves to a state-controlled economic environment. Consequently, family farms obtained their own specificities and, hence, cannot be understood in the same way as private family farms in a market economy. Halamska (1993) describes this as the symbiotic relation between Polish family farming and, socialized economy: Polish family farms as they existed on the eve of the 1989 Revolution could only survive in a state-controlled economy.

Without neglecting the impact of the Communist past on Poland's institutional environment, it seems reasonable to conclude that the Polish tradition of private family farming created an institutional environment which was, on the eve of the fall of the Communist regime, more favorable to further decollectivization, *at least when compared with other CEECs.*

Political economy factors

Does an analysis of the political costs and benefits of decollectivization explain the low degree of Polish decollectivization from 1991 to 1993? One cannot ignore the importance of other factors, including economics and institutions, in analyzing the causes of this process. But here we focus primarily on the political incentives for the government to break up the state farms. The *political costs* of farm decollectivization were relatively low for two reasons. First, while agricultural production decreases in state and collective farms during a decollectivization process, agricultural production is less affected on private farms. A large private sector plays the role of a buffer for food security. Therefore, the loss of political support from consumers would have been lower in Poland than in other CEECs. Moreover, when the farms emerging from decollectivization fit relatively well into an agricultural sector dominated by family farms as in Poland, this also deminishes disruption in agricultural production. Second, Poland's economic and informal institutional environment, which was favorable to decollectivization, decreased, the political cost of Polish decollectivization by making it easier for state farm employees or collective members to start independent family farms.

However, also the *political gains* from decollectivization have been lower in Poland than in other CEECs. Since most of the Polish land was already owned by private farmers during the Communist regime, the expected gain in support from new peasant landowners was low when compared with gains in other CEECs. An additional factor was the absence of land restitution. Privatization of land by sale has a smaller impact on decollectivization than restitution, especially when a low demand for land retards the privatization process and the production structure of the state farms remain intact during the transition period.

Finally, long-term political strategies were less affected by decollectivization in Poland. Poland was a pioneer of democratic and economic reforms in Central and Eastern Europe (see appendix 9.1). Unlike governments in such countries as Bulgaria, the government of Poland was not induced to stimulate the breakup of state farms in response to the threat of a Communist comeback. In most CEECs collectivization helped the Communist Party to strengthen its power in rural areas. Political organization was built upon the collective production structure. This was not the case in Poland, where the Communist Party had initially failed to strengthen its support base in rural areas.[3] In 1949 the Communist Party reorganized the strong rural anti-Communist *Polish Peasant Party* (PPP) and renamed it the *United Peasant Party* (UPP). The UPP had only members loyal to the Communist Party and became the Communist Party's most important organ in rural areas. During the first years of its existence, the UPP had responsibility for the collectivization campaign. When the collective production structure collapsed at the end of the 1950s, the Communist Party promised the UPP more authority to increase peasant input in agricultural policy matters. Throughout the following decades the UPP became a considerable force in rural areas, a force on which the Communist Party could rely (Sokolovsky, 1990; White, 1990).

These political developments under the Communist regime had an impact on post-Communist politics. In 1989 the UPP tried to change its image as a Communist Party alliance by using its pre-Communist name the Polish Peasant Party. In May 1990 the PPP merged with the Polish Peasant Party-Wilanow from the democratic opposition. This move had benefits for both parties: the PPP-Wilanow gave democratic credibility to the party, and the PPP supplied the party with organizational strength and the broad membership it had gained during the Communist regime (Vinton, 1992b). The PPP's main rival was the *Peasant Alliance* (PA), composed of members of the rural faction of Solidarity. While the PPP often attacked the Solidarity government's policies, the PA was more loyal to the government (McQuaid, 1991a). In the elections of 1991, the PPP gained 8.7 percent of the votes, the PA, only 5.5 percent (McQuaid, 1991b). On the eve of the elections of 1993 it was expected that the PA's popularity had decreased even further. Therefore, in contrast to other CEECs, where agricultural collective enterprises remained local Communist support bases, in Poland private farmers strongly supported a former Communist-satellite party. As a result, a more radical decollectivization was of little use in the battle of the reformers against the Communists.

In conclusion, the empirical evidence regarding Polish state farm decollectivization suggests that the lower political cost of decollectivization were more than offset by the combination of low political gains from decollectivization and important economic factors that worked against decollectivization from 1991 to 1993. With little political incentives to force a breakup of the state farms, the economic environment was the main determinant of state farm restructuring. Economic factors did not stimulate restructuring and the creation of individual private farms in the first years of the reforms (Swinnen and Mathijs, 1997). Only later, when risk reduced and terms of trade improved, did they stimulate important restructuring.

Conclusion

Compared with other CEECs, the absence of an intense political debate on restitution in agriculture in Poland is striking. The main reason for this is the nature of former landownership. Most Polish land was already owned by private farmers during the Communist regime, and most of the remaining land was, prior to World War II, owned by Germans who left te regions which became part of Poland after 1944. As land restitution would in many cases involve giving land property rights to former German owners, the vast majority of the Polish population opposed such policy, and it never became a serious issue in the privatization discussions. Further, more than half of that land is presently used by private farmers, increasing further resistance to the idea of restitution.

A key factor contributing to the relatively slow privatization and decollectivization of Polish state farms was the low demand for state farm assets by private agricultural producers because of low profitability in agriculture and scarce credit. The regional separation between supply and demand for land contributed to the low demand for privatized agricultural assets. Both the political costs and benefits of state farm decollectivization were low in Poland, when compared with those of other CEECs. Because only around 20 percent of Poland's land was state owned and collectivized, the privatization and/or decollectivization policy choice could have only minor effects on the political alignment of the rural electorate. This, in combination with the importance of the already established Polish Peasant Party in Poland's rural areas, reduced incentives for political parties to use the decollectivization policies to influence the social structure of the rural areas.

Notes

1   The authors thank Andrzej Kwiecinski and Jerzy Wilkin for critical comments on an earlier version of this paper.
2   For definition of restitution and decollectivization, see Chapter 1 of this volume.

3   In 1956 only 13 percent of the members of the Polish Communist Party
    were peasants (Sokolovsky, 1990).

References

Agra Europe. East Europe & USSR, Agriculture and Food, various issues.

Adamowicz, M. (1993), 'L'Agriculture et l'Agro-Alimentaire en Pologne: Situation et Facteurs d'Evolution', *Economie Rurale,* 214-215, pp. 82-88.

Blanchi, C. (1990), 'An Agricultural Strategy for Poland', in *An Agricultural Strategy for Poland*, Report of the Polish European Community-World Bank Task Force, Washington D.C.

Halamska, M. (1993), 'Les Cadres de la Mutation Fonctionelle de l'Exploitation Familiale sous la Contrainte du Marché en Pologne', *Economie Rurale*, 214-215, p. 71-75.

Jedrzejczak, G. T. (1992), 'Reprivatization in Poland', in *Reprivatization in Central and Eastern Europe, Country Privatization Reports and Specific Implementation Issues*, Central and Eastern European Privatization Network.

Kaser, M. C. and Radice, E. A. (1985), *The Economic History of Eastern Europe, 1919-1975, volume II*, Clarendon Press: Oxford.

Kusin, V. V. (1990), 'The Elections Compared and Assessed', *Report on Eastern Europe,* 13 July, pp. 38-47.

Kwiecinski, A. and Leopold, A. (1991), 'Polish Agriculture during the Transition Period', *PPRG Discussion Papers,* 8, Polish Policy Research Group, Warsaw University: Warsaw.

Maziarski W. (1992), 'The Republic at Risk?', *East European Reporter*, July-August, p. 3-6.

McQuaid, D. (1991a), 'The Political Landscape before the Elections', *Report on Eastern Europe*, 18 October, pp. 10-17.

McQuaid, D. (1991b), 'The Parliamentary Elections: A Postmortem', *Report on Eastern Europe*, 8 November, pp. 15-21.

OECD (1993a), *Agricultural Policies, Markets and Trade in the Central and Eastern European Countries, the New Independent States and China, Monitoring and Outlook 1993*, OECD: Paris.

OECD (1993b), 'Agricultural Policy and Trade Developments in Poland 1992-1993', paper presented at the OECD Seminar *Ad Hoc Group on East/West Economic Relations in Agriculture*, September, OECD: Paris.

Rembisz, W. and Rosati, D. (1993), 'Poland', in Braverman, A., Brooks, M. and Csaki, C. (eds.), *The Agricultural Transition in Central and Eastern Europe and the Former U.S.S.R.*, The World Bank: Washington D.C.

Rowinski, J. (1994), 'Transformation of the Food Economy in Poland', in Swinnen, J. (ed.), *Policy and Institutional Change in Central European Agriculture*, Avebury: Aldershot.

Sabbat, A. (1991), 'Mazowiecki's Year in Review', *Report on Eastern Europe*, 4 January, p. 25-31.

Slay, B. (1991), 'The Mass Privatization Program Unravels', *Report on Eastern Europe*, 1 November, p. 13-19.

Slay, B. (1992), 'Poland: The Rise and Fall of the Balcerowicz Plan', *RFE/RL Research Report,* 31 January, p. 40-47.

Sokolovsky, J. (1990), *Peasants and Power. State Autonomy and the Collectivization of Agriculture in Eastern Europe*, Westview Press: Boulder.

Swinnen, J. (1993), 'Politics and Economics of Land Reform', in Buckwell, A. and Swinnen, J. (eds.), *Policy and Institutional Change in Central European Agriculture and its Likely Impacts on Domestic and International Markets*, Final report to EU-ACE, The Leuven Institute of Central and East European Studies: Leuven.

Swinnen, J. and Mathijs, E. (1997), 'Agricultural Privatisation, Land Reform and Farm Restructuring: A Comparative Analysis', in Swinnen, J., Buckwell, A. and Mathijs, E. (eds.), *Agricultural Privatisation, Land Reform and Farm Restructuring*, Avebury: Aldershot.

Vinton, L. (1991), 'Bielecki Confirmed as New Prime Minister', *Report on Eastern Europe,* 25 January, pp. 17-19.

Vinton, L. (1992a), 'Poland's Governing Coalition: Will the Truce Hold?', *RFE/RL Research Report*, Vol. 1, No. 31, p. 34-40.

Vinton, L., (1992b), 'Olszewski's Ouster Leaves Poland Polarized', *RFE/RL Research Report,* Vol. 1, No. 25, pp. 1-10.

Vinton, L. (1993), 'Poland Goes Left', *RFE/RL Research Report,* 2 (40), p. 21-30.

White, S. (1990), *Political and Economic Encyclopaedia of the Soviet Union and Eastern Europe*, Longman Group: Harlow Essex.

Appendix 9.1
Political reforms 1989-1993

The transformation from a Communist regime to democracy started earlier in Poland than in other CEECs. In April 1989 an agreement was signed between the Communists and the opposition (Solidarity) regarding the future composition of the Polish Parliament: 65 percent of the seats of the Sejm were reserved for the Communists, the destination of the other seats in the Sejm and the seats in the Senate depended on election results. (The Polish Parliament

279

consists of two chambers, the Sejm an the Senate.) While this agreement was quite revolutionary at the time, it later became the main impediment to further political reforms. While other CEECs already organized fully free elections in 1990, the Polish elections of June 1989 were still burdened with a pre-arranged distribution of parliamentary seats (Sabbat, 1991). The first fully free elections were not held until October 1991.

In the parliamentary elections of June 1989 Solidarity scored extremely well, winning 161 of the 180 electable seats in the Sejm and 99 of the 100 seats in the Senate (Kusin, 1990). In September 1989 the Communist government was taken over by a Solidarity government with Prime Minister Tadeusz Mazowiecki. With the 'Government Program for Changing the Economic System', better known as the Balcerowicz Plan, the government succeeded in stabilizing inflation and balancing the budget (Slay, 1992). (Leszek Balcerowicz was Minister of Finance in the first two Solidarity governments.)

Although the Mazowiecki government laid the foundations for a democratic Poland and a free-market mechanism, opposition to the government arose for several reasons. First, part of the Solidarity Movement accused Mazowiecki of creating a new political elite which monopolized political power by blocking the influence of other political movements in the political decision making process. Second, the government was criticized for its 'no-witch-hunts policy', the policy that no one could be removed from his function on grounds of previous party affiliation. This meant that the Communist collective farm managers had good opportunities to reach advantageous positions in private businesses by using their functions, resources or contacts. This form of *spontaneous privatization* caused a lot of controversy. As a consequence, the Sejm passed a program for a more controlled privatization process in July 1990. Finally, the negative impact of the Balcerowicz Plan on employment and living standards decreased the popularity of the government's economic reform. Mazowiecki resigned, together with his government, in November 1990, after his defeat in the presidential elections by Solidarity leader Lech Walesa (Sabbat, 1991, Slay, 1991).

On 4 January 1991, the Sejm confirmed Krzysztof Bielecki, whose political roots were in the Solidarity Movement, as prime minister. Bielecki headed a government of apolitical experts, whose main task was to rebuild the economy (Vinton, 1991). The Bielecki government continued the Balcerowicz Plan of the Mazowiecki government (Slay, 1992).

By the eve of the October 1991 elections little progress had been made toward large-scale privatization, and discontent over the negative impact of the Balcerowicz Plan was increasing among the Polish people. More than 100 Polish political parties registered for the 1991 elections. These parties could roughly be divided into five groups, based on their economic programs: (1) parties that emerged from Solidarity, supporting the Balcerowicz Plan and the ongoing economic transformation, (2) parties emerging from Solidarity, but critical of the ongoing economic policies and accusing the two latest governments of 'building capitalism on a Communist foundation', (3) ex-Communists and their affiliates, (4) two peasant coalitions demanding government support for agriculture, and (5) parties like the nationalist Confederation of Independent Poland, the Greens, and Christian parties (McQuaid, 1991a).

After the 1991 elections Poland was left in a political deadlock. The new Parliament included representatives of 29 parties, with the 8 largest shares of seats in the Sejm ranging between 13.5 percent and 8 percent. The Democratic Union, the party of Mazowiecki, won only 13.5 percent of the seats in the Sejm. The Communist Democratic Left Alliance (12 percent) and the Polish Peasant Party, a former Communist ally, (8 percent), together received 20 percent of the votes. The combined Solidarity parties won less than 50 percent of the votes (McQuaid, 1991b).

On 23 December 1991, the government under Prime Minister Jan Olszewski took office. The election program of Olszewski's party, the Central Alliance, stressed the need for a 'break' with the Communist past, arguing that the economic programs of the first two Solidarity governments were too favorable for the Communist nomenklatura. This campaign also insisted on removing the Balcerowicz Plan and on providing more government intervention to make economic transformation more 'socially acceptable' (McQuaid, 1991a). The Olszewski government was soon voted out of office by the Sejm, on 5 June 1992. Pawlak, a member of the ex-Communist agrarian Polish Peasant Party, was proposed as Prime Minister, but failed to form a government (Maziarski, 1992). Finally, the government of Hanna Suchoka, a coalition of seven parties, took office on 10 July 1992. Although six of the coalition parties had Solidarity roots, the coalition presented a mix of ideologies: liberal, social-democratic, agrarian, Christian-democratic, Catholic-nationalistic (Vinton, 1992a). The Polish political situation remained unstable and early elections in September 1993 were unavoidable. With the prospect of new elections, the threat of a 'Communist revival' increased. Polish people were not satisfied with the results and the side effects of Polish transformation in the previous years. The 1993 elections did induce a major shift in the balance of power in Parliament: the ex-Communist Democratic Left Alliance (37 percent of the seats), and the Polish Peasant Party (29 percent) were the winners of the 1993 elections, with their combined 66 percent of the seats in the Sejm (Vinton, 1993).

10 Political economy of agricultural reform in Romania

Marvin Jackson

Introduction

Each transition country in Central and Southeastern Europe has special features that compel our examination. In Romania's case, its pre-Communist past, the grotesque distortions of the Ceausescu dictatorship, and the character of its transformation politics all demand attention by the comparative analyst.

For example, Romania's first step toward transition was singularly violent. What followed the December 1989 *coup d'état* was a five-year period of political domination by the forces around President Ion Iliescu, a parallel of which can only be found in the case of Vaclav Klaus in the Czech Republic. Although Iliescu and Klaus stand at opposite ends of the ideological spectrum, they share success in staying in power. Whether the comparison ends here or whether perhaps as political agents these men share other qualities deserves to be investigated.

The agricultural sector in Romania was badly abused under Ceausescu. Yet, according to the 1992 census, nearly half of Romania's population lives outside urban areas. And during the transformation, agriculture's share of employment has increased to more than a third of the total. Clearly, politics that affect the interest of those employed in agriculture should have an important impact on post-Communist Romania.

Indeed, it appears that the Iliescu forces would not have endured through the post-Communist elections without their special success in the small towns and villages. This connection will be explored as a central topic of this chapter.

The character of Romania's agricultural heritage

Agriculture and land before the Communists

Before 1918, Romania was composed of several areas – the Old Kingdom of Wallachia and Moldova, a region under Russia called Bessarabia, two regions under Hungary called Transylvania and the Banat, and a region under Austria called Bucovina. All came together in 1918 into what was called 'Mare Romania' (Great Romania, which also added Northern Dobroga, a slice of Bulgaria). Each had its own specific history, but all followed more or less the same patterns. In the mid-nineteenth century, the peasants were freed of serf status, under which they had worked on the basis of sharing production rather than providing labor services to the lord. After emancipation, large shares of the land continued to be owned by the nobility. This condition was quite different, for example, from the cases of Bulgaria and Serbia, where the native nobles were eliminated by the Ottoman occupation, or in Central-East Europe where labor services were turned into wage labor under an estate manager.

In 1918, Mare Romania, partly to keep the king's promise to soldiers in the First World War, undertook a radical land reform (Mitrany, 1931; Roberts, 1951). This reform had a significant impact on cropping patterns, with a great shift from wheat to maize as peasant smallholders were allowed to eat what formerly they had paid as rents. Yet (as in today's transition period), it proved difficult to undertake the verification of land claims and do the surveys necessary to grant private property. Often, former large estate holders managed to keep parts of the estate, renting out most of it. As a result, even on the eve of World War II, there were large landowners. Farming, nevertheless, remained mainly a small-scale family operation on scattered plots.

Even though a radical land reform was undertaken in 1945 by a 'popular-front' government, the actual size distribution of farming units on the eve of collectivization by Romania's Communists was not much different from what it had been before the war – something like 50 to 53 percent of farm units were under 2 hectares. Ownership units under 2 hectares actually increased from 53 percent before the war to 78 percent after the reform of 1945. In Romania there were proportionately more small ownership and farming units (under 2 hectares) than in neighboring Bulgaria and Yugoslavia (Jackson and Lampe, 1982).

Peculiarities of agriculture under Romanian Communists

Collectivization took place between 1949 and 1962. Its marked feature in Romania, in contrast with Bulgaria for example, was that it took place with far less substitution of machinery for labor. This is part of the reason that larger shares of Romanians continued to live in the countryside.

The other marked feature of Communist agriculture in Romania was the continuation of the 'machine-tractor stations' as separate from the collective farms. In the late 1970s and 1980s agriculture's special features under Ceausescu included severe limits on direct marketing of garden production by peasants and extensive exports of food and agricultural products. Consumption standards suffered more in Romania than in other countries. Ceausescu also forced upon the countryside a campaign to destroy the traditional village and force peasants into high-rise concrete flats, often without amenities, in a 'village systematization program'. The aim of this program was to eliminate the peasants' independence and spirit along with traditional elements of Romanian society.

Some important parameters on the eve of transition

Communist development strategy in Romania resulted in far less rapid urbanization than it did in neighboring Bulgaria. Romania remains today one of Europe's most rural countries. According to the 1992 census, 45.6 percent of the population still lived outside of the towns (only in 1985 did this share fall below 50 percent) (Shafir, 1992b). The number of rural dwellers age fifty and up still exceeds its cohort in the towns and cities, reflecting this shadow of the past. Moreover, the chance that a twenty-year-old in 1990 was born in the countryside is about 66 percent. Nearly all of these young adults have had contact with parents and grandparents who farmed before collectivization.

A second useful parameter is occupation of the population. At the end of 1990 some 29 percent of the working population was in agriculture and forestry. Of these 3.1 million persons, only 627,000 were 'employees and workers', occupied in state enterprises and administration in the sector. By contrast, we might note that only 259,000 persons were occupied in the food industry. Most of the others in agriculture fell into the category of 'collective farm peasants', although some were also busy on their own farms in the hill and mountain regions. What we know about those who were collective members is that 70 percent were women and a rather large percent were older persons, some only working part-time.

A third interesting parameter is information on the number of persons occupied in part-time or auxiliary farming. For example, nearly every rural family had at least one adult who was officially a member of the collective farm. That gave certain rights to garden farming that might otherwise be difficult. The most able were usually occupied outside the farm and commuted to a factory, sometimes for long distances. But even these able-bodied commuters usually worked in farming on the weekend. At the same time, around each larger city one could find many semirural houses with large gardens and/or smaller vineyards or orchards. The gardens might even have small hothouses or plantings under plastic. Usually both the husband and the wife of such a family worked elsewhere on salary, but on weekends and on holidays joined the children and the grandparents farming or building more houses. This third parameter of population is more difficult to quantify, but it probably indicates the most vigorous respondents to the opportunities for private agriculture that have been opened up by the transition in Romania.

A more comprehensive view of farm organization is given in table 10.1.

The evolution of transition politics

Events that ended Ceausescu's abusive regime started on 16 December 1989, when police and the army fired on demonstrators in Timisoara. Bloodshed increased the following day when thousands of demonstrators took to the streets. Ceausescu, still confident of his power to repress, actually left Romania on 18 December and when he returned delivered an especially abusive speech against Romania's enemies. The next day, at what was supposed to be one of Ceausescu's well-staged rallies, thousands booed him. Television caught him struck dumb in fear. Protesting students dared to gather that night in University Square, and the following day uncontrolled crowds stormed the Central Committee building in the center of Bucharest, forcing Ceausescu and his wife to flee. In the early hours of 22 December portions of the army and the Securitate abandoned Ceausescu. On 25 December after a secret trial Ceausescu and his wife were summarily executed (Tismaneanu, 1993).

On 28 December 1989, a group calling themselves the Council for National Salvation (NSF) declared that they were taking over the powers of the state and establishing a new Romanian government. Ion Iliescu, the council's head, became acting president, and Petre Roman became the country's acting prime minister. One of the council's first acts was to declare that free and open elections would be held as soon as possible (Socor, 1990).

In January the former pre-Communist parties – the National Peasant Party, the National Liberal Party, and the Social Democratic Party – were all reconstituted. The NSF Council responded by organizing its own party of the provisional government, even though it had expressly said that this was not its intention.

The NSF quickly gathered a formidable organization by taking over the regional structures of the old Communist party, including its assets, offices, equipment, means of transportation, and even its professional staff. It acquired privileged access to the media in the name of the government. It made use of a major component of the former secret police, the Securitate, which was quickly reorganized as the Romanian Information Service. At the same time, it declared that the Securitate's records would be sealed.

Table 10.1
Romanian farm organization on the eve of transition

Total persons occupied in
agriculture   3012.8 ths
  of whom, employees   609.9 ths

	State machine stations	State farms	Cooperative units	Personal farms gardens
Units	573	411	3,776 farms 3,172 other 604	
Persons (000)	163.3[a]	261.2[a]	1,910.7[a]	
Specialists (000)	8.1	17.1	31.7	
Agricultural land (000 ha)	[b]	2,055.5	8,963.7	852.8
Cultivated land (000 ha)	[b]	1,643.5	6,919.0	706.6
Fixed capital (million lei)	80,079	121,848	84,624	na
Tractors (physical units)	116,653	24,733	0	na
Animals				
Bovine (000)		1,144	3,064	2,082
Swine (000)		6,087	2,250	3,334
Sheep (000)		2,730	5,516	7,189
Poultry		57,736	14,849	41,382

a   For cooperatives, the number of persons able to work who actually worked; for state machine stations and state farms, the average employees during the year.
b   In 1989 the state machine stations plowed 9015 ths. ha.
Source: Romanian Statistical Yearbook, 1990.

The recently reestablished traditional parties could hardly match this political base. Two of them probably further disadvantaged themselves by nominating little-known émigrés as candidates for president against Iliescu. The National Liberal Party leader, Radu Campeanu, had been in Paris in exile. The National Peasant Party nominated Ion Ratiu, a successful British businessman of Romanian origin. Although Campeanu had spent a long time in Romanian political prison before his exile, he, like Ratiu, tended to talk down to Romanians who had suffered during the Ceausescu years.

The traditional parties found it even more difficult to take over the opposition. Many new parties and movements sprung up, some of which were deliberate satellites established by the NSF to confuse voters. On the eve of the election, some 82 parties were in the contest. Among other problems, this meant there was little available TV time for the traditional parties. In the meanwhile, the NSF figures dominated the media.

The NSF did not stop with simply co-opting the only available organizational base for political action. It launched a program of harassment and violence against the opposition, using the former security services and the network of the ministry of interior, even the village authorities. NSF worker rowdies threatened and then on 28 and 29 January 1990 went on a rampage in Bucharest, badly damaging opposition party facilities. Party workers and even their candidates were threatened (Ratiu's house was twice set on fire). Physical intimidation was worst in the factories and the rural countryside, where the opposition was effectively shut out. The Liberals gave up the rural areas, and the NSF rowdies then focused on the National Peasant Party.[1] International observers arrived only a day before the elections and could cover only a fraction of the polling stations (Socor, 1990).

Probably the NSF could have won without these illegal and violent measures. Its approach, which left little to chance, reflected its Leninist background and ideology. While the opposition did better in regions such as Cluj and Timisoara (where the revolution had started), it appealed mainly to students and intellectuals. The NSF had a wider political base, focused, of course, on professional Communists, higher-middle bureaucrats, and technocrats of the old system. The rural-agricultural bureaucracy, also mixed with former Securitate and Communist party officers, was another natural constituency. With these two groups and all but the worst of the Securitate, the NSF seems to have formed a social contract that would ensure their places at the top of a newly emerging Romanian society, no matter what political and economic form it might eventually take.

In order to broaden its political base, the NSF proved successful at rallying workers with the fear of unemployment and foreign takeovers. The NSF was even stronger in the countryside, partly because it had less organized opposition there. The source of its strength, again, was in the apparatus of local and agricultural administration, which the NSF used to generate fear of a complete collapse of order to divide and conquer the ordinary peasant.

Provincial and local administration. An important dimension of NSF strenght prior to the election became control of the provincial and local administrations. During and shortly after the revolution there was a great deal of spontaneous change in administration and economic organization, with both supporters of the old guard and radical anti-Communist factions gaining a measure of control. Voices were raised for a return to the pre-Communist district and commune boundaries (Ionescu, 1992b).

The NSF moved to extend its control through Decree-law 8/7 January 1990, which replaced the local People's Councils with more traditional mayoralties. A month later, Decree-law 21/7 February 1990 created an Office for Local Administration, headed by a minister state secretary whose main function was to ensure 'the unitary guidance of the activity of the mayoralties and their good collaboration with the central government'. There would be little doubt about the importance of NSF local control for the coming elections and post-election institutional decisions.

The NSF leadership decided to co-opt opposition initiatives and rebuild national consensus after the Bucharest violence in 27 and 28 January by establishing the Provisional Council of National Unity (PCNU), which included members of the opposition and counterpart councils at the local levels. Both the new local administration and the local PCNUs probably helped when bloody riots broke out on 20 March between Hungarians and Romanians in Targu Mures. Once the election was won, however, the PCNU and its local units were dissolved.

Political associates of the NSF. Two of the numerous parties that were sponsored by the NSF deserve some individual description.

The Democratic Agrarian Party (DAP) was set up as a NSF satellite for managers of state agricultural units, collective farm officials, and rural bureaucrats of the old system. Its head, Victor Surdu, was chairman of the NSF Committee for the Ministry of Agriculture and the Food Industry. He was reported to have said on 5 January that agriculture should be developed within its existing organizational structures (Gafton, 1990). The DAP received only 1.8 percent of the official vote in the May elections.

The Party of Romanian National Unity (PRNU) was first registered on 15 March 1990 as the Party of National Unity of the Romanians of Transylvania. It served as the political organization of a strongly nationalistic movement called *Vatra Romaneasca* (Romanian Hearth) which emerged into public view after the violent clashes between Romanians and Hungarians in Targu Mures. As a regional organization, it received only 2.12 percent of the national vote in May 1990, but it was stronger in Cluj District, with 13.5 percent, and in Mures District, where it received 34 percent. The party's head, Georghe Funar, had been an expert in the old collective farm system in Romania (Gallagher, 1994).

Results of the first elections in May 1990. By the time of the elections in May 1990, some 82 parties were registered. Iliescu claimed 85 percent of the votes for president, while the NSF gathered 66 percent of the votes of the lower house and 77 percent of the seats in the Senate.

The politics of opposition

The forces around Iliescu utilized almost every possible means to confuse the voters and weaken the opposition, but the opposition movement in Romania was itself so ineffective that one must wonder what other factors were involved. There was considerable public tolerance of Iliescu's undemocratic methods, particularly those regarding European socialist politicians and representatives of international agencies. Surely this tolerance reflected the intensity of the repression under the Communists. But other factors must have been involved, some going back to the weakness of pre-Communist political life, itself a product of Romania's position, squeezed between the Habsburg, Ottoman Turkish, and Russian empires. Political life in Romania never saw the emergence of a strong middle class. It is testimony to the weakness of opposition to the Communists, Ceausescu, or Iliescu that the most stable opposition group was not organized by political interests, but by ethnicity.

The Hungarian Democratic Union of Romania. The Hungarian Democratic Union of Romania (HDUR), represented the large Hungarian minority that lived mostly in Transylvania (Deletant, 1991). Organized in Cluj on 21 December 1989, it immediately issued a statement of goals, including (1) an educational system guaranteeing minority language instruction at every level; (2) a re-establishment of the Hungarian Bolyan University in Cluj; (3) mandatory bilingualism in Transylvania with administration and judicial proceedings in both languages, and (4) a ministry of nationalities.

The NSF initially responded to HDUR demands by restoring radio and TV in Hungarian and reopening the Bolyan University. It also announced a reorganization of primary and secondary schools in minority languages, a move that helped spark a violent reaction by Romanians of the region (see below).

As a regional party, the HDUR received a large share (7.2 percent) of the national vote, giving it 29 seats in the lower house and 12 senators. Thus, although far behind the NSF in the official count, it came in second. The

HDUR received 77 percent and 85 percent of the votes in the Covasna and Harghita districts, where Hungarians dominated. Also, in Mures District it took 43 percent of the vote.

The pre-Communist or traditional parties. The three traditional parties – National Liberals, National Peasants, and Social Democrats – signed a pact in which they agreed to refrain from attacking one another and to support the best-placed candidate to defeat Iliescu in the event of a second round in May 1990. After the elections, they all faced conflict about whether the older leadership was stuck on old issues and did not understand contemporary society. The National Liberal Party lost a splinter group (the National Liberal Party-Youth Wing) that soon was flirting with the NSF.

Besides the traditional parties and the parties that were set up as puppets and diversions by the NSF, other nontraditional groups and political movements quickly appeared (Shafir, 1990). One of the most important, the Group for Social Dialogue (GSD), was composed mainly of intellectuals. Rather than organize a political party as such, the GSD preferred the role of social conscience and educational force. Some GSD members ran individually as independent candidates in the election, but failed to gain representation.

The Democratic Antitotalitarian Forum (DAF), formed in August 1990 in Cluj, included representatives of the three traditional parties, the HDUR, which had been the most successful opposition party in the May elections, and others. The DAF's main aim was to unify all antitotalitarian forces and bring about a legal renewal of democratic institutions in Romania. Its first president was Cluj dissident Doina Cornea. Among other items, its program called for quick passage of legislation guaranteeing the peasantry's property rights to land and facilitating the purchase of the necessary means of production.

The Civic Alliance, set up in November 1990, set its aims as the development of civil society in Romania, with the immediate goal of reconciling intellectuals and students with workers and peasants. The Civic Alliance at first rejected normal political organization, preferring more direct action. It succeeded in gaining endorsements from the Romanian Orthodox Bishop of the Banat and from two main trade unions, Fratia and Alfa. Its demonstrations in Bucharest as witnessed by the author were indeed impressive. Nevertheless, the Civic Alliance was not well received by the traditional political parties, especially the National Liberals.

The more strictly political-organizational role of the DAF was taken over by the National Convention for the Establishment of Democracy (NCED), set up on 15 December 1990 with more or less the same parties as in the DAF. An important addition came in July 1991 when the political arm of the Civic Alliance, the Party of Civic Alliance (PCA), joined the NCED. In November the NCED announced that its member parties would run on joint lists and under one electoral symbol in the local elections that were scheduled for February 1992. With this it formally changed its name to the Democratic Convention of Romania (DCR).

Liberal dissent among the opposition. The National Liberal Party (NLP) suffered from more than just splintering. Its head, Radu Campeanu, was unhappy at not receiving the Democratic Convention's nomination as presidential candidate. The NLP wished to position itself so as to gain some of the nationalist electorate that had left the membership of the Hungarian Democratic Federation (HDFR) for the DCR (Ionescu and Shafir, 1993). In October 1991 two of the NLP's members accepted positions (as ministers of economy and justice) in the new Stolojan government. This happened without sanction from the NLP, even though it was also a leading member of the opposition DCR.[2] In March 1992, the NLP formally quit the DCR. Also, Campeanu, who had been on record as opposing the restoration of King Michael, did a turnabout with an offer to support him as a candidate for president, which the king turned down.

These political maneuverings did not bring results. In the September 1992 elections the NLP failed to gain even 3 percent of the vote necessary for representation. Thereafter, some members broke off and, with another group of former liberals who had splintered after the 1990 elections, formed the Liberal Alliance in the Democratic Convention.

Political fragmentation and public reactions. It appears that the problems of the NLP arose less over real political issues than over conflicts about leadership and personality. On the real issues there was endless hairsplitting, with opinion shaped more as a tactic for argument than for action. In this respect, the NLP, perhaps due to Campeanu's ways, only exaggerated this dominant characteristic of all Romanian politics.

By the end of 1990 there was a significant drop in support for the NSF and Iliescu (see below). At the same time, the combined support of the opposition parties did not increase and was still below that of the NSF, although by a much smaller margin than in the May 1990 elections. The preferred government, according to a poll taken in the spring of 1991, would have been made up of experts who were independent of the political parties. Also, the army and the Catholic Church were valued positively by the majority of persons polled, while the political parties and the Parliament were seen in strongly negative terms (Shafir, 1991b). Perhaps more than citizens of other transition countries, Romanians found it difficult to form a well-defined political culture.

The noncommittal turn of Romanian public opinion was not just a response to the ineffective and scurrilous behavior of the opposition politicians. The NSF and Iliescu seemed to block a further development of democracy while exposing most people to growing economic fears. At the same time, the governing group itself started to break up in pieces.

June 1990: Violence in University Square. The success of the May 1990 elections emboldened the more Leninist members of the NSF to move against both the opposition parties and the extraparliamentary opposition. The latter become more and more focused on University Square, where opposition groups set up protests beginning 22 April. Opposition was so vigorous that on 13 June Iliescu called upon the population to defend the new government from an attempted 'fascist coup d'état'. On 14 June the miners from the Jiu Valley descended on Bucharest again. Offices of opposition were again sacked and students were beaten. Before it was over, six persons had been reported killed and several hundred were injured.

Control over the district and local administrations. Another move came after the May 1990 elections, in the proposal and passage of a law providing for centrally selected prefects and for prefecture appointment of mayors in towns and villages. Although other countries, for example France, have centrally appointed prefects, the selection of mayors through means other than an election was an exceptional measure, widely seen in Romania as undemocratic. After the May elections and armed with this new law, the president and government moved to take control in all sensitive regions. These included strongholds of the opposition, such as Cluj and Timisoara, and places where local officials had aided spontaneous decollectivization (Ionescu, 1992b).

Dealing with Ceausescu's Gang and the Securitate. As Tismaneanu (1993) points out, in Romania the Communist past has been more effectively swept under the table than in any other post-Communist country. This was the result of a carefully managed process by the NSF and Iliescu's personal forces. It began with the hurried secret trial and execution of Ceausescu and his wife without a public hearing, which no doubt would have brought out all sorts of accusations. The archives have been closed, except possibly for some official leaks. According to Tismaneanu, 'once Ceausescu was ousted and liquidated [the NSF tried to act as if] Communism had ceased to exist, and Romania is another country'. Unlike former high Communists in other countries, Romania's former high officials have not published memoirs. Even Petre Roman, since 1991 ousted from power and often trading insults with Iliescu and his supporters, has not spoken about events before and leading up to 22 December 1989. He did not, however, refrain from describing the intervention of coal miners in Bucharest as a plot fomented by former Communists and unreconstructed Securitate members and has since turned on Iliescu. Nevertheless, on neither side did the combat turn to events before 22 December 1989.

The most popular document of the authentically democratic forces, the 11 March 1990 Proclamation of Timisoara, asked that 'the electoral law, for the first three consecutive legislatures, ban from every list all former Communist activists and Securitate officers'. Instead, under Iliescu more former highly placed persons from the Romanian Communist Party and its related state agencies have reappeared at high levels of government and political life than in any other post-transition country. In this there is a marked contrast between Romania's political system and the rehabilitated former Communist, now socialist, parties in Poland, Hungary, and Bulgaria, where the old generation (like Iliescu) was thoroughly replaced by young and seemingly better-educated politicians.

There were trials of former high officials beginning in January 1990 in Bucharest, which were limited to the former minister of interior and the most trusted members of Ceausescu's politburo. They were given life sentences. Ceausescu's son, Nicu, was finally sentenced in September 1990 to twenty years in prison. At his trial, it was revealed that such prosecutions would be limited only to events taking place in the last week of Ceausescu's rule, that is during the violence of 16-22 December. Nearly all of those imprisoned have been released or put in special facilities for medical reasons. But there have been no trials and not even any public hearings concerning earlier abuses of civil and human rights, including the thousands of documented cases of torture and murder of those who resisted Romania's Communists, before and during Ceausescu's rule.[3]

The Romanian Securitate was rehabilitated as the Romanian Information Service, headed by a former professor of the Communist party political academy, who had been sacked by Ceausescu in 1989. His position at that time without any doubt required him to have been highly placed in the security services.

Dealing with King Michael. Romania's living monarch, King Michael of Hohenzollern, who had been king briefly following the deposing of wartime leader Marshal Antonescu, was sent into exile by the Soviets and Romania's Communists. The question of his return to Romania was raised almost immediately after the revolution (Shafir, 1991a). King Michael's eventual appearance in the spring of 1992 was the occasion for an authentically emotional welcome, particularly from the more religious and traditional peasants. Nevertheless, the effects of a longer presence of the king has remained unclear. There has been sporadic, but perhaps symbolic, public support for the king as a figure of state in place of Iliescu. There has been no strong monarchist party, and support for the king by the opposition parties has been inconsistent. In any case, Iliescu and the NSF seem to have managed to keep this from becoming an issue.[4]

Falling support in opinion polls. Dealing with King Michael might have been easier than managing the political responses to economic reform measures, which saw limited price reforms in November 1990, followed by more extensive liberalization in 1991. Public opinion polls taken in January and March of 1991 indicated that most respondents felt great economic insecurity. Almost half wanted even slower reforms, while only one fourth wanted to see accelerated privatization (Shafir, 1991b). What is significant in these responses is that in both regards, compared with other transition countries, Romania had hardly moved.

It is not surprising that support for both Iliescu and the NSF fell. Some 55 percent of those polled in March 1991 still supported Iliescu, compared with his claim of 85 percent of the votes in May 1990. What probably spelled trouble was that Iliescu received somewhat less support than did Roman, the prime minister.

A December 1990 poll indicated that only 25 percent of respondents approved the NSF, compared with its claim of 66 percent of the vote in May 1990. Subsequent polls suggested only a slight recovery. Nevertheless, as already observed, the NSF continued to receive somewhat more support than the opposition (Shafir, 1991d). The average Romanian had little faith in politics, parties, or other political institutions.

Conflict within the NSF. Conflict between an Iliescu group, said to represent older (former) Communists and Securitate nomenklatura, and a Roman group, said to represent younger bureaucrats and some, like Roman, the spoiled children of old Communists, became more evident during the NSF national convention in March 1991 (Ionescu, 1991).

The point of stress seemed to be between Roman and his government and leaders of the Parliament, who in April refused two of Roman's appointments. Roman tried to make a coalition with genuine opposition. He opened contacts with the National Convention for the Establishment of Democracy (formed in December 1990), which failed. In July he formed a loose organization called the Charter for Reform and Democracy, which included the NSF, the Democratic Agrarian Party (DAP), the Ecological Movement of Romania, and the Liberal Party-Youth Wing. That effort also failed (Ionescu, 1992a).

Roman's fall and the change of government in September 1991. Roman's new April government was faced with the difficult task of introducing the main price reforms (in February, April, and September) at a time when the decline in industrial output was generating intense pressure. Industrial disruptions became more common, culminating in the September 1991 miners' riots and Iliescu's dismissal of Roman.

Whatever the nature of the Roman-Iliescu conflict, it did not lead to a sharp change in economic policy. If anything, the new government was more identified with economic reform than Roman's. The new prime minister, Theodor Stolojan, had been finance minister until March 1991, when he resigned to protest the slow pace of reform. His government, now a coalition, included economic and justice ministers from the National Liberal Party. Reversing none of the previous government's reforms, its first move was to introduce a scheduled internal convertibility of the national currency.

The government and Parliament went ahead with a new constitution, which had been under debate since July 1991. It was approved by referendum on 9 December 1991 (Shafir, 1991a).

Local elections and the split of the NSF. The change of government did not, however, relieve tensions between the forces of Roman and Iliescu. These were exacerbated by the NSF's poor showing in the local elections in February 1992. The NSF garnered only about half the percentage of votes, as it had in May 1990, while parties affiliated with the Democratic Convention gained significantly. In fact, the accumulated tally showed both gaining about one third of the votes.

After months of trading insults and of infighting, the NSF party congress approved Roman's program by 66 percent of the delegates. A group backed by Iliescu under the chairmanship of Ovidiu Gherman broke off and formed the Democratic NSF (DNSF) (Shafir, 1992a). Hence, the original NSF phalanx now found itself split as the campaign started for the country's first general elections scheduled for September 1992.

The general elections of September 1992 and beyond

In spite of the problems facing Iliescu and the DNSF, not the least of which were those of any incumbent party when the economy is highly depressed, the opposition failed to gain either Parliament or the presidency in the general elections of September 1992. An ominous sign was a better showing of the 'nationalist' parties.

In the first round of the presidential election, Iliescu counted 47 percent of the vote, while Emil Constantinescu, candidate of the Democratic Convention, won 31 percent and Georghe Funar of the Party of Romanian National Unity

(PRNU), 11 percent. In the second round, Iliescu's share was 61 percent while Constantinescu was 39 percent. Iliescu gained most of the support from the nationalists and neo-Communists, as well as others who had voted for favorite sons in the first round.

Choices for a coalition. The DNSF Party, associated with Iliescu and now without the support of Roman's group, led parties for Parliament with 28 percent of the vote and 34 percent of the seats in both houses. For Iliescu and his supporters, the question was how to build a coalition that would serve their interests through control of the government and its measures for appointments and changes in institutions and policies.

There appeared to be two alternatives, one that stressed economic reforms and political liberalization, the other with more nationalistic and conservative interests (in the sense of preserving the former Party nomenklatura and bureaucrats' interests). Either way, both Iliescu and the DNSF faced potentially competing personalities and programs.

The choice also seemed to question the role of Iliescu and the DNSF in the coalition. If it went with the reform elements, the DNSF would appear to be a competitor against the national-Communist right. If it went with the nationalistic and conservative interests, it would appear to compete with the reform elements in both the DCR alliance and in Roman's NSF party. In going with the reform elements, the government would more easily gain international support but would not appeal to the general Romanian population, who feared the economic consequences of reforms. Voter sympathy seemed to indicate the increasing appeal of the nationalistic message.

After several attempts, a new government was finally set up on the basis of a coalition with the nationalist-Communist 'right' based on about 52 percent of the seats in the lower house and 55 percent in the upper house. The parties included were the PRNU of Funar, the Greater Romanian Party (which promoted super-nationalist and racist causes), the Socialist Labor Party (the official successor to the old Communist Party), and the Democratic Agrarian Party.

The new cabinet had only members of the DNSF and so-called independents. The latter included the new prime minister, Nicolae Vacaroiu. Vacaroiu had had a long service in the former Communist regime, ending up as a director and Communist party secretary in the State Planning Committee. He reportedly was dismissed in October 1990 for being responsible for the price-liberalization policy opposing the price liberalization program initiated by Roman. His selection hardly suggests that Iliescu and those in his leadership group had a strong interest in the reforms demanded by the international community (Ionescu, 1993).

Still another interpretation can be given. Iliescu and the DNSF might have seen their general strength better served by more direct competition outside the coalition, with the DCR and Roman's NSF parties as the reform agents of Romania. After all, the DCR and Roman elements hardly provided a clear and convincing alternative reform program. Also, the Iliescu-Vacaroiu government had the advantage of controlling all contacts with the international agencies.

At the same time, Iliescu and the DNSF might have seen it better to compete with the right nationalist-Communist groups within the coalition. This way they could 'wear the colors' while perhaps moderating or at least suppressing the public image of the extremist elements. Still, this involved potentially dangerous concessions, for example, turning over to the PRNU increasing control over the appointment of local officials in Transylvania. Funar used this power to launch his role as a national politician and a potential competitor to either Vacaroiu or Iliescu himself.

Whatever might have been the strategical and tactical choices in setting up the coalition, it proved to be relatively durable. It seems to have been easier for Iliescu and the Vacaroiu government to compete against the DCR and Roman reform elements than to manage its partners in the coalition, especially Gheorghe Funar and the increasingly strident Greater Romanian Party. In the area of reform and economic policy, the greatest challenges were balancing pressures from the IMF and international agencies to suppress inflation and enhance privatization against the threats of increasingly militant groups of workers, who feared their continuing loss of real income and jobs.

The government has had more success in developing its international relations than it had in carrying out market reforms. A framework European Association Agreement was signed with the Commission in February 1993. In October 1993 Romania finally joined the Council of Europe and then received MFN status by the U.S. Congress, although neither step was easy or without conditions. Also, Romania was one of the first to sign a Partnership for Peace Agreement with NATO in 1994.

An overview of economic and institutional of reforms (Jackson, 1994, 1995). Although the government has undertaken a series of steps to reduce direct price controls and other distorting measures such as subsidies and structural monopoly, extensive instruments to affect prices have remained in place, including the Ministry of Agriculture's authority to set procurement prices for cereals and livestock, margin controls, and others. There have also been numerous ways of moving finance around. According to McKinsey and Co the economy in 1993 suffered from 'massive cross-subsidization between different companies and sectors, a lack of financial discipline and inadequate circulation of foreign exchange'.

Although, as elsewhere, an impressive number of new, mostly small, private companies and foreign joint ventures have been registered, Romania's industrial structure remains dominated by large noncompeting state-owned 'commercial companies' that need to be restructured and privatized. Such programs, which have received significant international assistance, have been characterized by organizational and political conflict as individual and special interests struggle for wealth and critical international funds and technical assistance.

A World Bank report characterized Romania as an 'outlier' with 'stop and go' macroeconomic policies resembling those of Russia. Following an IMF standby agreement negotiated in December 1993, Romania's National Bank did take important steps to liberalize exchange rates and to reduce the inflation rate in the second part of 1994. But in terms of microeconomic and reform policies, the government's main accomplishments still seem more the generation of bureaucratic jobs than the introduction of full market forces and private, competitive enterprise.

Implementation of the program during the course of 1994 and continuing into 1995 has brought the government into conflict with the most militant segment of Romanian labor – the workers in ferrous metallurgy and the coal miners. The government is now in a race to see if any benefits from its slight economic recovery will help it avoid a general labor crisis. Such a crisis would be most dangerous if it becomes mixed in some way with developing ethnic tensions in Transylvania, which provide the government with its second set of major challenges.

Three changes in the Vacaroiu government. It did not take long for the government's image in public opinion to fall. Polls in the first half of 1993 showed support down to 20 percent (Shafir, 1993). The connection between declines in the polls and the first cabinet change in August 1993 is unclear. This saw the reported 'resignation' of Economic Reform Minister Misu Negitoiu in protest over the slow pace of privatization and other reforms.

The next cabinet change took place in March 1994 when Iliescu reportedly ordered changes in response to opposition demands for stepped-up reforms. The changes involved the ministries of justice, defense, internal affairs, and transport.

A widening of the cabinet to coalition parties came after much discussion in August 1994. This was preceded, however, by a wider consideration of other coalition partners, including those from the DCR parties and Roman's NSF (Shafir, 1994). DCR opposition, rather than negotiate compromises, demanded fundamental concessions against extremists and those opposed to reforms. In June and July of 1994 the DCR initiated a series of no-confidence motions, intended to bring the government down. With no alternative than to make unacceptable concessions, the government turned back to the Party of Romanian National Unity and brought in two of its members, including one as minister of agriculture.

The continued instability of party politics. Numerous post-election adjustments took place in 1993. In July the Iliescu-oriented DNSF changed its name to the Party of Social Democracy of Romania (PSDR). The name change seems to have had no important effects, but it did threaten the traditional Social Democratic Party.

In November two of the PSDR coalition partners, the Party of Romanian National Unity and the Democratic Agrarian Party, formed an alliance called the National Unity Bloc. This move was probably based on their common interest in how reforms were taking place in agriculture, especially in Transylvania where there were strong factions of the Hungarian minority to compete with.

In May 1993, Roman's NSF merged with a politically insignificant Democratic Party to become the DP-NSF. It is now the Democratic Party. In the course of both 1993 and 1994 it adopted numerous joint positions with the opposition alliance DCR, but the two never set up a formal coordinating framework. In general, opposition maneuvering was very confusing and seemed only to reflect the lack of fundamental structure in Romanian opposition politics.

The Hungarian Democratic Union of Romania (HDUR) found itself supported by a relatively stable 7-8 percent of the national vote in the elections of May 1990, the local elections of February 1992, and the general elections in September 1992. As mentioned before, its voters were highly concentrated in two or three districts; in other districts the HDUR was in direct conflict with the PRNU. In March 1993 the government set up a Council of National Minorities. The HDUR first joined the council with scepticism, then suspended its council activities. During this time the party reportedly was also undergoing internal conflict between its moderate and more radical blocks.

During the course of 1994 the HDUR pressed harder for more radical minority political and civil rights in Romania. For example, it demanded the right to use the Hungarian language in any political unit where persons with Hungarian mother tongue made up 8 percent or more of the population. It has also started to press for the reestablishment of some sort of Hungarian autonomous unit in Transylvania.[5] In January 1995 the government denounced as illegal interference in local administration the setting up by the HDUR of a council of local administration with the participation of mayors and local councillors. Iliescu called for the council to be disbanded, which in turn brought expressions of concern from the Hungarian government. As of March 1995 these issues were holding up a Hungarian-Romanian treaty.

As expected, the demands of the HDUR brought the quickest and strongest reaction from the PRNU. In turn, the PRNU stepped up its pressure on the government and Iliescu (OMRI Daily Digest, 31 January 1995). Funar, in particular, used the occasion to move into the national arena by accusing Iliescu of seeking secret agreements with Hungary and other international organizations that would compromise Romanian sovereignty and of failing to defend the constitution and rights of Romanians (OMRI Daily Digest 7 and 8 February 1995). Iliescu, in turn, denounced both the HDUR and the PRNU leaderships.

The government has recently moved to dismiss the mayor of Brasov and twenty-seven other local officials, all of whom had been elected in 1992 through other parties associated with the Democratic Convention of Romania.

In turn, the DCR has come under great stress, as some members have threatened to quit over issues related to both the role of the HDUR in the Convention and moves by its chairman, Emil Constantinescu (who was the main opposition presidential candidate in 1992) to push himself forward as the DCR presidential candidate in the 1996 elections as well as his move to revise the DCR organization and its name (OMRI Daily Digest and BBC Survey of World Broadcasts in February and March 1995). By March 1995, the latest word on these maneuvers was the announcement of discussions between Roman's Democratic Party-NSF (now called the Democratic Party) and some members of the DCR (the Social Democrats, Civic Alliance, and Liberal Party '93) to set up a new coalition (OMRI Daily Digest, 2 March 1995).

Agrarian and economic reforms

On 22 December 1989, the Council of the National Salvation Front announced a ten point program that included two items on economics (Ionescu, 1990):

1 The restructuring of the entire economy in accordance with the criteria of profitability and efficiency: the elimination of command and bureaucratic methods of centralized economic management; and the promotion of initiative and skill in all economic sectors.

2 The restructuring of agriculture and support for small-scale production; a halt to the destruction of villages.

These points were repeated in the body of a decree on 28 December in which the council defined itself as 'the supreme body of state power'. Among the laws of the former regime abrogated at the same time were those concerning (a) the forced rural resettlement program, (b) per capita food consumption norms, (c) compulsory agricultural delivery quotas to the state, (d) compulsory prices for agricultural products sold on the private market, and (e) restrictions affecting the right to dispose freely of privately owned land.

Land and agricultural property reforms

The early NSF declarations said nothing about privatization or markets, which reflected the orientation of their formulators. In fact, Victor Surdu, NSF minister of agriculture and head of the NSF-satellite Democratic Agrarian Party, said that agriculture would be developed on the basis of already existing structures. Iliescu opposed dividing land again into small plots because he claimed it would reduce efficiency. There were significant differences in opinion. Corneliu Coposu, leader of the renewed National Peasant-Christian Democratic Party, called for full restitution to peasants with plots of 10 to 15 hectares. Peasants, in any case, were already taking matters into their own hands. So was everyone else, including the directors of collective farms and the state managers.

Decree Law 42/1990, promulgated 29 January 1990. The provisional NSF government moved quickly to provide some legal measure to control what was sure to become even greater spontaneous asset-grabbing in the countryside as spring approached. Decree Law 42/29 January 1990 raised the legal limit on garden plots of collective farm members from 0.15 hectares to 0.5 or more and made provisions for others to acquire garden land. Its provisions were:

1 In agricultural areas, any family, including town dwellers, could obtain up to 0.25 hectares, providing the land would be efficiently worked and the local cooperative paid a land-use fee.

2 Land covered by a cooperative member's house, garden, and front yard becomes the member's personal property and together with any new land received could be sold or inherited up to a limit of 0.6 hectares.

   Moreover,
   a in hill and mountain regions or in areas near towns, cooperative members could receive land up to a limit of that worked by a family without additional workers, with the allocation provided for 'long-term use' (i.e., not given as personal property); and
   b members of cooperatives in plains regions could be entitled to receive plots of up to 0.5 hectares but only for personal use. Former members wishing to return to agriculture could also receive this right.

This action did not appear to endanger the existing agricultural system. Nor did it appear particularly attractive, especially since according to the Romania Statistical Yearbook of 1985 members of collective farms who actually worked on the collective already had an average of 0.45 hectares of land (possibly this included the land of their house sites as well). Nevertheless, on 10 March 1990, provisional Prime Minister Roman announced that 3.0 million hectares of arable land, 30 percent of the total, had been leased to 'peasants'. Given that peasants only had 0.8 million hectares at their disposal before, this constituted a rather significant change in land-use patterns, particularly if peasants decided to farm individually (Gafton, 1990).

A May 1990 report on the strategy proposed by Roman for introducing a market economy (Postolache, 1990) claimed that individual peasant households (of private producers, cooperators, mechanics, specialist, workers of state farms, pensioners, and other village residents) 'hold in property or long-term use' [our emphasis] some 3.7 million hectares of agricultural land, of which 2.6 million hectares was arable land. The report stated that 'peasants, grouped within the agricultural cooperative' possessed 6.9 million hectares of agricultural land, of which 4.9 million hectares was arable land. Altogether, it claimed that the peasants held as property or in long-term use some 72 percent of agricultural land and 80 percent of the arable land.[6] The report also stressed that cooperatives could only remain if constituted 'freely' by the producers and 'freed of any administrative interference'.

We have found no official references to regulation of the terms of leasing; perhaps the report was simply an informal recognition of a *fait accompli*. There was government Decision 1228/1990, permitting the lease of machinery and equipment from the state-owned machine-tractor enterprises to 'farmers' associations' (Gavrilescu, 1994). But the land-lease law was not passed by Parliament until February 1993, so the measures must have been rather spontaneous and unregulated.

One other fact is important for understanding the forces that were motivating changes in the way farming would be carried out. The NSF had already taken measures, partly with an eye on the elections coming in May, to place trusted persons in the positions of district prefectures and communal mayors. This meant that they controlled simultaneously the law, administration, and police that might be involved in any interpretation of the decree.

At the same time, individual peasants who might want to acquire their own piece of land were subordinate to both the local authorities and the directors and managers of the cooperative farms and mechanization enterprises. The lease arrangements for both equipment and land favored continuing farming through larger management units, as well as *de facto* privatization of farming facilities.

The Land Law 37/1991. It took the new Parliament more than a half year to pass a law that more clearly set out the intention to privatize land property and the nonland assets of collective and state farms and mechanization stations (published 20 February 1991). Unlike the Bulgarian radical land restitution law, the Romanian law does not mandate the right of people to retrieve their property, but speaks of 'the reconstituting of the right to property' of those who brought (were forced to give) it to the collective. Principal elements of the law are as follows:

1 Land to be received could vary from 0.5 hectares up to 10 hectares per family, depending on the size of land originally taken (the law also sets a maximum cap of 100 hectares of arable land that could be owned by any person).

2 Land in most categories could be leased (although no lease law was provided until February 1993) and sold, but co-owners, neighbors, and local land authorities would have prior right of purchase. Transactions involving legal persons must receive approval of the Ministry of Agriculture or the Ministry of Environment. In three special cases of land distributed without prior contributions of labor or land, land could not be sold until after ten years (to prevent speculation).

3 Any changes in the uses of farmland must receive approval of the authorities, even changes in farming uses. Also, owners of arable land would be required to keep it in cultivation and would be subject to fines and eventual expropriation after two years of noncultivation.

4 Land was to be free of land taxes until 1996.

5 Land to be redistributed would not necessarily be the same land as that brought into the collective and would be subject to a formula of an 'arable equivalent' where as much as 2.5 hectares of pastures and as little as 0.4 hectares of vineyard might be equivalent to 1 hectares of arable land. Also, in areas of land scarcity, claimants might have to asked for allocations elsewhere.

6 Claimants were to present a written request indicating the amount of land claimed and a declaration of responsibility within thirty days after the law came into affect (20 February 1991), but later this was extended fifteen days. In addition, according to the administrative regulations set out on 4 March 1991, a number of other documents had to be included, ranging

from property acts to birth certificates, and legal heirs had to provide certificates of inheritance – all with certified copies.

7 Citizens could only benefit if they took up legal residence in Romania. Otherwise, those with claims would have to sell within a year or the land transferred to the state free of charge.

8 Articles 26 and 29 discuss provisions for the liquidation of nonland property of collective farms and intercollective associations in which liquidation commissions had up to nine months (basically to the end of the 1991 harvest year) to dispose of the actives and passives. Property of intercollective associations was to be first distributed to member collectives and then further processed. Structures that could not be divided were to become the property of a new type of cooperative (demolition of structures was expressly forbidden).

According to the OECD (Country Report 1993) members of former collectives were given the options of forming a new cooperative association, setting up a commercial company, or becoming independent farmers. When the members chose one of the first two options, ownership rights would be allocated according to the relative size of restitution claims. Members opting out would receive creditor status for their share of nonland assets. Those who wanted their land out would be allocated land that was inefficient for the collective unit to farm. In case no collective unit was set up, its nonland assets would be auctioned off and the proceeds distributed according to contributions.

9 If land had been taken into a state-owned agricultural enterprise, the claimant would receive ownership shares when the enterprise was commercialized and privatized (subject to Law 31/1990 and according to privatization legislation and regulations discussed below).

The Privatization Laws of August 1990 and August 1991. Law 15/August 1990 provided for the conversion of state-owned enterprises to forms defined in the commercial code: limited companies, joint stock companies, and state-autonomous companies. There resulted some 7,655 commercial companies in the first two categories and 701 state monopolistic companies in the second.

The law on privatization came out on 16 August 1991. Its main components were as follows:

1 Of the shares of commercial companies 30 percent were to be turned over to five 'private ownership funds' (POFs) that would act like mutual investment companies.

2 The POFs were to issue to each Romanian citizen one certificate that could be (a) sold to another Romanian citizen, (b) exchanged for shares in companies being privatized, or (c) kept for sharing in the profits of the POFs. Also, citizens could benefit from a 10 percent discount in share purchases, as well as have a POF act as a broker.

3 The remaining 70 percent of shares was turned over to one large State Ownership Fund (the SOF), which was to be divested of these shares at a rate of 10 percent per year through public auctions, negotiated sales, management-employee buy-out offers, etc.

4 In addition, the National Privatization Agency could sell up to 75 percent of certain enterprises on a piecemeal basis, thus effectively liquidating or downsizing an enterprise.

The last technique has been the most important way of privatization. Also, most enterprises privatized by the SOF have been forms of management buy-outs, sometimes with foreign participants. Both means have been used for enterprises in agriculture and industries upstream and downstream from those enterprises.

Changes in property rights and farming

At least four distinct actions were associated with the changes in rules regarding land and farm organization:

1 Recognizing claims on ownership of land by the award of (temporary) certificates;

2 Granting of an appropriate deed or title;

3 Taking over effective use rights by the new owners;

4 Changing the organization of farming.

Before discussing these changes, it is good to review the figures on farm organization at the end of 1989, as presented in table 10.1 and table 10.2. There were over 3 million persons occupied in agriculture, of whom 610,000 were 'employees', including 163,000 on state mechanization stations and 261,000 on state farms. Nearly 2 million were collective members who actually worked on the collective farms, and about 400,000 were in other categories, including private farmers. There were 3,172 collective farms and

604 intercooperative units, 411 state farms, and 573 state mechanization stations. Some 850,000 hectares were used for gardens by members of collective farms. Most of the agricultural and cultivated land was farmed under the collective farms with machinery from the state mechanization stations.

Table 10.2
Changes in farm units

Period	Number	Area (000 ha)	Persons (000)
1989			
State farms	411	2,055	261
Collectives	3,776	8,964	1,911
Other	na	3,740	840
Total		**14,759**	**3,012**
1990			
State farms		2,804	
Cooperatives		6,526	
Private farms		5,420	
Total		**14,750**	
1991			
State farms	411	1,919	
Agricultural societies	2,250	1,095	
Agricultural associations	8,338	1,226	
Individ. farms & groups in forms		7,997	
Individual farms	2 million		
Groups in form.	2,411		
Communal		2,561	
Total		**14,798**	
1991			
Cooperatives	2,641	1,276	683
Family farms	9,209	1,316	700
Private plots	98,100	177	98
Corporate farms	747	2,097	212
Other		9,933	1,402
Total		**14,798**	**3,095**

Table 10.2 (continued)

1992

State farms	411	1,919
Agricultural societies	4,050	1,916
Agricultural associations	11499	1,792
Individ. farms & groups in forms		6,610
Individual farms	2 million	
Groups in form.	1,515	
Communal		2,561
Total		**14,798**

1993

Cooperatives	5,205	1,908	1,200
Family farms	18,176	2,065	1,360
Private plots	3,130,000	5,639	1,000
Corporate farms	895	2,097	258
Other		3,306	582
Total		**14,710**	**4,400**

Source: OECD, 1993a,b.

The distribution of certificates and titles. Some 2,900 local land commissions were set up to handle land claims. In addition, there were 'liquidation councils' established for the former collective (cooperative) units. At the end of 1989 3,776 such units were registered in the statistics. We do not know how many liquidation councils were set up. There are a number of important questions that remain. We do not know who was appointed or how many people became occupied in these offices. Also, we have not been able to research how they were remunerated or their terms of appointment.

According to Gavilescu (1994), 6,236,057 claims were filed. These included some multiple claims for the same land by conflicting claimants, including different heirs of the same landowner. Also, there were 18-20 million individual plots of land involved; hence, there were multiple claims by one household because the previous land had not been consolidated.

By the end of 1992, 4,722,681 certificates had been awarded covering 75 percent of the claims, but only 35 percent of the land involved in claims. Thus, small claims were being processed faster than large claims. By June 1994 (OECD expert), 99 percent of the certificates covering 89 percent of the owners and 93 percent of the area had been awarded.

Distribution of legal titles went more slowly. Gavrilescu reports that only 2 percent of owners had received titles by the end of 1992. By the end of 1993 some 700,000 titles covering about 14 percent of the total had been granted.

The number of titles granted by June 1994 (OECD expert) went up to 1,095,000, covering 23.1 percent of the legal owners and 25 percent of the claims. At the end of August 1994, 28 percent of the titles were granted which involved 1.2 million 'proprietors' out of a total of 4.4 million (*Romania libera*, 2 September 1994). The official goal was to have all titles granted by the end of 1995 (that is, before the next general elections scheduled in 1996).

Reported changes in farming organization. There was no doubt much chaos and uncertainty regarding *de facto* control and use of land and farm capital during 1990 and 1991. The reporting sources also seem to have somewhat confused the record.

The OECD Romanian Country Study reported over a 2 million increase in total hectares under the heading 'private farms' at the end of 1990, compared with the total at the end of 1989 (but its figure for the latter date clearly exaggerates who controlled the land at that time). In place of private farms in the following years (see below) OECD reported 'individual farms and agricultural groups in formation'. Total land in this category was nearly 8 million hectares, another large increase over land of private farms at the end of 1990, by about 2.5 million hectares. In April 1992 and at the end of 1992, the amount of land in this category went down as the amount (and number) in 'agricultural societies' or companies organized under the commercial code (limited liability and joint stock) and 'agricultural societies' or new cooperatives went up.

A real issue in this case is whether the land was turned over to the new owner and farmed individually or was a certificate granted before the new association or society was formalized but while the land continued to be controlled by the former collective farm unit.

The different categories reported later by the OECD expert leave the precise 'ownership or organization' of 9.9 million hectares at the end of 1991 unidentified, and over 3.3 million still unidentified at the end of 1993. This is probably a wiser course since many arrangements were really in doubt. In this view, the numbers and the area of land in the two 'private' categories (family farms and private plots or gardens) go up rapidly. At the same time, the numbers of cooperatives and the amount of land so farmed also go up.

The third category in this report, corporate farms, shows an increase in numbers (from 747 to 895) and persons involved in the two year period, but a decrease in land area. This reference covers mostly former state farms, which numbered only 411 at the end of 1989. Some were probably broken up into smaller units, while other former state agricultural organizations probably also engaged in farming or acquired land to farm after 1989 (for example, animal-raising enterprises probably started to produce their own fodder).

Summary: The situation in late 1994. Romanian land reform is often referred to as 'radical', although there are good reasons to questions this characterization. It is certainly less radical than might be concluded on the basis of certificates of ownership issued. These have been given to private agents, mainly individuals and families for more than 70 percent of the agricultural land and 80 percent of the cultivated and arable land. Nevertheless, holding a certificate means far less than individual landownership in the Western European sense, even when we take into account the many restrictions on use and disposition in this part of Europe.

It is not clear to what extent a certificate defines the appropriate boundaries of a plot of land that might become, with some small adjustments, the certificate holder's property. That question is only clearly defined when a legal title is issued. At the beginning of September 1994, 28 percent of the 4.4 million claiming units (mostly family households) had been given legal titles.

More important questions have to do with use rights, income rights, and disposal rights – the fundamental components of property rights. There appear to be heavy restrictions on income and disposal rights even after legal titles are issued, more restrictions than are typical in Western Europe. Some of these restrictions are probably a consequence of contractual obligations imposed on the new owners so that legal authorities would move ahead on the certificates and titles in the first place. These obligations might have been 'encouragements' for lease agreements, agreements for the use of agricultural services, or memberships in new associations (cooperatives) for joint land leasing (out) and farming. There are no good statistics to present as evidence of these 'gray' transactions (although abundant anecdotes can be found in the press).

One finds information on the extent of land used under various new cooperative and corporative arrangements (see table 10.3). Thus, according to the statistical yearbook of 1994, at the end of 1993 70 percent of agricultural land (10.3 million ha.) and 80 percent of arable land (7.5 million ha.) were used 'privately' by individual households, family associations without legal entity (under Law 31/1990), and cooperative entities (under Law 36/1991). According to the OECD expert in May 1994, individual agriculturalists were in a minority – some 6,565 in farming and 5,810 in animal husbandry, beekeeping, horticulture, etc. More 'private entrepreneurs' were 'family associations' – some 13,508 in farming and 3,111 in animal husbandry, etc. These 16,555 family associations, which averaged 45 families per association (747,000 persons), used 1,872 thousand hectares of agricultural area. In addition, there were 4,054 'agricultural cooperatives' under article 5 of Law 36/1991, which averaged 185 families each (750,000 persons) and used 1,812 thousand hectares of agricultural area. Finally, some 374 commercial companies (under Law 31/1990 and article 30 of Law 36/1991) with 34,000 members (averaging 91 per company) had another 85,000 hectares of land.

The reported figure of 3,769,000 hectares of agricultural land is only 36.5 percent of the 1993 total (as given in the statistical yearbook). We assume that it does not include land farmed under informal arrangements, perhaps using common services for plowing, etc., and other arrangements made by the former agricultural mechanization stations in exchange for a share of the crops. Unfortunately, we do not have the independent comprehensive surveys that might allow us to estimate the true distribution of property rights.

The reported shares of farm units considered to be private follow in table 10.3.

Table 10.3
The reported shares of 'private' farm units (%)

Total arable areas	80.0
sown areas:	
Cereals	84.6
Maize	92.1
Barley	54.6
Sunflowers	70.7
Sugar beets	78.6
Potatoes	95.0
Vegetables	88.7
Animal herds	
Cattle	85.0
Swine	50.3
Sheep	89.0
Poultry	63.0

Privatization of agricultural services and the food industry. Company privatization in Romania has generally gone slowly. According to the OECD expert, by the summer of 1994 only 870 of the 2,200 commercial enterprises in the agricultural and food industries had been put on the list submitted to the State Ownership Fund to be privatized. This list included 511 mechanization companies, 30 supply companies, 92 transport companies, 22 land-improvement companies with construction and transport activities, 101 food-processing companies, and 41 other companies.

While 411 state agricultural mechanization enterprises existed at the end of 1989, 521 of 522 agricultural mechanization companies belonging to

AGROMEC were on the list to be privatized. Some 10.2 percent were supposed to have been privatized during the first half of 1994, another 22.5 percent were in the process of privatization, and the goal set for the end of 1994 was 98.0 percent.

According to another report (Romania libera, 15 August 1994), by August 1994, of the 2,204 commercial companies to be privatized in agriculture and the food industry, only 136 had been privatized, 79 had started negotiations, 155 had certificates of property for land, and 797 were proposed for privatization. Under the arrangements for privatization, special terms were offered to both employees and the associated farming units. It was hoped that 40 percent could be privatized by the end of 1994.

Romanian politics and the land reform

As a conclusion to this chapter, we now turn to what has been the more direct connection between Romanian politics and the land reform. In particular, we should try to explain the apparent contradiction between the relative success of Iliescu and his third chosen prime minister, Vacaroiu, in dominating Romanian politics, and the seemingly radical character of the land reform.

Special factors in the Romanian case

Before looking at possible specific connections, we want to point out some factors in the Romanian case that have influenced political developments and probably limited the nature of property settlements that might not be connected to the political maneuverings of Iliescu and those connected to him.

One condition is the seeming weakness of Romanian opposition politics. Only perhaps in Albania, but in no other Communist country (including the Soviet Union), did a regime devote as much effort to destroying and suppressing alternative political movements. Although there were some Romanian dissidents, they were weak. They often maintained some contacts with the Communist party. They received almost no support from the many Romanians who had run away or otherwise immigrated to the West during Ceausescu's time. There was no strong movement that united large numbers of free Romanians.

On the side of land disposition, it must be remembered that many Romanians still had their connections to the land. Surely for over half the population these ties were strong. Moreover, the term 'peasant' really describes the mentality of most Romanians who depended on agriculture, even those who were still members of collective farms. Unlike Bulgaria, where those providing labor on collective farms had been turned into wage-

agricultural workers, the Romanian farmer tended to be close to his household and village and was still, in the manner of the original collective farms, the residual income claimant with no guarantee of, and in recent years little or no, residual income. Consequently, the family continued to survive mostly on what could be provided by its household and stolen from the collective fields. *It is difficult to imagine a property settlement in Romania that would not have included at least a gesture towards the peasants' need for more land.*

Spontaneous land reform and the first elections (May 1990)

As we have noted, there quickly appeared a contradiction between the leaderships' statements about working within the existing collective corporate framework of farm organization and the quick, but limited, recognition of rights to 0.5 hectares per family. Various statements above suggest that by the time of the May 1990 elections, land plots claimed by the peasants (and seemingly recognized, if only *de facto*, by the provisional government) amounted to nearly 4 million hectares of agricultural land, quite an increase over the 0.8 million in collective households at the end of 1988.

We do know that this was a time of significant conflict in the rural areas. Sometimes the local authorities were part of the anti-Communist opposition and simply dissolved the local collective units. There is no record of this happening on a state farm or a state mechanization station that was under direct management of the Ministry of Agriculture. Also, the cases of liquidation sponsored by local authorities were surely in the minority. As we have seen, the NSF placed a high priority on extending tight controls over the district prefects and community mayors.

The other limit to spontaneous land takeover was the fact that most of the peasants had no means whatsoever to undertake farm work. According to a World Bank survey in 1991, only 9 percent had anything resembling a tractor, 28 percent had either a horse or a buffalo, but only 12 percent had a plow (Brooks and Meurs, 1994). The time of the takeovers was dead winter and early spring – time to prepare the fields. But which peasant would have had seeds to plant?

Of course, there is a second side to spontaneous takeovers. The rural and agricultural bureaucracy carried on their official and unofficial organizational structures. They even had their own NSF-satellite party in the form of Surdu's Democratic Agrarian Party as a speaking platform for their interests. Unlike the peasants, the NSF had all means at their disposal, the machinery and the seeds. Also, they were allied with the authorities, so it would not have been difficult for them to force favorable deals even with the most persistent peasant family. In this situation, we imagine that most peasant households just tried to extend the margin of their gardens to whatever could be tilled by the family

313

and agreed to any terms set by local authorities. To have had any bargaining power, they would have had to be united in village networks and to have labor that the bureaucrats and managers would need. *There is no good reason to believe regime statements about how much land was 'leased' or otherwise permitted to be taken over. But in any case, much of it was to be farmed under the old management forms.*

Politically, Iliescu and Roman did very well in the May 1990 election, even if part of the reported vote was fraud and gained by violent tactics. Their support appeared strongest in rural areas both because it was easy to cheat there, and because the NSF appealed to both rural factions. To the ordinary peasant, some land had been given, some prices freed, and a vague promise made to give back to families nearly all of the land that had been taken in the collectivization. The rural-agricultural bureaucracy already knew who was on their side and had at least an implicit contract to support the NSF.

The land reform laws and the general election of September 1992

Once Iliescu and the NSF claimed the election, the July law on district and local administration made their position in the countryside even stronger. With the summer well underway, peasants had little time for the political maneuvring that might have been necessary at the local level to extend their interests. Probably there was great quarreling over who could claim the crops during the summer and autumn. By that time, of course, the debates were going on over the new land law.

The political effects of the land law of February 1991 seemed to focus on three parameters.

First, the law provided in principal a potentially radical 're-propertization' of land to families from whom land had been taken between 1948 and 1962 and also to rural families who had no other land claims. The law set up procedures either to 'liquidate' or to convert to new voluntary associations the former collective farms and their nonland assets. Also, state farms, mechanization stations, and other service organizations were to be privatized under arrangements that would give insiders a privileged position. The law seemed to provide something for everyone. It even should have pleased the urban consumer, who could look forward to abundant supplies of good quality food in the peasant markets that dominated even Bucharest household purchases.

Second, the law offered a radical departure from the system under the Communists. But, because under that system legal traces of the past were often obliterated, the new law could not easily be put into practice. The special character of the law of February 1991 made it even more complicated. On the one hand, the law gave claimants very little time to file claims and required from them a collection of often hard-to-find records. On the other hand, the

314

law gave the administering authorities rather wide discretion in the precise way that any claim might be satisfied. For example, different qualities of land even in different locations could be given from either the originally collectivized land or the immediately farmed land.[7]

Third, with the law passed in February, and with the immediate necessity of preparing for another crop season, there was little or no time for most peasants to press their cases. In fact, the regulations simply prohibited disturbing the land farmed by the former collectives until the end of harvests. This provided more time for the authorities and the better-represented rural-bureaucratic interests to press their own cases for landed property and to legally and politically maneuvre peasants into accepting collective and corporative farming arrangements.

During the course of 1991 and 1992, as a prelude to the election, one can find a steady flow of anecdotal evidence of dissatisfaction with the land reform program. Nearly every possible complaint can be found: claims were not recognized, claimed land was being given to others, relatives and associates of the members of local land commission and local or district authorities were receiving special treatment, given land was not in the right location or of the right quality, etc. The minister of agriculture even complained that some local commissions disbanded themselves as soon as their members' own claims on land had been satisfied (OECD, 1993a).

There were also many complaints from peasants that they were forced to join associations, in some cases with the threat that their land claims would not otherwise be recognized. Many complained of being charged high monopoly prices for agricultural services or of being discriminated against in the distribution of credits or low-cost seeds and fertilizers.

There can be little doubt that many such problems arose. The problem is that, so far, at least, we have found no systematic evidence of their extent. According to the Economist Intelligence Unit in 1994 there were still over 1 million land cases still being decided in the law courts.

There were sure to have been negative impacts on agricultural output. Reported output did fall in 1991 and 1992 by significant amounts. Unfortunately, there is no way to know how much underreporting took place because there were incentives not to report output and income. In both years, and especially in 1992, there was reported drought.

There would appear to have been little in the government's land reform program for either the peasants or the urban consumer population to be pleased about as the elections came up in September 1992. There were other reasons to expect a change in political leadership. In June 1990, right after the elections, the government and Iliescu personally were widely condemned for the miners' bloody rampage in Bucharest. The handling of King Michael's attempted visits was clumsy. There was a growing split within NSF ranks, which led to

315

Roman's dismissal as prime minister a year before the election. Although this might have been seen as an attempt to make Roman the scapegoat for the unpopular price liberalization measures and the chaos of the land reform, during the year before the elections the Stolojan government was still associated with the country's continuing difficulties. A change of government might have been more convincing had it taken place in the early summer just before the 1992 elections.

In any case, the government and Iliescu fell in the public opinion polls. Voting for the NSF candidates in the local elections in February 1992 seemed to verify a voter shift towards the opposition.

The land reform was a major issue in the September 1992 general election campaign. Iliescu, the DNSF, and its allied forces in the DAP claimed that the opposition parties wanted to give land back to the former large landowners and to sell it to capitalist exploiters, especially foreigners. A new theme was that all of the shortcomings could be blamed on former Prime Minister Petre Roman. His government was blamed for having pushed through a land reform in which peasants were given land but no other means of production.

As in the 1990 election, the Iliescu forces did better in the rural areas than in the cities. And, as before, what this result represented cannot be judged on the basis of evidence so far found by our research. Surely part of it represented better access for campaigning in the countryside and arm-twisting by the authorities (who could still threaten not to cooperate in the administration of land claims). But the weight of positive views of Iliescu and/or negative views of the opposition is difficult to tell.

Land reform issues in the post-election politics

The strong turnout for the nationalist Party for Romanian National Unity, the switch of Iliescu's party towards a coalition with the Communist-nationalists, and the character of Romanian politics over the last two years – especially the increasingly bitter debates over the issues of Hungarian rights in Transylvania – possibly reveals a new side of land reform politics. This is suggested by table 10.4 on the percentage of titles granted to land claimants said to represent the situation as of September 1994.

Although there are one or two exceptions, there is a clear pattern showing a low percentage of titles granted in districts with high shares of Hungarian Romanians. This probably means that the local politics of these districts has been embittered by conflict between Hungarian-speaking claimants and Romanian-speaking claimants, or more likely, between the former and the authorities, who are dominated by activitists in the party of Iliescu, the PNUR, and the Democratic Agrarian Party.[8] The conflicts at this level would surely have also included accusations and fear mongering about possible Hungarian money coming in to the region.

Our problem is that we have only this inference, with no direct evidence of the problem. That is not to suggest there would be a lack of evidence. Probably evidence would be found in the Hungarian press.

Table 10.4
Share of legal titles issued by district, September 1994

District	Share (%)	District	Share (%)
Alba	*17.8	Gorj	13.0
Arad	35.0	Hargita	*17.8
Arges	41.8	Hunedoara	31.7
Bacau	25.3	Ialomita	27.5
Bihor	*17.4	Iasi	25.3
Bistrita Nasaud	37.6	Botosani	25.4
Brasov	12.8	Mehedinti	21.6
Braila	25.8	Bucharest	16.0
Buzau	44.9	Neamti	17.2
Calaras	23.4	Olt	26.6
Caras-Severin	28.4	Prahova	22.4
Cluj	*19.3	Salaj	49.0
Constanta	54.7	Satu Mare	*18.9
Covasna	*16.1	Sibiu	28.9
Dambovita	38.0	Teleoman	23.4
Dolj	27.5	Timis	32.0
Galati	53.0	Tulca	45.0
Giurgiu	38.0	Vaslui	21.6
		Valcea	25.0
		Vrancea	36.0

* Districts wih important areas of Hungarian-speaking inhabitants.
Source: Romania libera, 2 September 1994.

Finally, as one looks at the state of Romania's opposition politics, one can not overlook the lack of visible opposition programs for both land reform and agricultural policies in general. So far, there is no strong political formation with a clear message meant to appeal to successful emerging private farmers or, for that matter, to their counterparts in small urban businesses. Romania is still a society without a middle class based on small- and medium-sized businesses, and it clearly lacks politicians who might find their political market niche among such voters.

Notes

1   An incomplete record indicated two party organizers killed, 113 hospitalized with serious injuries, and 577 beaten in party offices and in their homes.

2   In April 1991 Roman had included one member of the NLP in his government, who was promptly repudiated by his party. Also, Dinu Patriciu, who had left the NLP after the elections in 1990 to form the breakaway NLP-Young Wing, was nominated by Roman but refused by Parliament.

3   According to Tismaneanu (1993), even Minister of Interior Draghici – the executor of the 'Stalinist terror' of Ceausescu's predecessor, Gheorghe-Dej – reportedly was allowed to leave Romania in 1992 with his wife in order to avoid a trial.

4   It is worth pointing out that Romania does not differ from other post-Communist countries where the issue of royal restoration has been raised.

5   Such a unit was established in the early years of Communist Romania under Soviet pressure. It was then disbanded by Ceausescu.

6   The state's share was only 4.1 million hectares of agricultural land and 1.9 million hectares of arable land.

7   'Unconfirmed reports indicate that in many localities agricultural specialists have often been allocated the full 10 hectares allowed, putting them in powerful positions in their multiple roles as MAFI employees, advisors to societies and associations, and independent landowners'. (Quotation from the OECD, 1993a, in endnote 3, p.113).

8   'The PDAR has a large membership among agricultural specialists and tends to represent their interests. Agricultural specialists occupy a unique place in Romanian agriculture; many still work for the state; at the same time they are often significant landholders as a result of privatization, and have become members of agricultural societies and associations'. In a press release in late 1992, the PDAR cited the lack of diesel fuel, fertiliser, credits, and animal feed as causing food shortages. They requested that the government roll back price increases in agricultural inputs and meat resulting from the devaluation (from 220 to 430), which was 'giving rise to speculation and unjustified dissatisfaction'. In 1993 the president of the PDAR announced 'the only way to save this year's crop ... 300 billion lei [of low interest credit] would be needed for the completion of the farming work during this spring' (OECD 1993a, endnote 23, p. 114).

References

BBC, *Survey of World Broadcasts*, various issues.

Brooks, K. and Meurs, M. (1994), 'Romanian Land Reform: 1991-1993', *Comparatieve Economic Studies*, Vol. XXXVI, No. 2, Summer, pp. 17-32.

Deletant, D. (1991), 'The Role of Vatra Romaneasca in Transylvania', *Report on Eastern Europe*, 1 February.

Gafton, P. (1990), 'Measures and Half-Measures to Stimulate Agriculture', *Report on Eastern Europe*, Vol. 1, No. 19, 11 May, p. 34-37.

Gallagher, T. (1994), 'The Rise of the Party of Romanian National Unity', *Report on Eastern Europe*, 18 March.

Gavrilescu, D. (1994), 'Agriculture Reform in Romania: Between Market Priority and the Strategies for Food Security', in Swinnen, J. (ed.), *Policy and Institutional Reform in Central European Agriculture*, Aldershot: Avebury.

Ionescu, D. (1990), 'The NSF starts to implement its Program', *Report on Eastern Europe*, Vol. 1, No. 5, 2 February, pp. 26-29.

Ionescu, D. (1991), 'National Salvation Front Holds Convention', *Report on Eastern Europe*, Vol. 2, No. 13, 29 March, pp. 6-11.

Ionescu, D. (1992a), 'Romania: Charter for Reform and Democracy withers away', RFE/RL Research Report, Vol. 1, No. 5, 31 January, p. 14-17.

Ionescu, D. (1992b), 'Social Tension threatens frail Romanian Economy', *RFE/RL Research Report*, Vol. 1, No. 10, 6 March, pp. 32-36.

Ionescu, D. (1993), 'Romania's Cabinet in Search of an Economic Strategy', *RFE/RL Research Report*, Vol. 2, No. 4, 22 January, pp. 45-49.

Ionescu, D., and Shafir, M. (1993), 'Political Change and Economic Malaise', *RFE/RL Research Report*, Vol. 2, No. 1, 1 January, pp. 108-112.

Jackson, M. (1994), *East-Central Europe in Transition*, papers presented to the Joint Economic Committee, Congress of the United States, U.S. Government Printing Office: Washington D.C.

Jackson, M. (1995), 'The Economic Penetration between the EC and Eastern Europe: The Romanian Case', *European Economies*, European Commission: Brussels.

Jackson, M. R. and Lampe, J. R. (1982), *Balkan Economic History, 1550-1950. From Imperial Borderlands to developing Nations*, Indiana University: Bloomington.

Mitrany, D. (1931), *The Land and the Peasant in Romania*, Yale University Press: New Haven.

OECD (1993a), *Romania: An Economic Assessment*, OECD: Paris.

OECD (1993b), *Agricultural Policy and Trade Developments in Romania in 1993-1994*, OECD: Paris.

OMRI Daily Digest, various issues.

Postolache, T. (coordinator) (1990), *Schita Privind Stragegia Infaptuiri Economiei de Piata in Romania* (An Outline of Strategy for Introducing a Market Economy in Romania), Bucharest, May.

Roberts, H. (1951), *Rumania: The Politics of an Agrarian State*, Yale University Press: New Haven.

Romania libera, various issues.

Romanian Statistical Yearbook and monthly statistical review, various issues.

Shafir, M. (1990), 'Oppositional Regrouping: the Democratic Anti-totalitarian Forum and the Civic Alliance', *Report on Eastern Europe*, Vol. 1, No. 50, Dec. 14, pp. 13-22.

Shafir, M. (1991a), 'King Michael's Second Expulsion' *Report on Eastern Europe*, 18 January.

Shafir, M. (1991b), 'Public Opinion one Year after the Elections', *Report on Eastern Europe*, Vol. 2, No. 24, 14 June, pp. 22-27.

Shafir, M. (1992a), 'Romania National Liberal Party Quits Democratic Convention', *RFE/RL Research Report*, Vol. 1, No .24, 12 June, pp. 25-30.

Shafir, M. (1992b), 'Preliminary Results of the 1992 Romanian Census', *RFE/RL Research Report*, Vol. 1, No. 30, 24 July, pp. 62-68.

Shafir, M. (1993), 'Public Opinion One Year After Elections', *Report on Eastern Europe*, 14 June.

Shafir, M. (1994), 'Romanian Politics in Turmoil', *Report on Eastern Europe*, 22 July.

Socor, V. (1990), 'The New President', *Report on Eastern Europe*, Vol. 1, No. 23, 8 June, pp. 38-41.

Tismaneanu V. (1993), 'The Quasi-Revolution and its Discontents: Emerging political Pluralism in Post-Ceausescu Romania', *East European Politics and Societies*, Vol. 7, No. 2, Spring, pp. 309-348.

11 Agrarian reform in Post-Soviet Russia

Don Van Atta

Introduction

Public discussion of the denationalization of agricultural land in the Russian Federation began in 1989. The basic mechanisms for land redistribution were worked out during the next two years. Because the reform measures were largely decided before the Soviet Union dissolved in late 1991, they evolved from Soviet forms. No restitution of agricultural land, either to peasants who had lost land during collectivization or to landlords who were dispossessed at the time of the Revolution, seems to have been seriously considered. Nor, despite measures to compensate victims of Stalinism since 1991, does restitution seem likely to be considered. Because of the landholding patterns in prerevolutionary and Soviet Russia, there has not been and there is very unlikely to be a sharp break with Communist-era land tenure and farm organization, as has happened in the Baltic States and much of Central and Eastern Europe. The most thoroughgoing attempts to reorganize landholding patterns towards individual ownership more suited to a market economy have not yet succeeded in changing the basic patterns of communal tenure. Even the most ardent proponents of these efforts suggest that land patterns will not change for at least another generation. This essay examines the historical and political reasons for this situation and considers its implications for the future of Russian agriculture and for post-Soviet Russia as a whole.

Traditional Russian agriculture

In principle, the Czar owned all land in the Russian Empire until the end of serfdom. But noble holders of land grants from the Czar treated them as very much their own. When serfdom was abolished in the 1860s, nobles and peasants received the right to own land, under certain conditions and with many restrictions on its sale or transfer. A land market of the type that emerged in much of Western Europe by the end of the nineteenth century did not appear in Russia before collectivization in the 1930s because of the relatively late abolition of serfdom and because of the legal procedures adopted for its abolition.

Russian peasant households usually clustered together in a village rather than situating themselves on individual farmsteads (*khutora*). The residents of a village normally farmed a single set of fields as part of a unified working 'commune', the *mir* or *obshchina* (Grant, 1976). The 1861 law that abolished serfdom gave land to the commune, not to the households or individual peasants. The communal assembly (*skhod*), a meeting of all the male household heads, allocated land to its members, arranged for the upkeep of local roads and bridges, acted as the village court, and was responsible for taxes and other state levies (Male, 1971; Mironov, 1985; Lewin, 1985). The communal assembly remained the major local government until collectivization (Atkinson, 1983). These institutional arrangements were supported by, and helped to preserve, essentially medieval farming practices.

Until collectivization, the three-field crop rotation system (one field left fallow, one sown with winter grain, and one with spring grains) predominated (Matossian, 1968).[1] Families' landholdings were parceled out in small plots or strips throughout the several large fields supporting common crop rotations. Much of the arable land was occupied by access paths to the strips, and the distance between plots required families to spend much of their time trudging from place to place. A delegate to the XV Party Congress in the mid-1920s reported that in Riazan' there were families with as many as fifty or sixty strips (Nemakov, 1966). The land could seldom be worked with machinery because of the small size of the plots. Tractors cultivated only 1 percent of Russia's plowed land when wholesale collectivization began in 1929 (Ronina, 1987).

As long as the state enforced collective responsibility for redemption dues to pay off the land taken from the nobility when the serfs were emancipated in the 1860s (Watters, 1968), there was little scope for political or social entrepreneurs to escape the commune, even after farmers were formally free of serfdom. In any case, no individual or family could benefit from cultivating better than or differently from their neighbors because the strips were mixed together, and strip agriculture requires that decisions about how and when to conduct particular agricultural operations be binding on everyone whose strips are included in the fields (Block, 1966).

Government policy toward the village changed during the Stolypin Reforms after the 1905 Revolution. The state then began to encourage individual or familial land settlement – consolidation of families' strips from the common fields into larger plots or independent farmsteads. Under the reforms, individuals or families were freed from communal responsibility if they wished to leave the commune. By the beginning of World War I, about half of all peasant families had been affected by land consolidation under the reforms. However, peasants did not share the reformers' preference for consolidated farms with dwellings on the property, preferring instead to unite their holdings of agricultural land while continuing to live in the village (Pallot, 1984).

Following the fall of the Czar in March 1917, the peasants began seizing land. The integration of former estate, crown, and church lands, as well as the reassimilation of the Stolypin separators, into village societies proceeded at varying speeds and with different amounts of violence depending on the locality. The same processes unfolded throughout the countryside. Between the fall of 1917 and the spring of 1918, peasants largely accomplished the general redistribution of land, the 'black repartition' which had been the dream of Russian populists half a century earlier (Keep, 1976). In many areas physical symbols of the old order – the manor houses and outbuildings – were torched as 'the peasants ... sought ... by these acts of violence ... not only to drive all *pomeshchiki* [landlords] away, but also to erase the traces – the very memory – of their presence' (Haimson, 1988, p. 17). By the end of this great upsurge, 'the peasant communities had emerged more homogeneous and more self-contained than ever before in the memories of their members' (Haimson, 1988, p. 17). Almost all of the consolidated plots and individual farms created under the Stolypin Reforms reverted to the village fields during the Revolution (Conquest, 1986). Although the creation of compact farm plots under Stolypin-Reform style procedures did continue during the 1920s, changes in land tenure patterns and the improvements in agricultural productivity the reforms had promised largely fell victim to the peasants' desire to eliminate any vestiges of the large estates and to take over former crown lands.

Collectivization of Russian agriculture

The strengthening of local peasant government in the wake of the Revolution posed a political problem for the Bolshevik regime, which even more than its Czarist predecessor, had few mechanisms for exercising authority in the countryside other than force, although it had formally nationalized all land once again, legally extinguishing all individual property rights in agricultural land. Postrevolutionary Russian industry had relatively little to offer the countryside. Inept industrial and price policies made the situation worse. Ingrained Bolshevik distrust of market mechanisms and the cadres' military style developed during the years of civil war made them neither sympathetic to nor understanding of financial and economic levers for dealing with the countryside. When the market seemingly failed to supply adequate quantities of grain for the cities in 1927-1928, Stalin publicly interpreted falling state grain procurements as evidence of conscious political opposition by the mass of the peasantry – a 'grain strike' (Lewin, 1965; Karcz, 1979). By the winter of 1928-1929, bread rationing was in force in the cities. Rationing guaranteed every city dweller, including many people who only the day before had been peasants, a minimum of food (Zelenin, 1989).

The regime 'solved' the grain crisis by forcibly reorganizing the countryside, abolishing peasant farms and the commune and replacing them with large-scale collective farms (Tanuichi, 1981). The forcible procurements ruined the government's chances to persuade peasants through economic means to increase production. Along with 'extraordinary measures' to compel grain production, the government quickened the pace of collectivization to end village resistance by destroying and reconstructing rural society. Many apparently market-based devices, such as the conclusion of advance delivery contracts for produce (*kontraktatsiia*), became administratively enforced measures to beat down resistance. Punitive taxes and delivery quotas forced peasants into the new farms.

Mass collectivization became a continuous process of improvisation in response to events which the leadership could affect by brute force but could not control.[2] Although the wholesale creation of collective farms can be traced to certain Party and state decisions, it is highly unlikely that Stalin had a vision of what the countryside should look like after collectivization when the 'third revolution' began (Lewin, 1968; Millar, 1982). Local Party organs raced to distinguish themselves by fulfilling and overfulfilling their assignments for creating kolkhozy. Many of the structures and procedures characteristic of the Soviet countryside from the 1930s to the 1990s arose more or less spontaneously during collectivization as cadres, peasants, and political leaders improvised methods and organizations as they went along. Regional and national leaderships then ordered the general imposition of those new devices it found most congenial.

At the same time, village riots and semi-organized attempts to liberate collectivized property were widespread.[3] The Soviet historian Nikolai Ivnitskii, citing data that apparently do not cover the whole country, reports some 2,700 peasant riots (*vystuplenie*) against collectivization during the first three months of 1930 (Ivnitskii, 1987).

The campaign for the liquidation of the kulaks as a class in the winter of 1929-1930 culminated Stalinist collectivization. But by then the traditional village moneylender was long gone, eliminated in the civil war. There were no wealthy peasant kulaks to remove by the time 'dekulakization' began. Those identified as kulaks were simply the most efficient middle peasants or those who had opposed collectivization too loudly (Literaturnaia gazeta, 1987).[4] The kulaks' property and agricultural inventory was needed by the kolkhozy. If the better-off peasants were not to be allowed into the collective farms, and by late 1929 it was clear they would not be, they could hardly remain in the villages where their property had been expropriated. So they were forcibly exiled.[5]

Just how many of these supposedly rich peasants were eliminated is still uncertain. Ivnitskii said in late 1987 that in the three years 1930-1932 a total of 650,000 families were dekulakized. More than 250,000 of them were exiled – forcibly removed from their homes and sent into the wastes of Siberia or Soviet Central Asia. Another 250,000 families 'dekulakized themselves' by running from the villages. (Ivnitskii did not say what happened to the other 150,000 families.) If a peasant family included four persons, a conservative estimate, perhaps 2.5 million people were officially counted as killed or exiled by Stalin's war on the kulaks. Viktor Danilov reported that a total of 381,000 families were deported as kulaks by the end of 1931. His figure did not include deaths or individual family members sentenced to labor camps (Emmons, 1991). Whatever the true numbers, it is clear that essentially every peasant household lost someone to the collectivization and its associated terrors.

It is hardly surprising that the collective farm maintained many of its repressive features for a generation, offering peasants little incentive for good work and giving managers little room for initiative until the mid-1960s. Even in the 1970s and 1980s, as the countryside received an increasing share of state investment and the authorities declared their goal of bringing rural standards of living up to those of urban areas, the collective farms maintained many repressive features. As long as the farm managers and local party authorities remained, the farms continued to be 'total institutions' in which managers controlled the work, leisure, and living conditions of their workers.

The development of Russian agrarian reform

Open political debate about agricultural landownership, farm organization, and the need for agrarian reform began in the former Soviet Union as a result of former General Secretary Mikhail Gorbachev's attempts to save the Soviet system by transforming its political institutions. These issues developed as part of the general drive for democratization, and were used by reform forces in attempts to break the power of the Communist party. Once again, ownership and forms of economic organization were politicized.

The creation of new Congresses of People's Deputies for the entire USSR and then for Russia provided a forum for debate on agricultural policy in which an organized bloc of 'agrarian deputies', whose power ultimately rested on their positions as successful farm managers under the existing system, eventually emerged. Soviet farm managers, rather like American college presidents, were at least as much politicians as managers. A successful farm manager often spent more time dealing with local and national officials to ensure a steady flow of resources and favorable economic treatment, than he did managing his own farm. These managers resented their dependence on officialdom and increasingly argued during the final years of the Soviet Union that the collective farm system from which they had benefited could solve the country's chronic food-supply uncertainties if only they were liberated from official interference. To the extent that market-oriented economic reform implied an end to local and national officials' interference in the management of their farms, and even promised that they might be able to assume ownership of their enterprises, successful farm managers were in favor of market mechanisms. These farm managers were opposed by a less homogeneous group of 'democrats' who believed that without land reform neither political nor economic transformation was possible.

The agrarian issue also became entangled in the breakup of the Soviet Union, as the Russian Federation emerged as an increasingly autonomous unit within the USSR and then an independent state. The coalitions made possible by the coincidence of the issues of democratization, agrarian reform, and the dissolution of the USSR allowed land reform legislation to be adopted, but they also explain why restitution was never a real possibility.

When the first Congress of People's Deputies of the USSR opened in 1989, many of the rural deputies expressed unhappiness with its disorganization and concern for broad philosophical and political issues rather than what they saw as the immediate, practical demands of the country's economic crisis. As a result of this perceived lack of attention, some 417 agrarian deputies (*deputaty-agrarnikov*) issued a manifesto on peasant interests demanding immediate attention to their concerns at the end of May 1989. In particular, they called for immediate reform (meaning a reduction) of the prices paid by farms for equipment and other inputs.[6] During that first session of the Congress of People's Deputies in June and July of 1989, the agrarian deputies were united in their demands for more resources for agriculture and an end to party interference in agricultural management.

Debate on the USSR Land Law in the fall and winter of 1989-1990 divided the agrarian deputies as the basic political issue shifted from demands for more resources for agriculture to the question of who would control the farms. Several drafts of the USSR Land Law were proposed to the Committee on Agrarian Questions and Food Supply in early October 1989. Although the draft texts are not available for comparison, their principal differences concerned the related questions of allowing private property in land and the need for a general land reform. The most radical of the four drafts came from agricultural economist Vladimir Tikhonov. Even this version of the law would apparently not have explicitly allowed land as private property, but it would have permitted individual control of the land, amounting to private ownership. Tikhonov sought to take control, management, and use of the land (which he defined as the three component parts of *zemlevladenie*, or landownership) away from the state (Konovalova, 1989). However, his conceptions were not fully adopted in the final law, which the Supreme Soviet adopted on 28 February 1990. The USSR Council of Ministers was to identify unused and irrationally used lands, create or strengthen state agencies for monitoring land use, and develop a special program of support for peasant farms. The government was also to bring existing legislation into accord with the new law and propose whatever additional legislation might be necessary (Pravda, 1990). Farm enterprises and individuals were to be allowed to hold land on lease from the state or in lifetime, inheritable tenure (*vladenie*). However, land was defined as a national resource (*dostoianie*), and true private ownership, including the right to freely resell land, was not permitted.

The USSR Land Law was only a statement of basic principles. Despite a demand from radical deputies that a law on land reform should be adopted simultaneously, no implementing legislation was passed (Boikova and Virkunen, 1990). The struggle over agrarian reform, the introduction of private property in land, and the future organization of the countryside, devolved to the union republics.

Russian republican elections were held in March 1990. On 21 April 1990, approximately 120 deputies to the new Russian Republican Congress of People's Deputies met in the offices of the Russian Republican State Agro-Industrial Committee (*Gosagroprom*) to work out their line of action at the Russian Congress.[7] After heated discussion, they organized themselves as a formal parliamentary faction. Mikhail Lapshin, a Moscow-area *sovkhoz* (state farm) director, was elected chairman of the group (Mikhailov, 1990; Petrakov, 1990). (Lapshin later became the chairman of the Agrarian Party of Russia, organized by the agrarian parliamentary faction.) Their concerns, their choice of a meeting place, and the presence of senior officials of the Russian Soviet Federated Socialist Republic (RSFSR) state committee on agriculture, suggested that these deputies were not by any means radical opponents of the existing system of agricultural organization. In accord with the growing self-definition of the agrarian deputies as a conservative group, the RSFSR Committee on the Social Development of the Village, Agrarian Problems, and Food Supplies has been markedly more united in its opposition to land reform that would threaten the existing farms' control over arable land than its all-union analog.[8]

In June 1990, the First Russian Congress of People's Deputies resolved that the issue of revitalizing the countryside and improving agricultural productivity should be examined at a special session of the Congress. Many of the deputies supported the resolution because they expected to use the session as a wedge to further increase government subsidies to the countryside. They argued that they should be allowed to charge the state whatever they wished for their produce, even as they expected that state subsidies for their inputs and subsidies for consumers to be continued. This is the most plausible reading of RSFSR Agrarian Committee Chairman Valentin Agafonov's critical support of the Iavlinskii economic reform plan at a session of the RSFSR Supreme Soviet the day after the deputies had demanded wider publicity be given to a resolution allowing farms to sell more of their produce to the general population.[9]

The Second RSFSR Congress of People's Deputies, called as a result of the First-Congress's resolution, opened on 27 November 1990. Its initial agenda included just two main items: land reform and overall economic stabilization and reform.[10] The Law on Land Reform explicitly abolished the state monopoly on landownership in the Russian Federation, providing that a land division (*nadelenie*) would occur, with individuals and all types of legal entities able to hold land on lease directly from the local soviet or from collective or state farms, with lifetime use-rights, or as private property with the right to resell only to the state. Land denationalization was to be done by the local soviets, the RSFSR State Committee on Land Reform (*Goskomzem*), the Ministry of Agriculture and Food Supplies, and the Ministry of Forestry, 'with the participation of other interested ministries and departments, *Goskomzem*, specifically created to carry out the reform on the basis of land-use administrations in the Ministry of Agriculture and headed by the former rector of the Institute of Land Surveyors, Viktor Khlystun, was to be the lead agency in this work.[11]

Since the farm managers and their allies in Parliament controlled the existing farms and other institutions in the countryside, few of them had any objection to taking control of the nation's farmland, a change which reinforced their own power and further freed them from domination by the state. The Congress amended Article 12 of the Russian Constitution to give state farm property to the labor collectives, effectively transforming them into collective farms (Uzun, 1993). So ended the legal distinction between state farms (sovkhoz) and collective farms (kolkhoz) that had existed since the 1920s, although it had become almost purely formal since all collective farms were ordered to introduce guaranteed wages and pensions in the 1960s.[12]

The real issue, however, was not formal ownership of the land and production facilities, but their control. The collective farms effectively occupied all the country's arable land. Inputs and equipment could be gotten only from monopoly suppliers legally permitted to sell only to economic entities with an account in the state agricultural bank – collective and state farms. The standard farm rules provided that members or families wishing to leave the farm had no right to a share of the collective assets or farmland, even though the collective farms, as 'cooperatives', had been created in the 1930s by the 'voluntary' union of peasant lands and equipment. Pensions and other social benefits were also administered by the farms for their members; therefore, leaving the farm also meant losing one's retirement income. Indeed, until the late 1960s, peasants were not even allowed to hold their own internal passports, the basic Soviet identity document without which it was difficult to travel and impossible to obtain legal employment or housing off the farm.

The basic thrust of the reform forces, therefore, was not the denationalization of land but providing a way for families to secede from the large farms with a share of the farm's land and production assets to set up their own family farms. They would have full property rights, including the right to free purchase and sale, over the production assets they received, but would not necessarily own the land. The key legislation in the package of measures prepared for the Congress was the Law on the Peasant Farm which gave individuals and families the right to leave the collective and state farms with a share of the communal land and assets, set up their own independent farms, and organize associations to provide services or even to work the land in common. A small group of agricultural economists organized by Vladimir Bashmachnikov, then a staff member in the CPSU Central Committee's Socioeconomic Policy Department, wrote the original Law on the Peasant Farm.[13] Their draft first appeared in early July 1990 (Bashmachnikov et al., 1990).

The peasant farm law provided that a separate 'entitlement' of land (*uslovnaia zemel'naia dolia*) and nonland assets (*uslovnyi imushchestvennyi pai*) should be determined for each adult on the farm, including retirees. Land entitlements were to be equal in size. The size of each nonland asset entitlement depended on how long the individual had worked on the farm and the total amount he or she had earned.[14] Entitlements were to be determined for the whole farm, but neither land nor nonland assets were actually to be generally distributed unless the farm voted to dissolve itself, creating an 'association of peasant farms' in its place. If the farm did not vote to liquidate completely, individuals and families were to have the right to receive physical shares on demand, however.

This right to leave with a share of farmland and assets was hotly contested before and during the Congress. The Law on the Peasant Farm was eventually passed, giving the right to obtain physical shares of land and assets on demand, but with the determination of what land and what physical items would be given out as the share left to the farm's general meeting. There have been widespread reports of marathon meetings and bitter wrangles as peasants fight over who should receive what physical assets.[15]

Since everyone had worked to create the national wealth that was being redistributed, everyone on the farm had long since earned their shares. Moreover, these land and property shares would be the major source of income for former farm members too old to work. Since in developed Western agriculture there are far more people involved in serving the farmers than there are people involved actually in plowing the land and milking the cows, the size problem did not bother supporters of reform. Let the pensioners, the teachers, and the other nonfarmers either lease or sell their land shares to individuals who intended to work the land. By this process of redistribution, the needs of the elderly and of the young for a steady income, formerly provided by the kolkhoz from its own funds, would be met, and commercially viable farms would be assembled.

The RSFSR Supreme Soviet refused to confirm the Law on the Peasant Farm unless the introduction of free purchase and sale of agricultural land was delayed. So the land reform legislation included a ten-year waiting period from the moment the land was acquired during which the plot could be sold only to the local soviet.[16] This measure was justified by fears that all the land shares would be bought up cheaply by urban speculators. This 'moratorium', and a provision for amending the law either by a vote of the Congress of People's Deputies or by a national referendum, were added to the Russian Federation Constitution at the Congress.[17]

The land-sales moratorium created an enormous land-assembly problem for would-be family farmers since it made it much more difficult for them to buy or purchase shares from other former farm members. The moratorium was a compromise forced by some deputies ideologically opposed to private landownership (Emel'ianov, 1993). Supporters of the Peasant Farm Law assumed that the moratorium was relatively harmless. It would, they apparently thought, be fairly easy to amend the Constitution and remove the moratorium. Just amending the existing Constitution to allow land sales turned out to be far more difficult than the reformers expected. Only the new basic law adopted at the 12 December 1993 referendum finally did away with the constitutional prohibition. However, even then a functioning land market did not really emerge.

The reformers made a second compromise at the Second Congress of People's Deputies in December 1990. The Congress had been called in order to improve conditions in the agricultural sector and, implicitly, to demand more state subsidies. The Congress accordingly passed a motherhood-and-apple-pie general statement on agrarian reform. This Program for the Revival of the Russian Countryside included the outlandish promise that an amount equal to 15 percent of the country's annual national income would be spent on agriculture and rural development.[18] One knowledgeable Russian explained this promise away in an interview by saying that 'there are laws that you have to pass that you know can't ever be implemented'. The law certainly has not been put into effect, and the agrarian lobby has repeatedly screamed betrayal because the Russian government has failed to provide legally obligated investment funds.[19] In retrospect, the tactic may be understandable, but it has helped contribute to a sense that the letter of the law does not matter and that uncomfortable legislation need not be obeyed which has hardly contributed to the country's stability.

The provisions for farm division in the Law on the Peasant Farm were voluntary. But, there was a struggle at the Second RSFSR Congress about granting the right to leave the farms, and that Congress' resolution on the land reform program, provided that the reform would be generalized at a second stage. In other words, the law's provisions would be generally applied.[20] Unprofitable and low-profit farms were required to reorganize in 1991 (Ministry of Agriculture and Food Supplies, 1991). At the end of 1991, Yeltsin issued a decree requiring that all farmland be denationalized, becoming the property of the farmers by the end of March 1992. All farms were to reorganize and recharter, completing that process by the end of 1992.[21] A subsequent Council of Ministers resolution provided that each collective farm had to choose one of four options for reorganizing.[22] By the end of 1992, about 80 percent of all farms had reorganized. By the time the (extended) deadline expired in March 1993, all collective and state farms had reorganized, most becoming some kind of joint-property farm (Craumer, 1994). Although this meant little or no change in day-to-day farm work, and the peasants never saw their physical shares of land and capital assets, completion of the registration process meant that the Russian state no longer held title to the farmland. It had been denationalized, if not quite privatized.

The large farms are currently beginning to be restructured, often with substantial foreign aid. However, the emerging entities generally are smaller collectives, not individual farms. Until the problems of what to do with the very large elderly rural population dependent on large farms for support and the associated issue of the distribution of 'social assets' (roads, hospitals, schools, housing, utilities, etc.) supported by the farms are resolved, farm restructuring cannot go very far. Nor will farming become an attractive business until macroeconomic stabilization is largely achieved.[23]

Will there be a restitution of agricultural land?

Since these basic laws were put into place, land and property entitlements have been determined for most farm members and pensioners. A string of presidential decrees intended to allow free resales of land have been adopted and disputed by the Parliament. By early 1996, little progress towards an agricultural land market had been made. Even that small progress was threatened by the possibility of a victory in the June 1996 Russian presidential elections by the Communist Party of the Russian Federation, which included in its platform the renationalization of all agricultural land.

There are scattered suggestions that restitution should be made. New York Times reporter Serge Schmemann, heir of a noble family, reported that his visit to the family's former holdings led to rumors that he might be taking it back (Schmemann, 1991, 1992). In a few cases, victims of Stalinist repression have won some property back (Kireev, 1995).

Even if the Communists do not carry out their threat to undo the reforms entirely, a general restitution is unlikely. Although some small restitution has been made to individual religious institutions, the old nobility will not retrieve their land. Organizations of descendants of prerevolutionary nobles have emerged since 1991, but their claims on their old estates are not likely to be taken seriously by any conceivable Russian government. Unlike the situation in some other ex-Communist states, where explicit land reforms eliminated large estates and gave the land to farmers after World War I (the Baltic States) or World War II (Poland), post-1917 changes in land tenure in Russia eliminated the old landlord class without giving their land to individual owners. Although some peasants may still know where their land was before 1930, a general attempt to return it to those who held it in, say, 1928, could never be carried through because of the lack of documentation, the loss of population, and the complications introduced by communal tenure. Nor, after so much time, does there seem to be much political support for restoring land to peasants' heirs, although some monetary compensation to the victims of Stalinism, including victims of collectivization, has been made.

Current land property rights are based on legal acts that descend from Soviet times. The Russian Federation has asserted that it is the legal heir of both the Russian Soviet Federated Socialist Republic and the Union of Soviet Socialist Republics. This means that there is no 'past' for Russian landownership to return to. Rather, the principle of 'land to the tillers' implicit in the 1991 farm reorganization is probably the best the reform designers could have created. Making that reform work is still a formidable task, and one that is far from accomplished.

Notes

1 For general description, see Robinson (1967).
2 On the regime's lack of control over collectivization and industrialization, see Narkiewicz (1966, 1968); Lewin (1976, 1977).
3 Women often took the lead in these disturbances. See Viola (1986).
4 The classic western attempts to define 'kulak' is Lewin (1966).
5 This argument is made by Viola (1986).

6   'Obrashchenie Ks'ezdu Narodnykh Deputatov SSSR', *Sel'skaia Zhizn'*, 1 June 1989, p. 1.

7   A later meeting, held in the 'Rossiia' hotel, attracted more than 200 participants (Baklanov, 1990).

8   I base this judgment on interviews conducted with members of the committee and others 15-20 October 1990 in Moscow. Compare Nikulina (1990).

9   'Nadezhda na Rynok', *Sovetskaia Rossiia*, 11 September 1990, p. 2, and the introduction to 'Postanovlenie Soveta Ministrov RSFSR: O Rasshirenii Prav Proizvoditelei Skoroportiashcheisia Sel'skokhoziaistvennoi Produktsii na ee Realizatsiiu za Nalichnyi Raschet i Ispol'zovanie Poluchennykh Denezhnykh Sredstv', ibid., p. 1.

10 'Postanovlenie S'ezda Narodnykh Rossiiskoi Sovetskoi Federativnoi Sotsialisticheskoi Respubliki: O Povestke Dnia Vtorogo (Vneocherednogo) S'ezda Narodnykh Deputatov RSFSR', 27 November 1990, p. 9 in *Zakony i Postanovleniia, Priniatye Vtorym (Vneocherednym) S'ezdom Narodnykh Deputatov RSFSR, 27 noiabria-15 dekabria 1990 goda* (Moscow: Izdanie Verkhobnogo Soveta RSFSR, 1991).

11 'Zakon Rossiskoi Sovetskoi Federativnoi Sotsialisticheskoi Respubliki S Izmeneniiami i Dopolneniiami, Vnesennymi Zakonom RSFSR ot 27 dekabria 1990 goda: O Zemel'noi Reforme (Law of the RSFSR with Amendments and Additions, Made in the Law on 27 December 1990: On Land Reform)', pp. 19-24, in Rossiisko-Amerikanskii universitet (1992). On Goskomzem's establishment, see 'Sovet Ministrov RSFSR Postanovlenie: Voprosy Gosudarstvennogo Komiteta RSFSR po Zemel'noi Reforme (RSFSR Council of Ministers' Resolution: Matters of the RSFSR State Committee on Land Reform)', No. 466, 25 October 1990, pp. 99-101 in *Kak Poluchit' Zemliiu?*

12 Not all state farms accepted ownership of their assets from the state, however, leading to later legislation regulating such 'unreconstructed' farms.

13 Uzun credits Bashmachnikov with initiating the drafting work. Author's interview.

14 The 'Statute' on kolkhoz and sovkhoz privatization adopted almost two years later changed these provisions by requiring that land shares be equal for everyone and allowing the farm general meeting to exclude workers in the 'social sphere' (schools, hospitals, etc.) from receiving a property share (Rossiiskie vest, 1990).

15 For instance, peasants on the 'Belaia dacha' kolkhoz, Glinka raion, Smolensk oblast', which the author visited in November 1993, had spent two years attempting to divide up the farm. The militia had been called in several times to break up fights over the division.

16 'Postanovlenie S'ezda Narodnykh Deputatov RSFSR: O Programme Vozrozhdeniia Rossiiskoi Derevni i Razvitiia Agropromyshlennogo Kompleksa [Resolution of the RSFSR Congress of People's Deputies: On the Program for the Revival of the Russian Countryside and the Development of the Agroindustrial Complex]', *Sovetskaia Rossiia*, 5 December 1990, p. 3.

17 Article 12, paragraph 3 of the Russian Federation Constitution. *Konstitutsiia (Osnovoi zakon) Rossiiskoi Federatsii Rossii* (Moscow: Izdanie Verkhovnogo Soveta Rossiiskoi Federatsii, 1992), p. 7.

18 'Postanovlenie S'ezda Narodnykh Deputatov RSFSR: O Programme Vozrozhdeniia Rossiiskoi Derevni i Razvitiia Agropromyshlennogo Kompleksa [Resolution of the Congress of People's Deputies of the RSFSR: On the Program for the Revival of the Russian Countryside and the Development of the Agroindustrial Complex]', *Sovetskaia Rossiia*, 5 December 1990, p. 3.

19 The Parliamentary Agrarian Committee, which worked out and verified the implementation of the laws on the social development of the countryside and 'On the priority supply of the agro-industrial with material-technical resources' certainly took those laws as seriously as they took the Law on the peasant Farm. For a complaint about the laws' non-fulfillment, see N. Radugin, 'Ternistyi Put' k Vozrozhdeniiu Sela [The Difficult Path to Revival of the Village]', *Zemlia i Liudi*, No. 13, 27 March 1992, p. 3.

20 RSFSR Law on Land Reform.

21 'Ukaz Prezidenta Rossiiskoi Federatsii: O Neotlozhnykh Merakh po Osushchestvleniiu Zemel'noi Reformy v RSFSR [Decree of the President of the Russian Federation: On Immediate Measures to Realize the Land Reform in the RSFSR]', *Rossiiskaia gazeta*, 31 December 1991, p. 3.

22 'Postanovlenie Pravitel'stva Rossiiskoi Federatsii: O Poriadke Reorganizatsii Kolkhozov i Sovkhozov, 19 December 1991' and 'Rekomendatsii po Reorganizatsii Kolkhozov i Sovkhozov', both in Kalinin (1992).

23 For recent surveys, see Part II, sections 1 and 4 of OECD (1995), and OECD (1996).

References

Atkinson, D. (1983), *The End of the Russian Land Commune 1905-1930*, Stanford University Press: Stanford.

Baklanov, I. (1990), 'Za Prioritet Selu', *Sel'skaia Zhizn'*, 17 May, p. 2.

Bashmachnikov, V., Kharitonov, N., Uzun, V., Vershinin, V., Kaiiali, Z. Beliaeva, Z., Ustiukova, V., Kadyrov, T., Zakharov, I., Obushenkov, N.

(1990), 'Proekt: Zakon Rossiiskoi Sovetskoi Federativnoi Sotsialistichekoi Respubliki: O Krest'ianskom Khoziaistve (Draft: Law of the Russian Soviet Federated Socialist Republic: On the Peasant Farm)', *Ekonomika I Zhizn'*, No. 28, July, pp. 15-17.

Bloch, M. (1966), *French Rural History: An Essay on its Basic Characteristics*, University of California Press: Berkeley.

Boikova T. and Virkunen, V. (1990), 'Zakon o Zemle Priniat!', *Sel'skaia Zhizn'*, 1 March , p. 1.

Conquest, R. (1986), *The Harvest of Sorrow: Soviet Collectivization and the Terror-Famine,* Oxford University Press: New York.

Craumer, P. R. (1994), 'Regional Patterns of Agricultural Reform in Russia', *Post-Soviet Geography*, Vol. 35, No. 6, June, pp. 329-351.

Emel'ianov, A. (1993), 'Do not do it Wrong, Russia! In What Kind of 'Wrapper' is the Idea of a Referendum on the Land Question Being Presented, and What Does it in Fact Contain?', *Sel'skaia Zhizn'*, 4 February, pp. 1-2, as translated in FBIS Daily Report: Central Eurasia, No. 20, 25 February 1993, pp. 64-67.

Emmons, T. (1991), 'Recent Developments on the Historical Front: Excerpts from an Interview with Viktor Petrovich Danilov', *Slavic Review*, Vol. 50, No. 1, Spring, pp. 150-156.

Grant, S. A. (1976), '*Obshchina* and *Mir*', *Slavic Review*, Vol. 35, No. 4, December, pp. 636-651.

Haimson, L. H. (1988) 'The Problem of Social Identities in Early Twentieth Century Russia', *Slavic Review*, Vol. 47, No. 1, Spring, pp. 1-20.

Ivnitskii, N. (1987), 'Oglianut'sia v Razdum'e', *Sel'skaia Nov'*, No. 12, December, pp. 14-17.

Karcz, J. F. (1979), 'Thoughts on the Grain Problem' and 'Back on the Grain Front', in Wright, A. W. (ed.), *The Economics of Communist Agriculture: Selected Papers*, International Development Institute: Bloomington.

Kalinin, A. A. (1992) (ed.), *Agrarnaia Reforma v Rossii: Dokumenty i Mterialy*, Respublika: Moscow.

Keep, J. L. H. (1976), *The Russian Revolution: A Study in Mass Mobilization*, W.W. Norton and Company: New York.

Kireev, N. (1995), 'Zhizn' Kk ona est: Kto Tut Vremennyi, Osvobozhdai Dom. Priekhal Ego Khoziain', *Rossiiskaia Gazeta*, 27 December, p. 2.

Konovalova, I. (1989), 'Akademik V.A. Tikhonov: Zhit' Bez Illiuzii', *Ogonek*, No. 36, September, p. 2.

Lewin, M. (1965), 'The Immediate Background of Soviet Collectivization', *Soviet Studies*, Vol. 17, No. 2, October, pp. 162-197.

Lewin, M. (1966), 'Who was the Soviet Kulak?', *Soviet Studies*, Vol. 18, No. 2, October, pp. 188-212.

Lewin, M. (1968), *Russian Peasants and Soviet Power: A Study of Collectivization*, W.W. Norton: New York.

Lewin, M. (1976), 'Society and the Stalinist State in the Period of the Five Year Plans', *Social History*, No. 2, May, pp. 139-175.

Lewin, M. (1977), 'The Social Background of Stalinism', in Tucker, R. C. (ed.), *Stalinism: Essays in Historical Interpretation*, W.W. Norton: New York.

Lewin, M. (1985), 'Customary Law and Rural Society', *Russian Review*, Vol. 44, pp. 1-19.

Literaturnaia gazeta (1987), 'LG'v Derevne: Tak Kuda zhe nas Zovut: Akademik VASKhNIL V.A. Tikhonov i Obozrevatel' 'LG' Kapitolina Kozhevnikova Obsuzhdaiut Polemicheskie Mis'ma Chitatelei', No. 15, 8 April, p. 12.

Male, D. J. (1971), *Russian Peasant Organization before Collectivization: A Study of Commune and Gathering, 1925-1930*, Cambridge University Press: Cambridge.

Matossian, M. (1968), 'The Peasant Way of Life', in Vucinich, W. S. (ed.), *The Peasant in Nineteenth-Century Russia*, Stanford University Press: Stanford.

Mikhailov, V. (1990), 'Krest'ianskii Nakaz', *Sovetskaia Rossiia*, 22 April.

Millar, J. R. (1982), 'Collectivization and Its Consequences: A New Look', *Russian Review*, Vol. 41, No. 1, January, pp. 60-67.

Ministry of Agriculture and Food Supplies (RSFSR) (1991), 'O Preobrazovanii Ubytochnykh i Nizkorentabel'nykh Kolkhozov i Sovkhozov v Assotsiatsii Krest'ianskikh Khoziaistv, Kooperativov i Malykh Predpriiatii [On the Transformation of Unprofitable and Low-Profitability Collective and State Farms into Associations of Peasant Farms, Cooperatives and Small Businesses]', 5 May.

Mironov, B. (1985), 'The Russian Peasant Commune After the Reforms of the 1860s', *Slavic Review*, Vol. 44, No. 3, Fall, pp. 438-467.

Narkiewicz, O. A. (1966), 'Stalin, War Communism and Collectivization', *Soviet Studies*, Vol. 18, No. 1, July, pp. 20-37.

Narkiewicz, O. A. (1968), 'Soviet Administration and the Grain Crisis of 1927-28', *Soviet Studies*, Vol. 20, No. 2, October, pp. 235-241.

Nemakov, N. I. (1966), *Kommunisticheskaia Partiia - Organizator Massovogo Kolkhoznogo Dvizheniia: 1929-1932*, Izdatel'stvo Moskovskogo Universiteta: Moscow.

Nikulina, N. (1990), 'Na Sessii Verkhovnogo Soveta RSFSR: Sverim Pozitsii!', *Sel'skaia Zhizn'*, 4 October, p. 2.

OECD (1995), *Agricultural Policies, Markets and Trade in the Central and East European Countries, Selected New Independent States, Mongolia and China: Monitoring and Outlook 1995*, OECD: Paris.

OECD (1996), *Agricultural Policies, Markets and Trade in the Economies in Transition: Monitoring and Evaluation 1996*, OECD: Paris.

Pallot, J. (1984), '*Khutora* and *Otruba* in Stolypin's Program of Farm Individualization', *Slavic Review*, Vol. 42, No. 2, Summer, pp. 242-256.

Petrakov, E. (1990), 'Soveshchaiutsia Deputaty', *Sel'skaia Zhizn'*, 22 April.

Robinson, G. T. (1967), *Rural Russia under the Old Regime*, University of California Press: Berkeley.

Ronina, G. (1987), 'Oglianut'sia v Razdum'e', '*Sel'skaia Nov'*, No. 12, December, pp. 14-17.

Rossiisko-Amerikanskii universitet (1992), *Kak Poluchit'zemliu? Sbornik Osnovnykh Dekumentov po Zemel'noi Reforme v Rossii*, Joint Venture 'Lexica': Moscow.

Rossiiskie vest (1992), 'Polozhenie o Reorganizatskii Kolkhozov, Sovkhozov I Privatizatsii Gosudarstvennykh Sel'skokhoziaistvennykh Predpriiatii', 22 September.

Schmemann, S. (1991), 'Once a Rich Farm, Now a Soviet Casualty', *New York Times*, 17 November, pp. a1, a6.

Schmemann, S. (1992), 'Fears Deep as Russia's Snow, but Poetry, Too', *New York Times*, 17 February, pp. a1, a6.

Taniuchi, Y. (1981), 'A Note on the Ural-Siberian Method', *Soviet Studies*, Vol. 33, No. 4, October.

Uzun, V. I. (1993), 'Last Month for a Peasant to Decide if He Wishes to Become a Landowner or to Reject this Right', *Izvestiia*, 13 January, p. 4, as translated in FBIS-USR, No. 20, 25 February 1993, pp. 57-58.

Viola, L. (1986), '*Bab'i Bunty* and Peasant Women's Protest During Collectivization', *Russian Review*, Vol. 45, pp. 23-42.

Viola, L. (1986), 'The Case of Krasnyi Meliorator or 'How the Kulak Grows Into Socialism', *Soviet Studies*, Vol. 38, No. 4, October, pp. 508-529.

Watters, F. M. (1968), 'The Peasant and the Village Commune', in Vucinich, W. S. (ed.), *The Peasant in Nineteenth-Century Russia*, Stanford University Press: Stanford.

Zelenin, I. E. (1989), 'O Nekotorykh 'Belykh piatnakh' Zavershaiushego Etapa Sploshnoi Kollektivizatsii', *Istoriia SSSR*, No. 2, March-April, pp. 3-19.

12 Privatization of Slovenian agriculture: Process and politics

Štefan Bojnec and Johan F. M. Swinnen[1]

Introduction

Political factors caused the nationalization of most of Slovenia's economy after World War II, and in recent years political factors have determined the recent process of privatization in Slovenia. The purpose of this chapter is to analyze the impact of those political factors and to consider as well the historical and economic influences on the privatization of agriculture in Slovenia.

Slovenia was part of the former Yugoslavia. Like Poland, former Yugoslavia was a socialist country with a noncollectivized agriculture. Most land was privately owned and used privately by peasants. But there was also an important state sector in agriculture, usually referred to as the 'social' sector.[2] Furthermore, institutional limitations were imposed on private farms, including regulatory and policy measures unfavorable for private farmers.

Agriculture in Slovenia contributed less than 5 percent to gross domestic product by the end of the 1980s. However, the share of agriculture in overall employment was around 10 percent. The majority of those employed in agriculture were in small-scale private peasant agriculture. In Slovenia, natural conditions are generally less favorable for crop production, and the rural areas are dominated by forests and grasslands. Still, Slovenia was around 90 percent self-sufficient in food products before the reforms. A significant share of animal feed was imported. The main export products were milk, poultry meat, potatoes, and hops (Bojnec, 1994).

This chapter focuses on the privatization process in general and on land reform and the restructuring of agricultural ownership in particular. The next section describes the historical and political events that led to Slovenia's independence and analyzes political events and institutional changes during the transition to democracy and a market economy. Then we discuss the policy options for the privatization process and the political constraints. In the fourth

339

section we discuss the collectivization and nationalization of agriculture under the old regime and the recent progress and problems of restitution of agricultural land and forests through the Fund of Agricultural Land and Forests (FALF). Finally, we draw some conclusions about the political economy of Slovenia's agricultural privatization process.

An overview of Slovenia's political developments

Slovenian territory came under the control of the Habsburg Empire in the thirteenth century and remained under Habsburg rule for about eight centuries. The Slovenian population consisted mostly of South Slavs with their own language and West European cultural influence. These people had been caught between movements in Central and South Europe and the Balkan States (Vodopivec, 1992). The Austro-Hungarian Monarchy collapsed after World War I, and a new state, the Kingdom of Serbs, Croats, and Slovenes – later called Yugoslavia emerged in 1918. Originally, the people of Yugoslavia were mainly the South Slavs of the former Kingdom of Serbia and of the Austro-Hungarian Monarchy. There were cultural, economic, and social differences between people of the former Austro-Hungarian Monarchy and those of the Ottoman Empire. During World War II, Yugoslavia collapsed after a couple days of German attacks. Slovenia was divided among Germany, Italy, and Hungary. After World War II, Slovenia became one of six constituent republics of the new Communist Yugoslavia. Slovenia's population is ethnically largely homogeneous: about 88 percent of Slovenia's inhabitants are of Slovene origin. The main religion is Roman Catholicism.

Slovenia held its first multiparty parliamentary and presidential elections in April 1990 while it was still part of Communist Yugoslavia with the Yugoslav People's Army still present in Slovenia. The parliamentary elections were won by the Democratic United Opposition of Slovenia (DEMOS) coalition with 52.9 percent of the seats (table 12.1). This reflected the result of the anti-Communist sentiments among voters and the success of DEMOS in the countryside and in small towns. DEMOS was a coalition of six center-right and center-left parties. The main parties in DEMOS were the Slovenian Christian Democrats (SKD) and the Slovenian Farmers Alliance (SKZ)[3]. The SKZ represented private family farmers and advocated radical land reform, privatization, and restitution. On the other side, three parties emerged from the former Communist Yugoslav regime to form the opposition against DEMOS: the League of Communists of Slovenia-Party of Democratic Renewal (ZKS-SDP), the League of Socialist Youth of Slovenia-Liberal Party (ZSMS-LS), and the Socialist Alliance of Slovenia-Socialist Alliance of

Working People (SZS-SZDL). All claimed to be independent from similar organizations in former Yugoslavia.

Table 12.1
Results of the 1990 Slovenian parliamentary elections

Proposer	Seats
a. Socio-Political Chamber	(total number of seats: 80)
DEMOS	47
SKD	11
SKZ	11
SDZ	8
ZELENI	8
SDZS	6
SOS	3
ZKS-SDP	14
ZSMS-LS	12
SZS-SZDL	5
Community of Italians	1
Community of Hungarians	1
b. Chamber of the Municipalities	(total number of seats: 80)
DEMOS	51
ZKS-SDP	16
ZSMS-LS	5
SZS-SZDL	5
Local Community	1
Community of Italians	1
Community of Hungarians	1
c. Chamber of the Associated Labor	(total number of seats: 80)
DEMOS	29
Enterprises, Societies, and Associations	20
ZSMS-LS	9
Slovenian Trade Unions	7
Chamber of Economy	7
ZKS-SDP	5
SZS-SZDL	3

Source: Statistical Yearbook of Slovenia (SY SLO), 1992, p. 93, and SY SLO, 1993, p. 77.

Slovenia's parliamentary system was inherited from Communist-era Yugoslavia (Andrejevich, 1991). The Slovenian Parliament had three 80-member chambers: the Chamber of Associated Labor, the Chamber of Municipalities, and the Socio-Political Chamber. A majority of votes in each of the three chambers of the National Assembly was needed for parliamentary decisions. This institutional setting created an important constraint on possible reforms because anyone of the parliamentary chambers could block a proposal. This was especially important after the 1990 election because DEMOS did not obtain a majority in the Chamber of Associated Labor.

Lojze Peterle, president of the SKD, was elected Slovenia's prime minister by the three chambers of the 240-seat Slovenian Parliament on 16 May 1990. Of 23 portfolio ministers 3 were from the former League of Communists (the ZKS-SDP), and 1 was from the opposition ZSMS-LS. Another 5 seats of the new government were held by independents. The SKZ and SKD were the largest parties within the government and the parliamentary DEMOS coalition. Joze Osterc of the SKZ became Minister for Agriculture, Forestry, and Food. Private peasants, the people most dominant in Slovenia's agriculture, had high expectations. They expected help with family farm development as well as full restitution of lost property rights and compensation for damages and discrimination caused by the former Communist regime, especially during the first two decades after World War II.

Elections were also held for the 5-member State Presidency of Slovenia. These elections preserved the former Communists' majority in the State Presidency: Communists and Socialists retained 3 of the 5 seats. Milan Kucan, candidate of the ZKS-SDP and SZS-SZDL, became president (Andrejevich, 1990a). After the elections, the Slovenian Parliament and government were therefore dominated by the anti-Communist coalition while the State Presidency was controlled by the ex-Communist parties.

Between 1990 and the beginning of October 1991, former Yugoslav and Slovenian economic, institutional, and political systems coexisted. The federal Yugoslav government of Prime Minister Ante Markovic controlled most of the economy. The Yugoslav expansionary monetary policy after mid-1990 and the federal legislation for privatization and restructuring of social enterprises had an important impact on Slovenia's economic performance.

On 25 June 1991 Slovenia declared its independence. Slovenia's movement for independence was initiated by the DEMOS coalition and supported by all major political parties. On 7 July 1991 the Brioni Peace Treaty was announced, in which Slovenia agreed to suspend its independence for three months. Slovenia became for the first time fully independent on 8 October 1991, when it also introduced its own currency.

The new Slovenian political leaders were blamed by the former Communists and the media for their lack of political, organizational and professional experience. The government was criticized for not having a comprehensive economic reform program, especially for privatization. Criticism increased as Slovenia's economic situation worsened, with a decline in the standard of living, a rise in poverty and unemployment, a drop in production, and increased business losses (Andrejevich, 1991). This also stirred trouble within the DEMOS coalition. The coalition fell apart in December 1991 because of internal disagreements.

In response to discontent shown toward the government, including a series of strikes organized at the beginning of 1992, three votes of confidence for Peterle's government were held. The third vote, on 22 April 1992, was successful in bringing down Peterle's government because the moderate parties no longer supported him.

In May 1992 Janez Drnovsek, the leader of the Liberal Democratic Party (LDS), formerly the ZSMS-LS, formed a center-left coalition government of six parties (Andrejevich, 1992).

The first Drnovsek government focused on a one-year economic program of market reforms and privatization. Macroeconomic policy to reduce inflation, fiscal and banking reform, privatization, and the reorganization of company management were given priority up to the elections in December 1992. Compared with the DEMOS government, the Drnovsek government argued for less radical privatization and restitution policies. Strong controversies arose between the Drnovsek government and the peasant party SKZ, which argued for a radical restitution process and the liquidation of state farms, both of which were opposed by the Drnovsek government.

The Drnovsek government lasted only seven months. In December 1992, Slovenia held its first post-independence elections to determine the 90 seats of the lower chamber (the National Assembly) and the 40 seats of the State Council, the upper chamber of the Slovenian State Parliament. The Slovenian State Presidency was replaced by the State Council, a supervisory body with the opportunity to veto laws proposed by the National Assembly. The State Council was divided among various local, professional, and economic interests: 22 seats went to representatives of municipality interests, and the remaining 18 seats went to representatives of farmers, industry, and self-employed professionals. The elections were based on a system of proportional representation, with at least 3 percent of the vote required for a seat in the Parliament.

Table 12.2 presents the election results for the 88 seats in the lower chamber of the National Assembly (the remaining 2 seats went automatically to the Community of Italians and the Community of Hungarians).[4] No single party won a majority in the National Assembly. The LDS got most of the seats (22 seats). Its popularity was strengthened in the urban and industrial centers (Andrejevich, 1992), where it had ties to the management of state companies and financial institutions as well as to reform-minded Communists. The Unity List (ZL), also headed by former Communists, got 14 seats. Due to internal personal divisions, the peasant party SKZ split into the Slovenian People's Party (SLS), which represented peasants interests and won 10 seats. Those who did not become SLS members joined the SKD, which won 15 seats. The Slovenian National Party (SNS), which was established after a split in the former SDZ, earned 12 seats.

Table 12.2
Results of the National Assembly elections in December 1992

Party	Total number of seats: 90
LDS - former ZSMS-LS	22
SKD	15
ZL - former ZKS-SDP	14
SNS	12
SLS - former SKZ	10
DEMOKRATI - former SDZ	6
ZELENI	5
SDSS - former SDZS	4
Community of Italians	1
Community of Hungarians	1

Source: SY SLO, 1993, p. 78.

After the December 1992 elections, a coalition of national unity supported a new government under Janez Drnovsek of the LDS. The SKD's 3 ministers included Joze Osterc, who after his move from the SKZ to the SKD again became Minister for Agriculture, Food and Forestry. The SLS remained in the opposition.

The privatization laws

The last federal government of former Yugoslavia, under Prime Minister Markovic, began a 'shock therapy' macroeconomic program on 1 January 1990. It included an anti-inflation program, privatization, and restructuring (including bankruptcy and liquidation) of enterprises as well as laying off workers. The process of privatization was initiated by the former Yugoslav Law on Social Capital (LSC) in 1990.[5] It tried to reform ownership rights for the creation of a 'market socialism'. The LSC and its amendment in 1990 opened the door for spontaneous and wild privatization, which was carried out by insiders and mainly benefited managers of state enterprises and representatives of ex-Communist institutions.[6]

Privatization and restitution of property that had been nationalized and confiscated under the Communist regime was an important part of the DEMOS coalition's political program. Compensation to owners of expropriated and confiscated property was seen both as an action of correcting past injustices and as part of the general privatization process. However, the priorities and the means for compensating former owners and their heirs was hotly debated: should one compensate former owners in-kind (e.g., for agricultural land and forests, flats and buildings, art and similar property), or when restitution in-kind is impossible, should one compensate with property of comparable value (in the case of land) with shares of privatized enterprises, or with government securities?[7]

The Law on Denationalization, proposed by the DEMOS government and adopted by Parliament in November 1991,[8] was the first important privatization law in Slovenia. It dealt with the restitution of most property nationalized and confiscated by the Communist regime. 'Denationalization' refers to reprivatization of nationalized and confiscated properties to former owners through restitution in real boundaries or through compensation in the form of comparable property or securities. The Law on Denationalization specified conditions under which citizens could apply for the return of confiscated property. Former owners were relatively well organized from the beginning. Restitution of small agricultural properties was an especially sensitive issue for the former SKZ, one of the most important groups within the DEMOS coalition at the time, and one of the first Slovenian opposition parties. However, the DEMOS coalition did not control all chambers of Parliament and the final Law on Denationalization was a compromise bill on land restitution. It included the concept of 'co-ownership on land' for former owners when land was currently in use by the larger land units or plantations. It also allowed for an 'adjustment period' on land operation by the state farms.

Privatization of cooperatives was regulated by the Law on Cooperatives, which was passed in March 1992 and amended in February 1993. This law dealt not only with agricultural cooperatives but also with other cooperatives (e.g., housing, retail trade, etc.). Agricultural cooperatives in Slovenia were not 'classical' socialist collective farms like those found in most of the CEECs. The process of agricultural collectivization was abandoned in 1953, and after the mid-1960s no classical socialist collective farms existed. The agricultural cooperatives were not important in terms of land use. However, they provided marketing, extension services, and credit to the private peasants. Agricultural cooperatives, subject to privatization, had contracts with private peasants for the supply of agricultural inputs and the procurement of peasants' agricultural output. After the mid-1970s the savings and loan services of agricultural cooperatives played a significant role in providing credits to those private peasants who cooperated with the state sector. The agricultural cooperatives transformed themselves according to the new Law on Cooperatives to become the legal property of private peasants. Private peasants also established new and specialized cooperatives (e.g., for wine, milk).

Political disagreements regarding the Law on Privatization, the main privatization law, delayed the implementation of all the other reprivatization programs with the exception of privatizing flats and apartments. Restitution of land was delayed due to disputes over the organization of an institution to carry out the land restitution by transferring land from state farms to their former owners. No significant progress was made in legal privatization for about two years as the government and Parliament debated different privatization proposals (Jones, 1992; Stiblar, 1992; Pleskovic and Sachs, 1994). (This created an environment for spontaneous and wild privatization.) Most of the discussion was on how to divide 'social capital' and very rarely on how to improve efficiency. Among the approaches and methods of privatization discussed were partial and voucher privatization. The Law on Privatization was submitted to the Slovenian Parliament in two substantially different draft proposals – first a 'gradual' and later a 'radical' privatization approach.

The gradual privatization package was similar to the former Yugoslav privatization program and close to the Hungarian approach at that time. It stressed a decentralized and spontaneous privatization process (except for enterprises operating at a loss) in which insiders, especially the management of the state enterprises, would be given preference in ownership allocation. This package was rejected by Slovenia's Parliament in the spring of 1991.

The radical privatization proposal was submitted later. It was similar to the Polish and Czech approaches. It emphasized mass voucher privatization and investment funds schemes. This proposal passed two chambers of Slovenia's Parliament, which was dominated by DEMOS, in the fall of 1991. However, the third assembly, the Chamber of Associated Labor which was dominated by managers of state enterprises and representatives of ex-Communist institutions, rejected this privatization package.

The Law on Privatization (and Ownership Transformation of Enterprises) in Slovenia was finally adopted by Parliament in November 1992 and was amended in 1993. Assets of agricultural farms (with the exception of agricultural land and forests which were to be restituted), agricultural enterprises, and most food-processing enterprises were privatized under this law. Exceptions were those food-processing enterprises privatized under the Law on Cooperatives and state enterprises operating at a loss considered public property and owned by the Development Fund.[9]

346

According to the Law on Privatization, 60 percent of a company's social capital would be transferred free of charge. Employees would receive 20 percent and state funds 40 percent (10 percent of shares transferred to the Pension Fund, 10 percent of shares transferred to the Compensation Fund to compensate former owners of nationalized property, and 20 percent of shares transferred to the Development Fund to be reserved for distribution through authorized investment funds).

The remaining 40 percent of a company's social capital could be privatized by several methods. Company managers and employees would be allowed to choose the method of privatization, and the Company Privatization Agency must agree with the proposal. It is possible for the 40 percent, in addition to the 20 percent of the enterprise shares transferred to employees, to be offered to managers and employees for an internal buy-out for which payment at a discount would be required. The remaining 40 percent might also be sold to domestic and foreign investors.

Several deadlines in the privatization program were extended due to amendments to the privatization legislation. Exchangeable ownership certificates were issued to Slovenian citizens for less than 20 percent of the social capital in the fall of 1993. The long delays in passing and implementing the Law on Privatization are an important reason for the current delays in the privatization process. All state-owned enterprises included in the privatization program, that is, state agricultural farms and food-processing enterprises, were given several deadlines to submit their privatization proposals to the Company Privatization Agency. The state farm assets (buildings, mechanization, plantations), with the exception of land and forests, are subject to privatization. The privatized state farms will become joint stock companies. However, the situation of those farms will be clear only after the land restitution process is finalized, because in many cases state farmland will be restituted in-kind to former owners.

Privatization and restitution of agricultural land and forests is handled by the State Fund for Agricultural Land and Forests (FALF). The Law on the Fund of Agricultural Land and Forests (the Law on the FALF) was adopted in February 1993 to deal with the organization of the State FALF and with the transfer of agricultural land, forests, and farms into the FALF. The Law on the FALF introduced the concept of a 'good landlord', which would allow state farms to continue to operate on state land for several years as long as they take 'good care' of the land during the 'adjustment period'. Social and political pressures from those employed in state farms, which continue to operate on former state agricultural land, in many cases have prevented restitution thus far.

Land restitution and reform

Collectivization and land nationalization under the Communist regime

Land structure in Slovenia is dominated by less fertile soil. More than half of the present area of Slovenia is forests, more than onequarter is grassland (meadows and pastures), and a significant share is barren earth, especially higher up in the Alps. The share of arable land for crop production is relatively low.

Between the first agrarian reform in 1918 and the end of World War II, most land was owned in small- and medium-size (up to ten hectares) peasant holdings. In 1931, in the Drava Province, a major part of present-day Slovenia, the average area per farm was 8.3 hectares, agricultural land per farm 4.8 hectares, and arable land per farm 4.0 hectares (Ministry for Agriculture and Forestry, 1992). There were a few big landowners, and some large farms were owned by churches and monasteries. The collectivization policy in 1945 expropriated ownership and user rights on land above 25 to 35 hectares of cultivated land per private farm holding, or above 45 hectares of poor soil and forests. At the same time a major part of land and forests owned by big landowners, by private companies, banks, and churches and religious communities was expropriated. Land owned by expelled minorities (i.e., Italian citizens) was also confiscated. This expropriated land is now mostly used by the state farms and, along with expropriated forests, is to be restituted to the original private owners. Alternatively, compensation is to be given for the lost properties. The main beneficiaries of land restitution are therefore the heirs of former larger landowners, heirs of peasants whose farms were over a certain land size, and churches.

Collectivization after World War II proved difficult because private peasants revolted against the collectivization. The economic results were poor, and the collectivization policy was abandoned in 1953 (Bergman, 1975). Peasants kept their land up to the maximum size of private farm landholding. After 1953 the rights to landownership and use and land trade were formally assured for private peasants. Within an upper limit of land per private peasant farm, land could be traded and taken on lease. By the mid-1960s, collective farms no longer existed. Only private and state sectors were present in agriculture. Thus, private landownership and private land use were always predominant. In 1992 about 70 percent of total land was privately owned (table 12.3). The share of state ownership differs strongly in arable land and forests: 11.2 percent of arable land, 16.8 percent of agricultural land, and 36.9 percent of forests.

Despite failed collectivization, agrarian land reform in 1953 further reduced the maximum size of private farm landholdings to 10 hectares of cultivated land, or 15 hectares of poor soil and forests.[10] This imposed limit on landownership and use was included in the Constitution since 1963 and had a significant impact on the structure and fragmentation of peasant farms.

Table 12.3
Structure of land area in Slovenia in 1992

	Land area (in 000 ha)	Share (in %)	% in private sector	% in state sector
1 Plough-land and gardens	244.8	12.1	87.5	12.5
2 Orchards	35.3	1.7	91.8	8.2
3 Vineyards	21.8	1.1	82.6	17.4
4 Meadows	347.5	17.2	89.8	10.2
5 Arable land (1+2+3+4)	649.4	32.1	88.8	11.2
6 Pasture land	212.6	10.5	66.6	33.4
7 Ponds, reeds and swampland	2.0	0.1	52.2	47.8
8 Agricultural land (5+6+7)	864.0	42.7	83.2	16.8
9 Wooded	1016.7	50.2	63.1	36.9
10 Barren earth	144.8	7.1	22.6	77.4
11 Total (8+9+10)	2025.5	100.0	68.8	31.2

Source: SY SLO, 1993, p. 199.

Peasant farmlands were further split into separate smallholdings and smaller plots. In 1973 the Law on Agricultural Inheritance specified that only the subdivision of so-called 'protected'[11] peasant farms was officially prohibited. Only the heir of a farm could legally inherit in-kind the property of the protected farm. Through the Law on Agricultural Land, the state sector enjoyed preferential rights over private peasants in buying available land. In February 1991, the amendment to the Law on Agricultural Land abolished these preference rights.[12] The amended law gave the neighboring farmers preference, and after that other buyers. Furthermore, the new law discriminated in favor of full-time farmers.

In 1990, the maximum size of private peasants' farms was increased from 10 to 30 hectares of owned cultivated land. This maximum was abolished in 1991. Land can now be freely traded among Slovene citizens. Private economic rights and property ownership are protected. Direct foreign ownership of land by foreign citizens is still prohibited, but foreigners can own land through a Slovenian-registered company.

Transfer of land into the FALF

On the basis of the Law on Cooperatives, the Law on Privatization, and the Law on the FALF, the state of Slovenia and local communes (municipalities) became the temporary owners of the former state agricultural land and forests. Those properties were to be transferred into the newly established FALF, whose role is to manage and lease those properties and deal with the process of restituting land and forests to previous owners. Land reform is intended to be mostly in the form of restitution in-kind.

The FALF was established in May 1993 (three months after the Law on the FALF was adopted) as the body that represents the state as owner. The FALF is responsible to the government. The council of the FALF has nine members, including five representatives of the state (appointed by Parliament), one representative of former owners, two representatives of present users or tenants, and one member representing the employees of the FALF.

There was extensive debate between the central and the local governments over the organization of the FALF. The FALF now administers on the state level with experts for agriculture, forestry, finance, and juridical services and coordinates the restitution process on regional and local levels. For the implementation of the process, local branch offices and regional coordination centers were established at the local level.

The final deadline for the transfer of state land and forests into the FALF was 11 September 1993. About 210,000 hectares of agricultural land and about 350,000 hectares of forest land, on about 988,000 pieces of land and with about 84,000 ownership certificates, were to be transferred to the FALF. This represents 27.8 percent of the area of Slovenia. Almost 100,000 hectares of formerly nationalized land have been used for urban and industrial use after its nationalization. The FALF will have only about 140,000 hectares of agricultural land and about 320,000 hectares of forest land for restitution and compensation. The FALF will return about 112,000 hectares of agricultural land in-kind to the original owners. The remaining 28,000 hectares of agricultural land will be used for compensation as substitute agricultural land.

Restitution of land to original owners

The Law on Denationalization became effective on 7 December 1991. The deadline for eligible persons to register claims for denationalization of agricultural land, forests, and other real estate was 7 June 1993. With the amendment to the Law on Denationalization in June 1993, the deadline was

350

extended to 7 December 1993. More than 20,000 claims for denationalization of agricultural land, forests, and farms were received, of which more than 14,0000 claims included the necessary documentary evidence. Persons with former Yugoslav citizenship[13] at the time their properties (or those of close relatives or heirs) were nationalized and religious communities were made eligible for denationalization involving restitution in-kind or compensation through substitute property and securities. By 31 May 1994, 5,191 cases for restitution were approved (Ministry for Jurisdiction, 1994).

A special problem is land that prior to 1945 belonged to Italian citizens who had emigrated from areas in the Slovenian coastal region (Gow, 1994). In this case, the solution will probably be some form of compensation instead of in-kind restitution.

By 31 May 1994, 16,592 hectares of agricultural land and 51,943 hectares of forest land were restituted, mostly in historical boundaries (see table 12.4). This represented about 8 percent of the agricultural land and 15 percent of the forest land subject to restitution. However, restitution of agricultural land declined in mid-1994. According to the Law on Denationalization and the Law on the FALF, agricultural land was to be returned in-kind to original owners only if the restitution process would not result in either a disruption of existing agricultural production units (e.g., orchards or vineyards) or induce a large and economically irrational fragmentation of land. In cases where restitution in-kind could have a significant negative impact on the economic or technological functions of an enterprise (for example, lead to its bankruptcy or liquidation or to a significant collapse of output and decrease in employment), the former state agricultural enterprise would continue to operate for a certain adjustment period. The law allows for 'co-ownership rights' on agricultural land used by such units, to be reestablished by agreement or by a court. This is an important reason why most former state land is currently frozen: property rights will be returned to the original owners in the form of co-ownership shares, and agricultural complexes will continue to use the former state land. As explained earlier through the Law on the FALF, former state agricultural enterprises or other former users may continue to use and manage 'their' transferred agricultural land, if they use it as a 'good landlord', for a defined period. The original owner has a right to land use after a defined adjustment period: five years after denationalization of the property rights in the form of co-ownership share, or until 7 December 1998. In the meantime, political pressure to adjust the regulations is expected from both the original owners of the property rights and from the former state sector as present users of larger agricultural complexes. Lease contracts made before the denationalization process, especially in the case of plantations, are valid no longer than ten years after the Law on Denationalization was approved. To break the contracts, the original owners must prove that they have a more rational and efficient use for the property. New lease contracts should then be made between the original owner and present users. However, in many cases an agreement between former owners and tenants (usually former state enterprises) has not been reached, and the claims have gone to court.

Table 12.4
Denationalized agricultural land and forest land (in hectares) by 31 May 1994

	Total	Municipalities	Ministry for culture	Court
1. Agricultural land	16,592	16,093	148	351
- Real property		14,531		
- Co-ownership share		1,359		
- Substituted land		83.5		
- Compensation payments		38.5		
- Encumbered with mortgages		81		
2. Forest Land	51,943	51,548	132	263

Source: Ministry for Jurisdiction, 1994, p. 6.

Problems also arise in the compensation of former owners through comparable substitute property when land was urbanized or when the value of the property has changed. Former owners prefer restitution of land in its original boundaries or a substitute property over compensation in the form of securities in the Compensation Fund. The Compensation Fund was established to compensate original owners with compensation bonds when return of property in-kind is impossible or when previous owners choose this form of compensation. The Compensation Fund obtains resources from housing and state enterprises privatization, as well as from sale and leasing of agricultural land and forests through the FALF during the process of denationalization.[14]

Leasing of land owned by the FALF

In cases where land transferred into the FALF is not subject to restitution, the FALF or the local municipal body can confer the concession or make a lease contract with the present user and other tenants for a period equivalent to the amortization period of investment in agricultural land, or, in the case of plantations, the period of fertility. However, existing lease contracts expire at least ten years after the Law on FALF (11 March 2003).

Use of land managed by the FALF for improving the structure of family farms has been limited. Instead, most of the land has been leased to state enterprises (usually plantations, such as vineyards and orchards) that used the land prior to 1990. Agricultural land was rented on short-run leases with about 60,000 leasing contracts. A problem was that most lease contracts were not made by the FALF in 1993. Instead, tenants made contracts with former administrators of state land. Rent for agricultural land was between 40 and 400 DM per hectare in 1993, depending on its quality, location, and other factors. Former state enterprises usually have not paid rent because the transfer of land into the FALF was going on during that time. Several spontaneous activities emerged in privatization and contracting, such as the sale of former state land, more intensive cutting of state forests, and subtenancy from the state sector to the private peasant sector. Consequently, a temporary moratorium on cutting trees and on selling state real assets was imposed. Detailed information is lacking on the registration of state enterprises' real assets and on the transfer of land into the FALF, as well as on land registration and delays in the registration process in general.

When land is subject to restitution, leasing contracts are limited to one year. This creates problems for the management of plantations (vineyards, orchards, and hop gardens). The state is the temporary owner of the land, while the plantation assets remain the property of the investors, usually former state enterprises. The compulsory lease agreement, by the Law on Denationalization, has a maximum of five years, with an exception of ten years for land under agricultural plantations.

The politics of Slovenia's agricultural privatization

Several observations can be made about the agricultural privatization process in Slovenia. First, like Poland, Slovenia is characterized by the failure of collectivization policies in the 1950s and, consequently, by an agricultural sector dominated by small-scale private farms. Those private farms coexisted with large-scale state enterprises in agricultural production. As in Poland, those state enterprises operated on state land, most of which was nationalized after 1945.

As in Poland, privatization and land reform has been limited to those state production units. However, unlike in Poland, this state land has been restituted in-kind to its former owners, if possible. The exception is where former owners were foreign citizens who left the country. These former owners might be compensated through means other than restitution in-kind. This is again consistent with the Polish situation, in cases where previous owners of the state land were Germans who no longer live in Poland.

353

This suggests that land restitution in historical boundaries where possible or in comparable boundaries has been a politically irresistible policy choice wherever the previous owners of the land (or their heirs) are (still) domestic citizens. Despite opposition from current users of the land (state farms, or, in other countries, collective farms) and efficiency arguments against the inherent fragmentation of landownership, the demand by domestic previous owners for restitution has been too strong politically to be resisted by policymakers.

The choice for land restitution in-kind was made under the Law on Denationalization. This law was approved early on under the anti-Communist DEMOS government. It was expected to overturn previous spontaneous privatization activities under the former Yugoslav Law on Social Capital, which mainly benefited insiders and managers of state enterprises and representatives of ex-Communist institutions.

The DEMOS government relied heavily on rural votes, captured by the peasant party SKZ, as well as the SKD. As in Poland, but unlike most other CEECs, the rural votes were mostly captured by a party favoring land restitution and supporting agrarian concerns that reflected the domination of private farmers in rural areas.

The SKZ not only favored restitution of land but also the liquidation of current state farms. However, implementation of land restitution and, especially, of liquidation of state farms, was slowed and possibly reversed during subsequent discussions in Parliament regarding additional privatization laws. When the DEMOS coalition consequently disintegrated and the government fell, some former Communists came back to power.

Their opposition to the liquidation and breakup of state farms is reflected in new regulations of the 1993 Law on the FALF. These allow state farms to continue to operate on land managed by the FALF pending restitution. The concepts of 'co-ownership of land' and 'good landlord' were introduced to give state farms more security in their operation of land identified for restitution.

In conclusion, the return to power of the ex-Communists has not led to a reversal of restitution regulations, but it has slowed down the restitutions and in several cases has inhibited implementation. In addition, the Law on the FALF protects the state farms from external efforts to break them up or to liquidate them for several years to come. Political pressure to adjust this regulations is building on both sides: landowners want the lease contracts dissolved earlier, while the people whose interests are aligned with the continuation of state farms demand an extension of the rules.

Notes

1   Štefan Bojnec gratefully acknowledges financial support from the ACE Program of the Commission of the European Communities and from the Katholieke Universiteit Leuven.

2   The 'social' sector of agriculture was based on 'social' land and assets, and was managed by the system of worker self-management. 'Social' property was at the same time everyone's (all people's) property and no one's property. The user rights were allocated to farms and enterprises. In this article we will refer to this sector as the 'state sector' instead of the 'social sector'.

3   For a summary of the parties and their backgrounds, see appendix 12.2&3.

4   Milan Kucan was reelected State President in the first round on 6 December 1992.

5   Slovenia's legal and regulatory frameworks for privatization are discussed in detail in Gray et al. (1993) and appendix 12.1.

6   Lee and Nellis (1990) point out financial, economic, political, and organizational deficiencies of 'spontaneous privatizations' as negative outcomes of the first phase of the privatization process. For a discussion of such developments in Hungary, see Canning and Hare (1993).

7   See Pirkmajer (1992) for a discussion of former owners' expectations and the different options in searching for compromise regulations and practical solutions between the Association of Owners of Expropriated Property and the Slovenian government.

8   For the Slovene Law on Denationalization in English translation, see the Appendix of CEEPN Workshop Series No. 1.

9   The Development Fund carries out a government program for restructuring those enterprises in public property.

10 In 1973, the maximum size for private farm landholdings in mountain and hill districts (over 600 metres height above sea level) increased from 15 to 20 hectares of poor soil and forests.

11 A farm could be registered as a 'protected' farm, with its heir, in which case the farm could benefit from state support to agriculture.

12 A new Law on Agricultural Land is expected at the end of 1996 or in 1997.

13 A foreign citizen is a person who did not have citizenship in former Yugoslavia at the time of nationalization of its property, recognized after 9 May 1945. The exception is a person who had permanent residence on the territory of the present Slovenia at the time their property was nationalized and whose former Yugoslav citizenship was recognized after 15 September 1947.

14 There have also been intensive political discussions about agricultural land and forests formerly belonging to churches and other religious institutions

operating on the territory of Slovenia in 1991, which are subject to denationalization.

References

Agricultural Extension Service (1993), 'Feasibility of Ecosocial Agricultural Development in Slovenia', Collection of Scientific Papers, Conference on Bled, November.

Andrejevich, M. (1990a), 'Communist Wins Presidential Runoff in Slovenia', *Report on Eastern Europe*, Vol. 1, No. 18, 4 May, pp. 38-39.

Andrejevich, M. (1990b), 'Slovenia's New Government: The First 30 Days', *Report on Eastern Europe*, Vol. 1, No. 26, 29 June, pp. 45-51.

Andrejevich, M. (1991), 'Slovenian Government Faces Challenges', *Report on Eastern Europe*, Vol. 2, No. 11, 15 March, pp. 30-33.

Andrejevich, M. (1992), 'Elections in Slovenia Maintain Status Quo', RFE/RL Research Report, Vol. 1, No. 50, 18 December, pp. 28-31.

Bergman, T. (1975), *Farm Policies in Socialist Countries*, Saxon House, D.C. Heath Ltd.: Westmead.

Bojnec, Š. (1994), 'Agricultural Reform in Slovenia', in Swinnen, J. (ed.), *Policy and Institutional Reform in Central European Agriculture*, Avebury: Aldershot.

Canning, A. and Hare, P. (1993), 'The Privatization Process - Economic and Political Aspects of the Hungarian Approach (From Goulash Communism to Goulash Capitalism?)', unpublished manuscript.

Central European (1994), 'Slovenia Accelerates Sales of State Companies', April, p. 5.

Duric, B. (1990), *The Law on Enterprises with the Law on Foreign Investments*, Poslovna Politika: Beograd.

Fund of Agricultural Land and Forestry (1994), 'Information about the Activities of the Fund for Agricultural Land and Forestry of the Republic of Slovenia in 1993', unpublished manuscript: Ljubljana.

Gow, J. (1994), 'Slovenia: Stabilization or Stagnation'? *RFE/RL Research Report*, Vol. 3, No. 1, 7 January, pp. 135-138.

Gray, C. W. and Associates (1993), 'Evolving Legal Frameworks for Private Sector Development in Central and Eastern Europe', *World Bank Discussion Papers*, No. 209, The World Bank: Washington, D.C.

Jones, C. (1992), 'Privatization in East Europe and in the Former Soviet Union', *Financial Times Business Information*.

Lee, B. and Nellis, J. (1990), 'Enterprise Reform and Privatization in Socialist Economies', *World Bank Discussion Papers*, No. 104, The World Bank: Washington, D.C.

Ministry for Agriculture and Forestry (1992), 'Strategy of Agricultural Development in Slovenia', unpublished manuscript: Ljubljana.

Ministry for Agriculture and Forestry (1994), 'Privatization of Enterprises under the Law on Cooperatives', unpublished manuscript: Ljubljana.

Ministry for Agriculture and Forestry (1994), 'Programme of Activities and Measures for Implementation of the Strategy of Agricultural Development in Slovenia in the period 1994-1996', unpublished manuscript: Ljubljana.

Ministry for Jurisdiction (1994), 'The Seventh Report on Realization of the Law on Denationalization', unpublished manuscript: Ljubljana.

Pirkmajer, E. (1992), 'Denationalization in Slovenia: The Former Owners' Point of View', in *Reprivatization in Central and Eastern Europe*, The Central and Eastern European Privatization Network Workshop Series No. 1, pp. 50-55.

Pleskovic, B. and Sachs, J. (1994), 'Political Independence and Economic Reform in Slovenia', in Blanchard, O., Froot, K. and Sachs, J. (eds.), *The Transition in Eastern Europe*, NBER and University of Chicago Press: Chicago, pp. 191-230.

Statistical Yearbook of Slovenia (SY SLO) (1992) and (1993).

Stiblar, F. (1992), 'Privatization in Slovenia', *Development and International Cooperation*, Vol. 8, No. 14-15, pp. 185-196.

Swinnen, J. (1994), 'Political Economy of Reform in Bulgarian Agriculture', in Schmitz, A., Moulton, K., Buckwell, A. and Davidova, S. (eds.), *Privatization of Agriculture in New Market Economies: Lessons from Bulgaria*, Kluwer Academic Publishers: Boston, London, and Dordrecht.

The Denationalization Act (Slovenia) (1992), The Central and Eastern European Privatization Network Workshop Series, No. 1, pp. 63-88.

Vodopivec, P. (1992), 'Slovenes and Yugoslavia, 1918-1991', *East European Politics and Societies*, Vol. 6, No. 3, pp. 220-241.

Appendix 12.1
Important legislation

Constitution of the Republic of Slovenia	OG SLO 33/1991
Law on Agricultural Inheritance	OG SLO 26/1973
Law on Agricultural Land	OG SLO 26/1973, 1/1979, 11/1981, 1/1986, 17/1986, 9/1990, 5/1991
Law on Foreign Investments	OG YU 77/1988
Law on Social Capital	OG YU 84/1989, 46/1990
Law on Ownership Transformation of Enterprises - Law on Privatization	OG SLO 55/1992, 7/1993, 31/1993

Decree on Preparation of Transformation Program and on Implementation of Single Methods of Ownership Transformation of Enterprises	OG SLO 13/1993
Decree on the Issue, Distribution, and Disposal of Ownership Certificates	OG SLO 40/1993, 72/1993
Law on Agency of the Republic of Slovenia for Restructuring and Privatization	OG SLO 14/1990 and 7/1993
Law on Development Fund of the Republic of Slovenia	OG SLO 14/1990 and
Law on Denationalization	7/1993
Law on Temporary Moratorium on Felling Trees and on Trade with Real Assets in the Social Property	OG SLO 27/1991, 31/1993
Instructions to the Law on Denationalization	OG SLO 26/1990, 43/1990, 2/1991
Decree on the Methodology for Valuation of the Value of Agricultural Land, Forests and Land Used for Building, in the Process of Denationalization	OG SLO 32/1991 OG SLO 16/1992, 21/1992
Ordinance on the Leasing of Agricultural Land and Farms	OG SLO 7/1994
Law on Slovenian Compensation Fund	OG SLO 7/1993
Law on Cooperatives	OG SLO 13/1992, 7/1993
Law on Protection of Competition	OG SLO 18/1993
Law on Companies	OG SLO 30/1993
Law on Fund of Agricultural Land and Forests of the Republic of Slovenia	OG SLO 10/1993
Guidelines on Documentation for Transfer of Agricultural Land, Wood Land and Farms into the Fund of Agricultural Land and Forests	OG SLO 32/1993
Law on Reestablishment of Agricultural Communities and on Return of Their Properties and Rights	OG SLO 5/1994

Source: Official Gazette of the Republic of Slovenia (OG SLO) and Official Gazette of the former Yugoslavia (OG YU).

Appendix 12.2
Main parties in the first Slovenian multiparty elections in April 1990
(Slovenia was still part of Yugoslavia)

Parties	*Abbreviation*	*Brief description*
Democratic United Opposition of Slovenia	DEMOS	DEMOS was an anti-Communist coalition founded in December 1989. The coalition collapsed due to serious internal rivalries and divisions in December 1991. Its program was a mixture of traditional social democratic and Christian democratic agendas with an emphasis on agrarian and ecological concerns.
- Slovenian Christian Democrats	SKD	SKD prime minister in 1990
- Slovenian Farmers' Alliance	SKZ	
- Slovenian Democratic Alliance	SDZ	
- Greens Alliance of Slovenia	ZELENI	
- Social Democratic Alliance of Slovenia	SDZS	
- Slovenian Craftsmen Party	SOS	
League of Communists of Slovenia - Party of Democratic Renewal	ZKS-SDP	The party in power 1945-1990. The ZKS changed its name in February 1990 to the Party of Democratic Renewal and announced its independence from the federal Communist Party of Yugoslavia.
League of Socialist Youth of Slovenia - Liberal Party	ZSMS-LS	The ZSMS was founded in 1974 and was open to all people from the ages of 15 to 35. The ZSMS-LS declared its independence from the federal party in November 1989.

Socialist Alliance of Slovenia - Socialist Alliance of Working People	SZS-SZDL	The SZDL was founded in February 1953, and was the ZKS's mass front organization. The SZDL declared itself an independent political party, the SZS-SZDL, in February 1990. The alliance advocates a new form of socialism.

Appendix 12.3
Main parties in the second Slovenian elections in December 1992
(Slovenia is independent)

Parties	Abbreviation	Brief description
Liberal Democratic Party	LDS	The LDS, formerly the ZSMS-LS, attaches importance of ensuring the continuation of Slovenia's political, economic, and social reforms.
Slovenian Christian Democrats	SKD	The SKD emphasizes political stabilization.
Unity List	ZL	The alliance of four parties (Labor Party, Democratic Party of Pensioners, Social Democratic Union, and SDP of Slovenia) headed by the former Communists.
Slovenian National Party	SNS	The main voters of this party were discontented young people between the ages of 18 and 30 (problem of unemployment).

Slovenian People's Party	SLS	The SLS, formerly the SKZ (the Farmers Alliance), advocates privatization and restitution.
Democrats - Democratic Party	DEMOKRATI	The democrats, formerly the SDZ.
Greens Alliance of Slovenia	ZELENI	The leftist Greens have been members of all three the post-1990 Slovenia's coalition governments.
Social Democratic Party of Slovenia	SDSS	The SDSS, formerly the SDZS.

Source: SY SLO, Report on Eastern Europe, and RFE/RL Research Report, various issues.

13 The choice of privatization and decollectivization policies in Central and Eastern European agriculture: Observations and political economy hypotheses[1]

Johan F. M. Swinnen

Introduction

This chapter first summarizes some general observations on privatization and decollectivization policy choices based on the ten Central and Eastern European countries (CEECs) studied in this volume. Then I will present political economy hypotheses to explain these observations.

The focus here is primarily on political economy factors and the extent to which they can account for the variation in policy choices in CEECs. I do not in any way argue that economic efficiency criteria are unimportant. However, in the framework of this volume, economic considerations are discussed only in their relation to political economy incentives and equilibria. I refer to the first chapter for definitions of the concepts used here and to the various country studies for background information and details.

Empirical observations

Observation 1. *Important changes in agricultural reform policies during transition are closely related to political changes.*

Most CEECs have approved several substantially different versions of privatization and transformation laws. The changes in the laws and their amendments often reflect different stages in the political reforms and changing power balances at the decisionmaking level. For example, many CEECs first witnessed the emergence of an anti-Communist opposition front[2] and the decline of Communist power at the end of the 1980s, then a fall from power of the Communist Party, and a period when anti-Communist reformers were in charge of government. This was consequently followed by a political revival of ex-Communist parties. These political changes have been reflected in the implementation of agrarian reform policies, and later in changes to the reforms, such as amendments to the privatization laws, revised transformation rules, new policy initiatives, or policy reversals.

Observation 2. *CEECs vary substantially in their reform policy choices.*

Table 13.1 summarizes the differences in land reform policies in CEECs and shows the variety of processes used. Collective farmland has been restituted in several CEECs, but in Albania it is distributed on an equal per capita basis to farm workers. Hungary sold part of the collective farmland for compensation bonds. Most state farmland is restituted in the Baltic countries and Slovenia, distributed to farm workers in Albania, and leased, pending sales in other CEECs.

Even when governments have chosen the same process, there might be subtle, but important, differences in their restitution regulations. For example, the details of the Romanian land restitution law allowed for much discretion in implementing the law. In contrast, the amended Bulgarian land law provided strict rules for its implementation and was much more favorable to former owners. Another example is from the Baltic states. In Latvia, former owners and, after them, individual farmers have been given the highest priority in land restitution and allocation. The lowest priority went to reforming cooperative farms. In contrast, in 1993 Lithuania passed a regulation allowing for allocation of urban land to former owners of agricultural land willing to postpone their claims on agricultural land used by former collective farms.

Observation 3. *Restitution of collective farmland to former owners and sale of state farmland are the most common forms of land privatization in CEECs.*

With the exception of Russia and Poland, an important share of collective farmland is restituted to its former owners in all CEECs included in this study (see table 13.1). Typically, former owners are restituted the land in historical boundaries, if possible. Otherwise they receive property rights to a plot of land of comparable size and quality. This has been the main process of collective farmland privatization in CEECs. The main exceptions to restitution of collective farmland are the compensation bonds for two thirds of the land used by Hungarian cooperatives, and land distribution to the rural population, in Albania. But even in Albania collective farmland property rights have been restituted to former owners in some mountainous regions

In the majority of CEECs, state farmland is to be sold. In most, the land is leased pending sales. For example, in East Germany nationalized land is managed by the Land Utilization and Administration Company (BVVG) and leased to former owners who lost their ownership titles and to legal entities. The main exceptions are the restitution of state farmland in Slovenia and distribution to farm workers in Albania. Initially, farm workers received privatization vouchers as state farms engaged in joint ventures. As most joint ventures failed, farm workers then received user rights, but ultimately were allocated full property rights.

Table 13.1

Most important land reform procedures in CEECs[a]

	Collective farmland		State farmland[b]	
	Procedure	% in TAL	Procedure	% in TAL
Albania	Distribution	76	Distribution[c]	24
Bulgaria	Restitution	72	Miscellaneous[d]	9
Czech Republic	Restitution	61	Sale (leasing[e])	25
East Germany	Restitution	82	Sale (leasing[e])	7
Hungary	Restitution+ distribution+sale for compensation bonds[f]	70 57	Sale for compensation bonds + sale (leasing[e]) + sale (leasing[e])	12 38
Latvia	Restitution	62	Restitution	30
Lithuania	Restitution	4	Restitution	19
Poland	-	58	Sale (leasing[e])	28
Romania	Restitution+distribution	71	Undecided[g]+Restitution	15
Slovakia	Restitution	0	Sale (leasing[e])	17
Slovenia	-		Restitution	

a   Special procedures for marginal amounts of land are not included in the table.

b   Excluding research farms which are nowhere privatized.

c   Farm workers received vouchers in newly established joint ventures. However, as most of these joint ventures failled, farm workers received first user richts and eventually full property rights.

d   In Bulgaria, the distinction between state and collective farms is more complicated than in other CEECs because of the creation and later abolishment of the so-called Agro-Industrial Complexes. Part of the land classified under 'state farmland' is restituted, because it was intially collective farmland and has a similars status; another part will not be privatized; and yet another part is the land on which large pig and poultry enterprises are built and which will be privatized separately.

e   Land is leased to individuals or entities pending sale.

f   Each of the land reform procedures applies to approximately onethird of the collective farmland.

g   The Romanian government has not decided how to privatize the state farms, including the land, on twothirds of the state farmland.

Observation 4. *Land reforms implemented under Communist-dominated governments after World War II have been acknowledged as legal, and the resulting landownership has been used as the basis for restitution in several CEECs.*

In the 1930s and immediately after World War II, CEECs witnessed several (attempts at) land reforms, which altered the landownership patterns (Mathijs, 1997a). In some cases the land reforms consisted of transferring land from one group of the population to another (e.g., from large landowners to peasants and landless agricultural workers). Other land reforms distributed land from foreign landowners or land owned by institutions such as the Catholic Church to domestic peasants. Because of the precollectivization land reforms, some plots of land had more than one 'previous owner'. Hence, when the restitution of land was discussed, the choice of reference date had important distributional implications.

In Romania, Hungary, and former Czechoslovakia, current land restitution is (explicitly) *not* based on the 1945 ownership situation, but on the ownership situation strongly influenced by a post-World War II land reform and implemented by a government dominated by the Communist Party (CP). Many reformers claim that the political basis on which these land reforms were decided and implemented was undemocratic, but they have still chosen to use the post-1945 landownership distribution date (when the collectivization process was started) as the basis for restitution. For example, in Czechoslovakia, between 1945 and 1948 many (especially large) landowners lost a major share of their land in CP-inspired land reform. Many Czechs claim that the 1946 elections won by the CP were manipulated. Still, the Czech (reform) government decided to use 25 February 1948 as the reference date for restitution. Similarly, Hungary took 1948 and Romania took 1947 as reference dates. Hungary compensated pre-1948 former owners with vouchers with which they could buy land in auctions.

Observation 5. *Land that was formally privately owned under collectivization has been restituted to those owners.*

All agricultural land was nationalized during the Communist regime in the former Soviet Union (FSU) and Albania. In all other CEECs, most of the land was never nationalized under collectivization, and at least part of the land remained *formally* privately owned by individuals who joined the collectives (or by their heirs). The agricultural collectives as they existed in most of Central and Eastern Europe were an intermediate step towards the type of full collectivization that existed in the former Soviet Union and Albania. Even in Bulgaria, where collective farms were reorganized into huge state enterprises called the Agro-Industrial Complexes, formal landownership remained in private hands.

Brooks et al. (1991) claim that while originally there were important differences between state and collective farms and how they remunerated employees and members, by the 1980s the difference between formal individual, collective, or state ownership of land mattered little. This implies that effective property rights, as Barzel (1989) defines them, were by all means strongly in the hands of collective farm management or the state. Legal owners had little or nothing to say in the allocation of their land.

However, the difference in formal *asset* ownership seems to have affected agrarian reform in several countries. Without exception, CEECs have restituted property rights to land which was still formally privately owned in 1989 to their 'formal' owners (or their heirs) (see table 13.2).

Table 13.2
Entitlement basis for the restitution of property rights on land

| | *Former owners* | | *Workers* |
	who always kept legal title to the land	*who lost their legal title to the land*	*who are not former owners*
East Germany	yes	no	no
Czech Republic	yes	no	no
Slovakia	yes	no	no
Hungary	yes	partial and indirect	yes
Bulgaria	yes	-	no
Romania	yes	yes	yes
Slovenia	yes	-	no

Hungary is a special case because after 1968 people who were no longer active in the collective farm were forced to sell their land to the collective farm. Afterwards, Hungarian collective farms used a mixture of privately owned and collectively owned land. By the end of the 1980s, most of the land used by collective farms was owned by them. Only approximately one third of the land was still formally privately owned. This privately owned land has been restituted to its owners, while land owned by the collective farm has been used partly for compensation via auctions and partly for distribution among collective farm employees. Former owners who were forced to sell the land (at artificially low prices) were not restituted their land.[3] Such former owners

367

have been compensated with vouchers, which they could use, among other things, to purchase land set aside for this purpose (Mathijs, 1997b).

The privatization of collective farmland and state farmland has often been treated differently. For example, in Bulgaria and Romania most collective farmland has been restituted to former owners, but state farmland has been privatized as part of the general privatization process, thus without restitution of the land.[4] In some cases the state farmland was state land before 1940. In other cases it was nationalized after the war (taken from foreign landowners or from the Catholic Church).

Observation 6. *Different methods have been used to privatize nonland agricultural assets.*

Whereas land has mostly been restituted in-kind, this has not been the general rule for other assets. Nonland assets have been restituted in some countries, but in many cases were privatized using vouchers that could be turned into capital shares in the new cooperative farm or used for purchasing nonland assets for private use. The distribution of those vouchers was the subject of much debate. In general, the principle was that members (or their heirs) who had contributed land, labor, or other assets to the cooperative over the forty-five years of its existence should receive some share of the remaining assets. To implement this required an inventory of the cooperative's assets, their value, and a formula to determine the shares of each contributor. Both aspects posed great difficulties. The solutions chosen have varied substantially in the CEECs, as they were also driven by political considerations.

Table 13.3 shows how active members received only 20 percent of nonland assets in Slovenia, versus 40 percent in Hungary and 100 percent in Lithuania. In Lithuania farm equipment could be purchased with investment vouchers (which everybody received), money, or 'green vouchers' (which were only distributed among agricultural workers, based on the number of years they worked in the collective). The consequence was that rural pensioners obtained a disproportionate share of the nonland assets. In former Czechoslovakia, vouchers were distributed according to a 50/30/20 scheme: 50 percent for former landowners, 30 percent for former nonland assets (capital) owners, and 20 percent for labor contributors. In contrast, Bulgarian and Romanian labor contributors received 50 percent and 60 percent, respectively, of the nonland assets.

Observation 7. *Foreign former owners have not been restituted their land.*

In several CEECs, former owners of land included foreigners. An example is state land in Poland, a large share of which was owned by Germans who emigrated from West Poland after World War II. Similarly, land in the western border regions of the Czech Republic was owned by Sudeten Germans until 1945. In Slovenia, Italians owned some of the land nationalized after World War II. In all these cases, foreigners were not restituted the land.

Observation 8. *Several CEECs, mostly under the influence of the ex-Communist parties, have taken measures to restrict the transfer of full property rights to land to individuals.*

The return of the ex-CPs to power in many CEECs (e.g., Hungary, Bulgaria, Poland, Lithuania, Slovenia) has resulted in amendments to reform laws, new regulations, and adjustments of incentives for reform implementation. These policy changes have, in general, not resulted in changes in the legal privatization process. Instead, the regulations and adjustments have reduced or complicated the transfer of effective property rights regarding assets to individuals and have reduced the impact of decollectivization. Examples are the increase of (opportunity) costs for submitting land claims, giving former collectives more rights and authority to decide about the use of assets under privatization, and limiting new owners' rights in transferring and using the assets.

Table 13.3
Distribution of nonland assets: dividing rules[*]

	Latvia	Lithuania	Bulgaria	Czech & Slovak	Hungary	Slovenia
Active members	(yes)	100 %	(yes)	(yes)	40 %	20 %
Contributors of:						
- Labor	n.a.	n.a.	50 %	20 %	n.a.	100 %
- Land	n.a.	n.a.	50 %	50 %	n.a.	0
- Capital	n.a.	n.a.	0	30 %	n.a.	0
Former Owners	n.a.	0	(yes)	(yes)	20 %	10 %
Pensioners	n.a.	0	0	0	40 %	10 %
State fund	n.a.	0	0	0	0	20 %
Sale	n.a.	0	0	25 %	0	40 %

[*] '(yes)' refers to 'eligible for allocation of nonland assets, but detailed information on the share is unavailable' (see Swinnen and Mathijs, 1997, for more details).

The Slovenian government has gone the furthest and, under pressure from former Communists, introduced the concept of 'co-ownership of land' to give the former state farms more security of operation. In addition, it has introduced an 'adjustment period' of several years during which the large-scale state plantations (vineyards and orchards) can continue their operation on land destined for restitution without fear of being disrupted. Similar options were proposed by an ex-Communist Party government in the 1995 Bulgarian land law amendments to limit new owners' rights to use and transfer the land.

Whereas in the Czech Republic a 'Sanction Law' was approved to penalize cooperatives that did not fulfill property claims, such a law was not approved by the Slovak government. Rather, cooperatives there are allowed to issue vouchers, tradable only after seven years, further restricting the property rights of Slovak former owners (Kabat and Hagedorn, 1997).

Observation 9. *Radical decollectivization policies are not a general rule.*

In some CEECs, spontaneous decollectivization led the way and left the government with few options other than to support the process. For example, in Albania the government faced a spontaneous and almost complete breakup of the collective farms and could have done little to stop it. If anything, most CEEC governments have tried not to increase the disruption caused to state and collective farms beyond that resulting from the privatization policies. This argument may be best understood if one compares the most common transformation regulations with the 'radical' policies that have been proposed (and in some cases implemented).

Key characteristics of decollectivization policies are (a) the role they allocate to the management of the collective and state farms, and (b) the incentives they provide for leaving the collective farm. Two examples where radical decollectivization policies were chosen can be cited. First, the 1992 UDF government in Bulgaria decided to throw out the old management of the collective farms and replace it with special institutions to effectively liquidate the collective farms, appropriately called 'liquidation councils'. Second, the 1991 Sajudis government in Lithuania removed the existing management from its controlling positions and created the Municipal Agrarian Reform Services (MARS), chaired by outsiders. Not surprisingly, in both countries the role and the composition of these institutions was changed when the ex-Communists came back to power.[5]

In contrast, other CEECs have opted for a less radical approach, emphasizing the need to minimize further disruptions. They have done so by giving the members and old management a place in the transformation of their collective and state farms. For example, in Hungary, Slovakia, and the Czech Republic, former management has played an important role in the transformation of the collective farms: they were made the main agents on the 'transformation boards' which draw up the plans for transforming the organization. Individuals have been discouraged from leaving the transformed collective farm to start up their own individual farms, for example, by imposing on them a share of the former collective's debt and the administration costs of parceling out the land. Such policies have been criticized by the peasant parties (e.g., the Peasant Party in former Czechoslovakia and the Independent Smallholders' Party in Hungary) as favoring the former Communists.

Stages in political and economic reforms

The change from Communist Party dictatorship to democracy took various forms,[6] but one can distinguish a series of phases in the political reforms most CEECs passed through (see table 13.4). The first stage is the emergence of an anti-Communist opposition front during the 1980s. In the face of rising opposition and declining USSR hegemony, the CP introduced minimal reforms and changed its name, e.g., the Socialist Party (SP). Anti-Communist coalitions eventually defeated (ex-)Communist parties in elections in most CEECs (the only exception being Romania). Typically, the anti-Communist coalition felt apart before or quickly after their first election victory. As their uniting force was opposition against the Communist regime, discussions of specific reforms and policies made the fragility and the heterogeneity of the coalitions apparent. In many CEECs, descendants of the Communist Party have been returned to government at a later stage.

Table 13.4
Styles of political changes

Stage	Characteristics
0.	CP monoply
1.	Emergence of anti-CP coalition
2.	CP remains itself SP and introduces minimal reforms
3.	Reformers form government
4.	Falling apart of anti-CP coalition
5.	Return of SP in government

One can distinguish several stages in the economic reform process coinciding with the political changes shown in table 13.4.

Stage I: A dramatic political crisis as precondition for economic reform

Hayami (1991), de Janvry (1981b) and Mathijs (1997a) conclude that in East Asia, in Latin America, and in Central and Eastern Europe earlier this century effective land reforms have only occurred after a dramatic decline in the ruling elite's power and confidence. The most successful reforms occurred in countries and time periods when political crises (or shifts in power balances) were most dramatic. For example, after World War II, landowners who had supported the Germans or Nazi allies during the war were the main victims of the land reform movements in Europe, and in Japan land reform was imposed by the American government. In CEECs, the current reform of the property rights system after the collectivization drives of the 1950s and 1960s required a dramatic shift in political institutions. The privatization and land reform programs only occurred after the decline of USSR hegemony in Central and Eastern Europe. This shift in political power allowed the approval and implementation of, by all measures, dramatic property rights reforms in most countries.

Stage II: Conceding minimal reforms as a legitimation strategy

As some of the CP leaders realized that a dramatic change in political institutions was inevitable after the decline of Soviet hegemony, they wanted to use limited reforms to influence the electorate in upcoming elections, elections which they could not prevent. As long as the CP was in power it could design the reform process in a way to allow CP members and individuals sympathetic to the CP to shift their 'political power' into 'economic power'. This could be done by using their central and local monopoly on information and enforcement to steer the reform program.

This argument is also consistent with observations on land reform elsewhere. Both de Janvry (1981a) and Hayami (1991) argue that one of the most important factors in explaining land reform failures is that the ruling class, which opposes reforms, will concede to reform pressures for the sake of legitimizing their dominance (i.e., de Janvry's 'Conservative Model'). When political crises occur, the ruling order will 'allow' land reforms to take place because the probability of remaining in power without some reforms has declined and because the chance that without reforms a revolution will occur has increased. Allowing limited reforms is hoped to reduce the pressure for more substantial reforms. Hence, from this perspective, land reform programs are expected to be as limited as possible while achieving their political purpose. A typical way of achieving such an objective is to deliberately choose a reform process with complex rules and insufficient means to execute it (see Junguito, 1991). This logic leads to the following hypothesis: *When the political challenge to the CP's power monopoly increased, the CP has responded with limited reform proposals to fend off this challenge and/or to use reforms to its own advantage. Actual changes in property rights resulting from these reforms were intended to be limited, or to benefit the nomenklatura.* One should expect such reforms to be characterized (1) by great complexity and uncertainty, e.g,. by including few details regarding how to implement and execute the law, and (2) by much discretion left to local governments and collective farm management regarding the law's implementation.

Many of the CP-initiated reforms have such characteristics. For example, before the first democratic elections in former Czechoslovakia, a coalition government of the CP and non-Communists under Calfa approved the first agricultural restitution law. The law had little impact because its scale was limited and there were no specifications as to how the reform should be implemented (Lindemans, 1997a). In Hungary, the last important measure taken by the CP before the April 1990 elections was the passage of a law to allow members of collective farms who had formally retained title to their land to withdraw it from communal cultivation and farm it privately. The law had little impact at that point (although it would affect future discussion and regulations) and can be seen as an attempt to influence rural voters in the upcoming elections (Mathijs, 1997b).

In Bulgaria, the Lukanov government issued a decree in February 1990 allowing private farmers to lease up to 30 hectares of farmland, with little effect. Bulgaria also had a law that permitted the conversion of state enterprises into so-called private firms, which was rather actively used (Jackson, 1991). The hypothesis that this mainly benefited nomenklatura interests is supported by one of the first actions of Zhelyu Zhelev, a member of the anti-Communist coalition, after his election as president in August 1990 – suspending privatization. The 1991 land reform law, which was approved by a government coalition of (ex-)Communists and nonpartisan experts, included restricted land restitution. The latter was initially vigorously opposed by the ex-Communists but approved under growing extra-parliamentary pressure. However, the law resulted in little, as details on implementation and execution were missing. At the government level, publications of necessary supplementary regulations were continuously delayed, and at the local level, collective managers and political agents obstructed the process (Swinnen, 1994).

Jackson (1997) suggests that the Romanian reform was to an important extent an attempt by the National Salvation Front (NSF) government to legitimize its dominant position after the 'revolution' and to win the rural electorate's support for the upcoming elections. The reform legislation gave important discretion to local authorities (often NSF allies) in implementation. On the other hand, the reform did have an important impact on land use and

373

effective property rights in the Romanian countryside, including effective restitution to families of use rights to land – an important implication emphasized by Brooks and Meurs (1994).

Stage III: Reformer policies of anti-CP coalitions

In all CEECs except Romania, anti-CP coalitions won elections and came to power in the early 1990s. The governments they formed decided on land reform, privatization, and transformation legislation. We observe remarkable similarities, but also important differences, between CEECs (see above). What determined their policy choices?

When the reform-minded parties came to power in CEECs, they experienced a 'honeymoon period' following their election. But as the former Communists reorganized in opposition and new opposition parties emerged, governing parties and politicians had to weigh political costs and benefits of the various reform options, given their political and institutional constraints and their proper objectives. A key factor in their choice was implicit change in the distribution of income, wealth, and political influence in CEECs (Hillman, 1992),[7] including a trade-off between economic efficiency, social (equity) objectives, and legal (historical justice) demands.

The next section presents detailed hypotheses on how these (and other) factors have influenced reform choices. We distinguish between the determinants of the privatization and decollectivization policy choices because – as I will argue in the next section – the factors which have most influenced them differ.

Stage IV: Return of the ex-Communists and reform policy adjustments

In most CEECs, Socialist (ex-Communist) parties returned to power by the mid-1990s, either following new elections or when the initial anti-Communist coalitions broke down and became part of new coalition governments. In many CEECs amendments and adjustments of the reform laws were introduced after the ex-CP parties returned to power. It is difficult to find hard evidence that the objectives of the adjustments were either economic (to improve the efficiency of the reform implementation or the reform outcome) or distributional (to increase rents for certain groups in society). But, in virtually all cases, the adjustments had both distributional and efficiency consequences.

For example, a regulation such as the Slovenian 'co-ownership' of land during an adjustment period prevented the breakup of plantations and orchards and provided incentives to the current management to maintain the crops. At the same time, it distributed (potential) rents from the new owners to the current management and farm workers. In general, the coincidence of many such changes with a shift of power, i.e., the return of former CP allies in government, suggests that at least part of the objectives were distributional.

Determinants of agricultural privatization and land reform policies

In this section I will argue that three legal and historical factors are key determinants of the choice of privatization and land reform policies in CEECs. They are (in declining order of influence) (1) postcollectivization asset ownership status, (2) the ethnicity of precollectivization asset ownership, and (3) the equality of precollectivization asset distribution.

Postcollectivization ownership status

The most important factor determining privatization policy choice is the status of an asset's legal ownership at the outset of the reforms: *agricultural assets which were still legally privately owned in 1989 have been restituted in all CEECs.* This factor is the main reason land is generally treated differently from nonland assets in privatization. During collectivization, private farmers and landowners were forced to bring their assets into a collectively organized production unit. Many of the assets that the collective used were initially privately owned, but gradually most assets became collective property when the original assets (buildings, animals, machinery) were physically replaced by new assets. The main exception is land. Land could be changed quite dramatically in qualitative terms, because the collectivization process resulted in a consolidation of fields, in a new infrastructure, destruction of old buildings and roads and construction of new ones. Plots of land which prior to collectivization were adjacent to a road might now be in the middle of a vast grain field. Plots previously located close to villages might now be far away. Or plots that had little infrastructure might now have drainage and irrigation facilities, or even buildings on them.[8] However, land as an 'area on the map' was not replaced, and that land remained legally privately owned throughout the Communist regime in many CEECs. Only in the Baltic countries, as well as in the rest of the former Soviet Union and in Albania was land legally nationalized.

As a consequence, CEEC governments could not use a process other than land restitution unless they first took away the legal ownership rights from the former, and also formal or legal, owners. Indeed, some economists even argue that one should not refer to land restitution as 'privatization', because the land was always legally privately owned.[9] One can imagine that in this situation the political costs of not restituting the land are considerably higher than when legal landownership was not private. First, opposition from the legal owners is likely to be stronger because of the legal status of the land. Second, a policy of nonrestitution would be inconsistent with the political and economic reforms. It would be quite ironic if private ownership rights, after surviving forty years of collectivization and state control, would be taken away by democratically elected governments supporting a market economy.

The principle that agricultural assets still formally privately owned should be restituted to their formal owners contributes to the explanation of several observations:

1 Differences between CEECs: where land is not restituted to former owners (such as in Albania, Russia, and Poland), the land was state-owned.

2 Differences within CEECs: where part of the land is restituted, the difference is due to legal ownership (e.g., in Hungary).[10]

3 State farmland has not been restituted when collective farmland is, because state farmland was generally state-owned.

4 In several CEECs the basis for land restitution was the ownership distribution after the land reform(s) implemented under Communist-dominated governments after World War II, because this land reform determines the 1989 legal ownership status.

5 The difference between land and nonland assets: nonland assets were no longer formally privately owned.

Ethnicity

Another factor in a country's choice of privatization and land reform policies is the ethnicity or nationality of the former owners. The choice of privatization policy affects the future asset ownership distribution among ethnic groups, both *inside* and *outside* the country. Therefore, one can expect that the resulting choice will depend on the political rules, and more specifically, on how various ethnic groups have access to the political system (e.g., by voting rights) and how this affects the distribution of political gains and costs.

As former owners who are not (or are no longer) citizens of the country do not belong to the domestic political constituency, there are few political gains in restituting land to them. Moreover, given the nationalistic feelings that have emerged in most of the CEECs, opposition to such policies, and thus political costs, could be quite important in proposing land restitution to foreigners. This explains the observation that foreign former landowners have not been restituted land. In addition, governments have restricted land sales and even

376

land rental to foreigners. Neither potential benefits from attracting foreign capital and knowledge nor pressure from foreign countries[11] has been strong enough to alter this position.

The comparison between land reform in Slovenia and in Poland provides interesting empirical evidence. Slovenia's pre-1989 farm structure was similar to Poland's (at least when compared with those of other CEECs). Both countries were characterized by the absence of collective farms and the coexistence of many small private farmers and some large state farms. Both have transferred the state farmland into a state fund responsible for privatizing the land and managing its use during transition. However, while Poland is selling most of this land, Slovenia is restituting most of its state farmland to former owners, with the exception of land formerly owned by Italian citizens.[12] So, both Poland's and Slovenia's privatization policies, while very different at first sight, follow the same rule of nonrestitution to foreigners.

Ethnic arguments have played a role in the choice of which date to use as the basis for land restitution in former Czechoslovakia. The Christian Democratic parties proposed to shift the reference date for land restitution from 1948 to 1945. This would allow land confiscated from the Catholic Church between 1945 and 1948 to be restituted. However, there was little support for this proposal. One important reason was that it would also imply restituting land to two to three million heirs of Sudeten Germans who had emigrated in the wake of World War II and whose land had been confiscated (and also to Czechs and Slovaks who had collaborated with the Nazis during the war).

The concept of 'foreign owner' is not always defined in the same way. In many CEECs, only current citizens residing in the country have been restituted land. However, Slovenia has based its restitution policy on the citizenship of the land's owner in 1945. If this person was Slovenian and the heirs have a different citizenship, they are still restituted the land (Bojnec and Swinnen, 1997). A similar rule has been used in Latvia. The Latvian government restituted land to Swedish citizens of Latvian descent as part of its strategy to secure independence from Russia. Interestingly, the motive behind this seems to be consistent with the motive behind the general rule – national control over the land (see Rabinowicz, 1997, for an excellent discussion).

The choice of privatization process depends on the influence of ethnic minorities on the decisionmaking and how this influence could affect the distribution of political gains and costs. I will illustrate this point with two examples. In the case of nonland asset privatization in Bulgaria, the privatization choice benefits ethnic minorities. The second case, land privatization in the Baltics, is an example of a privatization choice being used against ethnic minorities.

In Bulgaria, most land was still formally privately owned and was restituted to the formal owners. An important consequence of this land restitution policy was a rather egalitarian distribution of land, except to the Turkish minority. This Turkish minority represents almost 10 percent of the population and is mainly employed in agriculture. They did not receive any land under the restitution program. Buckwell et al. (1994) argue that the allocation of 50 percent of nonland assets to labor contributors (which was much higher than, e.g., in the Czech Republic (see table 13.3) and which benefited Turkish agricultural workers) was supposed to placate the Turkish minority. The political costs and benefits distribution has to be seen in light of the 1991 election results. Turkish minority interests were represented by the Movement for Rights and Freedoms (MRF), which obtained 10 percent of the seats in Parliament. This put the MRF in a strong position, as the rest of the seats were divided equally between the Union of Democratic forces (UDF) with 45 percent and the Bulgarian Socialist Party (BSP) with 45 percent. The MRF provided the crucial votes for the respective UDF- and BSP-dominated governments between 1991 and 1994. While it could not prevent the UDF government's choice of land restitution program, the MRF did win compensation in the form of generous nonland assets distribution to agricultural workers.[13] For the UDF government, the political costs in terms of allocating more nonland asset shares to labor than they preferred was more than offset by their political gains from pushing through the 1992 radical land reforms with MRF support.

Rabinowicz (1997) shows how ethnic factors have had an important influence on privatization policies in the Baltics. In those countries, all land was nationalized after 1945 and reforms covered not only the internal conversion of a socialist economy towards a market economy, but also independence, in their separation from the Soviet Union. The independence problem was complicated by the large share of ethnic minorities, especially Russians, many of whom had immigrated after 1945. For example, in Latvia, ethnic non-Latvians make up 46 percent of the population (compared with only 12 percent in Lithuania). The major share of this group are Russians (34 percent of the Latvian population) who are mainly employed in industry.

In both Latvia and Lithuania the first privatization effort was under the CP regime, which gave land on a usufruct basis to rural workers. However, after anti-Communist coalitions overwhelmingly defeated the CP in the 1990 elections, the new government implemented land restitution to former owners as a key strategy in securing independence, because former owners were all native Latvians and Lithuanians. As such, the restitution policy secured landownership in the hands of native citizens.

This emphasis on a radical and rapid agrarian reform is in stark contrast to the Latvian government's reluctance to privatize industry. Restitution of industrial capital to former (Latvian) owners was impossible, because most of the industry was built after 1945. Any other privatization policy was likely to give an important share of the capital stock to the management and employees of the industrial enterprises, many of whom are Russians. Thus, while ethnic motivations induced a fast privatization in agriculture, they had the opposite effect in industry.

Ethnic factors have further influenced the implementation of the restitution policy and the decollectivization policy. In Lithuania, rural opposition against the radical Sajudis government reforms was captured by the Lithuanian Democratic Labor Party (including the majority of the ex-CP) which won the first election after independence in 1992 with more than 50 percent of the seats. Consequently, the Lithuanian DLP government reduced its commitment towards restitution and individual private farming. In contrast, the Latvian Democratic Labor Party was much less successful after independence. In both Latvia and Lithuania, the former Communist Party had split into a pro-independence and an anti-independence party. In Lithuania (with 12 percent non-Latvians) the majority of the CP sided with Brazauskas' pro-independence Lithuanian DLP. In contrast, the majority of the Communist Party members in Latvia were Russians who sided with the anti-independence Latvian DLP. This significantly reduced their authority after independence. Furthermore, in post-independence Latvia the Parliament decided that voting rights would be restricted to long-term residents who spoke the local language. This decision effectively excluded most of the ethnic non-Latvians, including Russians, from voting. As a consequence, the Latvian DLP (including the majority of the ex-CP) won less than 1 percent of the votes in the June 1993 election. The Latvian government continued to pursue a radical reform policy, supporting individual private farming over other farm enterprises, giving it the highest priority and transformed collective and state farms the lowest priority in land use.

In addition to the choice of policies, the implementation may also be influenced by ethnic issues in those cases where policies or the legal status of the assets did not allow for ethnic discrimination. For example, Jackson (1997) presents evidence that in the districts in Romania with a large Hungarian population the allocation of land titles was significantly lower than in other districts.[14]

Precollectivization landownership distribution

Precollectivization landownership distribution has determined to what extent the objectives of historical justice and social equity conflict are consistent with one another. If precollectivization landownership was egalitarian, as in Bulgaria, restitution of land promotes historical justice as well as social equity. However, if it was more unequal, historical justice and social equity become conflicting objectives. For example, in Albania, two different political parties

379

within the anti-Communist group represented these conflicting objectives, and while both strongly supported privatization and decollectivization, the parties have fought each other strongly over whether land should be restituted to former owners (Cungu and Swinnen, 1997).

How does the precollectivization landownership distribution influence the choice of the agrarian reform? It is not immediately clear in what direction a more egalitarian distribution would influence such as choice, because there appear to be offsetting effects on the political costs and benefits balance. Political support (or opposition) from former owners has depended on the quality and the size of land that they might be restituted.

First, a less egalitarian precollectivization distribution implies that some former owners would receive a larger plot. Political support from those individuals would be stronger because their 'vested interest' increases. On the other hand, fewer former owners would benefit from restitution, decreasing the number of people supporting restitution. These effects tend to offset one another.[15]

A second effect has to do with the transaction costs involved in privatization and how transaction costs differ between rural and urban people. Transaction costs in agricultural privatization are typically lower (and therefore the net benefits are higher) for the rural population (and especially for collective farm employees and members). Therefore, a more egalitarian precollectivization land distribution reduces opposition to restitution from the rural population in general (and collective farm members in particular). On the other hand, it has the opposite effect of reducing incentives for urban former owners to demand restitution.

Third, effective collective action is likely to be positively related to the concentration of (potential) landownership (Olson, 1965). On the other hand, the more unequal the precollectivization land distribution (and thus future distribution in the case of restitution), the more those opposed to restitution will be able to gather political support for opposition using equity arguments. Their claim that the reform policies will create a new feudal system will be perceived as being more justified in this case.

In summary, an egalitarian precollectivization land distribution will have both positive and negative effects on the choice of restitution. What can we learn from our empirical findings?

The most striking case of the impact of the precollectivization land distribution on the choice of current privatization policies is Albania. In Albania land distribution was unequal prior to collectivization. The land in the best agricultural regions of the country was owned by a few families. Therefore, as soon as the reform-minded government announced its intention to break up the collective farms, an intensive debate erupted between two groups within the anti-Communist bloc. The first group, representing most of the (rural) population and politically represented by the Social Democratic Party, favored distribution of land among the rural population on an equal per capita basis. The second group, representing the interests of the former landowners, favored land restitution to the former owners. As land was nationalized during collectivization and no longer legally privately owned, the Albanian government had several options. The government, dominated by the Social Democratic Party, chose to redistribute land to the rural population on an equal per capita basis. With a large share of its population in agriculture, and the Social Democratic Party relying on support from many of the people favoring the distribution program, winning a large number of votes seems to have been a more important factor than the large vested interests of the few former landlords: social equity was chosen over historical justice.

The most important effect of precollectivization land distribution was the increase in opposition from collective farm employees (and other rural inhabitants) to restitution of land in cases of an unequal precollectivization land distribution. This has probably also played a role in Romania with its large rural population. Furthermore, this situation induced adjustments in the reform policies in CEECs where restitution was chosen because of legal ownership or ethnic factors. For example, in both Lithuania and Latvia, the reformers' governments chose for land restitution in historical boundaries in the 1990-1992 period. The motivation for this decision was to secure the reforms and the countries' independence (see the previous discussion on ethnicity). However, the privatization and decollectivization policies after 1992 have diverged substantially in Lithuania and Latvia (Rabinowicz, 1997). Why? One reason is their precollectivization land distributions. Lithuania had a rather uneven land distribution, while Latvia had a much more equal distribution. As a consequence, many workers in agricultural collectives in Lithuania did not receive land under restitution.[16] This increased opposition to the reforms in the rural areas and has led, in turn, to much stronger support for the ex-CP in those areas than in rural Latvia, where most of the agricultural workers were restituted land. When the Lithuanian Democratic Labor Party (i.e., ex-CP) returned to power in 1992, it introduced measures to reduce the impacts of restitution and give rural workers more security in agricultural production by enhancing land leasing and transfer of land to rural workers and management.[17] While it did not change the process of restituting ownership titles, the Lithuanian government tried to limit the transfer of effective property rights to individuals outside the former collectives. This is in contrast with the Latvian government's continued support for restituting full property rights to former owners (Rabinowicz, 1997).

Precollectivization land distribution has influenced the choice of the date for determining rights to restitution in some CEECs. While the 1948 land distribution was relatively egalitarian in both Hungary and Czechoslovakia, this was not the case in the pre-war period, or even in 1945. In both countries, former owners who had lost land prior to 1948 have fought hard to obtain restitution or compensation, claiming that the 1945-1948 land reforms were inspired by the same Communist Party that afterwards collectivized agriculture, and therefore land distribution from the two periods should be equally regarded. Because of the large vested interests in this debate, political demand for pre-1948 restitution or compensation has been strong. In Hungary, the government has partially agreed to this demand (and the Constitutional Court has insisted on this action), and it has also compensated owners who lost their land after 1939. In former Czechoslovakia, the date-for-restitution debate has centered mostly on restitution of former Catholic Church property, most of which was expropriated in 1946. The Christian Democratic parties have put strong pressure on the government to restitute former Church land. In the Czech Republic, thus far, they have not succeeded in shifting the government's policy. After the split of the country, the Meciar government agreed to restitution of former Church land in the Slovak Republic in exchange for political support for his minority government during a political crisis in 1993 (Lindemans, 1997).[18] However, one should keep in mind that an important factor in the 1945 - 1948 debate was the potential restitution of land to Sudeten Germans, which may be a more important factor in explaining the difference between the Czech and Slovak policies (see previous section).

Determinants of the decollectivization policy choice

Decollectivization policies can be grouped into three classes:

1 Those trying to preserve the large-scale farming structures after the transformation to private asset ownership;

2 Those that are 'structure-neutral', i.e., which specify general transition regulations, allowing for the creation of individual farms but without specific incentives for either preserving or breaking up the old collective farm structure (beyond a transition towards private asset ownership) and leaving the restructuring to market forces; and

3 Those intended to break up the collective and state farms in the short run (a policy we refer to as 'radical').

Key characteristics of a decollectivization policy are (a) the role it allocates for the management of the collective and state farms, and (b) the incentives it provides for individuals to leave the collective farm.

In some CEECs, governments appear to have chosen land restitution because of the legal ownership factor, while they might have preferred a less disruptive privatization process for economic reasons. Our empirical observations suggest that in these cases governments have tried to limit further disruptions. For example, in Hungary, the government allowed land restitution to legal owners – all of whom were active in agriculture – but tried to avoid further disruptions by refusing other restitutions and by choosing transformation regulations which had less disruptive impacts. A remaining question, then, is why some other CEECs have intentionally pursued a more radical decollectivization program (see observation 9).

Besides the direct income distribution effects discussed in the previous section, another set of political costs and benefits influences the choice of an agrarian reform strategy. The process of privatization and decollectivization affects the distribution and use of asset endowments in society. As such it affects the distribution of economic interests throughout society and will determine social classes, based on endowment ownership and, hence, future political alignments. It also affects the main organizational structure of the rural areas, the base for the CP's advantage in political organization. The importance of such structures is reflected in how the electorate can be mobilized and influenced. Finally, the privatization-decollectivization process also affects the ability of former management to influence the reform implementation.

Asset distribution, policy preferences, and political parties

Long-term political benefits for reform-minded parties may result from the creation of a 'class' of small- and medium-scale private property owners. Such a rural population will have different preferences than one based on large-scale farming enterprises where the relationship between management, workers, and production factor ownership reflects more closely the organization and ownership relations of large-scale industrial enterprises. The reformed CP will most likely have a much greater chance to obtain rural votes under an organization involving larger-scale enterprises. Agricultural workers have preferences similar to those of industry workers and feel that their interests will be better protected by parties, like the 'left-wing democratic labor' parties in the West. Several former Communist parties in CEECs are presenting this image. In addition, close ties between former collective management and CP officials might survive through the transformation process, turning the reformed CP into a party defending interests of the former nomenklatura, now in charge of reformed collectives. Interests of large-scale farms are often defended by former Communist parties. For example, in Lithuania several directors of 'agricultural associations' ('transformed' collectives) and the

383

chairman of the Union of Agricultural Workers were elected as deputies of the Lithuanian Democratic Labor Party in the 1992 elections. Those parties have been the strongest opponents of restitution of land or other agricultural production factors and of decollectivization.

Private owners of small- and medium-sized properties might form a long-term base for securing anti-Communist political and economic reforms. The creation of such a conservative group is more likely with a restitution and radical decollectivization policy. A farming structure that is largely decollectivized, with a much closer link between landownership, labor input, and management, as is typical the case in the average Western European family farm, will shift political preferences of the rural population towards parties that defend private landownership and family farm operations. Such preferences, and their associated vested interests, are typically defended by 'right wing' parties in the West. In CEECs the political representation of small farmers' interests is either through so-called peasant parties (like the Bulgarian Agricultural National Union (BANU),[19] the Latvian Farmers Union, and the Independent Smallholders' Party in Hungary), or Christian Democratic parties (in the Czech and Slovak republics and in Slovenia where the farmers' alliance was associated with the Christian Democrats). In general, those parties have been the strongest advocates of radical reform, including land restitution in-kind and the complete liquidation of collective farms.

The usual support base for the political and economic liberalizations would be the middle class. However, such a middle class was largely absent from pre-1989 CEEC societies. In addition, the logical beneficiary of market reforms, the emerging business class, does not provide a guaranteed support base for the reform-minded parties, especially because many of the new managers and businessmen have nomenklatura backgrounds. For example, Rabinowicz (1997) reports that in Lithuania businessmen reaping the profits of so-called nomenklatura privatization were much more supportive of the ex-Communist LDLP than of the radical reformers. Similarly, in Bulgaria, the anti-Communist UDF has generally been suspicious of this group and its demands, viewing businessmen as natural allies of the ex-Communist BSP (Engelbrekt, 1992). Instead, the UDF focused on the restoration of the pre-Communist hierarchy as their 'natural' long-term support base. Given the egalitarian pre-Communist distribution of land, the restitution of property rights would create a large class of small- to middle-size property owners (Davidova and Buckwell, 1994).

While in many cases the restituted property would be too small for the owners to aspire to the 'middle class', reformers might still consider this group of owners a safe long-term base for preserving their anti-Communist stance. This is consistent with Hungtington's (1968) argument that no social group is more conservative than a landowning peasantry. A quote of Anastasia Moser, leader of the Bulgarian unified agrarian party BANU illustrates our argument:

> The middle class is the basis of democracy worldwide and there can be no democracy in Bulgaria without it. That is why land restitution and privatization are so vital. It is the farming sector that will allow the emergence of a solid middle class: people owning private property which makes them independent (Radeva, 1993, p. 5).

Political organization

The overwhelming influence of the Communist organization for the past forty years has left the ex-CPs with well organized structures throughout the country, while new parties have had to establish a structure, especially in the countryside. In some CEECs, such as Poland, opposition movements could rely on alternative structures such as the Catholic Church to develop their political organization.[20] However, in countries such as Bulgaria and Romania, the absence of such structures heavily favored the ex-CP in rural political activities in general and in elections in particular (Jackson, 1997).

In several CEECs (ex-)Communist parties continue to show strong electoral support in rural areas. There are several reasons or this. Collectivization and central planning in agriculture have dramatically transformed the rural areas throughout Central and Eastern Europe. Because of the strong interaction of political and economic goals, economic, social, and political organization were closely intertwined under the Communist regime. Management positions in important economic units, such as collective farms were reserved for individuals loyal to the regime, if only because of the Party's near monopoly in regional employment. Moreover, collective farms and their management have played an important role in political organization for the Communist Party. Collective farm management supported the old regime because they derived their position from them and because management's future position depended on substantial support for the agricultural production system. Further, many of the most dynamic people have left the rural areas over the last thirty years leaving many older, less dynamic 'employees'. Consequently, the rural managers and workers have the most to fear from a dramatic reform of the Communist welfare system, including the removal of price controls and welfare (pension) schemes.

While the emerging non-Communist parties have tried to set up local chapters of their parties, the relative success of the ex-CPs in maintaining political support in most of the rural areas must partly be attributed to their superior organizational structure. In this, economic organization plays a key role in rural political organization.[21] One way to reduce the support base of the ex-CP is to destroy a crucial part of their political organization, that is, the collective farm organization, as the main economic and social structure in the rural areas.

The political calculus of decollectivization policies

The discussion so far suggests that the main political benefits for reformers' governments to choose a radical decollectivization policy – intended to break up the state and collective farms into individually farmed enterprises – are that such a policy (a) damages the organizational structure from which the ex-CP derives its remarkable electoral strength; (b) creates a long-term political support base for the reforms, and (c) removes the nomenklatura from those key positions from which it could block the implementation of the reforms. The main political costs of radical decollectivization policies during transition are increasing opposition because of induced disruptions and (perceived) efficiency losses. However, these political benefits and costs are not fixed. Both are conditional on other factors, such as the economic and political environment and the duration of transition.

Efficiency effects

Efficiency losses depend on the productivity of the large-scale farms versus the productivity of smaller-scale farms. It is beyond the scope of this chapter to analyze the efficiency of the various farm structures, and I refer to a large literature on this. It suffices here to summarize that relative efficiency depends on a variety of factors, including the functioning of input and output markets, the specific production activity (wheat, pigs, ect.), and the technology used. In some cases, there may not be any efficiency loss at all, and there may be efficiency gains even in the short run. In other cases efficiency losses may result in the short run, but individual farms may prove more efficient in the long run. In fact, some experts argue that agricultural production in collective farms is always less efficient in the long run (e.g., Schmitt, 1993). If so, structure-neutral policies will probably also lead to a breakup of the collective and state farms into individually operated farms in the longer run, but this may take time to emerge.

In Mathijs and Swinnen (1996), we present a series of hypotheses regarding the impact of the economic environment on the relative incomes of collective farms versus individual farms. Key factors include prices, risk, productivity of farm workers under both frameworks, and exit costs (influenced by privatization and decollectivization policies). Our empirical analysis shows that average prereform productivity of the collective farms and relative access to appropriate technology are key factors influencing the individuals' preference to remain in the collective farms. In those countries where prereform productivity of collective farms was very low (such as in Albania and Romania), peasants have preferred to leave the collectives and start up their own private farms. In those cases where prereform productivity was low, efficiency losses were small or nonexistent even in the short run. For example, overall agricultural productivity has increased with the breakup of the collective farms in Albania (Cungu and Swinnen, 1997). In contrast, in countries such as Hungary, where the collective farms were relatively more efficient and also better equipped with machinery and capital-intensive technology, efficiency losses may be greater in the short run.

Brooks and Meurs' analysis (1994) confirms that the main factor limiting individual farming in Romania was the availability of appropriate machinery, itself correlated with the main agricultural production specialization of the region.

For our analysis, relative efficiency losses are not only important government considerations in themselves, but also affect the political reactions of various interest groups to proposed reform policies. For example, political opposition to radical decollectivization policies is likely to be much stronger in countries such as Hungary, the Czech Republic, and Slovakia, where large-scale farming heavily depended on capital investments and large-scale technology. In Bulgaria, the share of people involved in agriculture was much less than in Romania, while the capital-intensity in agricultural production (reflected in the number of machinery per hectare) was much higher. These factors reflect the stronger opposition of these countries to radical decollectivization in comparison with such countries as Albania and Romania. Furthermore, the welfare especially of the poorest groups in rural society may have been more affected than has been suggested by the efficiency increases. This is because prereform food shortages existed even in the rural areas, and the distribution of land and individual farming has increased food security in these poorest groups, substantially improving their welfare. In such situations, governments have followed these preferences and not prevented the breakup of the farms.

Political benefits

Political benefits of radical decollectivization policies depend on the political equilibrium. The political importance of support for (ex-)Communist parties in the rural areas depends on the overall strength of the Communist Party and on that of the reformers. If the reformers are supported by a large majority or if they feel that the democratic political regime and the market economy are 'relatively safe', they may feel less threatened by a continued support base for the (ex-)Communists. If this is not the case, and if such a support base preserves the continuing threat of a 'Communist revival' which could undo many of the political and economic reforms, reformers will be more inclined towards a strategy to reduce this support base.

The more likely it is that Communist parties will return to power, the more likely a reformers' government is to choose a radical decollectivization policy. The motivation to create an enduring anti-Communist and proreform political support base will play an important role when democratic reforms are insecure, when Communist support remains strong, especially in the countryside, and when reformers perceive a strong link between Communist support and collective and state farm production organizations. My hypothesis is that *the 'radicalness' of agrarian reforms chosen by a reformers' government is inversely related to the 'security' of the overall political reforms.*

One could also relate this argument to the importance of a 'political center', which we define as a political group that takes the middle ground on agrarian reform between the left-wing ex-Communists, typically opposing reforms, and right wing parties advocating restitution and radical decollectivization. Typically such centrist parties are committed to democracy and a market economy, but favor privatization with minimum disruptions. When in government, they have allowed for restitution of part of the land, but have opposed radical breakup of the farm structures. This suggests that *the presence of an important political center has moderated reform policies and is therefore inversely related to the radical agrarian reforms.*

Is there any empirical evidence supporting this argument? Our study indicates that in those CEECs where a reform-minded center has been strong and where reforms were perceived as more 'secure', moderate decollectivization policies have been chosen. Let us compare the position of the reformers' governments in Hungary and former Czechoslovakia, which have opted for less radical decollectivization, with some of the reformers' governments in Bulgaria, Lithuania, and Latvia (see observation 9).[22]

Both in former Czechoslovakia and in Hungary there was a strong political center (as defined earlier) and reforms seemed quite secure during the 1990-1992 period when the main agrarian reform decisions were made. In Hungary, the traditional Communists of the Hungarian Socialist Workers Party obtained no seats and the more reform-minded ex-Communists of the Hungarian Socialist Party (HSP) obtained only 11 percent of the seats in the April 1990 elections. The anti-Communist Hungarian Democratic Forum and Alliance of Free Democrats together won 66 percent of the seats. Both parties wanted privatization but were opposed to radical decollectivization. Even in 1993, most polls indicated little chance for a revival of the former Communists, not even for their reform-minded section, organized in the HSP, which ultimately won the 1994 election.

In former Czechoslovakia, the Civic Forum - Public Against Violence coalition got a majority in Parliament after the first elections.[23] The former Communists (the Left Bloc in the Czech Repubic and the Party of Democratic Left in the Slovak Republic) obtained about 16 percent of the seats in both the federal and the republican parliaments in 1990 and, importantly, only slightly improved that share in the 1992 elections (17.5 percent in the Czech Republic and 19.3 percent in the Slovak Republic), although the ex-Communist parties did perform relatively better in rural areas.

In both Hungary and former Czechoslovakia the political competition in the countryside was much less between the former Communists and the centrist parties than between the ex-CP and parties advocating more radical agrarian reforms, such as the Independent Smallholders' Party in Hungary and the Christian Democrats in former Czechoslovakia. This made, as long as overall support for the ex-CP was not increasing, the issue of decollectization much less key for the governing center parties.

The conditions that made the Bulgarian Union of Democratic Forces (UDF) government choose a radical transformation process, including the explicit liquidation of collective farm structures by outsiders, were extreme and have only occurred (for a limited period) in Bulgaria. They were the consequence of a series of developments. The ex-Communists of the Bulgarian Socialist Party (BSP) won the first elections in June 1990. The BSP land reform and agricultural privatization program had little effect because the implementation was effectively blocked. An important consequence was that the reformers realized that an effective agrarian reform would not result unless they devised some way of ensuring implementation as well. Two additional factors are important. First, in the months before the fall 1991 elections, several centrist factions of the UDF created their own parties, but none of these centrist parties got beyond the 4 percent vote required for parliamentary seats. The result was that 25 percent of the votes which made up the aggregate political center were not represented in Parliament. The Parliament had two large (extreme) blocs: former Communists (BSP) and radical reformers (UDF), each with aproximately 45 percent of the seats.[24] The elections not only showed that the BSP still had a very important share of the votes but that it got much of its support from the rural areas. The UDF realized that it had to reduce the power of Communist strongholds in rural areas to secure reforms.

The results of these combined factors were (1) that the UDF's stance was radicalized by the disappearance of the centrist factions from the UDF coalition; (2) that the UDF was strongly determined to pursue a radical land reform and to decollectize agriculture; (3) that the UDF realized it had to specify explicit and simple rules in the law regarding how to implement reforms to remove uncertainty; (4) that it attempted to reduce local opposition by removing collective farm management and bringing in outsiders to form liquidation councils to effectively liquidate collective farm assets; and (5) that it had the power to do all this because of the lack of representation by a political center in Parliament.

It is worth emphasizing that the radical agricultural reform pursued by the UDF government contributed to its fall when the MRF withdrew its support after the reform brought few benefits and much loss to the Turkish minority. Many of the Turkish people were employed on collective farms and none of them were to receive land under the restitution program.[25] The next Bulgarian government, a coalition which relied on BSP and MRF support, replaced 75 percent of the liquidation council chairpersons. After the 1994 elections in which the BSP won the majority, the BSP government abolished the liquidation councils.

Observations of the Baltic reforms also support our conclusion. After the 1990 elections, the Lithuanian Sajudis government aimed at destroying collective farms by a radical reform program. The reform program included land restitution and the explicit removal of agricultural specialists, assumed to defend nomenklatura interests, from the reform-implementing institution (Rabinowicz, 1997). The program created new institutions, including the municipal agrarian reform services (MARS), chaired by outsiders. While Sajudis won two thirds of the votes in the 1990 elections, the Communist influence remained strong. This was reflected in the results of Brazauskas' Lithuanian Democractic Labor Party (LDLP), including the majority of the ex-CP, which won the first election after independence in 1992 with more than 50 percent of the seats. Its comeback resulted to an important extent from rural opposition to the agrarian reform because many agricultural workers did not receive any land under the Lithuanian restitution program. The LDLP government reduced its commitment towards restitution and decollectivization and increased its support for collective farm employees. For example, they offered former owners compensation in the form of urban land if they would postpone land claims. As with the BSP in Bulgaria, the LDLP, after returning to power, changed the role and the composition of the reform-implementing institutions (the MARS).

In Latvia, Communists were heavily defeated in the 1990 election. The Latvian government pursued a radical reform policy, explicitly supporting individual private farming, e.g., by giving those farmers the highest priority and collective and state farms the lowest priority in land use. The fact that the Latvian ex-CP had less than 1 percent of the votes in the June 1993 election seems to be inconsistent with our argument. However, in post-independence Latvia voting rights excluded most ethnic non-Latvians (46 percent of the population). Most of this group are Russians who support the Latvian ex-CP. This fact has to be seen in perspective with Russian interventions to support the interests of its citizens living in Latvia. The election results were therefore not a good reflection of the security of the reforms.

Conclusions

In all CEECs privatization and decollectivization policies have been chosen and implemented following the collapse of the Communist regime. Reform policy choices differed greatly, both during transition within each country and from one country to the next.

A first, not surprising, general conclusion is that policy changes within CEECs are strongly influenced by changes in political institutions and by power balances. More specifically, we conclude that when the political challenge to the CP's power monopoly increased, the CP responded with limited reform proposals to fend off this challenge. Actual changes in property rights resulting from these reforms were intended to be limited, or to benefit the CP nomenklatura.

Three historical-institutional factors have influenced the choice of agricultural privatization policies. The most important determinant has been the postcollectivization ownership status of the asset. All assets that were legally privately owned in 1989 were restituted to their 'formal' owners. The second factor is ethnicity. The privatization policy choice affects the asset distribution between ethnic groups. The choice of privatization policy therefore depends on how important the concentration of asset ownership in an ethnic group's hands is for the ruling government and on the political influence of ethnic minorities. One general observation is that foreign owners are not restituted their assets and at best receive some compensation in value. Third, the precollectivization asset distribution determines the potential conflict between historical justice and social equity. The most important effect of this factor is the rural population's increased opposition to restitution in the case of an equal prereform distribution of assets. In those CEECs where restitution was not chosen because of postcollectivization ownership or ethnic factors, this has induced a land distribution (on an equal per capita basis) program rather than restitution.

The return of the ex-CPs to power in many CEECs (Hungary, Bulgaria, Poland, Lithuania, Slovenia) later resulted in amendments to reform laws, new regulations, and adjustments of incentives for reform implementation. These policy changes have, in general, not resulted in changes in the legal privatization process. Instead, the regulations and adjustments have reduced or complicated the transfer to individuals of effective property rights to assets and have reduced the impact of decollectivization. Examples are the increase of (opportunity) costs for submitting land claims, giving former collectives more rights and decision authority regarding the use of assets under privatization, and limiting new owners' rights in transferring and using the assets.

Most CEEC governments have not chosen a decollectivization policy that would induce disruptions beyond the disruptions already caused by the privatization policies. Those reform-minded governments that chose radical decollectivization policies did so because they calculated that the long-run gains outweighed short-run costs. This could be due to the fact that short-run efficiency losses were small or nonexistent, as in the least productive agricultures. In these areas, the increasing importance of individual farms increased food security, further contributing to general support for decollectivization. In countries where widespread decollectivization would create production declines in the short run, radical decollectivization policies were used for political purposes. They were intended to change the social structures and political organizations and preferences in the countryside in order to create a long-term political base for securing political and economic reforms. The political gains of this strategy outweighed its political costs only when (a) the 'security' of the overall reforms was low (reflected in continued political strength of the CP and a small political center); (b) the rural areas' political preferences could significantly alter the power balance; and (c) the radical reformers had sufficient votes in Parliament to push through the policy.

Notes

1   The author gratefully acknowledges financial support from the Leuven Institute for Central and East European Studies (LICOS), the Belgian National Foundation for Scientific Research (FKFO-grant), and the K.U.Leuven Department of Agricultural Economics. The author thanks Erik Mathijs for many discussions and research assistance, James Garrett, Ewa Rabinowicz, Isabelle Lindemans, Sophia Davidova, Zvi Lerman and participants at seminars in Stanford University, Cornell University, University of Cambridge, UC Berkeley, Wye College, The World Bank IFPRI, Sinaia and Edinburgh for critical comments on earlier versions of the paper.

2   Examples are Solidarity in Poland, the Civic Forum in former Czechoslovakia, Sajudis in Lithuania, and the Union of Democratic Forces in Bulgaria.

3   Law proposals which included restitution of land to former owners of land sold to the collective farms were ruled unconstitutional by the Hungarian Constitutional Court, because they differentiated between land and other assets owned by collective farms.

4   The activities of state farms are often different than those of collective farms, e.g., they include agricultural research stations, seed production farms, intensive animal husbandry enterprises. For some intensive animal husbandry enterprises, the importance of the land is relatively limited compared with overall capital assets.

5   The 1993-1994 Bulgarian coalition government, which relied on socialist party (BSP) support, replaced 75 percent of the liquidation council chairpersons. After the 1994 elections in which the BSP won the majority, the BSP government abolished the liquidation councils.

6   In Hungary and Poland change was gradual. In former Czechoslovakia the Communist Party collapsed quickly. Bulgaria's Communists went in two steps. Reform-minded Communists won a first democratic election in June 1990. But then, as trouble overwhelmed them, they lost a second election in October 1991 to the Union of Democratic Forces, a combined anti-Communist opposition. In Romania the break with the old regime was more ambiguous. In December 1989 the Communist dictator, Nicolai Ceaucescu, was overthrown and put to death along with his wife. An umbrella group called the National Salvation Front (NSF) took over. This was undoubtedly anti-Ceaucescu. How democratic it was is still disputed. In the Baltics, the key issue during the end of the 1980s and beginning of the 1990s was independence from the former USSR. With the collapse of the former USSR, this became possible. In Lithuania, the Communist Party was most successful in translating nationalistic ideas and support for independence into political support and power. In Latvia, the opposite occurred, and the CP crumbled.

7   Many analyses of land reforms elsewhere (e.g., Allen, 1982; de Janvry, 1981a,b; Hayami 1991) or of institutional change in general (Bardhan, 1989) emphasize the prime importance of the distributional issue. See Rabinowicz and Swinnen (1997) for a more extensive discussion.

8   In general, these changes are more important when the land is situated in better agricultural areas. Plots in mountainous and agriculturally disadvantaged rural areas often have undergone less change. Change in quality and use of land affects the administrative difficulties in restituting land to previous owners. It also induces compensation claims. Non-landowning members and management of collective farms have claimed that they should be compensated if the quality of the land has been improved and the land is restituted to previous owners.

9   The formal owners were devoid of virtually any authority regarding the use of the land. This fact provides a good illustration that legal ownership rights are not a sufficient condition for the existence of effective property rights. Privatization in this case has to do more with the transfer of property rights than (legal) ownership rights. In other cases privatization

393

concerns the allocation of both legal ownership rights and effective property rights to individuals or private institutions.

10 The Hungarian debate on agricultural privatization is an excellent illustration of our argument. That part of the land still legally owned by individuals, all of whom were members of the collectives, was restituted to them. The two thirds of the land no longer privately owned was privatized differently, i.e., through distribution to farm workers and through a voucher process. The importance of legal asset ownership was emphasized by the Hungarian Constitutional Court, which ruled against treating land differently from other assets legally owned by the collectives or the state in privatization procedures.

11 The Czech Republic and Slovenia are pressed by Germany and Italy, respectively, to restitute land to German and Italian former owners.

12 Under pressure from the Italian government, the Slovenian government is negotiating a possible compensation (in value) to the former owners.

13 There is an important additional (ethnic) reason why the MRF supported the UDF government's agricultural policy despite the fact that the MRF's view on agricultural privatization was closer to the BSP's. The BSP had attempted to gain suppport on the basis of nationalistic sentiments and had taken a very strong anti-Turkish position in previous years and in the election campaign. The result was that after the elections, it was unimaginable that the MRF would form an alliance with the BSP. Interestingly, the MRF stepped out of the UDF-MRF coalition after less than one year, effectively bringing down the government, partly because of increased opposition from the Turkish agricultural population to the agricultural reform implementation. After that, the MRF and the BSP entered into a 'devil's coalition' supporting the 1993-1994 Bulgarian government.

14 The average share of legal titles issued in September in 37 Romanian districts was 28.5 percent. In the 6 districts with an important share of Hungarian-speaking inhabitants, the average was 17.9 percent and all of those districts had fewer than 20 percent of titles issued. In contrast, the average was 30.6 percent in the other 31 districts, with only 3 out of 31 having fewer than 20 percent. (The difference was significant at the 1 percent level).

15 This issue is strongly related to the so-called number paradox in the political economy of redistributive policies. Swinnen and de Gorter (1993) show that with redistributive policies the increase in political support due to the higher per capita benefits more than offsets the decrease in political support due to the decline in the relative number of supporting individuals.

16 Many of the larger Lithuanian farmers ('kulaks') were deported to Siberia after 1945.

17 The reason the Lithuanian DLP returned to power, while the Latvian DLP was wiped out, was likely influenced by this process, but the most important factor was ethnic differences in both cases (see above).

18 The proposal was initially vetoed by the Slovak president, but a revised version was accepted.

19 Part of BANU was associated with the Communist Party and was a satellite party represented in Parliament under the Communist regime. After the removal of many of its old leaders, several BANU-parties merged into the current BANU (Swinnen, 1994). A similar reorganization of the peasant party occurred in Poland.

20 The use of existing social or cultural organizations for political organization of the rural areas played a crucial role in Western Europe at the turn of the century. For example, in Belgium and France the existing organization of the Catholic Church helped right-wing political parties to 'capture the rural electorate'. It is remarkable that former Communist parties won the first free elections only in the parts of Eastern Europe with a predominant Eastern Orthodox culture. Penev (1991) argues that while the pervasive influence of the Communist Party in social, economic, and political life was overwhelming everywhere in CEECs, most CEECs went through dramatic political destabilization, because of those countries' traditionally closer links to West Europe and an independent religion. Public opinion in those Catholic or Protestant countries regarded the ruling Communist Parties as national traitors. Conversely, the prevailing religion in Bulgaria is Eastern Orthodox Christianity, which has been a part of ideology tightly controlled by politics. Religious destabilization was just as impossible because religion has a low social standing and the governing institutions of the church were bound with the Communist state (Dimitrov, 1991).

21 Olson (1965) has used a similar argument to explain the strength (and existence) of farmers organizations in the West. His by-product theory claims that only those political organizations that could offer their members selective economic incentives to overcome the free-riding problem in political organization have been successful (see Moe (1981) and de Gorter and Swinnen (1995) for a critical discussion).

22 In Poland and Slovenia the rural areas were mostly populated by private farmers (and most of their votes went to peasant parties). Those countries do not provide evidence because reformers' parties have not been able to decide on reform policies.

23 Recall that 'radical' in our discussion refers to the decollectivization policy. For example, the Czech government under Vaclav Klaus' CDP is widely referred to as pursuing a 'radical liberalization' policy. However,

his party did not support radical decollectivization (and was criticized for that by the Christian Democratic parties) (Lindemans, 1997).

24 The remaining 10 percent was in hands of the Turkish minority party (MRF), which mainly defends Turkish minority issues and which could swing the balance. The strong anti-Turkish stance in the past and during the election campaign by the BSP made a BSP-MRF coalition virtually impossible.

25 Many changes were introduced when the BSP returned in government (see discussion in first section).

References

Allen, R. (1982), 'The Efficiency and Distributional Consequences of Eighteenth Century Enclosures', *Economic Journal*, 92, pp. 937-953.

Bardhan, P. (ed.) (1989), *The Economic Theory of Agrarian Institutions*, Clarendon Press: Oxford.

Barzel, Y. (1989), *Economic Analysis of Property Rights*, Cambridge University Press: Cambridge.

Bojnec, S. and Swinnen, J. (1997), 'Privatization of Slovenian agriculture: Process and politics', chapter 12 in this volume.

Brooks, K., Guasch, J. L., Braverman, A. and Csaki, C. (1991), 'Agriculture and the Transition to the Market', *Journal of Economic Perspectives*, Vol. 5, No. 4, pp. 149-161.

Brooks, K. and Meurs, M. (1994), 'Romanian Land Reform: 1991-1993', *Comparative Economic Studies*, Vol. 32, No. 2, pp. 17-32.

Buckwell, A., Davidova, S. and Trendafilov, R. (1994), 'Land Reform: How Will the Future Look?', in Schmitz, A., Moulton, K., Buckwell, A. and Davidova, S. (eds.), *Privatization of Agriculture in New Market Economies: Lessons from Bulgaria*, Kluwer Academic Publishers: Boston, London, and Dordrecht.

Cungu, A. and Swinnen, J. (1997), 'Agricultural privatization and decollectivization in Albania: A political economy perspective', chapter 3 in this volume.

Davidova, S. and Buckwell, A. (1994), 'Agriculture Reform', in Schmitz, A., Moulton, K., Buckwell, A. and Davidova, S. (eds.), *Privatization of Agriculture in New Market Economies: Lessons from Bulgaria*, Kluwer Academic Publishers: Boston, London, and Dordrecht.

de Gorter H. and Swinnen, J. (1995), 'The Economic Polity of Farm Policy: Reply', *Journal of Agricultural Economics*, Vol. 46, No. 3, pp. 403-414.

de Janvry, A. (1981a), 'The Role of Land Reform in Economic Development: Policies and Politics', *American Journal of Agricultural Economics*, May, pp. 384-392.

de Janvry, A. (1981b), *The Agrarian Question and Reformism in Latin America*, The Johns Hopkins University Press: Baltimore and London.

Dimitrov, R. (1991), 'Formation of the Bulgarian Opposition 1989-1991', *Bulgarian Quarterly*, No. 1, pp. 53-65 and No. 2, pp. 43-52.

Engelbrekt, K. (1992) 'The Fall of Bulgaria's First Noncommunist Government', *RFE/RL Research Report*, Vol. 1, No. 45, pp. 1-6.

Hayami, Y. (1991), 'Land Reform', in: Meier, G. (ed.), *Politics and Policymaking in Developing Countries. Perspectives on the New Political Economy*, ICS Press: San Francisco, pp.155-171.

Hillman, A.L. (1992), 'Progress with Privatization', *Journal of Comparative Economics*, 16, pp. 733-749.

Hungtington, S. (1968), *Political Order in Changing Societies*, Yale University Press: New Haven.

Jackson, M. (1991), 'The Rise and Decay of the Socialist Economy in Bulgaria', *Journal of Economic Perspectives*, Vol. 5, No. 4, pp. 203-209.

Jackson, M. (1997), 'Political economy of agricultural reform in Romania', chapter 10 in this volume.

Junguito, R. (1991), 'Comment', in Meier, G. (ed.), *Politics and Policymaking in Developing Countries. Perspectives on the New Political Economy*, ICS Press: San Francisco, pp.171-173.

Kabat, L. and Hagedorn, K. (1997), 'Privatization and Decollectivization Policies and Resulting Structural Changes of Agriculture in Slovakia', in Swinnen, J., Buckwell, A. and Mathijs, E. (eds.), *Agricultural Privatization, Land Reform and Farm Restructuring in Central and Eastern Europe*, Avebury: Aldershot.

Lindemans, I. (1997), 'Process and politics of agricultural privatization: The case of the Czech and Slovak Republics', chapter 6 in this volume.

Mathijs, E. (1997a), 'An historical overview of Central and Eastern European land reform', chapter 2 in this volume.

Mathijs, E. (1997b), 'Process and politics of agrarian reform in Hungary', chapter 8 in this volume.

Mathijs, E. and Swinnen, J. (1996), 'The Economics of Agricultural Decollectivization in Central and Eastern Europe', Working Paper Series of the joint Research Project: *Agricultural Implications of CEEC Accession to the EU*, Working Paper No. 3/1, Department of Agricultural Economics, K.U.Leuven.

Moe, T. M. (1981), *The Organization of Interests. Incentives and the Internal Dynamics of Political Interest Groups,* The University of Chicago Press: Chicago.

Olson, M. (1965), *The Logic of Collective Action,*Harvard University Press: Cambridge.

Penev, V. (1991), 'Chances of political stability', *Bulgarian Quarterly*, No. 1, pp. 44-52.

Rabinowicz, E. (1997), 'Political economy of agricultural privatization in the Baltic countries', chapter 4 in this volume.

Radeva, N. (1993), 'Market Economy Starts from Farming: Interview with Agrarian Leader Anastasia Moser', *Bulgarian Economic Review*, 4-17 June, p. 5.

Schmitt, G. (1993), 'Why Collectivization of Agriculture in Socialist Countries Has Failed: A Transaction Cost Approach', in: Csaki, C. and Kislev, Y. (eds.), *Agricultural Cooperatives in Transition*, Westview Press: Boulder, pp. 143-159.

Swinnen, J. (1994), 'Political Economy of Reform in Bulgarian Agriculture', in Schmitz, A., Moulton, K., Buckwell, A., and Davidova, S. (eds.), *Privatization of Agriculture in New Market Economies: Lessons from Bulgaria*, Kluwer Academic Publishers: Boston, London, and Dordrecht.

Swinnen, J. and de Gorter, H. (1993), 'Why Small Groups and Low Income Sectors Obtain Subsidies: The 'Altruistic' Side of a 'Self-Interested' Government', *Economics and Politics*, Vol. 5, No. 3, pp. 285-296.

Swinnen, J. and Mathijs, E. (eds.) (1997), *Agricultural Privatization, Land Reform and Farm Restructuring in Central and Eastern Europe: A Comparative Analysis*, in Swinnen, J., Buckwell, A. and Mathijs, E. (eds.), *Agricultural Privatization, Land Reform and Farm Restructuring in Central and Eastern Europe*, Avebury: Aldershot.